*Also in the Variorum Collected Studies Series:*

**MARGARET GIBSON**
'Artes' and Bible in the Medieval West

**MARCEL PACAUT**
Doctrines politiques et structures ecclésiastiques dans l'Occident médiéval

**SUSAN REYNOLDS**
Lay Ideas and Loyalties in the Medieval West

**KENNETH PENNINGTON**
Popes, Canonists and Texts, 1150–1550

**JOHN GILCHRIST**
Canon Law in the Age of Reform, 11th–12th Centuries

**PIERRE RICHÉ**
Education et culture dans l'Occident médiéval

**CYRILLE VOGEL**
**Ed. ALEXANDRE FAIVRE**
En rémission des péchés: recherches sur les systèmes pénitentiels dans l'Eglise latine

**JEAN GAUDEMET**
La doctrine canonique médiévale

**ROGER E. REYNOLDS**
Law and Liturgy in the Latin Church, 5th–12th Centuries

**KARL F. MORRISON**
Holiness and Politics in Early Medieval Thought

**ANDRÉ GOURON**
Etudes sur la diffusion des doctrines juridiques médiévales

**CHARLES MUNIER**
Vie conciliaire et collections canoniques en Occident, IVe–XIIe siècles

**STEPHAN KUTTNER**
The History of Ideas and Doctrines of Canon Law in the Middle Ages

**ROBERT SOMERVILLE**
The Papacy, Councils and Canon Law in the 11th–12th Centuries

COLLECTED STUDIES SERIES

# Innocent III: Studies on Papal Authority and Pastoral Care

Photograph: Louise Bourdua

Brenda Bolton

Brenda Bolton

# Innocent III: Studies on Papal Authority and Pastoral Care

VARIORUM
1995

Published by VARIORUM
Ashgate Publishing Limited
Gower House, Croft Road,
Aldershot, Hampshire GU11 3HR
Great Britain

Ashgate Publishing Company
Old Post Road,
Brookfield, Vermont 05036
USA



ISBN 0-86078-489-4

**British Library CIP Data**
Bolton, Brenda
Innocent III: Studies on Papal Authority and Pastoral Care.
(Variorum Collected Studies Series; CS 490)
I. Title II. Series
282.092

**US Library of Congress CIP Data**
Bolton, Brenda
Innocent III: Studies on Papal Authority and Pastoral Care /
Brenda Bolton. p. cm. — (Collected Studies Series: CS490)
Includes bibliographical references and index.
ISBN 0-86078-489-4 (alk. paper)
1. Innocent III, Pope, 1160 or 61–1218. 2. Popes—Primacy—History of doctrines—Middle Ages, 600–1500. 3. Pastoral theology—Catholic Church—History of doctrines—Middle Ages, 600–1500. 4. Catholic Church—History of doctrines—Middle Ages, 600–1500. 5. Europe—Church history, 600–1500. I. Title. II. Series: Collected Studies: CS490.
BX1236.B66 1995 95–3349
282'.09'022—dc20 CIP

The paper used in this publication meets the minimum requirements of the American National Standard for Information Sciences - Permanence of Paper for Printed Library Materials, ANSI Z39.48-1984. ™

Printed by Galliard (Printers) Ltd
Great Yarmouth, Norfolk, Great Britain

COLLECTED STUDIES SERIES CS490

# CONTENTS

PASTORAL CARE

This volume contains xvi + 318 pages

# Preface

Of the successors to St Peter, only Gregory the Great and Gregory VII have received closer attention than that given to Innocent III. Yet, as the Eight Hundredth Anniversary of his accession approaches, it is to be hoped that the increasing interest and awareness arising will shift the balance more markedly towards Innocent III. This pope surely deserves no less. To this end, I have taken a determinedly revisionist line. I trust that additional evidence will be advanced to support this approach as the interpretation comes to receive more prominence, and the accompanying searching scrutiny, which the assessment requires.

The Imperial struggle - as recorded in the *Regestum super negotio Romani imperii* (*RNI*)[1] - is not really the concern of this Collection. It has been amply covered elsewhere and by many significant scholars[2]. Instead, in seeking a spiritual dimension, I have sought the inspiration of Innocent's own letters and sermons[3]. These, together with related accounts by contemporaries and eye-witnesses, often working openly or at times covertly, can reveal a spirituality which many have either neglected, discounted or not even looked for. Although the nature of this type of evidence is often elusive, the resultant profit is so rewarding as to make the effort well worth while. This is emphatically so since, when Innocent makes clear the intention of the message

---

1 F.KEMPF, *Regestum Innocentii III papae super negotio Romani imperii*, *Miscellanea Historiae Pontificiae*, xii (Rome, 1947).

2 R.L.BENSON, 'Political *Renovatio*: Two Models from Roman Antiquity', *Renaissance and Renewal in the Twelfth Century*, edd. R.L.BENSON and G.CONSTABLE with C.D.LATHAM (Oxford, 1982), pp. 339-86 provides an excellent overview of this area. For another see also H.FURHMANN, '*Quis Teutonicos constituit iudices nationum?*: The Trouble with Henry', *Speculum* 69 (1994) pp. 344-58.

3 J.-P.MIGNE, *Patrologia Latina* 214-217 (Paris, 1855).

he is putting forward through an apposite Biblical quotation, he usually caps it with one of his characteristically fleeting interventions, always incisive, often humorous, sometimes ironic, but unfailingly relevant. This was in keeping with the linguistic style of the time and Innocent's own approach was one for which he was renowned amongst his contemporaries.

However, the language of history and of legend was not the only medium he sought to use. Rome itself, the City, its buildings and its art were all to play important roles[4]. To remember this is to develop our understanding of Innocent and the importance to him of Rome as the City of the Faith, the City of the Church and the City of the People. His aim was to ensure that it was also the City of God in the service of Christ. My regular visits to Rome and the Patrimony over the years have confirmed this view. In support of this history and its legends Innocent himself would have had access to the topography and archaeology of Rome[5]. The physical examination of this could be made on foot and can be followed even today despite the many changes since his time. I have handled the exquisite small works of which he was the proud patron and have gazed at the earliest representation of him in the *Sacro Speco*, St Benedict's Cave at Subiaco. There he wears a square nimbus, a symbol of sanctity in his own time but one which all later generations have categorically denied him[6].

An analysis of Innocent's mission as pope has underlain much of my work for more than twenty years. What his real intentions may have been has always exerted a power to attract, perplex and intrigue me in equal measure. In spite of a high-profile visibility in the history of the papacy which has

---

4 *Mirabilia Urbis Romae*, ed. R.VALENTINI and G.ZUCCHETTI, *Codice topografico della città di Roma* 4 vols, 3 (Rome, 1946); *The Marvels of Rome*, ed. and trans F.M.NICHOLS (London, 1889), 2 ed. E.GARDNER (New York, 1986); Master Gregory, *The Marvels of Rome*, trans. J.OSBORNE, Medieval Sources in Translation, 31 (Toronto, 1987).

5 J.R.PATTERSON, 'Survey Article: The City of Rome: from Republic to Empire', *Journal of Roman Studies* 82 (1992), pp. 186-215 provides an admirable example of methodology for an earlier period.

6 G.B.LADNER, 'The So-Called Square Nimbus', *Images and Ideas in the Middle Ages: Selected Studies in History and Art*, Storia e Letteratura 155-6, 2 vols (Rome, 1983) I, pp. 115-70.

aroused frequent and much less than favourable comment, Innocent has attracted surprisingly little study which breaks really new ground. The appended short bibliography will help but much remains to be done to elucidate wider aspects of his pontificate. These, in the past, have either been neglected or developed only so as to sustain other issues.

A high proportion of the studies contained in this volume have developed out of my involvement as a member of the Ecclesiastical History Society for nearly thirty years. Seven are from the collection of my communications given in support of the themes chosen annually for the Society's Summer Conferences. In addition, Essay VI resulted from an invitation from Henry Chadwick to give a Main Paper at the Winter Meeting of the Society in January 1985 while Essay V was first presented to the Anglo-American Conference of Historians at the Institute of Historical Research in July 1989 before being developed in honour of Michael Wilks. Thus, my work on Innocent III has greatly benefited from the Ecclesiastical History Society's existence. It is a unique forum which allows the ideas of both younger and older scholars to be presented, tested and subsequently published. Three of the essays given elsewhere (II, X and XIII) have had to be re-set for reasons of format or typography. All remain essentially unaltered save that I have taken the opportunity to reproduce the slightly fuller version of X as delivered at Kalamazoo in May 1990. I am grateful to the publishers who have allowed me to reproduce these articles.

This volume falls into two parts, papal authority and pastoral care, but there is inevitably much blurring at the edges so essays in the first section may well refer forward to the theme of the second and *vice versa*. The first eleven essays deal with aspects of Innocent's exercise of papal authority. Essays II and III show how essential it was for the Pope as Bishop of Rome to establish personal control over his City and the Patrimony of St Peter in order to achieve a position which would allow him to implement his reforms. His use of the Cistercians in Essay II refers forward to later studies in this Section. Essay IV argues that the anonymous biography, the *Gesta Innocentii PP III*, represents a celebration and prose justification for papal actions marking what may have been seen at the Curia as only a limited victory by 1208. Essay V investigates the spiritual motivation behind Innocent's exercise of authority, traditionally seen in strictly political terms, to bring the kings of France and England to a perpetual peace or a long truce. Innocent saw clearly that, without lasting pacification, the subjects of these rulers, however willing they might be, would never be free to take up the Cross and recover the Holy Land for Christ.

Essays VI to X deal with aspects of the organisation and uniformity of observance of the Rule of St Benedict which made the Cistercians the first real Order in the Church. Although their actions frequently exasperated the Pope, he saw it as his task to try to contain and humour them for there were no more effective agents than the Cistercians, whether as missionaries in the field or as implementers of General Chapter legislation. Essay X was written for the nonacentenary celebration of the birth of St Bernard in 1990. Innocent's appreciation of Bernard's organisational and spiritual qualities was expressed in a collect which the Pope composed in the saint's honour in 1202[7]. The first section ends with the Fourth Lateran Council, the ultimate expression of papal authority but revealing also of the Pope's proud pleasure at showing the city of which he was Bishop to the notables who had gathered in Rome in November 1215.

The second Section takes pastoral care as its general theme. Innocent III was quite exceptional in treating so responsively those accused of heresy. Whether humiliati, Waldensians, religious women or the earliest mendicant friars, he wished to include all of them within the Church rather than risk keeping them outside. His genuine concern for the religion of ordinary people also led him to channel their enthusiasm towards visual images which both deepened and enriched their spiritual experience through focusing attention on their presence in Rome and the Patrimony. His response as Bishop to the physical needs of the poor, to widows and orphans in general and specifically to abandoned children was always humane and often far ahead of its time.

These essays have appeared over a period of more than twenty years and my views have undergone a similar process of ageing. Were I starting again, I would doubtless have written several of them very differently or perhaps not at all. Only Essay I appears for the first time and represents an attempt to fly

---

[7] *PL* 214, cols 1032-33.

a few kites and draw together some threads, particularly the Roman ones, running through these papers. It is not the purpose of this Collected Studies Series to provide a platform for major alterations although I have taken the opportunity to correct the misprints and add a few afterthoughts.

This selected Collection has grown out of the stimulation of vigorous discourse with scholars of different views and from the challenge presented over the years, both in Rome and in London, by all those undergraduate and postgraduate students who have worked with me in constructive disagreement to achieve insight into the life of this great Pope. To them all, I am eternally grateful.

Brenda Bolton

Queen Mary and Westfield College,
London
*December 1994*

***PUBLISHER'S NOTE:*** *The articles in this volume, as in all others in the Collected Studies Series, have not been given a new, continuous pagination. In order to avoid confusion, and to facilitate their use where these same studies have been referred to elsewhere, the original pagination has been maintained wherever possible.*

*Each article has been given a Roman number in order of appearance, as listed in the Contents. This number is repeated on each page and quoted in the index entries.*

ACKNOWLEDGEMENTS

The author and the publisher acknowledge copyright and express their appreciation for permission to reprint the essays in this volume to the following editors and publishers: Judith Loades, Headstart History, Bangor (II and XI); Cambridge University Press (III); Martin Sheppard, Hambledon Press (UK), London (IV); Dr R.N. Swanson, Ecclesiastical History Society and Basil Blackwell, Oxford (V, VI, VIII, IX, XII, XV, XVI, XVII and XIX); Professor Marcel Pacaut and the Centre Interuniversitaire d'Histoire et d'Archéologie médiévales, Lyon (VII); Simon Winder, St Martin's Press, New York (X); Professor Harry Lenhammar, Department of Theology and Church History, Uppsala University (XIII); Herr Stephan Gutowski, Dietrich-Coelde Verlag, Werl (XIV); Professor R.V. Schnucker, Director, Thomas Jefferson University Press (XVIII).

For permission to reproduce the photographs in this volume grateful acknowledgement is also given to: P. Carlo Morandin, osb, Prior of the Monastery at Subiaco for the 'Fresco Representation of Innocent III'; the Soprintendenza per i Beni Artistici e Storici di Roma for the 'Lunette of Mentorella'; and The British School at Rome.

*

* *

I would personally like to acknowledge The British School at Rome and The British Academy, whose provision of grants in 1982 initiated the Italian dimension of this work. Since then the British School at Rome has continued to provide a secure and invaluable base, an outstanding library and a unique forum for the exchange of ideas, both for myself and my Innocent III students.

The great support of Father Leonard Boyle, Prefect of the Vatican Library, and Monsignor Charles Burns of the Vatican Secret Archive has strengthened me at every stage, while the Luiselli family have visited, with great patience, many sites associated with Innocent III.

My grateful thanks are due to Brian Place of the Arts Computing Unit at Queen Mary and Westfield College for the exceptional camera-ready copy for essays I, III, X and XIII; and finally to John Smedley and Ruth Peters at Variorum for their kind patience and tolerance at all stages of preparation on this volume.

Margaret Gibson

In gratitude and esteem

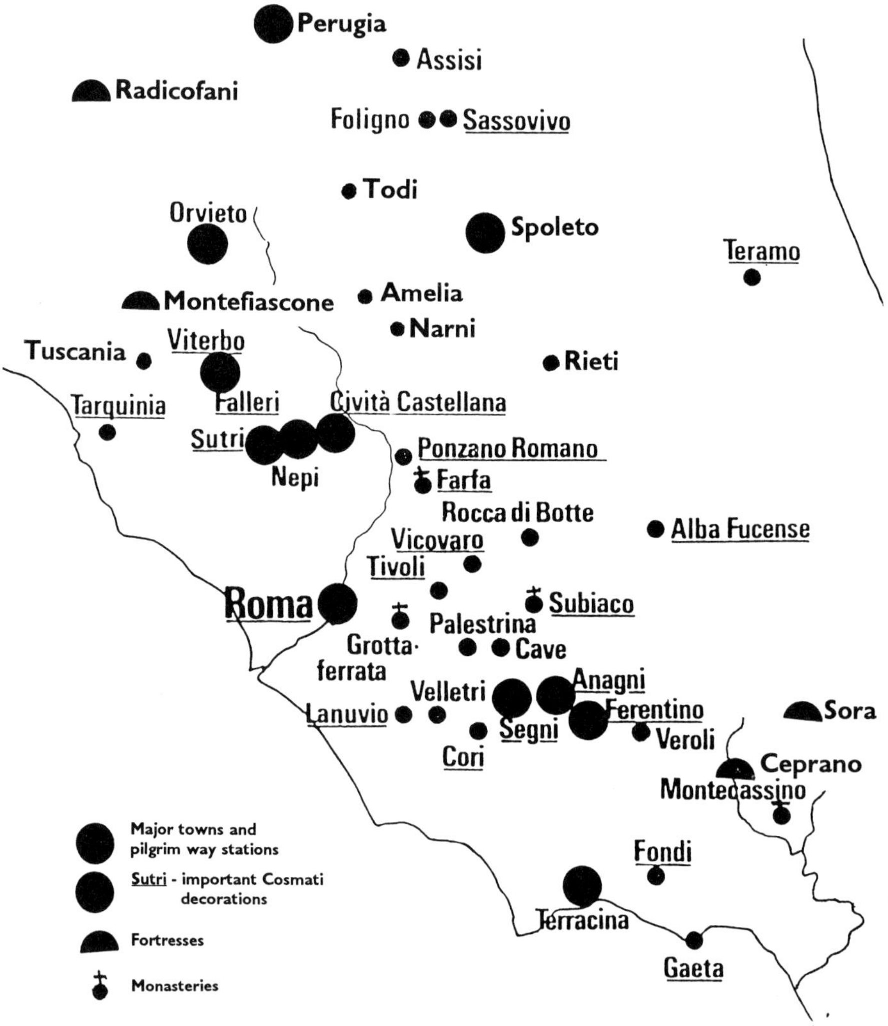

Perugia
Assisi
Radicofani
Foligno
Sassovivo
Todi
Orvieto
Spoleto
Teramo
Montefiascone
Amelia
Narni
Tuscania
Viterbo
Rieti
Tarquinia
Falleri
Civitá Castellana
Sutri
Nepi
Ponzano Romano
Farfa
Rocca di Botte
Alba Fucense
Vicovaro
Tivoli
Roma
Subiaco
Palestrina
Grotta-
ferrata
Cave
Velletri
Anagni
Lanuvio
Ferentino
Sora
Segni
Veroli
Cori
Ceprano
Montecassino
Fondi
Terracina
Gaeta
Major towns and pilgrim way stations
Sutri - important Cosmati decorations
Fortresses
Monasteries

**The Patrimony of St Peter, 1198–1216**

I

# Rome as a Setting for God's Grace

'The awakening of an active awareness of human history was one of the achievements of Latin Christendom in the twelfth century'[1]. If this is acceptable as a frame of reference, it might justifiably be assumed that Innocent III, pope and long-time effective servant and member of the Curia[2], would have shared this awareness. Importantly, the twelfth century was the time when Christendom began to realise its historical evolution[3] and Innocent often referred to the path of history from Adam through Moses to the coming of Christ and on to his own day[4]. It also came increasingly to grasp the significance of other lands outside its influence[5].

---

1 M.-D.CHENU, *Nature, Man and Society in the Twelfth Century: Essays on New Theological Perspectives in the Latin West* edd. J.TAYLOR and L.K.LITTLE (Chicago, 1968) pp. 162-201, especially p. 162.

2 See particularly M.MACCARRONE, 'Innocenzo III, prima del pontificato', *Archivio della Società Romana di Storia Patria* 20 (1942), pp. 3-78; W.MALECZEK, *Papst und Kardinalskolleg von 1191 bis 1216: die Kardinäle unter Coelestin III und Innocenz III* (Vienna, 1984) pp. 101-104.

3 CHENU, *Nature, Man and Society*, p. 201.

4 *Patrologia Latina* 217, ed. J.P.MIGNE (Paris, 1855) col. 634. (Cited as *PL*).

5 For example, the papal correspondence between Alexander III and Prester John in 1177. See R.C.SMAIL, 'Latin Syria and the West 1144-1187', *TRHS*, 5th series, 19 (1969), pp. 1-20; J.R.S.PHILLIPS, *The Expansion of Europe*, (Oxford, 1988) pp. 60-2.

Innocent, himself, had been educated in the late 1170's in the School of Pastoral Theology within the nascent University of Paris[6]. Over many years, debates about the nature of human history had flourished at this institution[7]. On top of this, he was most decidedly a new young pope whose origins were in Rome itself[8]. His own City of Rome was to play a particularly acute role in his awareness of the century in which he lived. Few have denied Rome's place in history and Innocent III was certainly not one of them[9].

In the body of a letter dated 30 October 1198, addressed to the officials of Tuscany and the Duchy of Spoleto, Innocent III emphasised the importance of Rome and its surrounding territory, the Patrimony of St Peter[10] - so much so that he defined the area as '*Italia*'. By divine disposition, *Italia* had obtained principality over all the provinces of Christendom but it was in *Italia* alone that it was clear beyond doubt that the pope exercised both papal authority, *pontificalis auctoritas*, and royal power, *regalis potestas*. That this papal responsibility extended outwards through all other regions of Christendom, no matter how distant they might be, was accepted but the finer detail and interpretation attached to 'responsibility' gave rise to conflict. The difference of view between 'spiritual' and 'temporal' which had played so large a part in previous papal history, particularly in the time of Gregory VII

---

6 J.W.BALDWIN, *Masters, Princes and Merchants: the Social Views of Peter the Chanter and his Circle*, 2 vols (Princeton, 1979); Idem, 'Masters at Paris from 1179 to 1215', *Renaissance and Renewal in the Twelfth Century*, edd. R.L.BENSON & G.CONSTABLE (Oxford, 1982), pp. 138-72.

7 BALDWIN, *Masters, Princes & Merchants*, I, pp. 161-79.

8 MACCARRONE, 'Prima del pontificato', pp. 11-14.

9 M.MACCARRONE, *Chiesa e Stato nella dottrina di papa Innocenzo III*, Lateranum, NS, (Rome, 1942).

10 *Register* I, 401, pp. 599-601; *PL* 214, col 377. Compare the review by L.E.BOYLE, *Speculum* 42 (1967), pp. 153-62.

(1073-85) and repeated reference to the Donation of Constantine[11], was one aspect with which Innocent had to come to terms[12]. His attitude to Rome or *Italia* gives an understanding of the approach he took. Although all regions of Christendom merited equal treatment in the service of Christ, Innocent claimed *specialiter* a feeling of paternal solicitude - with all that entailed - for Rome and the Patrimony[13]. Not only was this solicitude a special commission from St Peter, given to him as to each pope in turn[14], but there was also the daily impact of the City's history. Tradition and meaning, both classical and Christian, were everywhere. The physical evidence of this impact so constantly confronted Innocent that he could not ignore it. Nor, indeed, would he have wished to do so. On the contrary, his intention would be to increase the spiritual message of the impact.

Many and varied were the communications which had flowed from all popes to the recipients who made up Christendom. Innocent did not change the pattern. In so doing, his letters, and particularly his sermons, make constant reference to earlier works available to him[15]. The Bible was obviously foremost amongst these but, when it came to references to Rome, he added frequent citations from the Classics and from Christian literature. The latter stretched from the Early Christian Fathers to the writers of his own time. In this manner, he linked together the three historical strands on which the Rome of his day was based. Classical Rome was revealed through the

---

[11] Compare H.E.J.COWDREY, 'Pope Gregory VII', *Medieval History* 1 (1991), pp. 23-38 for Gregory's complete identification with St Peter. He was 'in St Peter and St Peter was in him', *IBID*, p.26.

[12] See particularly Innocent's sermon for the Feast of St Silvester, *PL* 217, cols 481-4.°

[13] M.MACCARRONE, *Studi su Innocenzo III*, Italia Sacra 17, (Padua, 1972), pp. 9-22.

[14] Compare the statement of Nicholas I (859-67), *PL* 119, col. 888. 'Romanus pontifex sollectitudinem (sic) habet non solum unius provinciae sed et totius ecclesiae'.

[15] J.LONGÈRE, *Oeuvres oratoires de Maîtres parisiens au xiie siècle*, Etude historique et doctrinale, I (Paris, 1975); compare *Selected Sermons of Stephen Langton*, ed. P.B.ROBERTS (Toronto, 1980).

works of Virgil, Horace, Ovid and Juvenal[16]. The Bible provided the Judaeo-Christian inheritance, particularly the New Testament with its Gospel message. The works of later christians from the Early Fathers to earlier popes such as Leo I (440-61) and Gregory the Great (590-604) passed on the faith. By using these citations, Innocent attributed to Rome not only a special place but also a special purpose[17]. In the setting of Rome, the glory of God's grace would be praised; the grace that saved through Christ crucified and through which the faith was strengthened[18]. The implications for the Church whose centre was Rome were to be far-reaching[19]. There, too, God's grace needed to be found and salvation obtained through Christ crucified.

Innocent develops this significance of Rome in a sermon written for the Feast of the Apostles Peter and Paul, 29 June. In this he first expounds at some length on the burden of labour and grief which Adam's yoke had brought upon mankind. He cites in evidence the well-known proverb of Horace: 'Whatever errors the great commit, the people must atone for'[20]. Innocent's message is that wherever the Gospel is preached, there salvation will be found. On this particular feast day, Rome itself is the very place concerned. He proceeds to take as his theme Christ's command to Peter[21], 'Put out into the deep of the sea and let down your nets for a catch' - it was indeed a miraculous draught! Innocent then turns to allegory. Rome is the deep of the sea because she used to have and still has primacy and sway over the whole world and in her, many may be caught for Christ. In pagan times, Rome alone of all cities had sole dominion over the Gentiles. In the Christian era which followed it was right that she should have *magisterium* over all the

---

[16] MACCARRONE, 'Prima del pontificato', p. 16, note 6.

[17] For Leo I's view of Rome, *PL* 54, col. 424, 'Civitas sacerdotalis et regis per sacram beati Petri sedem caput orbis effecta'.

[18] Ephesians 1:2.

[19] 1 John: 4, 15.

[20] 'Quicquid delirant reges plectuntur Achivi', Horace, *Letters* I, ii.14; *PL* 217, col. 556.

[21] Luke 5: 4.

faithful. 'God so loved Rome that he had made the City both royal and priestly, imperial and apostolic. Through divine authority, Rome held the primacy of honour and was greater and more noble by far than ever she had been by earthly dispensation. By the former, she has the keys of the kingdom, by the latter, the reins of the whole world'. 'Indeed', says Innocent, 'through the disposition of a perpetual law, it has been decreed that such an honour of dignity or dignity of honour as belongs to her should never pass to any other city but remain forever Rome's.'

Rome, therefore, according to Innocent, had been divinely chosen as the perpetual seat of Peter and of his successors[22] and it was particularly appropriate that the bishop who was at the head of the Church should have his see in Rome. He was not the first to say this. The first Pope Innocent (401-17), having witnessed the Visigothic Sack of the City by Alaric in 410, had made substantial claims for Rome to be the *caput ecclesiarum* spread throughout the world[23]. He had begun the process of bringing all major legal cases, *causae maiores*, under the general competence of the Bishop of Rome[24]. Innocent II (1130-43), whilst he had been driven out of Rome for much of his pontificate, had succeeded in achieving recognition of his view of Rome and the papacy from such powerful external forces such as St Bernard and the kings of France and Germany[25]. He still had to face continued hostility from the people of the City. It is not known what importance Innocent III attributed to the name he shared with these predecessors but it can be assumed that he felt a significant bond with the two previous Innocents in their insistence on the City of Rome being the centre for the papacy. The foundation and cornerstone of the Christian religion had been set down there and, through the primacy of the apostolic see, Rome's principality dominated both priests and kingdoms. Innocent III thus took

---

22 *PL* 217, col. 556, 'quantum Deus urbem istam dilexerit'.

23 *PL* 20, col. 527, Innocent I to the bishops of Macedonia in 414.

24 W.ULLMANN, 'The Papacy as an institution of government in the Middle Ages', *Studies in Church History* 2 (1965), pp. 78-101.

25 B.SCHIMMELPFENNIG, *The Papacy* (New York, 1992), pp. 154-5.

seriously the historical obligations attaching to his office. He saw it as his responsibility to maintain the battle lines of the faith and to extend them wherever possible, whether in Rome herself, within the Patrimony of St Peter or elsewhere[26].

To Innocent it was significant that the City of Rome was the See of the Bishop who claimed descent from Peter. This same Peter was the Prince of the Apostles and, as Apostle to the circumcised, took the message to the Christian Jews in Rome itself. Rome had become the sole Patriarchate in the West and the acknowledged centre of the whole of Christendom. But Rome was also the City of St Paul, the Apostle to the Gentiles - the uncircumcised. It was the centre in which Paul had undertaken his mission of preaching and had composed many of his Epistles. It was where he too was to meet his death. As the heir to both Peter and Paul, Innocent III recognised the spiritual importance of the inherited task which he had to undertake[27]. This was to make of Rome a City acceptable to God through Jesus Christ and dedicated to His service; the centre of His Church where all could serve in the manifold grace of God[28]. Rome, therefore, according to Innocent, had been divinely chosen as the perpetual seat of Peter and of his successors.

Innocent follows Ambrose of Milan (337/9-97) in adding a vivid reminder for those listening to his sermon of the legend by which Christ himself had actually set foot in Rome. When Peter was fleeing from the City, Christ himself had appeared to him. 'And when Peter asked "Lord, whither goest thou?", he replied, "I am going to Rome to be crucified again". Peter, realising that the head could be crucified through its members' actions, turned

---

[26] See Essay II, pp. 1-20 in this volume.

[27] J.M.HUSKINSON, *Concordia Apostolorum: Christian Propaganda at Rome in the Fourth and Fifth Centuries: a Study in Early Christian Iconography and Iconology*, BAR International Series, 148, (Oxford, 1982), especially pp. 77-107 for a valuable discussion on Peter, Paul and the Primacy of Rome.

[28] I Peter, 4:10; M.MACCARRONE, *Romana Ecclesia: Cathedra Petri*, 2 vols, Italia Sacra. 47-48, edd. P.ZERBI, R.VOLPINI, A.GALUZZI, (Rome, 1991).

back to suffer the ultimate penalty of martyrdom[29].' Yet Peter had not been alone in Rome. Paul had been his companion and Innocent in the Sermon resorts to grammatical constructions to explain to his listeners that the singular *duc in altum* had been followed by the plural *Et laxate retia in capturam.* Peter alone had been fishing in the depths of the Sea of Galilee but in Rome both Peter and Paul had together let down the nets of preaching for the catch of men[30].

'Surely', argues Innocent, 'it is through the action of divine providence that this City, founded physically by Romulus and Remus, two brothers in the flesh who lie honourably entombed there, should also house the basilical tombs of Peter and Paul, two brothers in the faith who were responsible for its spiritual foundation?' In common with contemporary twelfth-century belief, Innocent places the tomb of Romulus near Peter's burial place[31] and that of Remus near Paul's. From these tombs all four founders guarded this City with their favour.

Having dealt with the matter of the first foundation of Rome by Romulus and Remus and its spiritual refoundation by Peter and Paul, Innocent goes on to explain the purpose for which Rome had been singled out. 'The Church is the ship[32], the world is the sea and Rome is the deep water. The nets represent preaching for a net is woven with inter-connecting threads just as a sermon is composed and strengthened by using inter-connecting authorities[33]. All men are saved by being caught in the nets of gospel preaching and Rome

---

29 *PL* 217, col. 557. The church known as *Domine, quo vadis?* on the Appian Way was so called to commemorate this legend.

30 *IBID*, col. 558.

31 Master Gregorius, *Marvels of Rome*, ed. and trans. J. OSBORNE, (Toronto, 1987) pp.32-3, 86-8. A pyramid near Castel Sant'Angelo, described as '*meta que vocatur Memoria Romuli* was matched by the '*meta Remi*' on the Via Ostiensi on the other side of Rome.

32 See I.R.ROBINSON, 'Church and Papacy' in *The Cambridge History of Medieval Political Thought c.350-c.1450* ed.J.H.BURNS (Cambridge, 1988) especially pp. 255-57 for the concept of the Church as *navis*.

33 *PL* 217, cols 557-8. Compare Innocent's Prologue to his Sermon Collection presented to Arnald Amaury, Abbot of Cîteaux, in 1204, *IBID*, cols 309-12.

therefore is the universal city of Christian salvation. Peter and Paul together had let down their nets for the catch. Through their preaching Rome was converted from error to truth, from vice to virtue. All the apostles should be venerated at Rome but especially these two, who should be particularly honoured as fathers and patrons of the City[34]. Their prayers and merits keep the City healthy on earth just as it will be happily crowned in heaven.

Although Innocent's main preoccupation appears to be with Peter, he once addresses himself directly to the importance of St Paul[35]. This was in a letter to the monastery of S Paolo *fuori le Mura* dated early in June 1203 and written from Ferentino where he was ill and in self-imposed semi-exile. The letter confirmed the monastery's privileges and in taking it under papal protection, he describes St Paul as 'the most worthy preacher, chosen vessel and preacher of grace'.

Innocent's interest in the use of Roman legend, folklore and the continuity of popular devotion is revealed through the insights found in several of his works. In a Sermon for the Purification of the Virgin Mary on 2 February, he expounds the historical development of the liturgy for that day. 'Why', he asks rhetorically, 'are lighted candles carried on that day?' The Gentiles, as he calls the Romans, had habitually sacrificed at the pagan feast of *Amburbale*[36] at the beginning of February. At this time too Pluto had carried off Proserpina to the Underworld. Her mother, Ceres, had sought her with torches beneath Mount Etna and with lights throughout the island of Sicily. When the Fathers of the Church had been unable to extirpate this pagan custom, they had transformed *Amburbale* into a celebration of the Virgin Mary at which lighted candles were borne aloft in special veneration of the Mother

---

34 *IBID*, col 558, 'sed hos duos quasi primos et praecipuos, quasi patres et patronos ipsius specialiter honorare'. See also H.CHADWICK, 'The Circle and the Ellipse: Rival Concepts of Antiquity in the Early Church', *History and Thought of the Early Church*, (London, 1982) I, pp. 4-17, especially p. 15.

35 *PL* 215, cols 91-5. I am indebted to John Doran for drawing my attention to this reference. See also, HUSKINSON, *Concordia Apostolorum*, pp. 77-107 for a valuable exposition of the decline in Paul's popularity.

36 *PL* 217, col. 510.

of Christ. Elsewhere, Innocent refers to the Feast of the Purification by its Greek name, *Ypopanti* or *Hypapandi*, explaining that Simeon had seen in Christ 'a light to lighten the Gentiles'[37].

Innocent was also adept at using 'real History' to bring home his point. After all, he had been consecrated in St Peter's own Chair[38]. In explaining the historical development of the Mass, he found it necessary to explain why the Bishop of Rome was unable to use St Peter's own pastoral staff. Peter himself had entrusted it to Eucharius, the first bishop of Trier, who had gone to evangelise the German people. In Innocent's day, the staff was still used with great reverence by the Church of Trier[39].

In a Sermon for the Feast of the Annunciation[40] and another for Christmas Day, Innocent wrote in the tradition of those earlier christians who had been already looking forward to the day when the Roman Emperor himself would be converted to the faith[41]. He reminded the congregation how, during the reign of the Emperor Octavian Augustus (27BC-14AD), a sudden fountain of oil had miraculously spouted from the *taberna meritoria*, an inn on the other side of the Tiber and had flowed continuously all day into the river to the great surprise of the Romans. The so-called *fons olei* was thus a portent of the Nativity, occurring at the very hour of Christ's birth. In his Second Sermon for Christmas Day[42], Innocent linked this miraculous

---

37 *PL* 217, *De Sacro Altaris Mysterio*, cols 763-914, especially col. 800, 'In Ypopanti propter puritatem Mariae, quae juxta canticum Simeonis obtulit lumen ad revelationem gentium'.

38 M.MACCARRONE, 'La "Cathedra Sancti Petri" nel Medioevo: da simbolo a reliquia', *Rivista di Storia della Chiesa in Italia*, 39 (1985), pp. 349-447, especially pp. 422-3.

39 *PL* 217, cols 796-7.

40 *PL* 217, col. 524.

41 *PL* 217, cols 455-60.

42 *PL* 217, cols. 455-60 especially col. 456, 'Octavianus Augustus fertur in caelo vidisse virginem gestantem filium ad ostensionem Sibyllae'. Compare B.McGINN, '*Teste David cum Sibylla*: The Significance of the Sybilline Tradition in the Middle Ages', *Apocalypticism in the Western Tradition*, (London, 1994), pp. 7-35.

happening to the prophesy of the Sybil, also in the time of Augustus, that a child would be born who would be 'King of Kings and Lord of Lords'. As if for good measure he coupled this with the witness of Virgil's Fourth Eclogue[43], perhaps being influenced by St Augustine's adoption of its prophecy of the Virgin Birth. The message of the Fourth Eclogue lay not merely in its prophetic character but also in the spirit it represented. The inherited Sibylline tradition was based on materials handed down from antiquity and the patristic era. The Sybil was seen as the prophetess of Christ by Christian ecclesiastical writers, pronouncing Christ to the Gentiles as the Old Testament prophets had announced him to the Jews. In the pagan past, Sybilline prophecies had been traditionally used to sanction Rome's religious expansion and could often be involved with the fate of dynasties. What, of course, we cannot know is whether Innocent was aware of more than one dimension of the classical tradition but he quite specifically cites line 7 of the Eclogue[44].

We are particularly well informed about this pope's use of the legend of the miraculous *fons olei* as a stimulus to popular religious feeling in Rome itself[45]. The tradition of the fountain of oil signifying the grace of God born of mankind was not officially associated with S.Maria in Trastevere until 1079. Its importance increased when Calixtus II (1119-24) established the Feast of the Circumcision on 1 January, the octave of the Nativity, and transferred the station - the place at which the liturgy was traditionally performed - from S.Maria *ad martyres* to S.Maria in Trastevere. The transfer of stations was rare for stational liturgy was regarded as perfect and not to be

---

43 Virgil, *Bucolics*, *Eclogue* iv, 7. Composed 40 BC and first published 27 BC when Octavian took the title Augustus. See Stephen BENKO, 'Virgil's Fourth Eclogue in Christian Interpretation', *Aufsteig und Niedergang der Römischen Welt*, II, 31.1 (Berlin, 1980) pp. 646-705, especially pp. 671-76; P. COURCELLE, 'Les exégèses chrétiennes de la quatrième éclogue', *Revue des ètudes anciennes* (1957) pp. 294-6; B.LUISELLI, 'Il profetismo virgiliano nella cultura veterocristiana', *Virgilio nel Bimillenario, Sandalion* 6-7 (Sassari, 1983-84), pp. 133-49.

44 *PL* 217, col. 457, 'Unde poeta: In nova progenies coelo dimittuntur alto'.

45 *Mirabilis Urbis Romae: The Marvels of Rome or a picture of the Golden City*, ed. F.M.NICHOLS, (2nd ed. New York, 1986), pp. 35-8.

tampered with[46]. The readings and prayers associated with individual stational churches were attributed by Jerome and Gregory I to the Holy Spirit working through its agents. Perhaps Innocent would have understood the willingness of Calixtus to change the liturgy on this matter. His approach to the revisions of liturgy which he himself wanted would have been to claim that they also were 'spirit-led'[47]. It has, however, been argued that Calixtus must have had a very special reason for wishing to relocate the liturgy for 1 January at S.Maria in Trastevere. Could he have been influenced by the large Jewish population of the area or was it perhaps a reminder that Christ himself was a Jew? Or perhaps the transfer represented instead a Papareschi family enterprise for its members were responsible for renewing the church *sumptibus propriis*[48]? Possibly it was for the far simpler reason that if the Christmas Day station was at S.Maria Maggiore with its relic of the *praesepium*, Christ's own crib, then the Octave of Christmas and the Feast of the Circumcision should be celebrated at S.Maria in Trastevere, the site of the second *praesepium* and of the *fons olei*.

Innocent III was also interested in S.Maria in Trastevere because of its association with his predecessor of the same name, Innocent II (1130-43). This is clear from three sources. The entry in the *Liber Pontificalis* of Martin Polonus *c.*1280 mentions the consecration of this church by Innocent III on Sunday 15 November 1215 in the presence of those attending the Fourth Lateran Council[49]. This used to be categorically rejected by scholars on the grounds that the consecration must have already been performed by Innocent II and that no evidence existed to substantiate the claim of Martin Polonus. In 1964, the publication of the so-called Giessen manuscript proved the point

---

46 V.PERI, '*Nichil in Ecclesia sine causa*', *Rivista archeologia cristiana* 50 (1974) pp. 249-73.

47 S.J.P.VAN DIJK & J.HAZELDEN WALKER, *The Origins of the Modern Roman Liturgy*, (London, 1960), pp. 79-80, 91-113.

48 H.TOUBERT, 'Le renouveau paléochrétien à Rome au début du xii siècle', *Cahiers archéologiques* 20 (1970) pp. 99-154.

49 *Liber Pontificalis*, ed. L.DUCHESNE (Paris, 1892), pp. 451-3.

irrefutably[50]. The Anonymous German Eyewitness had been present there and had seen the whole ceremony with his own eyes.

The *Acta* of the Consecration has survived in a seventeenth-century manuscript, formerly in the Chapter Archives of S.Maria in Trastevere but now in the Vatican Library[51]. It provides a clue as to how this confusion could have come about[52]. Innocent II, himself of the Papareschi family, had renewed the *capella praesepis* with its altar and had consecrated it on the Feast of the Purification, granting an indulgence of forty days to those who visited it. Fully intending to mark his restoration of the whole church by a suitably honourable consecration, Innocent II had died without seeing the completion of his project. Although his relations completed the building, they could not consecrate the church. A further fifty-five years then elapsed before the accession of Innocent III on 8 January 1198. Innocent's decision to summon a General Council of the Church in November 1215 aroused the interest of Guido, Cardinal Bishop of Palestrina (1206-1221)[53], titular priest of S.Maria in Trastevere and a descendant of that same Papareschi family. In a divine revelation, the venerable Guido heard a voice saying that the right time for the consecration of S.Maria in Trastevere[54] would be during the opening stages of the Council. Thus, on 13 October, the eve of the Feast of S.Calixtus, in either 1213, 1214 or even 1215, Guido began diligently to discuss with his brother clerics the matter of the proposed consecration. On the Sunday following the Feast, Guido summoned together the entire

---

50 S.KUTTNER and A.GARCIA Y GARCIA, 'A new Eyewitness Account of the Fourth Lateran Council', *Traditio* 20, pp. 115-78, especially pp. 143-6; D. KINNEY, *Santa Maria in Trastevere from its Founding to 1215* (University Microfilms International, Ann Arbor, Michigan, 1975).

51 Vat.Lat 8429 folios 160r-165r, *De Abstrema Dedicatione Insigna Basilicae S.Marie Transtyberim Fontis Olei nuncupatur an. 1215.*

52 Compare L.E.BOYLE, 'The Date of the Consecration of the Basilica of San Clemente, Rome', *Archivum Fratrum Praedicatorum* 30 (1960), pp. 417-27.

53 W.MALECZEK, *Papst und Kardinalskolleg*, pp. 99-101. Guido was created Cardinal Priest of S.Maria in Trastevere in 1191.

54 'Nunc esse aptum tempus consecrandi...'.

population of Trastevere before the solemn mass so that all could deliberate and reach a unanimous decision on what they should do. When he explained his idea, everyone applauded and so, after three o'clock on that same day, a delegation met Innocent to beg him to agree to the consecration of their church. All the clergy, knights and men on foot came to the pope *maxima cum alacritate* and he heard them in a most kindly way. John James Crassus, bearing the petition of consecration, spoke up eloquently on behalf of the inhabitants of Trastevere. When he had heard their spokesman, the Pope replied: 'This is the Lord's work that you should seek the consecration of this Church and it is marvellous in our eyes, because Innocent made the body and Innocent will instill the soul, wishing that statement to mean that the former (Innocent) renovated it, now I shall consecrate it'. And thus, he willingly agreed to their petition and added: 'The sign is that this place in which the Lord allowed oil to flow at the time of his birth should be honoured by all. When they heard the Pope speak thus, they rejoiced greatly and returned whence they had come. At length, when everything had been appropriately prepared for the consecration, the same glorious Pope in the company of a great number of illustrious men who had come to the Council from all parts of the Christian world entered the Basilica on 15 November with all solemnity for the ceremony of consecration'. Not only did Innocent bestow great wealth and gifts upon the church but to the faithful he granted an indulgence of three years for every visit of eight days and conceded one year of remission of penance, *vera indulgencia*, to anyone visiting it on the anniversary of its dedication. He also consecrated the main altar in honour of the Blessed Virgin Mary under which rested the bodies of SS Calixtus, Cornelius, Julius, Calepodius and Quirinus, surely the greatest concentration of papal bones together in one place.

All the churches of Rome had, in varying degrees, significance for Innocent. After all, they most readily gave the evidence of history and faith on which he was so determined to base his own message on the importance of Rome. The papal biography, the *Gesta Innocentii PP III* is valuable in indicating his approach to all of them[55]. He was always keen to use the

[55] *PL* 214, cols xvii-ccxxviii.

churches and their history as points from which the mission of the Gospel could be proclaimed. Many of them were linked in the processions he inherited or arranged on important religious occasions. Most had specific relevance, such as the Basilica of St Peter with its *confessio* which he wished to raise to co-equal status with the Constantinian Basilica of the Lateran[56]. One much smaller but no less interesting case was that of SS Sergio e Bacco, mentioned in two passages in the *Gesta*[57]. On becoming Cardinal-Deacon in 1189 or 1190, Lotario dei Conti di Segni took this church as his *titulus* in succession to Paolo Scolari (1179-80), later Clement III (1187-90) and Octavian (1182-89), later Cardinal-Bishop of Ostia (1189-1206). Was it perhaps a *titulus* marked out for those destined to hold high office in the Church? If so, it is hard to explain the apparent neglect in which Lotario found it. It was in such a ruinous condition that one could see more of the crypt beneath than of the church above. The *Gesta* records the essential repairs to roof and walls which Lotario undertook within two years of his elevation to the Cardinalate, together with the construction of new steps leading up to a new altar and a new *pectoralia* or enclosure for the *schola cantorum* in the choir.

The *Gesta* identifies a second campaign of decoration by Innocent when he became Pope. Then and immediately he ordered a portico with columns to be built, paying for this ‘from the goods which God had conferred upon him during his Cardinalate’. He also gave expensive gifts and patronised exquisite small works for use in the liturgical ceremonies in the church. The *Gesta* records a purple silk cope with an orphrey, a *baldachino* and altar frontal, a cope and alb, a *corporale* and pyx for the Eucharist, a basilica-shrine in Limoges enamel work together with the sum of twenty pounds. To enhance the altar, he gave various small silver dishes and receptacles - a tiny silver dish shaped like a boat, a silver *cochlear* or spoon weighing seven and a half ounces as well as vestments, a chasuble of red silk with an orphrey, a silken

---

56 MACCARRONE, *"Cathedra Sancti Petri"*, pp. 428-32.

57 *Gesta*, cols. xviii, ccvii; M.BONFIOLI, ‘La diaconia dei SS.Sergio e Bacco nel Foro Romano: fonti e problemi’, *Rivista di archeologia cristiana* 50 (1974), pp. 55-85.

fringe and a silver-gilt chalice. He also ensured an income of one hundred pounds to SS Sergio e Bacco.

SS Sergio e Bacco, first mentioned as a *diaconia* in 684, was important during the pontificate of Leo III (795-816)[58]. After many years it ceased to exist, some time between 1518 and 1562 - possibly even as early as 1532. A road was then cut through the Forum for the visit of the Emperor Charles V. Innocent had already defined the curtilage of SS Sergio e Bacco when he took it under papal protection on 2 July 1199 and the location of the new road seems to have confirmed Innocent's view of the church's central position[59]. Elsewhere it is also identified as located at the *umbilicus* of Rome, *SS Sergii ubi umbilicum Romae* or *fons Sancti Petri ubi est carcer eius*, from its proximity to the Mammertine prison. It was close to the church of S.Adriano, the former Senate House or *Curia*, itself significant as a liturgical station at the end of the Via Sacra[60].

Interesting manuscript evidence for this reveals that an inscription existed over the portico[61]. A rough translation might be + ALMOST RUINED AS IF THERE WAS NOTHING THERE; BUT LOTHAIR, THE BRIDEGROOM, FIRST RAISED UP THE BRIDE AND THEN BEING MADE THE FATHER OF THE CITY AND THE WORLD AT LENGTH RENEWED MY NAVE FROM HIS OWN POSSESSIONS, THUS I WAS TWICE RENEWED +. It is possible that the inscription is contemporary with Innocent's III's pontificate for it stresses the important two-stage restoration of the Cardinalate and of the

---

[58] IBID, p. 60.

[59] *Register II*, p. 102; *PL* 214, col. 651.

[60] A,MANCINI, 'La chiesa medioevale di S.Adriano nel Foro Romano', *Pontificia Accademia Romana di Archeologia. Rendiconti*, 40 (1967-8), pp. 101-45.

[61] + PENE RUI QUASI NULLA FUI: SED ME RELAVAVIT LOTARIUS SPONSUSQUE PRIUS SPONSAM RENOVAVIT DEQUE MEO GREMIO SUMPTUS PATER URBIS ET ORBIS HOC TAMEN EX PROPRIO FECIT MIHI, SIC RENOVOR BIS + Vat. Lat. 3938, fol. 284, *In ecclesia SS Sergii et Bacchi supra porticum.* Compare Schede Corvisiero, Busta II.

pontificate as established by the *Gesta*. On the other hand, Sixtus IV's general interest in Innocent might suggest that it dates from his pontificate[62].

Innocent's liberality to SS Sergio e Bacco is clear from his list of gifts. The Limoges-enamel 'basilica' shrine, similar to those in the Musée de Cluny or the Museo del Duomo at Pisa was of the finest and most fashionable work and the young Lotario would have encountered similar examples first at Grandmont in the Limousin where he was in May-June 1187[63]. His generosity here can perhaps be linked with his veneration for the pope's personal chapel of St Laurence at the Lateran, known as the *Sancta Sanctorum*[64].

In all his actions, Innocent followed the stance taken by his predecessors; those of Peter and Paul; those of the two previous Innocents and particularly that of Gregory the Great. Rome, during his own pontificate, had again become the centre to which he could summon the men of the Church. It was the place to which many felt the call to come either to pilgrimage or to seek papal help. Innocent had, through his actions, opened to all those who came the mission and message of the churches of Rome and of Rome itself. He had built up a series of events and images, from his use of the *acheropoita* or image of the Saviour in the *Sancta Sanctorum* to an enhanced importance of the *pallium*, through which the faith was strengthened in Christ. To all who came, the crucified Christ and the message of God's forgiveness was preached, worshipped and followed. He had indeed made of Rome a setting for God's grace as he had wished.

In doing this, Innocent had learned from Rome's classical past, the City of Antiquity's importance as the Eternal City. Yet Rome had not only passed from Antiquity. It had come to represent the Christian faith's release from its

---

62 BONFIOLI, 'La diaconia dei SS Sergio e Bacco', pp. 66-7.

63 M.M.GAUTIER, 'La Clôture Emaillée de la Confession de Saint-Pierre au Vatican hors du Concile de Latran, 1215', *Bibliothèque des Cahiers Archéologiques*. II. *Synthronon: art et archéologie de la fin de l'Antiquité*, (Paris, 1968), pp. 237-46.

64 VAN DIJK & HAZELDEN WALKER, *Modern Roman Liturgy*, pp. 91-5.

old Jewish matrix[65]. In so doing, it showed that the faith had been saved from being Judaised; something which had been important in the message of St Paul[66]. As the Rome of the earlier Romans passed away, this developing Church enabled the City to become the centre of Christendom. As a further step in this progress during his pontificate, Innocent believed that his task was to make of the words of St Peter a reality in that 'the lively stones made up the spiritual house'[67]. Rome would be shown to be the habitation of the Spirit, the setting for God's grace and a worthy City of God.

---

65 CHADWICK, 'The Circle and the Ellipse', for a most interesting exposition on this problem.

66 Titus I: 14.

67 I Peter 2: 4-5.

G.B. Pittoni, The Church of Ss Sergio e Bacco on the Roman Forum
(Photograph: Frank Salmon; by permission of The British School at Rome.)

Marten van Heemskerck, A three-quarter rear view of the Church of Ss Sergio e Bacco, looking from the Tabularium towards the Colosseum, c. 1535 (Photograph: Frank Salmon; by permission of The British School at Rome.)

# Cistercians in the Papal States, 1198–1216

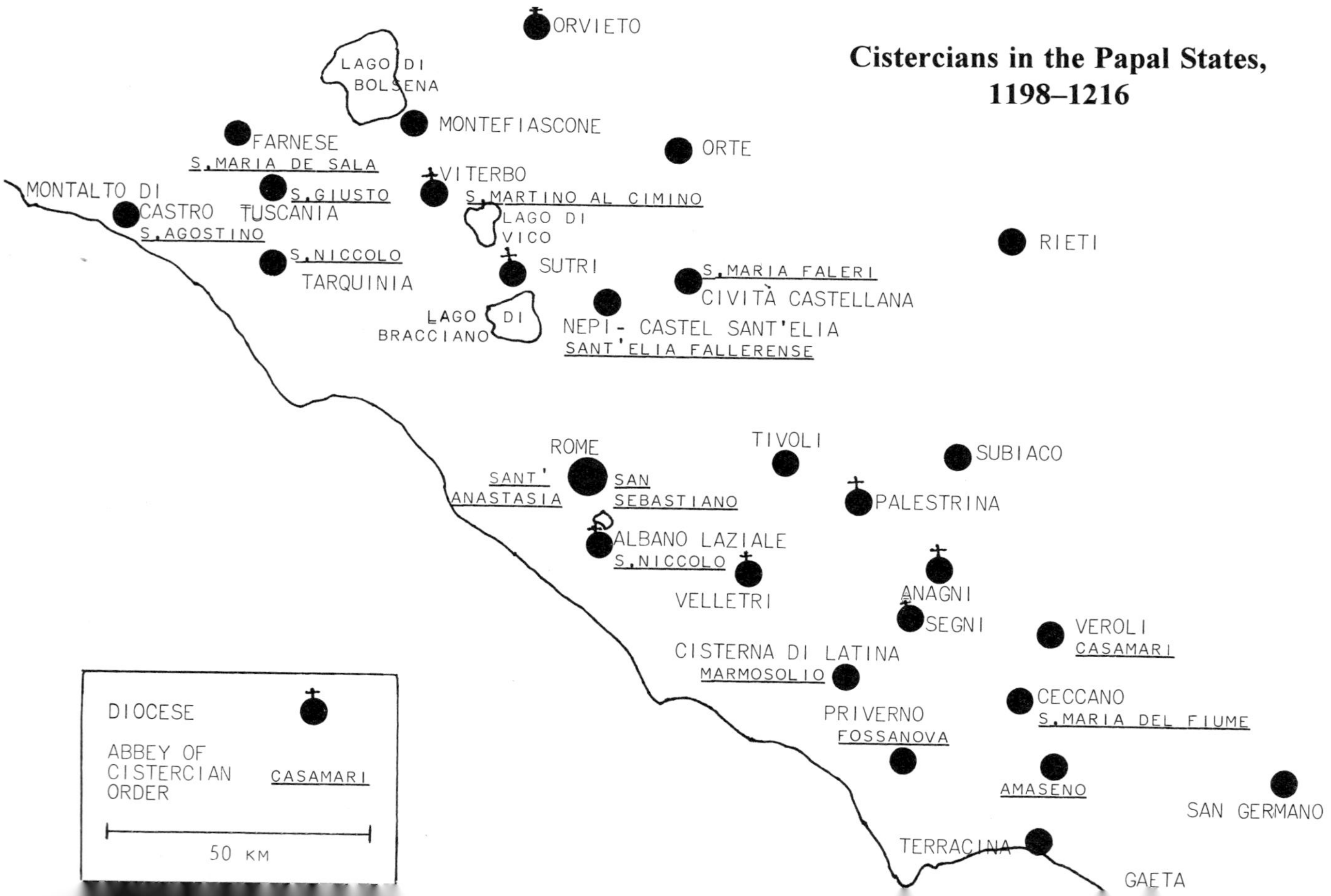
ORVIETO
LAGO DI BOLSENA
MONTEFIASCONE
FARNESE
S.MARIA DE SALA
ORTE
VITERBO
S.MARTINO AL CIMINO
MONTALTO DI CASTRO
S.AGOSTINO
S.GIUSTO
TUSCANIA
LAGO DI VICO
RIETI
S.NICCOLO
TARQUINIA
SUTRI
S.MARIA FALERI
CIVITÀ CASTELLANA
LAGO DI BRACCIANO
NEPI - CASTEL SANT'ELIA
SANT'ELIA FALLERENSE
ROME
SANT' ANASTASIA
SAN SEBASTIANO
TIVOLI
SUBIACO
PALESTRINA
ALBANO LAZIALE
S.NICCOLO
VELLETRI
ANAGNI
SEGNI
VEROLI
CASAMARI
CISTERNA DI LATINA
MARMOSOLIO
CECCANO
S.MARIA DEL FIUME
PRIVERNO
FOSSANOVA
AMASENO
SAN GERMANO
TERRACINA
GAETA
DIOCESE
ABBEY OF CISTERCIAN ORDER
CASAMARI
50 KM

# II

# For the See of Simon Peter: The Cistercians at Innocent III's Nearest Frontier

From the very first moment of his election on 8 January 1198 Innocent III was acutely aware that he was successor to the Fisherman of Galilee, the Apostle Simon Peter.[1] At his consecration on 22 February, coincidentally the Feast of St Peter's Chair in Antioch, he became even more convinced of his inheritance.[2] On this day, when he became Bishop of Rome, he believed that the chair on which he sat for the ceremony was that same one which the feast day celebrated.[3] As was to be expected, tales of a vision were brought to him to consolidate these feelings. This vision, told by an aged priest and recorded in the Chapter Archives of St Peter's, reported that, while the priest slept, St Peter himself had appeared saying 'Go to Pope Innocent and tell him from me that from the day of his birth, I have loved him like a son. Now, having been promoted through all the grades of the priesthood, he has at last come to my

---

1 O.HAGENEDER and A.HAIDACHER (eds), *Die Register Innocenz' III*, Bd I, *Pontifikatsjahr 1198/99* (Graz-Koln, 1964), [hereafter *Register* I], 3-5; J.P.MIGNE (ed), *Patrologia Latina* (Paris, 1855), *Innocentii III; Opera Omnia,* 4 vols [hereafter *PL*], 214, I, 1; A.POTTHAST (ed), *Regesta Pontificium Romanorum,* 2 vols (Berlin, 1874), [hereafter POTTHAST], I, 1.

2 *Gesta Innocentii III*, *PL*, xvii-ccxxviii, [hereafter *Gesta*], VII, xx; L.Duchesne, *Le Liber Pontificalis* (2 ed Paris, 1955-1957).

3 M.MACCARRONE, 'La "Cathedra Sancti Petri" nel Medioevo: da Simbolo a reliquia', *Rivista di Storia della Chiesa in Italia*, 39 (1985), 349-447; *Register* I, 296, 417-419; A.ALBANI (ed), *Collectionis Bullarum Sacrosanctae Basilicae Vaticanae* 3 vols (Rome 1747-1754) I, *Ad Sancto Leone Magno ad Innocentium VI*, 77.

seat'.[4] The message of this vision was crystal-clear reinforcing what Innocent himself believed. The work of the Apostle Simon Peter, whose faith Christ had prayed would not fail him and who had received the message to strengthen the brethren, was to be continued by his successor Innocent.

There was much work to be done and not withstanding his primacy of position as pope the help of others would be essential. Problems came right up to the gates of Rome itself and even arose within the City.[5] In the surrounding area, more German than Italian under Philip of Swabia and his henchmen, Markward of Anweiler, Conrad of Marlenheim and Diepoldo of Acerra, there was little interest in furthering the aims of the church.[6] The Patrimony belonged to St Peter in name alone[7] and while the Germans did not then control Campania they were still feared there more than the pope himself. In Rome the noble families, the *consortoria*, were linked and inter-linked by marriage ties and intrigue.[8] The support of a majority of these was vital to any new pope and could never be taken for granted even if the pope

---

4 *Ibid*, 79-80. Quod a nativitate sua, quasi filium illum dilexi et per diversos gradus promotum in mea tandem Sede constitui.

5 *Gesta*, VIII, xxi.

6 T.C.VAN CLEVE, *Markward of Anweiler and the Sicilian Regency* (Princeton, 1937); M.MACCARRONE, 'Innocenzo III e gli avvenimenti di Romagna del 1198', *Miscellanea Augusto Campana, Medievo e Umanesimo*, 45 (Padua 1981), [hereafter MACCARRONE, 'Gli avvenimenti'], 403-443.

7 For the view that a real Papal State existed before 1198 see T.F.X.NOBLE, *The Republic of St Peter: the birth of the Papal State 680-825* (Pennsylvania, 1984); M.Moresco, *Il Patrimonio di S.Pietro: studio storico-giuridico sulla istituzione finanziarie della Santa Sede* (Turin, 1916). For the opposing view, D.WALEY, *The Papal State in the Thirteenth Century* (London, 1916); P.PARTNER, *The Lands of St Peter* (London, 1972), P.TOUBERT, *Les Structures du Latium Mediévale* 2 vols (Rome, 1973); M.Laufs, *Politik und Recht bei Innocenz III* (Koln, 1980).

8 A.LUCHAIRE, 'Innocent III et le Peuple Romain', *Revue Historique*, 81 (1903), [hereafter LUCHAIRE, 'Innocent III et le Peuple Romain'], 225-277; D.HERLIHY, 'Family Solidarity in Medieval Italian History', *Economy, Society and Government in Medieval Italy. Studies in Memory of Robert L.Reynolds* (Kent, Ohio 1969); L.HALPHEN, *L'Administration de Rome au Moyen Age* (Paris, 1907).

was, as in Innocent's case, himself a Roman. These families were notoriously fickle. The caustic comments of St Bernard remind us of this when, in his own outspoken way, he called them both irreverent and factious.[9] Neither Germans nor Romans could be counted upon to support the pope, rather the reverse. Various measures would have to be taken to bring Rome and the Patrimony more into line with what was expected of the see of Simon Peter and Innocent seems to have decided quite early on that he could best work through monastic institutions.[10] The Cistercian Order seemed to him to be particularly suitable for the tasks he had in mind. His letter to the General Chapter in September 1198 asking for Cistercian help plays on the Martha-Mary, Leah-Rachel imagery where contemplation and action were both needed.[11] He refers to himself as the helmsman in the barque of St Peter, where on storm-tossed seas the Apostle stretches out his right hand to save those in danger. Further, he promises that with St Peter, their feet will be led to dry ground and there will be no danger to them of being drowned by worldly affairs.[12]

By the end of the twelfth century the Cistercians who, in St Bernard's words, were 'the restorers of lost religion'[13] had, through their remarkably

---

9 St Bernard, *Vita Prima, auctore Ernaldo*, *PL* 185 (1855), 4. I, Book II, VII, 291-293; LUCHAIRE,'Innocent III et le Peuple Romain', 226.

10 M.MACCARRONE, 'Primato Romano e Monasteri dal Principio del Secolo XII ad Innocenzo III', *Istituzione Monastiche e Istituzione Canonicali in Occidente (1123-1215)*, (Milan, 1980) [hereafter MACCARRONE, 'Primato Romano'], 49-132.

11 J.M.CANIVEZ (ed), *Statuta Capitulorum Generalium Ordinis Cisterciensis ab anno 1116 ad annum 1786*, 8 vols (Louvain, 1933-1941), I, *Ab anno 1116 ad annum 1220*, (Louvain, 1933) [hereafter CANIVEZ, I], 221-224. Compare C.J.HOLDSWORTH, 'The Blessings of Work: the Cistercian view', *Studies in Church History* 10 (Blackwell, 1973) [hereafter HOLDSWORTH, 'Blessings of Work'], 59-76.

12 CANIVEZ, I, 223.

13 For a description of his own ascetic practices, St Bernard, *Vita Prima*, *PL* 185, 250; J.F.HINNEBUSCH, *The Historia Occidentalis of Jacques de Vitry*, Spicilegium Friburgense, 17 (Fribourg, 1972), 112-115 on the novelty of the Cistercians.

strong organisation achieved much well-deserved acclaim.[14] However, the considerable donations, privileges and exemptions which had accumulated around them were contrary not only to the ascetic spirit of their founding fathers but also to that of St Benedict. Whilst the Cistercians themselves were open to criticism, the papacy too bore some responsibility for this situation.[15] Cistercians everywhere had sought and obtained a whole series of papal privileges which exempted their abbeys from local episcopal control and from paying tithes on their own lands. Such exemptions jeopardized the observance of their rule and their life of poverty at the desert margins and the order acquired instead a reputation for avarice and greed.[16] This caused Walter Map to rail and grumble that they had become the new Jews of Europe.[17] They were tempted to assert their independence not only from local bishops but also from the pope himself. But the responsibility of a pope as *abbas universalis* had become an increasingly important charge, transforming the apostolic protection of St Peter into a papal institution expressing the exercise of the pope's jurisdiction over the whole church. This reached its highest development during the pontificate of Innocent III, expressed as it was in his confident formula of association of the pope with St Peter *sub beati Petri et nostra protectione suscipimus*.[18]

---

14 C.H.LAWRENCE, *Medieval Monasticism* (2 edition London, 1989), 174-205; G.CONSTABLE, 'Renewal and Reform in Religious Life: Concepts and Realities',in R.L.BENSON and G.CONSTABLE (eds), *Renaissance and Renewal in the Twelfth Century* (Cambridge, Mass. and Oxford, 1982), 37-67.

15 B.M.BOLTON, '*Via Ascetica*: a papal quandary', *Studies in Church History*, 22 (Blackwell, 1985), [hereafter BOLTON, '*Via Ascetica*'], 161-191; MACCARRONE, 'Primato romano', 80-107.

16 R.W.SOUTHERN, *Western Society and the Church* (Harmondsworth, 1970), 259-261.

17 M.R.JAMES (ed), Walter Map, *De Nugis Curialium: Courtiers' Trifles*, revised and translated by C.N.L.BROOKE and R.A.B.MYNORS (Oxford, 1983), 85-113, especially 103-113.

18 7 July 1199. R.FANTAPPIE, *Le carte della prepositura di Prato, I, 1006-1200* (Florence, 1977), 488; MACCARRONE, 'Primato romano', 50-70, especially 58, 63-64.

Innocent clearly admired the undoubted qualities of the Cistercians, their organisation, filiation and mutual supervision. They were ideally suited as crusade preachers and organisers and as frontier guards of the faith in those areas where the Church's writ ran weakly. Other aspects did not please him so well - as when in 1198 he was blamed for having excused the Abbot of Sambucina from the General Chapter to allow him instead to preach the Crusade in Sicily[19] - or when the mother house of Cîteaux fell into internecine quarrelling in 1202 with her four daughters, La Ferté, Pontigny, Clairvaux and Morimond.[20] What was seen by Innocent as his duty to intervene when things needed to be remedied to improve the Order was seen by the Cistercians as an unwarranted intrusion into matters which only they could regulate through their institutions. Later Cistercian hagiography *c*1230 was to emphasize any resentment there may have been by indicating by just how narrow a margin Innocent had escaped going to Hell.[21] In actual fact, Innocent surrounded himself with able, intelligent and willing Cistercians, using them as legates, as commissioners of enquiry and as his confessors and chaplains. Spiritually outstanding amongst these was Brother Rainier,[22] the Andrew to Innocent's Peter.

---

19 CANIVEZ, I, 16; *Register* I, 302,430-433; 508, 741-743; POTTHAST I, 335.

20 *PL* 214, 1107-1108; POTTHAST I, 1772.

21 J.STRANGE (ed), *Caesarii Heisterbacensis Monachi Ordinis Cisterciensis Dialogus Miraculorum* 2 vols (Koln, 1851) II, 7-8: O.HOLDER-EGGER (ed), *Chronica Minor Auctore Minorita Erphordiensi*, *Monumenta Germania Historia*, Scriptores [hereafter *MGH, SS*] 24, 196; THOMAS DE CANTIMPRÉ, *Vita Lutgardis Virgine*, G.HENSCHENIUS (ed), *Acta Sanctorum Bollandia*, 3 June (Antwerp, 1701), 245-247; MACCARRONE, 'Primato romano', 111-112.

22 (?-d.1207/1209). H.GRUNDMANN, 'Zur Biographie Joachim von Flore und Rainers von Ponza', *Deutsches Archiv*, 16 (1960), [hereafter GRUNDMANN, 'Zur Biographie'], 437-546; B.GRIESSER, 'Rainer von Fossanova und seiner Brief an Abt Arnald von Cîteaux (1203)', *Cistercienser Cronik*, 60 (1953), [hereafter GRIESSER, 'Rainer von Fossanova'] 152-167; A.MANRIQUE, *Cisterciensium seu verius ecclesiasticorum Annalium a condito cistercio*, 4 vols (Lyon 1649-1657), [hereafter MANRIQUE] III, *ab anno MCLXXIV usque ad MCCXII inclusive*, 368-370.

Although Innocent enjoyed variable relations with the Order as a whole, the situation in the Patrimony closer to Rome meant that all minds, including those of the Cistercians, had to be concentrated upon the tasks in hand. The sudden death of the young German Emperor, Henry VI, in September 1197 was to present Innocent and his local Cistercian allies with a unique opportunity. Their nearest frontier was not in some far-distant place in Poland or Pomerania or even in the Baltic or Iberia. It was quite literally in those areas within the Patrimony in German hands and where ecclesiastical authority needed to be restored.[23]

Maccarrone has clearly shown how Innocent's policy towards the *Patrimonium beati Petri* was from the outset conceived in terms of reform and recovery expressed through his use of the terms *recuperatio* and papal *solicitudo.*[24] The Church, sometimes obliged to conduct political actions to restore papal territory, faced the risk that in a deteriorating situation it might be forced to resort to the same methods as those of the local lords.[25] Innocent balanced this with the need to bring peace and stability to the region. He sincerely believed that unless he could guarantee powerful overlordship, not only of Rome but of the whole Patrimony, he could not, as heir to the Apostle, carry out his duty to the universal church. His justification was that the Church had received its dominion from that power given by Christ to St Peter and his successors.[26] The programme of papal government for the area was both astute and appealing. After the yoke of unbearable German oppression, that harsh military government exercised by the functionaries of

---

23 MACCARRONE, 'Gli avvenimenti', 437-446.

24 M.MACCARRONE, *Studi su Innocenzo III*, *Italia Sacra*: Studi e documenti di Storia Ecclesiastica, 17 (Padua, 1972), [hereafter MACCARRONE, *Studi*], 9-22; *Register* I, 126-128; *PL* 214, 76; POTTHAST I, 82.

25 *Gesta* XVII, xxix-xxx; MACCARRONE, *Studi*, 10-13. Innocent used the text from Ecclesiastes 13:1, He who touches pitch shall be defiled.

26 M.MACCARRONE, 'Il papa "Vicarius Christi": Testi e dottrina dal secolo xii al principio del xiv', *Miscellanea Pio Paschini*, Lateranum, NS, 2 vols (Rome, 1948), I, 427-500 and especially 445-459.

Henry VI and so often experienced by the people of the Patrimony, Innocent's papal alternative offered an easy yoke and a light burden.[27] Apostolic protection and papal government in this region would be mild for laymen and monasteries alike. The pope's peace would lay stress on justice, peace and a secure road system where previously even a cardinal had been known to have been hijacked![28]

Along this road network, on the great Roman arteries going North and East, the Aurelia, the Clodia, the Cassia and the Flaminia, and the Appia and Latina running South, lay some of the sixteen or so strategically-placed and identifiable Cistercian houses of the Patrimony.[29] All seem to have been old foundations which became Cistercian later, for the most part during the pontificates of Adrian IV and Alexander III between 1154 and 1181.[30] Two houses were close to Rome itself - Sant'Anastasia,[31] the present-day Tre Fontane, on the via Ostiense and S.Sebastiano[32] near the catacombs of the same name on the via Appia Antica. Guarding the Patrimony's Northern

[27] Matthew 11:30; *PL* 214, 76; *Register* I, 126-128: POTTHAST I, 82.

[28] Octavian, Cardinal-Bishop of Ostia, captured c1192 by Conrad 'Flybrain' and held at Monte S.Maria. *Gesta* IX, xxiv-xxv; W.MALECZEK, *Papst und Kardinalskolleg von 1191 bis 1216: die Kardinale unter Coelestin III und Innocenz III* (Vienna, 1984), [hereafter MALECZEK, *Papst und Kardinalskolleg*], 82; O.HAGENEDER, W.MALECZEK and A.Strnad, *Die Register Innocenz' III, Bd II, 2 Jahrgang (1199/1200)*, (Rome-Vienna, 1979), [hereafter *Register* II], 166 (175), 322-323,

[29] L.JANAUSCHEK, *Originum Cistercensium* I (Vienna, 1877); F.CARAFFA, *Monasticon Italiae* I, Roma e Lazio (Cesena, 1981), [hereafter *Monasticon*]; M.MASTROCOLA, 'Il monachesimo nelli diocesi di Cività Castellana, Orte e Gallese fino al secolo XII', in *Miscellanea di Studio Viterbesi* (Viterbo, 1962) 352-419; *I Cistercensi e il Lazio*, Atti delle giornate di studio dell'Istituto di Storia dell'Arte dell'Università di Roma, 17-21 Maggio 1977, (Rome, 1978).

[30] *Monasticon*, 104-106.

[31] *Ibid*, 179, 84-85. Cistercian from 1140.

[32] *Ibid*, 154, 77. Cistercian from 1171.

frontier were S.Agostino at Montalto di Castro,[33] S.Maria de Sala at Farnese near Lake Bolsena,[34] S.Giusto at Tuscania[35] and S.Niccolo at Tarquinia,[36] all in that area known as *Tuscia Romana.*[37] In South Etruria between the northern frontier of the Patrimony and Rome were two houses, Sant'Elia *Fallerense* at Castel Sant'Elia[38] and S.Maria *Faleri* near Cività Castellana,[39] both still bearing place-name evidence of Etruscan origins. Outside Viterbo near the Lago di Vico was S.Martino al Cimino,[40] in many ways the most interesting monastery in the northern part of the Patrimony.

On his accession, Innocent acted to control this area. In the autumn of 1198 he had journeyed to Perugia returning by way of Todi, Amelia and Cività Castellana receiving the homage and fidelity of the people of those areas.[41] He went on to intervene directly in the affairs of these Cistercian houses of *Tuscia Romana.* The Cistercian General Chapter of September 1199 recorded their own visitation of Faleria, S.Giusto, S.Martino, S.Sebastiano,

---

33 *Ibid*, 132,149; *PL* 215, 703-705; POTTHAST I, 2198. Cistercian in 1215-1216.

34 *Monasticon*, 101, 141. Founded as a Cistercian house in 1189.

35 *Ibid*, 267, 186-187. Cistercian from 1146.

36 CANIVEZ I, 243.

37 *Gesta*, XIV, xxviii; J.RASPI SERRA, *La Tuscia Romana* (Rome, 1972); A.Diviziani, 'Il patrimonio di S.Pietro in Tuscia', *Bolletino dell'Istituto Storico-Artistico Orvietano*, 17, (1961), 3-41; J.RASPI SERRA and C. LANGANARA FABIANO, *Economia e territorio: il Patrimonium Beati Petri nella Tuscia* (Naples, 1987).

38 *Monasticon*, 70, 131-132. Taken into papal protection in 1178. In 1195 the Cistercian General Chapter ordered its reform.

39 *Ibid*, 98, 139. Became Cistercian in 1143.

40 *Ibid*, 299, 195; P.EGIDI, 'L'abbazia di San Martino sul Monte Cimino con documenti inediti', *Rivista di Storia Benedettina*, 1 (1906), 579-590; 2 (1907), 161-199.

41 *Gesta*, X, xxv-xxvi.

Sant'Anastasia and Sala so that reports of lax discipline could be investigated.[42] Apparently a number of monks were not living according to the Rule and few were sufficiently worthy to correct the rest. Further, at Sant'Anastasia silence was not observed and women had gained access. The Chapter claimed the competence to correct or to find the means of correction, asking Innocent with humility and reverence that John, monk of Casamari should explain the monastic *conversatio*[43]. Innocent himself was clearly hinting at the possible dissolution of these monasteries divided as they were by quarrels amongst themselves.[44] This dark threat seems to have produced the required remedy. For the rest of the pontificate the misdeeds of all Cistercian houses in the Patrimony as reported in the General Chapter were of the very slightest nature - trivial in the extreme. There was only one exception to this. The Statutes of the General Chapter in 1200 reveal something of the extent of indebtedness of S.Martino, the house in that year owing twenty shillings in money of Lyon for business undertaken at the Curia.[45] In 1206 the abbot of its mother house at Saint-Sulpice in Bugey was ordered to reform its wayward daughter.[46] In the same year Innocent wrote to Abbot Peter and the monks of S.Martino reminding them - lest they should be in any doubt - that they were by then in such an advanced state of poverty that scarcely three brothers could be maintained in the house.[47] Its possessions were all alienated and its debts formidable. Whilst the General

---

42 *PL* 214, 826-828, 1107-1108; POTTHAST I, 1772; MACCARRONE, 'Primato romano', 112-113.

43 John of Casamari, Papal Chaplain, Bishop of Forcone, L'Aquila, (1204-1207) and of Perugia (1207-1230).

44 *Ibid*, 243. Dominus papa pro dissolutione quarumdam abbatiarum de partibus illis. *PL* 214, 1107-1108; Potthast I, 1772.

45 CANIVEZ, I, 260.

46 *Ibid*, 327.

47 *PL* 215, 1309-1312; POTTHAST 2997.

Chapter seems to have taken the decision to abandon it altogether Innocent, 'wishing rather to encourage the spread of religion than to see it removed completely' from such a strategically-placed monastery, offered the vast sum of 1000 pounds to redeem its possessions and pay off the debts.[48] To ensure its income, Innocent granted the church of S.Salvatore near Orte with all its possessions. This lavish investment in the Cistercians of S.Martino *presso Viterbo* was by no means a waste of money, maintaining as it did a Cistercian house at an important frontier point. The size of the gift, however, was not typical. The 100 pounds in rent which he granted to the monastery of Faleria was a far more modest example of gifts by this pope to his Cistercians.[49] Successful strategy was worth paying for. In 1207 S.Martino was placed in the filiation of Pontigny and adopted as its 'special daughter'.[50] In the case of S.Martino, Innocent had not only acted as *abbas universalis*, over-ruling politely but firmly, the decision of the Cistercian General Chapter but also applied the same principle he was applying to Subiaco and Cassino; that modest corporate wealth was essential for the well-being of a monastery.[51] Innocent had other links with Viterbo and its region. It was a former imperial stronghold with a serious problem of heresy specifically legislated against in 1199,[52] 1205[53] and 1207.[54] In 1207 he held his great three-day Parliament

---

48 *Gesta* CXXVI, clxii-clxiv; POTTHAST 3291. For the gift of a red and gold altar frontal and 100 pounds in money of Siena, *Gesta* CXLV, ccviii, ccxxvii.

49 *Ibid* CXLIX, ccxxvii.

50 CANIVEZ I, 345.

51 BOLTON, '*Via ascetica*', 175-180.

52 *Vergentis in senium*, 25 March 1199. *Register*, II, 1, 3-5; *PL* 214, 537-539; Potthast 643; W.ULLMANN, 'The significance of Innocent III's decretal *Vergentis*', in *Etudes d'histoire du droit canonique dediées à Gabriel Le Bras*, 2 vols (Paris, 1965) I, 729-741.

53 *Cum lupi rapaces*, 16 June 1205. *PL* 215, 654-657, 673-674; POTTHAST 2539.

54 *Ad eliminandum*, 23 September 1207. *PL* 215, 1226-1228; POTTHAST 3187.

in the City, publicly receiving the homage of his vassals.[55] He spent that summer there with the Curia,[56] returning again in 1209[57] and 1214.[58]

It was however to the south of Rome, in Campania and Marittima, that the two greatest and most important Cistercian houses were to be found in the Patrimony. Fossanova near Priverno lay astride the via Appia[59] while Casamari near Veroli[60] guarded the approaches to the Regno by way of the via Latina and the Upper Liri Valley. There were others but they were small by comparison: Marmosolio at Cisterna di Latina whose abbot requested affiliation to both Fossanova and Casamari in 1206;[61] Amaseno,[62] S.Maria del Fiume at Ceccano[63] and S.Niccolo, a cell at Albano Laziale.[64] Innocent made his most generous gifts to the two great abbeys on his southern frontier. He gave 100 pounds for the completion of the new church of Fossanova begun in 1187 and was present at its consecration on 19 June 1208[65]

---

55 *Gesta*, CXXIV, clxii; MACCARRONE, *Studi*, 51.

56 William of Andres, *Chronicle*, MGH, SS, 24, (Hannover 1897), 690-773, especially 737.

57 His second and longest stay was from mid-May to mid-September 1209. L.V.DELISLE, 'Itinéraire de Innocent III dressé d'après les actes de ce pontife', *Bibliothèque de l'Ecole des Chartes*, (1857), [hereafter DELISLE, 'Itinéraire'], 500-534, especially 509. Also MACCARRONE, *Studi*, 56-57; POTTHAST 3727-3802.

58 23 June - 19 September, 1214. *Ibid*, 4932-4938.

59 *Monasticon*, 168, 159. Cistercian since 1125.

60 *Ibid*, 283, 190-191.

61 *Ibid*, 86, 135-136; CANIVEZ, I, 332. Cistercian since 1167.

62 *Monasticon*, 13,118. Unclear when this house became Cistercian.

63 *Ibid*, 79, 133-134.

64 *Ibid*, 11, 117. ? Cistercian.

65 *PL* 215, 1435-1437; POTTHAST I, 3465; G.H.PERTZ (ed), *Annales Ceccanenses*, MGH, SS, 19 (Hannover, 1866) 275-302, especially 297; F.FARINA and B.FORNARI, *L'architettura cistercense e l'abbazia di Casamari* (Frosinone, 1978).

donating a further 100 pounds in annual income.[66] He gave 200 ounces of gold *pro fabrica* for the rebuilding of Casamari together with a grange at Castrum and 100 pounds in annual rent.[67] His donation of 100 pounds income to the house of Marmosolio at Cisterna[68] was comparable to the small-scale gifts to houses in the northern part of the Patrimony.

The threat to the Patrimony in the South came not from heresy but from the considerable and long-lasting German occupation which even prevented Innocent from making the journey to Montecassino, mother house of all the Benedictines, until the summer of 1208 in the tenth year of his pontificate.[69] In the autumn of 1199, Casamari had been the stage for political intrigue, a spectacular banquet organised by the excommunicated adventurer Markward of Anweiler to welcome the papal legates.[70] Three cardinals were sent by Innocent to receive his submission, amongst them Hugolino, then Cardinal-Priest of S.Eustachio,[71] who outwitted the wily German after rumours were spread that the papal envoys risked capture if they dared to issue the papal mandate.[72] After Markward's death the German threat was greatly lessened when in 1205 the brother, Rainier of Fossanova, received the submissions of Conrad of Marlenheim and Diepoldo of Acerra and played a crucial role in ensuring that their oaths were binding.[73]

---

66 *Gesta*, CXLIX, ccxxvii.

67 *Ibid*, CXLV, ccviii.

68 *Ibid*, CXLV, ccxxvii.

69 A.GAUDENZI (ed), *Chronica Romanorum pontificium et imperatorum ac de rebus in Apulia gestis (781-1228) auctore ignoto monacho Cisterciensi, Società Napoletana di Sancta Patria*, I, Cronache, (Naples, 1888), 34; *PL* 215, 1593-1594; DELISLE, 'Itinéraire', 521.

70 *Gesta*, XXIII, lxviii.

71 MALECZEK, *Papst und Kardinalskolleg*, 126-133.

72 *Gesta*, XXIII, xliv.

73 *Ibid*, XXXVIII, lxviii.

In the North of the Patrimony Innocent had acted himself whereas in the South, mainly because of the German occupation he was forced to rely on others. In this the houses of Fossanova and Casamari were of great importance. Earlier, both had played a dual role on the pope's behalf in trying to bring the kings of England and France to lasting peace or at least a truce.[74] While Stephen of Fossanova was commended to John by Innocent,[75] Gerald, abbot of Casamari,[76] entrusted with the mission to Philip Augustus, ran backwards and forwards between France and England[77] *de Francia ad Angliam et de Anglia ad Franciam discurrendo* for a whole year between 1203-4 - medieval shuttle-diplomacy. Such sensitive diplomatic negotiations required trusted men, well-informed and authoritative who could also appear neutral and impartial. That Innocent should have turned to the Cistercians of the Patrimony and especially to Fossanova and Casamari, should not surprise us. One man, Brother Rainier, probably the most significant Cistercian since St Bernard, provided the link between these two houses and the pope himself.

It is now on Rainier that our full attention must focus. The consequences of his spirituality, faith, life and work are striking and he could not but fail to set the highest example for the Cistercians of the Patrimony. His monastic vocation began at Casamari for there he was certainly an *intimus* of Joachim of Fiore.[78] He was again with Joachim in 1188 at Petralata and both were

---

[74] M.MACCARRONE, 'La Papauté et Philippe Auguste: La decrétale "Novit ille", in R.H.BAUTIER (ed), *La France de Philippe Auguste. Le temps des mutations*, (Paris 1981), 378-397.

[75] MALECZEK, *Papst und Kardinalkolleg*, 179-183; V.J.KOUDELKA, 'Notes pour servir à l'histoire de S.Dominique', *Archivum Fratrum Praedicatorum*, 35 (1965), 5-20; *PL* 215, 182-184; C.R.CHENEY and W.H.SEMPLE (eds), *Selected Letters of Pope Innocent III concerning England*, (London-Edinburgh, 1953), 149-154.

[76] Abbot of Casamari (1183-1209), nephew of Gerald, sixth abbot of Clairvaux.

[77] *Gesta*, CXXIX, clxix-clxxi.

[78] GRUNDMANN, 'Zur Biographie', 437-546.

declared *fugitivi* by the General Chapter in 1192[79] although Rainier did not accompany him to La Sila.[80] In 1198 Rainier was Innocent's legate in Leon, Castile and Portugal[81] while in December of that year the Pope entrusted him with the official legation to Languedoc.[82] Here he was given powers of interdict and excommunication and was instructed to preach together with Brother Guy against the Cathars. His last act of legation seems to have been in July 1199 when he returned from Languedoc suffering from ill-health.[83] He was still mentioned as legate at the General Chapter of 1199[84] and about this time became the Pope's own confessor.[85] Rainier then moved to Fossanova but nevertheless remained within the papal entourage. In June 1201 he was one of an important three-man commission set up to investigate the First and Second Orders of the Humiliati,[86] that is, the canonical *praepositi* and the *religiosi* leading a regular, quasi-monastic life. In November and December 1201 he was with Innocent at Anagni and advised the pope, by his interpretation of a papal dream, on the canonisation process of Gilbert of Sempringham.[87] The author of *The Book of St Gilbert* provides valuable insight into the life of Rainier yet in so doing raises as many questions as he answers. Here Rainier is given the title of Abbot yet we do not know over which, if any house, he held this position. Already by 1201

---

79 CANIVEZ, I, 154.

80 GRUNDMANN, 'Zur Biographie', 441.

81 *Register* I, 92, 132-134; *PL* 214, 79-81; Potthast 81.

82 *Register*, II, 72 (75), 126-134; *PL* 214, 610-615; Potthast, 716.

83 *PL* 214, 1053-1057, de infirmitate.

84 CANIVEZ, I, 245, coram Renerio legato Curiae Romanae.

85 MANRIQUE, III, 369.

86 G.TIRABOSCHI, *Vetera Humiliatorum Monumenta* 3 vols (Milan, 1766-1768), I, 136, 140.

87 R.FOREVILLE and G.KEIR, *The Book of St Gilbert*, (Oxford, 1987), lxxx, 176-177.

he was renowned for his exemplary solitary life-style amongst the hills and greatly venerated, not only by the pope but also by the whole Church of Rome for his remarkable sanctity and knowledge. In truth, a holy man! Rainier interpreted the pope's dream with much confidence, in the best traditions of sacred history, and filled with the spirit of a Joseph or a Daniel, both great biblical interpreters of dreams.[88] His recommendation that Gilbert be canonised was judged by Innocent to require action without delay.

Innocent was also ready to receive Rainier's advice in regard to the Cistercian Order and to the memory of St Bernard for whom the pope had a special veneration. Rainier was eager to maintain the purity and stability of the Cistercians in the face of rash and childish behaviour. In 1202 Rainier encouraged Innocent to comply with the request of the Archbishop of Lyon to prepare a short collect in honour of St Bernard whilst he himself wrote a didactic letter[89] in 1203 to Arnald Amaury, new abbot of Cîteaux.[90] This letter,[91] rich in scriptural allusion from both Old and New Testaments, originated as an attempt to heal the divisions between Cîteaux and her four daughters over primacy. Much of the trouble, Rainier says, is that unsuitable people are entering the Order and asks that the Abbot should read a similar letter which Innocent had sent to him on this very question.[92] The General Chapter of 1204 placed this item on its agenda asking the abbot of Casamari and Brother Nicholas, the pope's chaplain, to deal with the matter.[93]

---

88 *Ibid*, lxxx. Daniel 2. 25-45; Genesis 41. 1-36.

89 *PL* 214, 1032-1033, ad instantiam dilecti filii fratris Rainieri.

90 Arnald Amaury (d. 1225), abbot of Poblet, Grandselve and Cîteaux (1202)

91 GRIESSER, 'Rainer von Fossanova', 163-166.

92 *Ibid*, 166. Compare *PL* 214, 1031-1034 for deserters to the Cistercian Order.

93 CANIVEZ, I, 304.

Even more striking was the remarkable letter,[94] written probably between 1207 and 1209 by Hugolino who had been elevated to the Cardinal-Bishopric of Ostia in 1206 and created Legate to Germany soon after.[95] It was addressed to the abbots and brothers of Fossanova, Casamari and Salem[96] in Germany where Hugolino then was. The substance of the letter which we may analyse under three headings - eulogy, biblical symbols and stimulation to the Cistercians of the Patrimony - is arcane, full of cryptic meaning and scriptural allusion. It would, however, have been perfectly comprehensible to those to whom it was addressed and exemplifies the model whereby ideals and experience are communicated through the vehicle of a friendship with a strongly autobiographical element.[97] Hugolino was not a Cistercian but he may well have been influenced by a literary lament such as that written by St Bernard on the death of his brother.[98] This letter is surely a unique outpouring of feeling and grief and would have been the very thing Cistercians would like to hear.

Following Rainier's death Hugolino is inconsolable and hence delivers his eulogy. Practically speaking we learn that the monk Rainier had retreated to the island of Ponza off Terracina but his death is untimely to say the least.[99] Hugolino describes himself as a premature child brought to birth with his

---

94 E. WINKELMANN (ed) '*Analecta Heidelbergensia*', *Varietà, Archivio della Società Romana di Storia Patria*, 2 (Rome, 1879), [hereafter, WINKELMANN, *Varietà*], 363-367. I am most grateful to Elizabeth A.Beckwith, University of Pennsylvannia, for rendering an unedited and difficult text both accessible and elegant.

95 MALECZEK, *Papst und Kardinalskolleg*, 126-133. Later Pope Gregory IX (1227-1241).

96 Eberhard, abbot of Salem (1191-1240).

97 B.P.MCGUIRE, 'Monastic Friendship and Toleration in twelfth-century Cistercian life', *Studies in Church History*, 22 (1985), 147-160.

98 *Ibid*, 155-156, note 24.

99 WINKELMANN, *Varietà*, 366.

spiritual characteristics as yet unformed.[100] Why, he asks rhetorically, did Rainier abandon him 'in the womb of the world' before he had been led to the point of spiritual birth and light 'with the result that you ceased to be my father before I could be called your son?'.[101] He next bewails the loss of Rainier's spiritual solace, not merely on his own account but for all men. Mauritania can say more about him than can Italy for there his miracles have 'softened the hardness of infidelity'.[102] His gift of prophecy, perhaps linked to his undoubted ability in the interpretation of miracles, his knowledge of both Old and New Testaments, his eloquence, elegance and urbanity was likened to that of Origen[103] and Didymus[104]. His anti-heretical, eremitical views may be compared to those of Hilarion,[105] Censorinus[106] and Victorinus[107] while his searching out of the real meaning of the Bible, like Gregory Nazianzus[108] and Gregory the Great,[109] meant that when, in Church, he opened his mouth 'rivers of living water seemed to flow from his inmost being'. Spain - where Rainier was legate in 1198 - knows all this as

---

[100] *Ibid*, 364.

[101] *Ibid*, 365.

[102] *Ibid*, 365.

[103] Origen of Alexandria d.254, most prolific writer of all the Fathers of the Early Church.

[104] Didymus the Blind of Alexandria d.395. Learned theologian, dogmatist and exegete.

[105] Hilarion (c291/292-371) left the Egyptian desert to establish anachoretism in Palestine. Loosing the solitude for which he craved, he retreated to Cyprus.

[106] Censorinus. I can find no trace of him.

[107] Victorinus, converted to Christianity 362. Rhetorician, theologian and teacher in Rome and enemy of the Arians.

[108] Gregory of Nazianzus d.390. Studied at Caesarea, Alexandria and Athens and composed sermons, letters and theological orations.

[109] Gregory the Great (590-604), the first monk to become pope. In spite of poor health, produced outstanding sermons and exegesis.

well. As does Pope Innocent and even more so since it was his innocence that Rainier used to commend to the Lord with prayers and tears.[110] Described by Hugolino as an angel of the Lord, this holy man descended from time to time from the heights of contemplation wrapped in a cloud of learning and wearing the crown of spiritual knowledge on his head, at whose roar seven thunderbolts spoke uttering allegorical and moral voices. Rainier may even have possessed the ability to speak in tongues - he was frequently snatched off to the third realm of heaven in the course of delivering his words and reported arcane things which none besides himself knew how to speak. When he crossed over to the Island of Ponza so that he might be free to contemplate, kings, princes and prelates begged to be allowed to give him assistance to mitigate the rigours of such a rigid devotion. Naturally the holy man denied them this pleasure.

The Biblical imagery used in this letter is also of considerable interest. Rahel's (Rachel's) voice is heard in Roma, surely a play on Rama, that holy place,[111] and Rainier's service and devotion to the Cistercian Order is paralleled by the allusion to Jacob's service for her. Although he occasionally clung to Leah, nevertheless he did not part from the embrace of Rachel. Just as Leah and Rachel are juxtaposed so too are Martha and Mary as we should expect in a Cistercian context.[112] Both sisters are to wear mourning until the infidel are restored to the faith. Rainier is equated with Abisaq, the beautiful Shunamite and virgin who is used to warm the bed of the aged King David and thus keep him alive.[113] The warmth of his faith will likewise keep the Patrimony in being.

The message to the Cistercians of Fossanova and Casamari is as telling as the message of Divine Providence which refused to allow Rainier to hide his light under a bushel. The holy man's virtues cannot be described, so

---

[110] WINKELMANN, *Varietà*, 366.

[111] Jeremiah 31.15.

[112] HOLDSWORTH, 'Blessings of work', 64-66.

[113] I Kings 1, 1-4.

immeasurable are they. He represents the lasting sweetness of the word of God - the contemplation of Mary - and, always obedient, he understands Martha's struggle with the brief reward of labour. The role of the Cistercian Order is for Hugolino as beautiful and as virtuous as the young virgin Abisaq by the heat of whose love the members of a chilly and aging world now grow warm.[114] The Order's special jewel is Rainier, learned and erudite and yet possessing the popular touch. He was an inspirational communicator, clearly active in preaching to Moslems in North Africa or Spain, although this letter is the only evidence we have. In his life as a monk his personal severity was much harsher than that of the Order in general. As the text says, he expressed in himself the full rigour and glory of the Cistercian Order. His retreat to Ponza is represented not as the flight of the youthful *fugitivus* but as the search for a desert solitude, that supreme *transitus ad arctiorem vitam* by which he mighty enter into more intimate association with God's word.[115] The Sons of the prophets have flocked to him as if to another Elysium, desiring to gain something from his spiritual joy but he would never tolerate any mitigation of self-imposed harshness. Preferring to read rather than to sleep, to fast rather than to speak, he emulated St Jerome and produced his own spiritual writings, a collection of letters and epistles. 'Oh, where is that collection now?' begs Hugolino. 'All would benefit by reading it, adorned as these works are with the flowers of his virtues. They would be ideal preparation for putting off "the work of the flesh" and obtaining spiritual ends'. Hugolino ends by stating how rapidly and in what an unpolished form he has written this brief note in the very early hours of the morning. What he intends to do, if God so wills it, is to set down the miracles, life and merits of this quite extraordinary abbot. That he does not appear to have done so is very much our loss.

---

[114] WINKELMANN, *Varietà*, 365.

[115] M.A.DIMIER, 'Saint Bernard et le droit en matière de *Transitus*', *Revue Mabillon*, 43 (1953), 48-82; G.PICASSO, 'San Bernardo e il 'transitus' dei monache', in *Studi su S.Bernardo di Chiaravalle nell'ottavo centenario della Canonizzazione* (Rome, 1975), 182-200.

Other events were soon to require attention. The growing importance of the urban environment required a new form of mission for which the Cistercians with their concentration on the desert margins were not suited.[116] Perhaps Rainier, had he lived, would have been able to change this emphasis in his role as the new southern Bernard and as such a major spiritual force in the Patrimony of St Peter. With his untimely death this was not to be so. Rather, it was to the new mendicant friars that Innocent looked to take the gospel message to the towns. Hugolino, at first bereft, was soon to find another inspirational figure to protect and advance. Less conventional than Rainier and of at least equal spiritual significance was Francis of Assisi who is revealed to us so much more clearly than Innocent's retiring monk-confessor. Nevertheless, in the recovery of the Patrimony at this time, the Cistercians had been agents of success, Rainier the inspiration and Innocent the guiding hand who, from the day of his election, had been determined to follow his predecessor Simon Peter to whom Christ had given the charge.

---

[116] L.K.LITTLE, *Religious Poverty and the Profit Economy in Medieval Europe* (London, 1978), 146-169, 197-217.

# III

## *'Except the Lord keep the city'*[1]*: towns in the papal states at the turn of the twelfth century*

With his surprise election on 8 January 1198[2] came Innocent III's first, immediate and practical concern. This was to remove from those lands around Rome the 'intolerable German tyranny' which was still oppressing the people.[3] The area of 'middle Italy' with its mountains and narrow coastal stretches consisted mainly of towns or fortified villages dominated by agriculture. Some of them had existed since Roman or even Etruscan times[4] but it would be a great mistake to think of them in any way as successors to the Roman cities or as forerunners of those great city-states of northern Italy.[5]

The structure of the region, Rome and the towns, both simplified and yet made more difficult Innocent's task.[6] It was

[1] Psalm 127 (126), verse 1.

[2] M. Maccarrone, 'Innocenzo III, prima del pontificato', *Archivio della Società Romana di Storia Patria* (hereafter *ASRSP*) 9 (1942), 1–78 especially 64–78; W. Maleczek, *Papst und Kardinalskolleg von 1191 bis 1216: die Kardinäle unter Coelestin III und Innocenz III* (Vienna, 1984), pp. 101–4; M. L. Taylor, 'The election of Innocent III', in *The Church and sovereignty*, ed. D. Wood, *Studies in Church History, Subsidia* 9 (Blackwell, 1991), pp. 97–112.

[3] 'Propter importabilem Alemannorum tyrannidem', *Gesta Innocentii PP III*, (hereafter *Gesta*) *PL* 214–17 (Paris, 1855), 17–228, especially 26–7.

[4] J. Ward-Perkins, 'Etruscan towns, Roman roads and medieval villages: the historical geography of southern Etruria', *The Geographical Journal* 128 (1962), 389–405; T. W. Potter, *The changing landscape of South Etruria* (London, 1979), pp. 138–67.

[5] P. Racine, 'Innocent III et les Communes italiennes', *Religion et culture dans la cité italienne de l'antiquité à nos jours*, Actes du Colloque du Centre Interdisciplinaire de Recherches sur l'Italie, des 8–9–10 novembre 1979, Bulletin du C.I.R.I., 2e serie (Strasbourg, 1981), 73–87. Compare M. Pacaut, 'La Papauté et les villes italiennes (1159–1253)', *I problemi della Civiltà Comunale, Atti del Congresso Storico Internazionale per il viii centenario della prima Lega Lombarda, (Bergamo, 4–8 settembre 1969)*, a cura di Cosmo Damiano Fonseca (Bergamo, 1971), pp. 33–46.

[6] P. Toubert, *Les Structures du Latium médiéval. Le Latium méridional et la Sabine du IX^e siècle à la fin du XII^e siècle*, 2 vols. Bibliothèque des écoles françaises d'Athènes et de Rome, vol. 221 (Rome, 1973). For two vastly different yet complementary studies of the historiography of the region see K. Walsh, 'Zum *Patrimonium Beati Petri* im Mittelalter', *Römische Historische Mitteilungen* 17 (1975), 193–211 and S. Rubin Blanshei, 'Perugia 1260–1340: conflict and

simplified because of its geographical connection with Rome or made more difficult because these towns were either isolated on their rocky promontories or were way-stations to meet the needs of trade or pilgrims passing through the area. Insignificant many of these towns may have been but their inhabitants were certainly not lacking in awkwardness, especially in relation to the church in Rome.[7] The death of the Emperor Henry VI in 1197 and the consequent attempt by the church under Celestine III to restore control only served to heighten this awkwardness.[8] Innocent, the new shepherd and bishop of the area, wasted no time in setting out on his task. His aim was to recover those lost areas of the patrimony of St Peter and to remedy the unhappy state into which they had sunk.[9]

The towns concerned surrounded the great city of Rome. Those to the north, in present-day Lazio, then proudly belonged to the area of Tuscia Romana,[10] which should not be confused with modern Tuscany, then known as Tuscia Lombarda. Towns to the south, also now in Lazio, were then in Campania and Marittima, stretching as far as the bridge over the River Liri at Ceprano in the shadow of Monte Cassino and with Terracina being one of the most important.[11] In the view of Innocent III, the patrimony covered the area from Radicofani in the north to Ceprano in the south[12] and although the actual borders may have reached further

change in a medieval Italian urban society', *Transactions of the American Philosophical Society* 66 (1976), 1–128, especially 7–11.

7 For example, L. Lanzi, 'Un lodo d'Innocenzo III ai Narnesi: specialmente per la terra di Stroncone', *Bolletino della Società Umbra di Storia Patria* 1 (1895), 126–35.

8 M. Maccarrone, *Studi su Innocenzo III*, Italia Sacra 17 (Padua, 1972), 9–22.

9 'Status Romanae Ecclesiae pessimus erat', *Gesta*, col. 21. See also C. Lackner, 'Studien zur Verwaltung des Kirchenstaates unter Papst Innocenz III', *Römische Historische Mitteilungen* 29 (1987), 127–214 for an extensive discussion of 'päpstlicher Territorialpolitik' and useful prosopographies.

10 *Gesta*, cols. 28–30; T. F. X. Noble, *The republic of St Peter: the birth of the papal state 680–825* (Pennsylvania, 1984), p. 37. For a visual and documentary record see J. Raspi-Serra, *La Tuscia Romana: un territorio come esperienza d'arte: evoluzione urbanistico-architettonica* (Rome, 1972).

11 G. Falco, 'I communi della Campagna e della Marittima nel Medio Evo', *ASRSP* 42 (1919), 537–605; 'Le origini ed il primo commune (sec. IX–XII)'; ibid., 47 (1924), 116–87. Neither of Falco's articles, although frequently cited by historians, contains much useful information for the period 1198–1216. See also A. Contadore, *De historia terracinensi: libri quinque* (Rome, 1706); A. Bianchini, *Storia di terracina* (Tivoli, 1952).

12 'A Radicofani usque Ceperano', *Gesta*, col. 24; Lackner, 'Des Kirchenstaates', p. 129, 117–86. See Noble, *Patrimony* pp. xxv–xxix for a persuasive discussion on the existence of a papal state before the eighth century and a critique of D. Waley, *The papal state in the thirteenth century* (London, 1961) and P. Partner, *The lands of St Peter* (London, 1972).

to the north east by the end of his pontificate, it is the towns of the smaller area which are most interesting in relation to Rome and the church.

One of our main sources will be the *Gesta Innocentii PP III* where the pope's biographer paints a most depressing picture of the grave servitude in which his subjects found themselves:[13] of dangerous assaults and hijackings on the roads; of a vastly depreciated currency; of oaths broken everywhere and the church's power usurped in town and village alike.[14] No one was safe. Had not even Octavian, cardinal bishop of Ostia been hijacked in 1192 at Monte S. Maria by Conrad 'Flybrain' and detained against his will?[15] Did not thugs abound, such as those at Rispampani where Guy and Nicholas, of noble origin, exacted illegal tolls[16] at the bridge where the Via Cassia from Radicofani to Aquapendente crossed the River Rigo?[17]

The *Gesta* goes on to give evidence of Innocent's practical help in regard to the roads of the region. He aimed to keep them open and Guy and Nicholas were, after, a hard fight, forced to swear that they would henceforth leave the roads in peace.[18] Papal peace was imposed for all faithful pilgrims and for travellers, particularly on that dangerous stretch of the Via Cassia between Vetralla and Sutri.[19]

[13] Y. Lefèvre, 'Innocent III et son temps vus de Rome', *Mélanges de l'Ecole Française de Rome* 61 (1949), 242–5; V. Pfaff, 'Die *Gesta* Innocenz' III und das Testament Heinrichs VI', *Zeitschrift der Savigny-Stiftung für Rechtsgeschichte, kanonistische Abteilung* 50 (1964), 78–126, especially 79–90; B. M. Bolton, 'Too important to neglect: the *Gesta Innocentii PP III*', *Church and chronicle in the middle ages: essays presented to John Taylor*, eds. G. A. Loud and I. R. Wood (London, 1991).

[14] *Gesta*, cols. 26–9.

[15] Ibid., col. 25; O. Hageneder, W. Maleczek and A. Strnad, *Die Regi:'er Innocenz' III. 2. Pontifikatsjahr, 1199/1200* (Rome–Vienna, 1979) (hereafter *Register* II), 166 (175), p. 322; PL 214. 725; Potthast, 826; Maleczek, *Päpst und Kardinalskolleg*, pp. 80–3 and especially p. 82 for the activities of Conrad von Lützelnhart.

[16] *Gesta* xv, col. 29; I. Ciampi, *Cronache e Statuti della città di Viterbo* (Florence, 1872), p. 325; Lackner, 'Des Kirchenstaates', p. 152, n. 77–9. 'Senescallo et rectoribus patrimonii S. Petri in Tuscia super captione Guittonis et Nicolai et super tractatu habito cum eisdem' in A. Theiner, *Vetera Monumenta Slavorum Meridionalium Historiam Illustrantia, 1198–1549* (Rome, 1863), doc. 187, p. 61.

[17] C. R. and M. G. Cheney, 'A draft decretal of Pope Innocent III on a case of identity', *Quellen und Forschungen* 41 (1961), 29–47, especially 31, n. 10; G. Caselli, *La Via Romea* (Florence, 1990), pp. 138–41.

[18] Compare the oath of 1201 taken by the citizens of Viterbo, 'Domnus papa Innocentius (III) fecit (? con) firmatione pacis...de Nicola et Guitto de Strata...firmiter servabo et fideliter adimplebo sicut exprimunt', Ciampi, *Cronache*, p. 325; Caselli, *Via Romea*, pp. 146–7.

[19] *Gesta*, col. xxix 'In super domino papae fidelitatem, secundum morem et consuetudinem aliorum fidelium, juraverunt.' Compare *PL* 214.359, n. 65 which Migne linked, perhaps erroneously, with this case.

In his general aim of returning the papal states to the sphere of influence of the church, some political measures would be needed to restore the temporal dominion and Innocent was well aware of what had gone before. The provisions of the *Ludovicianum*,[20] the pact of 817 between Louis the Pious (814–43) and Pope Paschal I (817–24) would have been well known at the Curia. It had, after all, been only recently copied into the *Liber Censuum*, or *Book of Taxes*, a compilation of the customs, rents and payments owed to the Roman church, made by Cencio, the papal chamberlain and completed by him in 1192.[21] Although the actual revenues received by the church were not very great, it was important to Innocent that he stated his right to them, even if he then generously waived them on suitable occasions as at Fossanova in 1206.[22] His main concern was to establish this part of central Italy as a unified region with its own special identity and purpose, having strong links with the church.[23] He was keen to establish a successful model which he could then use elsewhere. The region was quite simply to be one 'Italia' and in its creation the towns of the area were to be set apart as particular agents of the pope.[24] In return for their support, they were rewarded with a period of papal residence, an event which enriched them because papal favour brought real profit as the entourage and the inevitable hangers-on attracted traders of all descriptions.[25] Those towns not fortunate to be visited by the pope himself made the best of what they could with lesser visits by cardinal-legates.

The *Gesta* sets down the pope's deeds with considerable bravura. It gives a long list of those areas recovered in the first two years of the pontificate.[26] One by one, they come back into the fold – a medieval version of the 'domino theory' so beloved of today's strategists. The list seems endless: from the March of Ancona in the north east through the Duchy of Spoleto. It then

[20] Noble, *Republic of St Peter*, pp. 148–53.

[21] *Le Liber Censuum de l'Eglise Romaine*, ed. P. Fabre and L. Duchesne, 3 vols. (Paris, 1889–1905), I, pp. 363–5; J. E. Sayers, *Papal government and England during the Pontificate of Honorius III (1216–1227)* (Cambridge, 1984), pp. 1–12.

[22] W. E. Lunt, *Papal revenues in the Middle Ages*, 2 vols. (Columbia, 1934), I, pp. 57–136, especially 69; II, pp. 62–4; 'Chronicon Fossanovae', ed. L. A. Muratori, *Rerum Italicarum Scriptores* 7 (Milan, 1725), 853–97, especially 886.

[23] Maccarrone, *Studi*, p. 16, n. 1.

[24] O. Hageneder and A. Haidacher, eds., *Die Register Innocenz' III*, I. *Pontifikatsjahr 1198–99* (Graz-Vienna-Köln, 1964–68), 401, pp. 599–601; *PL* 214. 377–8; Potthast, 403.

[25] William of Andres, *Chronicon*, MGH SS, 24, ed. G. H. Pertz (Hanover, 1897), pp. 690–773, especially p. 743; Maccarrone, *Studi*, pp. 55–61.

[26] *Gesta*, cols. 24–30.

peters out towards the south where the Germans had been stronger and where it was 1208 before Innocent was able to make any substantial journey to this area.[27] This strong German influence must have been in Innocent's mind in his general approach to Campania and Marittima. He was eager to replace the scarce and short-weight money of Flora used in this region, by so-called 'money of the Senate', *de jure* papal but *de facto* Roman. In so doing, he hoped to increase commerce in the south.[28] The attention he gives to the town of Terracina is another indication of this concern.[29] The situation there had been made even more difficult by the strength of the Frangipani brothers.[30] Anything Innocent could do to demonstrate the benign influence of the papacy would have been useful. It is most likely that he improved the 'triumphal arch' of the duomo of Terracina as he had already done in Cività Castellana to indicate to the inhabitants the pride they should have in guarding these significant points of entry to the increasingly important patrimony.[31] All in all, the author of the *Gesta* is more accurate about the 'labour and expense'[32] involved in returning these towns to the pope than he is in his timescale. Recovery was a far longer process than the *Gesta* suggests, beginning in 1198 and still far from total in 1216.[33]

Innocent's approach to reclaiming what he felt belonged by right to the church was a mixture of temporal and spiritual, of 'force and blandishment'[34] and the power of his office together with the gospel message, pastoral care and the promise of salvation. He regarded his temporal activities as an unavoidable diversion.[35] He expressed his deep distaste at the thought that by using methods resorted to by factious local lords, the church might be said to have abandoned its spiritual principles. His letters continually express his awareness of the risk and his papal qualms appear perfectly genuine.[36] Indeed, it is precisely in this area that

[27] Lackner, 'Des Kirchenstaates', pp. 164–82.

[28] *Liber Censuum*, I, pp. 14–5.

[29] Contadore, *De Historia Terracinensi*, p. 174 for the text of the Bull *Satis Vobis*, 28 June, 1204.

[30] James, Deodatus, Manuel, Odo and Peter, Bianchini, *Storia di Terracina*, pp. 143–52; Lackner, 'Des Kirchenstaates', pp. 169–73.

[31] Ibid., pp. 205–8.

[32] 'Quia labor erat magnus et fructus parvus', *Gesta*, col. 30.

[33] Compare *Regestum Innocentii III papae super negotio Romani imperii*, ed. F. Kempf, *Miscellanea Historiae Pontificiae* 12 (Rome, 1947) 56, 150–3, especially 153 for Innocent's claim made at the end of October or early November 1201 that he held Rome. Also Bolton, *The Gesta Innocentii PP III*, pp. 95–7.

[34] Maccarrone, *Studi*, pp. 9–19.

[35] *PL* 214. 751; Maccarrone, *Studi*, p. 12.

[36] *Gesta*, col. 30; Maccarrone, *Studi*, p. 11.

the author of the *Gesta* comes closest to understanding Innocent's innermost feelings when he cites the text from Ecclesiastes, 13.1: 'Whomsoever toucheth pitch shall be defiled.'[37] There is no doubt that whatever method was used, the pope's solicitude for his subjects was paramount.[38]

In his activities around the patrimony, Innocent was well aware of the importance of both the historical and biblical dimensions of papal claims. He read avidly the *Liber Pontificalis*[39] and much admired his great predecessor, Gregory I (590–604) whose pragmatic and practical attitude towards the patrimony had led to a more systematic organisation[40] – even a 'Romanisation'[41] – whilst, at the same time, never losing sight of the pastoral duties involved. Innocent constantly used Bible references in the sermons which he, as a noted preacher, frequently delivered.[42] In the second of his *Sermones Communes* he develops the theme of Psalm 127.[43] 'Except the Lord build the house, they labour in vain that build it. Except the Lord keep the City, the watchman waketh but in vain.' His powerful text was composed for general use on feast days *in communi apostolorum* and also as a circuit-sermon for use on journeys around the patrimony. This is the guide to his approach to the towns and those who dwelt within them. 'The King of Kings, dearest brothers, has different cities in different regions, that is to say, heavenly and earthly, spiritual and corporal.' 'These four cities', he tells us, 'represent the Churches Triumphant and Militant, the whole body of the faithful and Jerusalem, the Wonderful.' The cities are threatened from above and below, from within and without by fallacious demons, 'the little foxes' of heresy, carnal concupiscence and alluring inducements. The rectors of the church are to keep the four watches: *conticinium*, the first part of the night, *intempestum* or dead of night,

[37] *Gesta*, col. 30; Maccarrone, *Studi*, p. 11.

[38] 'Propter curam et sollicitudinem apostolica patrimonium', 11 October 1199, *Register* II, 193 (202), pp. 367–8; *PL* 214. 750–1; Potthast 848.

[39] *Le Liber Pontificalis* ed. L. Duchesne, 3 vols. (Paris, 1886–92); *The book of pontiffs (Liber Pontificalis)* translated by R. Davis (Liverpool, 1989); S. J. P. Van Dijk and J. Hazelden Walker, *The origins of the modern Roman liturgy* (London, 1960), pp. 126–8.

[40] Sermo XIII, *De Sanctis, In festo D. Gregorii Papae, Hujus Nomine* I, *PL* 217. 513–22; Noble, *Republic of St Peter*, pp. 9–11; J. Richards, *Consul of God: the life and times of Gregory the Great* (London, 1980), pp. 128–39.

[41] Ibid., p. 132.

[42] *PL* 217. 309–688.

[43] 'De diversis civitatibus Dei, nimirum coelesti, terrestri, spirituali et corporali', *PL* 217. 601–6; Psalm 127 (126) verse 1.

*gallicantium* or cockcrow and *antelucanum*, just before daybreak.[44] They are the custodians of the cities, the *apostolici viri*, who ought to watch and take care of the flock throughout the night. 'Nothing', says Innocent, 'is to divide the head from the members, to keep fathers from sons, the shepherd from his sheep.' The gravest danger of all is heresy, to be guarded against as securely as men guard their riches.[45] Hence, the rector's rôle, as agent of the pope, is conceived of as highly supportive.

In a series of letters addressed to the cities of the patrimony, Innocent expatiates further on the implications of papal solicitude. The pope's yoke, like that of Christ, would be easy and the burden light.[46] Henceforth, all would walk, not in darkness but in the light and the recovered dominion would be a restored 'Italia', saved from foreign domination and kept in perpetuity for the church.[47] Innocent aimed to transfer to 'Italia' what Leo I and the medieval tradition had attributed to Rome.[48] In future, the towns would satisfy their desire for autonomy, linked together in the privilege of being the seat of the principality of the church as Rome had once been the seat of emperors. The sons of the patrimony would no longer be servants, nor would *minores* be oppressed by *majores*.[49] Some might even have the opportunity to be raised up to the status of *filii speciali*, an honorific title bestowed on prominent citizens and ecclesiastics whose activities the pope wished to recognise.[50] There would be a fair administration of justice and wherever necessary, the observance of a papally inspired truce would encourage *pax et concordia* in disputes amongst the towns of the patrimony.[51] Brotherly love would abound and the political fragmentation inherent in the geographical, historical and other characteristics of the patrimony would melt away before Innocent's unifying vision. Even with

44 *PL* 217. 604.

45 *PL* 217. 604–5.

46 'Jugum meum suave est et onus meum leve' (Matt. 11:30). Compare the parallel letter to the consuls and people of Sutri, *c.* 15 October 1199, *Register* II, 194 (203), pp. 369–71; PL 214. 751–2; Potthast, 849. A similar letter was also sent to the consuls and people of Nepi, Spoleto, Narni, Orte, Rieti, Cività Castellana, Amelia, Città di Castello, Tuscania, Vetralla, Todi, Assisi, Bagnoreggio, Centocello, Perugia, Foligno, Orvieto and Corneto. Compare Maccarrone, *Studi*, pp. 14–15.

47 *Gesta*, xxvi; Maccarrone, *Studi*, p. 15.

48 *Register* I, p. 600; *PL* 214. 377; Potthast, 403.

49 'Ne filii fiant servi, neque minores maioribus opprimantur', *Register* I, p. 600; *PL* 214. 377.

50 *Register* I, 1, p. 5; *PL* 214. 2; Potthast, 1.

51 For one such exhortation given on 23 September, 1207, *PL* 215. 1228; Maccarrone, *Studi*, p. 17.

Innocent, ambitious schemes did not always materialise; and by 1213, when he sent out his crusade encyclical *Quia Maior*, the hoped-for unity was still not achieved.[52] Perhaps he was expecting and demanding too much.

To return to his methods, we must first look at the way in which he presented his programme through the institution of rectors in various parts of the patrimony.[53] Regretting his inability to be everywhere at once, but rejoicing that others could act on his behalf, he sent circular letters to the bishops and leading citizens, asking them to receive his rectors.[54] Gregory I seems to have appointed only clerical rectors but Innocent had a mixture of both clerical and lay.[55] In 1203, he created as rector his *cognatus* and thus possibly a relation, one Stephen Romano Carsoli,[56] whom he strategically based at Montefiascone, a former imperial fortress. He praised the purity of the man's faith, his hard work and discretion and stated that he had absolute trust in him.[57] Obviously these were the qualities which the pope hoped for in all his rectors. Another relation, his cousin James the Marshall, was deemed worthy of this position in 1215.[58]

A rector's tour of duty seems to have lasted about a year, perhaps the limit of endurance and effectiveness which could be expected as the pressure of work was considerable.[59] Rectors were responsible for collecting the *fodrum*, the traditional hospitality tax,[60] for keeping the peace, for dealing with appeals from lower courts and arbitration in regard to claims made by one subject against another.[61] Should the rectors be also cardinals, they were

[52] L. and J. Riley-Smith, *The Crusades: idea and reality 1095–1274* (London, 1981), pp. 118–24.

[53] On the office of rector and the administration of the patrimony in general, see M. Moresco, *Il Patrimonio di San Pietro* (Turin, 1916); J. Richards, *The popes and the papacy in the early Middle Ages 476–752* (London, 1979), pp. 307–22; Waley, *Papal state*, pp. 52–3.

[54] 'Romanus pontifex pro defectu conditionis humanae per se ipsum omnia expedire non potest, iuvetur subsidiis aliorum', *Register* II, 194 (203), p. 369; *PL* 214. 750; Potthast, 849.

[55] Richards, *Consul of God*, p. 134; Lackner, 'Des Kirchenstaates', pp. 197–205.

[56] *PL* 215. 112; Lackner, 'Des Kirchenstaates', p. 200.

[57] 'Cum ergo de tuae fidei puritate indubitam fiduciam habeamus, et de tuae discretionis industria', *PL* 215. 112. [58] Prosopography in Lackner, 'Des Kirchenstaates', pp. 200–3.

[59] Waley, *Papal state*, p. 96.

[60] C. R. Brühl, *Fodrum, Gistum, Servitum Regis*, 2 vols. (Köln-Graz, 1968) I, pp. 578–761. For various insights into the imperial *fodrum* see *Chronicon Fossanovae*, ed. L. A. Muratori, *Rerum Italicarum Scriptores* 7 (Milan, 1725), 853–97, especially 886 and 889.

[61] For the oaths taken from rectors, Waley, *Papal state*, p. 97. See also G. Ermini, 'I rettori provinciali dello Stato della Chiesa da Innocenzo III all'Albornoz', *Rivista di Storia del Diritto Italiano* 4 (1931), 5–6.

made responsible for working with bishops in their dioceses.[62] A novel form of *Parliamentum*, consisting of all estates, clerics, nobles and citizens, was summoned by Innocent to meet together for three consecutive days at Viterbo in 1207.[63] On 21 September, he set out the law of the Roman church and received the oaths of the laity.[64] On 22 September, he adjudicated quarrels and complaints between his vassals[65]; whilst on 23 September, the last day, he promulgated statutes to promote peace and justice, including the repression of heresy.[66] At the same time, he formalised the office of rector. Thereafter, most appointments seem to have been laymen close to the pope, who could be trusted to carry out his policy, particularly when new fortifications, manned by Innocent's own castellans, were necessary.[67]

Whilst most rectors were concerned with large areas, the office itself also existed in some of the towns. The *Gesta* refers to the events of 1197 when the citizens of the northern part of the patrimony had appointed their own 'rectors' and joined in the league of Tuscan cities.[68] Whilst this league claimed to serve the Holy See, Innocent seems to have given them little more than a letter of greeting and commendation.[69]

In addition to the rectors, the bishops were most important agents of the pope, immediately subject as they were to him, in his position as archbishop of the region.[70] All these bishops were bound to swear an oath of recognition to the pope, promising obedience and reverence and, in return, receiving his special vigilance and protection.[71] As there were more than twenty episcopal towns throughout the patrimony,[72] Innocent might

[62] Compare the letter of March 1198 to all the bishops of the Marches, *Register* I, 38, pp. 56–7; *PL* 214. 31–2; Potthast, 40.

[63] *Gesta*, cols. clxi–clxii; *PL* 215. 1226–8.

[64] Ibid., 1227, 'Cum ex officii nostri'.

[65] 'Cum juratum sit', ibid., 1228.

[66] 'Ad eliminandum', ibid., 1226–7.

[67] Lackner, 'Des Kirchenstaates', pp. 197–205 for prosopographical studies of the rectors. In Tuscia Romana: John Cencio (1199); Gregory Ceccarello, Cardinal–Deacon of S. Giorgio in Velabro (1199–1200); Peter de Vico, Prefect of Rome (1199–1201/2); Stephen Romani Carsoli (1203), *cognatus*; James, the Papal Marshal (1213–16). In Campania-Marittima: Lando de Montelongo, *consobrinus* (1199–1203); Peter de Sasso (1208–12).

[68] *Gesta* cols. xxvi–xxvii; Lackner, 'Des Kirchenstaates', p. 147.

[69] *Register* II, 198 (207), pp. 377–9; *PL* 214. 55–6; Potthast, 870.

[70] C. Eubel, *Hierarchia Catholica Medii Aevi* (Regensburg, 1913), p. 540.

[71] Maccarrone, *Studi*, pp. 302–5, especially n. 1, p. 302.

[72] In the Province of Rome: Tivoli, Segni, Anagni, Alatri, Veroli, Ferentino, Terracina, Grosseto, Bagnoreggio, Montefiascone, Viterbo, Nepi, Sutri, Orte, Cività Castellana. In Umbria: Rieti,

have been forgiven for being complacent over this apparent support. He could not afford to be so. The problem of Catharism was a grave difficulty which had, before 1198, infiltrated Viterbo and Orvieto and was there for him to deal with.[73]

The task of each bishop was to defend his flock, maintain its faith by preaching and example, administer the goods of the diocese so that he could hand them on undiminished to his successor and generally to show united allegiance to the pope and the church in Rome. In Orvieto, the inadequacy of the aged bishop Richard (1178–1202) was so apparent in dealing with heretics and his sympathies were so much in doubt that Innocent was forced to keep him in Rome under house arrest for nine months in 1198.[74] The faithful of the city, seeking reconciliation with the pope, appealed for a 'rector' to extirpate the heresy.[75] Peter Parenzo was selected by Innocent and was then promptly murdered in May 1199.[76] The shock of his death provoked a reaction strong enough to eliminate heresy in Orvieto.

Orvieto's neighbour and the former imperial stronghold, Viterbo, proved a far more serious threat.[77] Heresy here was deep-rooted and one of Innocent's letters to the city became a model decretal forming the basis for Canon III of the Fourth Lateran Council.[78] *Vergentis in Senium* of 25 March 1199 and addressed to the clergy and people of Viterbo, established heresy as a treasonable offence.[79] *Si adversos vos* dated 4 June 1205,[80] in the opinion of Luchaire possibly the most virulent letter ever to emerge from Innocent's chancery,[81] revealed that the chief official of Viterbo, the *camerarius* John Tigniosi, and the consuls of the city were not only heretics but also excommunicates.[82] The Bishop

Narni, Terni, Amelia, Castro, Perugia, Città di Castello, Assisi, Foligno, Gubbio, Nocera, Orvieto, Todi and Spoleto.

[73] On Catharism in the region, see V. Natalini, *S. Pietro Parenzo: la leggenda scritta dal Maestro Giovanni, Canonico di Orvieto*, *Lateranum*, new series 2, (Rome, 1936); Maccarrone, *Studi*, pp. 30–51; Lackner, 'Des Kirchenstaates', pp. 148–54; D. Waley, *Mediaeval Orvieto* (Cambridge, 1952), pp. 12–21. [74] Natalini, *S. Pietro Parenzo*, p. 104; Maccarrone, *Studi*, pp. 28–9.

[75] Maccarrone, pp. 33–5. [76] Natalini, *S. Pietro Parenzo*, pp. 163–4.

[77] I. Ciampi, *Cronache e Statuti della Città di Viterbo* (Florence, 1872); P. Egidio, 'Le croniche di Viterbo', *ASRSP*, 24 (1901), 197–252; N. Kamp, *Istituzioni communali in Viterbo nel Medioevo. I. Consoli, Podestà, Balivi e Capitani nei secoli XII e XIII*, Biblioteca di Studi Viterbesi, 1 (Viterbo, 1963).

[78] *Conciliorum Oecumenicorum decreta*, ed. J. Alberigo et al. (3rd ed. Bologna, 1973), pp. 263–4.

[79] *Register* II, 1, pp. 3–5; *PL* 214. 537–9; Potthast, 643. [80] *PL* 215. 654–7; Potthast, 2532.

[81] A. Luchaire, *Innocent III: Rome et l'Italie* (Paris, 1905), p. 93.

[82] *PL* 215. 652; Potthast, 2532.

seemed to be nowhere. Two weeks later, in a joint letter to the Bishops, Rainier of Viterbo[83] and Matthew of Orvieto,[84] Innocent ordered that 'Brother Viterbo' should immediately go to the rescue of his flock whom he had deserted, whilst 'Brother Orvieto' was ordered 'not to wait at a distance with dry eyes' but must immediately assist, even if it meant laying down his own life.[85] The systematic, firm and energetic actions which followed were to be a model for use elsewhere, but there is evidence that the degree of success in Viterbo itself was very slight.[86] The Statute *Ad Eliminandum*, promulgated at the Viterban Parliament in 1207,[87] dealt harshly with heretics but the matter seems not to have been resolved. In due course, Bishop Rainier seems to have been suspended for incompetence and incapacity.[88]

In spite of heresy not having been eradicated, the bishops of the region began to play a greater part in restoring peace and concord, especially in negotiating the settlement of disputes between the cities. In so doing, they followed the pope's overall duty. The language Innocent uses in this is surprisingly similar to that he used to monarchs.[89] The Roman church is regarded as the pious mother, who is unable to forget the sons she has borne.[90] Yet he believes in firm, direct and hard-hitting intervention where needed. In 1198–9, he freed Aquapendente from domination by Orvieto[91] and protected Vitorchiano from its predatory neighbour Viterbo.[92] He showed himself willing to move firmly against Narni in 1208[93] where he accused the people of having been stained by pitch. He intervened to settle rivalries between Todi, Amelia and Orvieto[94] saying that too many casualties had been caused and that all their attempts at mediation had been in

[83] Rainier (1199–?1221): Eubel, p. 532, n. 1.

[84] Matthew of Orvieto (1201–?1221): Eubel, p. 508; Ciampi, *Cronache*, pp. 326, 335.

[85] *Cum lupi rapaces*, *PL* 215. 673–4; Potthast, 2539.

[86] Ciampi, *Cronache*, p. 326 cites an undated letter from Bishop Rainier about the heresy of Master Robectus who appears to have practised a thorough-going form of Cathar dualism, denying the value of baptism and using such obscenities that Ciampi felt unable to print them.

[87] *Gesta*, cols. clxi–clxii: *PL*. 214.1226–7.

[88] Eubel, *Hierarchia*, p. 532, n. 1: Ciampi, *Cronache*, pp. 326, 335–6.

[89] Compare B. M. Bolton, 'Philip Augustus and John: two sons in Innocent III's Vineyard?', *The church and sovereignty*, pp. 113–34.

[90] *PL* 214. 400–1; Maccarrone, *Studi*, p. 72, n. 1.

[91] *Gesta*, col. xxvii; Natalini, *S. Pietro Parenzo*, pp. 155–6; Maccarrone, *Studi*, pp. 22–30; Waley, *Papal state*, p. 36.

[92] *Gesta*, cols. clxxix–clxxxiii.

[93] *PL* 215. 1458–9; Lackner, 'Des Kirchenstaates', pp. 158–9; Lanzi, 'Un lodo d'Innocenzo III ai Narnesi', pp. 126–35.

[94] Maccarrone, *Studi*, pp. 70–3.

vain. When called upon by both sides to resolve the disputes, the pope insisted on receiving their oaths personally so that a real and lasting peace could be agreed.[95]

In some of these towns there already existed *podestà*, consuls and other urban officials; but the *ius elegendi potestatem*, that is, the right to elect their own, enjoyed by the Lombard League in the North, had not been easily transposed to Tuscia Romana.[96] Some towns had to ask permission or approval from the pope himself or from his rector. In May 1199, the citizens of Cività Castellana promised not to elect their rector without papal permission[97] and Innocent agreed to approve their candidate, John, as he had been elected *communiter*, by all the people.[98] Quite the reverse seems to have happened at Velletri in 1201 where John Nicholas was forced to step down.[99] In the same year, Innocent conceded that the people of Aquapendente might receive John of Orvieto[100] but, by 1203, the pope was intervening once more to prevent a Viterban noble from holding office there.[101] In 1206, he acted against the strategic frontier town of Radicofani.[102] 'On this occasion', says Innocent, 'the people have not lightly but seriously offended by electing consuls without his permission.'[103] The blessings of the Holy See which are extended to *nationes* ought to be shown equally to *domestici* and vassals who are the proper concern of papal solicitude. Interestingly, in the same year, the pope had written to the people of Sutri, a great pilgrim centre on the Via Cassia, instructing them at no time to receive strangers into the government of the town.[104] Sutri epitomised the problems faced by pilgrim towns in regard to the influence of strangers from outside its borders. Much of Sutri's prosperity derived precisely

[95] 'Receptis ab utraque parte iuramentis aliisque securitatibus ... talem inter eos pacem et concordiam ... duximus statuendam', Ibid.

[96] G. Ermini, 'La libertà communale', *ASRSP* 49 (1926), 4–7.

[97] Bonus de Fordevolie, elected without papal consent, PL 214. 617–18; Ermini, 'La libertà communale', p. 9; A. Theiner, *Codex Diplomaticus domini temporalis S. Sedis*, 3 vols. (Rome, 1961), I (756–1334), p. 32.

[98] 22 December 1199, *Register* II, 246 (256), p. 470 (where Cività Castellana and Città di Castelle appear to be confused); *PL* 214. 815–16; Potthast, 911; Waley, *Papal state*, p. 70.

[99] 'Quem contra inhibitionem sedis apostolice elegerunt in Rectorem', Theiner, *Vetera Monumenta*, 237, p. 54.

[100] Ibid., 235, p. 54.

[101] 13 January 1203, *PL* 214. 1147–9; Potthast, 1804; Maccarrone, *Studi*, p. 63.

[102] *PL* 215. 796–7; Ermini, 'La liberta communale', p. 55.

[103] 'Hac vice non leviter offenderitis', *PL* 215. 795.

[104] Theiner, *Codex Diplomaticus*, 48, p. 40.

from its position on the principal road to north Italy. Nepi enjoyed a similar position on the Via Amerina and Cività Castellana on the Flaminia.[105]

The patrimony was, in fact, much more than a papal dominion. It was a permanent area of transit with highways and byways all leading to Rome. The whole area between Sutri in the north and Albano to the south was regarded as a pilgrim zone in which papal protection was necessarily sought and freely given. In return, the pope possessed several rights there. For example, in Sutri, if a pilgrim fell so ill in the town as to need a priest for the last rites, he was warned that he should also have present either the administrative official known as the *gastaldus curie* or two vassals of the Roman church.[106] This was a necessary precaution to enable the pilgrim to dispose of his worldly goods as he wished. If this testamentary deposition was not carried out to the letter, the will of the pilgrim would be judged invalid. Priests were particularly instructed to point out to solitary pilgrims that if they were to die intestate, within the pilgrim zone, the Curia would have the right to claim all their goods. Perhaps some of these goods were used towards Innocent's hospital foundations for pilgrims and strangers in Rome (1204)[107] and Anagni (1208).[108]

The problems which arose in towns such as Orvieto and Viterbo exemplify the importance Innocent gave to the visits he made to different parts of the patrimony throughout the eighteen years of his pontificate.[109] In this time, Innocent made four visits to Viterbo, in 1207,[110] 1209,[111] 1214[112] and 1216,[113] totalling about twelve months in all, although his final visit there was fleeting. The amount of time spent in Viterbo was only matched

[105] Waley, *Papal state*, pp. 83–4.

[106] 'Consuetudines et iura, que habet dominus papa in Burgo Sutrino', Theiner, *Codex Diplomaticus*, p. 29. On the *gastald* see G. Tabacco, *The struggle for power in medieval Italy: structures of political rule*, translated by R. Brown Jensen (Cambridge, 1989), pp. 102–3.

[107] 19 June 1204, *Inter opera pietatis*, *PL* 215. 376–80.

[108] 26 August 1208. See R. Ambrosi de Magistris, 'Il viaggio d'Innocenzo III nel Lazio e il primo ospedale in Anagni', *Storia e Diritto* 19 (1898), 365–78.

[109] L. Delisle, 'Itinéraire d'Innocent III dressé d'après les actes de ce pontife', *Bibliothèque de l'Ecole des Chartes* 18 (1857), 500–34.

[110] William of Andres, *Chronicon*, p. 737.

[111] From mid-May to mid-September, Delisle, p. 509; Potthast, 3727–3802; Maccarrone, *Studi*, pp. 56–7.

[112] From 23 June–19 September 1214, Potthast, 4932–8.

[113] Maccarrone, *Studi*, pp. 7–8. Compare *Cronaca di Luca di Domenico Manente (1174–1413)* in *Ephemerides Urbevetanas*, in *Rerum Italicarum Scriptores*, 15, ed. L. A. Muratori, 2nd ed., ed. L. Fiumi, 2 vols. (Città di Castello, 1920), pp. 269–414, especially p. 288.

by his time in Anagni, a favourite southern seat and a safe refuge during times of difficulty with the city of Rome.[114]

The whole pattern of Innocent's itineration is of interest. Between July and October 1198, in a massive display of personal authority in towns which had recently returned to the dominion of the Church, he progressed to Rieti, Spoleto and Perugia, returning by way of Todi, Amelia and Cività Castellana.[115] His journey left behind tangible reminders of the papal presence. At Rieti, where he consecrated the churches of S. Eleuterio and S. Giovanni, he gave to both precious altar cloths, one decorated with lions, the other with leopards.[116] In Spoleto, where he dedicated an altar, he was attributed by his biographer with a small miracle.[117] A horse trough on which the city depended had dried up with serious consequences but, on the pope's arrival, an abundant spring began to flow and was known thereafter as the *fons papalis*. At Perugia he consecrated the high altar of the Duomo and at Todi, that of the church of S. Fortunato. For the decoration of all the altars, undertaken so personally, he obtained precious silken altar *pallia* and subtly worked covers.

At the Duomo of Cività Castellana, the most spectacular cosmatesque portico, facing out towards the Via Flaminia, has been attributed to his patronage.[118] Art historians have seen this as a Roman triumphal arch, proclaiming as it does, its message of peace and goodwill: +GLORIA IN EXCELSIS DEO ET IN TERRA PAX HOMINIBVS BONEVOLVMTATIS LAVDAMVS TE ADORAMVS TE GLORIFICAMVS TE GRATIAS AGIMVS+.[119] It has been suggested that the model was the antique arch of Gallienus,[120] used by the city of Rome in 1200 for the setting of the triumphal civic display of the key captured from the city of Viterbo.[121] A partly illegible

[114] *Gesta*, cols. cxcvi–cxcvii (1201–2), clxxxviii (1203). [115] Ibid., cols. xxv–xxvi.

[116] Ibid., col. ccx. [117] Ibid., cols. xxv–xxvi.

[118] P. Claussen, *Magistri Doctissimi Romani: die Römischen Marmorkünstler des Mittelalters, Corpus Cosmatorum*, I (Stuttgart, 1987), pp. 82–91.

[119] K. Noehles, 'Die Kunst der Cosmaten und die Idee der *Renovatio Romae*', *Festschrift Werner Hager*, eds. G. Fiensch and M. Imdahl, (Recklinghausen, 1966), pp. 17–37; H. Bloch, 'The new fascination with ancient Rome', in *Renaissance and renewal in the twelfth century*, eds. G. Constable and R. L. Benson (Oxford, 1982), pp. 615–36; E. Kitzinger, 'The arts as aspects of a Renaissance: Rome and Italy', ibid., pp. 637–70.

[120] Claussen, *Magistri Doctissimi Romani*, pp. 85–8 and Plate 105; S. G. MacCormack, *Art and ceremony in late antiquity* (Berkeley, 1981), pp. 32, 35 and Plate 10.

[121] Ciampi, *Cronache*, pp. 11–12; F. Cancellieri, *Le due nuove campane di Campidoglio* (Rome, 1806), p. 37.

inscription running along both sides of the portico could possibly tell us more.[122] Under the portico in the lunette above the right-hand doorway, a bearded Christ with a cruciform nimbus blesses with his right hand and holds a closed book in his left. The work, both portico and lunette, is signed by the Cosmati and dated 1210.[123] Claussen has suggested that on the portico of the Duomo at Terracina on the Via Appia to the south of the patrimony a similar inscription may well have matched that of Cività Castellana.[124] Other gifts were given to the churches Innocent visited to north and south of the patrimony[125] – chasubles in red and purple, elaborately worked orphreys and a silver crozier to the Duomo of Anagni[126]; but of all these rich gifts Viterbo became the greatest beneficiary. There he gave to the churches of S. Lorenzo, S. Angelo de Spata, S. Sisto and S. Maria Nova not only the usual chasubles, orphreys and altar cloths but also a papal ring.[127]

Viterbo offered great advantages as a papal summer residence, not merely on account of the pleasant summer climate but also because of the space available to visitors.[128] As we know from the eyewitness account of William, abbot of the Cistercian abbey of Andres in Picardy, who journeyed there in June 1207, it could easily house all the *curiales* and papal chaplains as well as petitioners and pilgrims hoping to see the pope.[129] William asserts that the presence of the Curia and its hangers-on had increased Viterbo's normal population by as many as 40,000.[130] Even if this usually precise abbot did exaggerate somewhat, the fact remains that Viterbo was a large, well-developed town, with a rich hinterland, situated on the Via Cassia leading to Tuscany and Lombardy. The pope's presence there – 'as if he were in his own city'[131] necessitated the establishment of a stable chancery so that work could continue uninterrupted throughout the summer months.

[122] + INTRANTES---ASC----S--POTESA-VA-----RANTESSICETSALVA-OP ECAI---CEXAVD---. Transcribed 3 April 1991. Compare Claussen, *Magistri Doctissimi Romani*, p. 86 for a slightly different reading.

[123] + MAGISTER IACOBVS CIVIS ROMANVS CVM COSMA FILIO SVO + CARISIMO FECIT OHC OPVS ANNO DNI M C C X.

[124] Claussen, *Magistri Doctissimi Romani*, p. 88; Bianchini, *Storia di Terracina*, pp. 207–8.

[125] *Gesta*, cols. ccviii–ccx. [126] Ibid., col. ccix. [127] Ibid., cols. ccxxviii–ccxxix.

[128] 'Viterbo ... una vera e grande città, non un "oppido", come erano le piccole citta del Lazio meridionale', Maccarrone, *Studi*, p. 58. [129] William of Andres, *Chronicon*, pp. 737–8.

[130] Ibid., p. 737. [131] 'In civitate propria manebat', Ibid., p. 737; Maccarrone, *Studi*, p. 61.

Whereas in 1207 the Chancery moved with Innocent when he visited Montefiascone for twelve days in August, by 1209, on his next visit, it was the pope who did the travelling while the Chancery stayed put in Viterbo.[132] By 1210, the city had what passed for a 'papal palace' and by that date, the two small and ancient ecclesiastical dependencies of Centocelle and Blera, had been transferred from Tuscania-Corneto to the bishopric of Viterbo.[133] Innocent thus combined his own preference for cooler summer places with the urgent need to create a political capital in territories likely to be contested by imperial forces. We also know, from the chance survival of uncensored remarks by papal chancery clerks, that the hard-pressed *curiales* did not care for such remote, stifling and mosquito-ridden towns as Subiaco where they stayed unwillingly throughout August and September 1202[134] or Segni where they endured three visits in 1201, 1212 and 1213.[135] While political events such as the troubles in Rome in the early years of his pontificate[136] or the incursions of Otto IV after 1209[137] limited or determined the extent and nature of the pope's itineration, Innocent used every opportunity at his disposal to show himself to the people of the patrimony for practical reasons, as well as for the customary crown-wearings. Wherever the pope had consecrated a church or dedicated an altar, he left behind a gift.[138] In whichever town he stayed, his patronage would benefit the citizens.

As he could not be everywhere at once, he needed a symbol as a reminder of the importance of the religion of the church in Rome, the foundation stone of 'Italia', and something which might help to suppress localism.[139] Innocent wished to unify his subjects throughout the patrimony by bringing them together in a particularly 'Roman' ceremony.[140] His success in this can be measured by the widespread veneration of images of the Saviour

[132] Ibid., pp. 58–9.
[133] *PL* 215. 1234; Ciampi, *Cronache*, p. 302.
[134] K. Hampe, 'Eine Schilderung des Sommeraufenthaltes der römischen Kurie unter Innocenz III in Subiaco 1202', *Historische Vierteljahrschrift* 8 (1905), 509–35.
[135] Potthast, 3727–3801; Van Dijk and Hazelden Walker, *Origins*, pp. 97–9.
[136] A. Luchaire, 'Innocent III et le peuple romain', *Revue Historique*, 81 (1903), 225–77.
[137] Lackner, 'Des Kirchenstaates', pp. 157–64.
[138] *Gesta*, cols. xxv–xxvi.
[139] *PL* 214. 377–8.
[140] W. Volbach, 'Il Cristo di Sutri e la venerazione del S. Salvatore nel Lazio', *Atti della Pontificia Accademia Romana di Archeologia. Rendiconti* 17 (1940–1), 97–127; B. M. Bolton, 'Advertise the message: images in Rome at the turn of the twelfth century', *Studies in Church History* 28 (1992), 117–30.

throughout the region, still perpetuated in Lazio even today.[141] The particular image which Innocent promoted was that in the *Sancta Sanctorum* or papal chapel of St Laurence at the Lateran, called by Gerald of Wales the *Uronica* and also known as the *Acheropita* or icon not made by human hand.[142] This venerable image was ritually processed through the streets of Rome on the night of 14 August, the Vigil of the Assumption, arriving early on the morning of 15 August at S. Maria Maggiore so that Christ could greet his mother on her special feast day.[143] In November 1207, when Innocent passed through Sutri, he rededicated the Duomo there to the Virgin of the Assumption and promoted the 'Roman' image of the Saviour in Majesty, a cruciform nimbus behind his head, seated on a throne with his right hand raised in blessing and holding in his left a closed book.[144] This image was identical to the Christ in the Lateran, although it is worth recording that Innocent later had the Roman image covered to the neck with a splendid silver cover to concentrate attention on the face.[145] Only one of the images in the patrimony is a direct copy in every sense. At S. Egidio at Palombara in Sabina, the fourteenth-century artist had only seen the covered image and so reproduced both cover and face as he had first seen them in Rome.[146] The image used in almost every small town in the region seems to have reproduced this particular Roman ceremony. Images of the Saviour on the Lateran model and associated with the Feast of the Assumption are known to have existed, not only at S. Maria Nova in Viterbo, right under Innocent's eye, but also at Trevignano, S. Andrea in Anagni, Velletri, Bracciano, Castel Sant'Elia at Nepi[147] and at Tivoli where the ceremony of *inchinata* – ritual bowing to each other – took place between Christ and his mother as recently as 1978.[148] All these many images were variants of the original Roman model of liturgical procession and possessed the same message.[149]

[141] E. Kitzinger, 'A Virgin's face: antiquarianism in twelfth-century art', *Art Bulletin* 62 (1980), 6–19.

[142] *Giraldus Cambrensis Opera*, eds., J. S. Brewer and J. F. Dimock, 8 vols., *RS*, (London, 1861–91), vol. IV, pp. 268–85; J. Wilpert, 'L'*acheropita* ossia l'immagine del Salvatore della Capella del *Sancta Sanctorum*', *L'Arte* 10, (1907), 159–77, 246–62, especially pp. 162–5.

[143] Volbach, 'Il Cristo di Sutri', p. 116.

[144] Ibid., p. 100.

[145] Wilpert, 'L'*Acheropita*', p. 174 and figure 9.

[146] Volbach, 'Il Cristo di Sutri', p. 114 and figure 11.

[147] Ibid., pp. 97–126.

[148] Kitzinger, 'A Virgin's face', p. 12, n. 46.

[149] Bolton, 'Advertise the Message', 125–8.

Marangoni in the eighteenth century believed that these processions were in the tradition of ancient imperial triumphal rites – based on the use of arches and marble sculpture and his views have been taken up with perhaps more enthusiasm than accuracy to show how, in the eighth century, the icon of Christ in Majesty replaced that of the Emperor.[150] Then it was associated with the idea of freedom from foreign usurpers.[151] Had not the *Liber Pontificalis* spelt out clearly how, in 752, Pope Stephen II had carried this image across the city of Rome on his own shoulders to gain divine intervention against the Lombards, themselves enemies of both liberty and religion?[152] Did this image bear similar associations of liberty through unity, this time against the 'tyrannical Germans'? Innocent, well-read in the *Liber Pontificalis*, would certainly have been aware of the image's history.[153]

Another unifying device was Innocent's apparent use of arches, antique and contemporary, as sites for the placing of a religious message. On two of the most important roads into the patrimony, the Via Appia to the south and the Via Flaminia to the north, at Terracina and Cività Castellana respectively, 'triumphal' arches have a most conspicuous position at the point of entry.[154] On the portico before each Duomo, the supremely 'Roman' cosmatesque decoration possibly reflects an anti-foreign emphasis. This Italian–Roman emphasis seems to have been a symbol of unity wherever it occurred. Each small town was thus a replica of Rome in this respect and a reinforcing message of one faith for 'Italia'.

In April 1216, Innocent set out on what was to be his final itineration throughout the patrimony with the intention of going north to settle a dispute between Pisa and Genoa. He hoped that this action would be both an example and a stimulus to those bishops subordinate to him in the Roman region. Already, Innocent had summoned the Fifth Crusade and legislated for it in

[150] G. Marangoni, *Istoria della Sancta Sanctorum* (Rome, 1747), p. 139; *Le Liber Censuum*, I, pp. 298–9; F. Gregorovius, *History of the city of Rome in the Middle Ages*, (*A.D. 1200–1260*), translated by A. Hamilton, vol. V (London, 1906), p. 14, n. 2; Compare S. MacCormack, 'Change and continuity in late antiquity, the ceremony of *Adventus*', *Historia* 21 (1972), 721–52; ibid., *Art and ceremony*, pp. 62–89.

[151] For a summary of these views, Volbach, 'Il Cristo di Sutri', pp. 121–6.

[152] *Liber Pontificalis*, ed. L. Duchesne, 3 vols. (Paris, 1886–92), I, p. 443.

[153] Van Dijk and Hazelden Walker, *Origins*, pp. 126–8.

[154] Figures 1 and 2. Claussen, *Magistri Doctissimi Romani*, figures 21, 22, 82, 99 and 105.

*Ad Liberandum* on 30 November 1215.[155] With this Crusade in mind, he wished Rome and the cities and towns of the patrimony to have a special and indeed 'peculiar' rôle.[156] It was part of his plan to make 'Italia' – middle Italy – the centre and pivotal force of the new crusade. For the very first time, crusaders from Rome and its surroundings were to be strongly encouraged to participate.[157] A ship and £30,000 were to be put at the disposal of these crusaders.[158] A further 3,000 silver marks which had come from the offerings of the faithful, personally given to the pope, would be passed on to the 'Italia' contingent. Finally, Innocent stated that he himself would travel in person to the south of Italy in June 1217 to bless the crusaders as they sailed away from Messina and Brindisi.[159] All he needed to do now was to encourage men and women alike to take the Cross. He hoped that his own preaching of the Cross would produce not only a great popular consensus – for crusading was, after all, a voluntary matter – but also that the efficacy of the appeal he preached would produce the manpower and finance which were so badly needed.[160] For a man of perhaps fifty-five, desperately affected by the heat, his proposal to travel the length of the peninsula in the height of summer, arousing popular religious enthusiasm as he went, was not without its own perils.[161]

The eyewitness account of Innocent's inspired preaching on Sunday 1 May 1216, during a torrential downpour, reveals the spontaneous, fascinating and truly evangelical aspect of the event.[162] By the end of the day, when Innocent was led away from the field in a triumphal procession, more than 2,000 men and many women had taken the Cross. Throughout the patrimony, his own bishops, like Innocent himself, had followed to the letter the instructions laid down in *Quia Maior*. In Bagnoreggio, for example, the bishop claimed for his diocese a very large number of crusaders.[163] From all the towns of the patrimony, therefore a definite Roman contingent emerged – a *magna turba*

[155] Riley-Smith, *The Crusades*, pp. 124–9.
[156] Macarrone, *Studi*, pp. 129–42.
[157] Ibid., pp. 137–8, especially n. 3.
[158] Riley-Smith, *The Crusades*, p. 126.
[159] Ibid., p. 125.
[160] Ibid., pp. 142–8.
[161] M. Petrucci, 'L'ultimo destino perugino di Innocenzo III', *Bollettino della deputazione di storia patria per l'Umbria* 64 (1967), 201–7.
[162] New York, Pierpont Morgan Library, M. 465, fo. 90 verso, printed in Maccarrone, *Studi*, pp. 8–9 and Plates I–II.
[163] Ibid., p. 138.

*Romanorum*.[164] In spite of everything which followed his untimely death on 16 July in Perugia, Innocent had brought together in unity, peace and concord the towns of the papal states in a common purpose.

[164] Ibid., p. 138, n. 3; *Lettres de Jacques de Vitry (1160/1170–1240) évêque de Saint-Jean-d'Acre*, R. B. C. Huygens, ed. (Leiden, 1960), p. 110, lines 227–32: 'novem vero naves cum domno Petro Hanibal et quibusdam aliis Romanis in ebdomada post festum sancti Bartholomei in portu Damaite applicuerunt.' Huygens suggests 22 September 1218 as the date of the letter.

# IV

## *Too Important to Neglect: The Gesta Innocentii PP III*

It is the purpose of any *gesta*, that most particularly medieval genre of historical prose, to provide a contemporary background to the outstanding deeds of its principal character, usually portrayed as the hero of the piece.[1] The form of the *gesta* originally followed the simple chronological framework used in the widely diffused *Liber pontificalis*.[2] Basic details such as family origins and length of career were followed by an account of striking achievements, concluding with a brief description of the subject's death. By the twelfth century it had become standard practice for material to be organised explicitly according to its bearing on separate topics such as personal attributes, the defence of lands and castles and gifts to local monasteries and churches. As kings began to realise the considerable potential of *gesta* their form was adapted to a more courtly context, while the authors became concerned to describe and justify the growth of royal authority.[3] By the second half of the twelfth and by the early thirteenth century, the *gesta* was at the height of its development and fashion. The Emperor Frederick Barbarossa (1152–90)[4] and Henry II of England (1154–89)[5] had their *gesta* as did Philip II Augustus (1179–1223).[6] One pope seems to have merited a *gesta*, namely Innocent III (1198–1216).[7] From this we should not be

[1] R.D. Ray, 'Medieval Historiography through the Twelfth Century: Problems and Progress of Research', *Viator*, v (1974), 32–59; C.B. Bouchard, *Spirituality and Administration: The Role of the Bishop in Twelfth-Century Auxerre*, Speculum Anniversary Monographs, v (Cambridge, Mass., 1979), pp.5–13; B.F. Reilly, 'The *Historia Compostelana*: The Genesis and Composition of a Twelfth-Century Spanish *Gesta*', *Speculum*, xliv (1949), 78–85.

[2] *Le Liber Pontificalis*, ed. L. Duchesne-C. Vogel, 3 vols., 2nd ed. (Paris, 1955–57); T.F.X. Noble, 'A new look at the *Liber pontificalis*', *Archivum Historiae Pontificae*, xxiii (1985), 347–58.

[3] R.R. Bezzola, *Les origines et la formation de la litterature courtoise en occident, 500–1200* (Paris, 1958–1963).

[4] *Ottonis et Rahewini, Gesta Friderici I imperatoris*, ed. G. Waitz and B. von Simson, *Monumenta Germaniae Historica, in usum scholarum* (Hannover, 1912); *The Deeds of Frederick Barbarossa: Otto of Freising and his Continuator Rahewin*, trans. C.C. Mierow (Columbia, 1953).

[5] *Gesta regis Henrici secundi Benedicti abbatis*, ed. W. Stubbs (London, 1867).

[6] *Oeuvres de Rigord et de Guillaume le Breton*, ed. H.-F. Delaborde, i, (Paris, 1882).

[7] *Gesta Innocentii PP. III*, in *Patrologia Latina*, ed. J.P. Migne, (Paris, 1855) ccxiv, I-CL, cols. xvii-ccxxviii.

misled into an overemphasis of Innocent's political activities. His *Gesta*, however, provides us with an important source, just as valuable as those of his secular contemporaries.

By Innocent's day the *gesta* had evolved into something far more dramatic and interesting than a mere factual chronicle. The worthy deeds of the individual could now be supplemented by the inclusion of *instrumenta* or documentary evidence from the growing collections of archives, charters, registers and judicial rolls. If the patron was sufficiently powerful, a Philip Augustus for example, the prose *gesta* might subsequently be transformed into verse.[8] If a suitable villain could be found to act as counterpoint to the hero the dramatic effect of prose or verse was all the more intense. The approach was strongly biographical and a *gesta* written from first-hand experience would enjoy an improved standing over one based merely on 'common report'. Many *gesta*, of course, incorporated a variety of approaches and methods. Often the work of several authors, although sometimes of one alone, they were frequently reworked to suit changing circumstances. Where an eyewitness was involved events and suitable anecdotes could sometimes be interwoven with privileged information obtained from private archival or documentary sources. In some ways then a *gesta* might have had something in common with a modern festschrift the purpose of which is well understood.[9]

To honour John Taylor's retirement and to convey my thanks, I want to attempt to rehabilitate Innocent III's *Gesta*,[10] that neglected and

[8] J.W. Baldwin, *The Government of Philip Augustus: Foundations of French Royal Power in the Middle Ages* (Berkeley, 1986), pp.362–93, 420–23.

[9] I stand eyewitness to John Taylor's excellence as a tutor. Thirty years on I can still relate a particular event which typifies the concern for and availability to students which was always linked to the fine teaching and scholarship of the Leeds History School. One typically Yorkshire autumn day five of us, two of the three History Johns (John Cox and John Taylor; the third was John Le Patourel, Professor of History, 1945–1974, died July 1981) and three students, drove deep into the Dales. Our conveyance was a splendid and aged Rolls-Royce hearse; our mission was to rub the great brass of Simon of Wensley as a joint effort for the department. Mission accomplished saw us playing darts in the local inn where three inexperienced students were encouraged to defeat two kindly and considerate staff. I cherish my memories of John Taylor's encouragement in other fields as well, although neither of us would have suspected at the time that I might come to work on the Medieval Church, that area which he has made so much his own.

[10] H. Elkan, *Die Gesta Innocentii III im Verhältnis zu den Registen desselben Papstes* (Heidelberg, 1876); Y. Lefevre, 'Innocent III et son temps vus de Rome: étude sur la biographie anonyme de ce pape', *Mélanges d'archéologie et d'histoire de l'École Française de Rome*, lxi (1949), 242–45; V. Pfaff, 'Die Gesta Innocenz' III und das Testament Henrichs VI', *Zeitschrift der Savigny-Stiftung für Rechtesgeschichte: kanonische Abteilung*, 1 (1964), 78–126, especially 79–90; W. Imkamp, *Das Kirchenbild Innocenz' III (1198–1216)*, Päpste und Papsttum, xxii (Stuttgart, 1983), pp.10–46.

undervalued source which seems to have lain so long dormant, as did my interest in church history after my time at Leeds. The *Gesta Innocentii PP III* is a unique source for the life and work of its hero during the first ten years of his pontificate. The *Gesta* was apparently not well known in the middle ages[11] and seventeenth-century copies seem to have survived in greater number than manuscripts of the time. The transmission of the text of the *Gesta* has been painstakingly reconstructed by Imkamp who identifies two sources, one in France, the other in Rome.[12] In France, two fourteenth-century manuscripts,[13] one possibly from Toulouse, the other from Autun, both end at chapter CXLV and make no mention of Innocent's *Commentary on the Penitential Psalms*. These appear to have been used in the editions of Bosquet (1635)[14] and Baluze (1682).[15] In Rome, Vat. Lat. 12111, written in a late thirteenth- or early fourteenth-century hand, can be identified from the Papal Library Catalogue as being in Avignon in 1411.[16] It seems to have arrived back in Rome before the end of 1604.[17] The death of Giacomo Grimaldi, Archivist of St. Peter's, on 7 December of that year is recorded on the first folio.[18] This manuscript may well have been Vallicelliana J49, used by La Porte du Theil and Brequigny in 1791 and published again by Migne in 1855.[19] More comprehensive than its counterparts it includes a further six chapters, CXLVI to CL, with detailed and significant lists of gifts and promotions made by Innocent to the Roman church. The manuscript also includes the pope's *Commentary on the Psalms*.

Today the text of the *Gesta* is still most readily accessible at the beginning of Migne's four-volume edition of Innocent's *Opera omnia* where it occupies 211 columns.[20] As Innocent is the first medieval pope to have anything approaching a complete set of surviving registers, the attention of historians has been concentrated on the official chancery documents which make up the main body of Migne's four volumes. The *Gesta* has usually been discounted in a few dismissive words. How

[11] K.W. Pennington, *Pope and Bishops: The Papal Monarchy in the Twelfth and Thirteenth Centuries* (Philadelphia, 1984), p.54.

[12] Imkamp, *Das Kirchenbild*, pp.10–20.

[13] Paris Bibliothèque Nationale, MS Lat. 5150; 5151.

[14] F. Bosquet, *Epistola Innocentii pontificis maximi notae* (Toulouse, 1635), pp.1–150.

[15] E. Baluze, *Epistolarum Innocentii III Romanorum pontificis libri undecim; accedunt Gesta eiusdem Innocentii et prima collectio decretalium composita a Rainerio diacono et monacho Pompostino; Stephanus Baluzius Tutelensis editionem Tolosanum innumeris propemodum in unum colligit, magnam partem nunc primum editit, reliqua emendavit*, 2 vols., (Paris, 1682).

[16] Imkamp, *Das Kirchenbild*, p.14.

[17] *Ibid.*, p.15.

[18] MS Vat. Lat. 12111, fo. 1r.

[19] Imkamp, *Das Kirchenbild*, pp.17–19.

[20] *Gesta*, I-CL, cols. xvii-ccxxviii.

could a biography by an anonymous contemporary, which does not even cover the whole pontificate match more official sources of greater validity? It was all too easy to denigrate with the words 'enigmatic',[21] 'partisan', 'panegyric' and 'pro-papal'.[22] It is now high time to redress the balance. This will reveal the *Gesta* to be unique as a source for the better appreciation of Innocent III's activities, particularly as they apply to Rome and the Papal States.

The official biography of Innocent III, entered in the *Liber pontificalis* by Martin of Troppau (d. 1279),[23] merely outlines Innocent's career to 1216 as it would have been known and remembered in the third quarter of the thirteenth century. A poor thing it is too, both brief and uninspiringly terse. It follows a simple chronological framework: a few sentences on his family origins in Campania; the length of his pontificate; an account of his main achievements; and finally a brief description of his death. Martin's work cannot be compared either in quality or in quantity with the *Gesta*'s rich detail and vivid narration of events.

The *Gesta* of Innocent III is attractive and exciting. Its author must have seen the pope frequently, worked closely with him and understood and sympathised with his feelings. It helps us to come closer to the person of the pope. Other eyewitness accounts that we have of the pontificate serve to increase the credibility which the *Gesta* has for the period it covers. Two of these are chance survivals. One is a private letter from an official of the Curia at its summer retreat at Subiaco in 1202 and possibly addressed to Rinaldo, archbishop-elect of Capua.[24] This reveals how by sheer force of his personal example, Innocent inspired his officials to work through the full heat of every day no matter how they yearned for their siesta.[25] The so-called Giessen Manuscript contains a letter by a German cleric,[26] who attended the Fourth Lateran Council (11–30 November 1215) and who records not only Innocent's impressive chairmanship of the greatest assembly of the church since Chalcedon (451) but also registers the pope's spontaneous and proprietorial delight in showing Rome to his distinguished visitors. The third eyewitness, a continuator of the Chapter Archives of S. Costanzo in Orvieto, is perhaps more conscious of the need

[21] Lefevre, 'Innocent III', p.243.

[22] T.C. Van Cleve, *Markward of Anweiler and the Sicilian Regency* (Princeton, 1937), pp.119–21.

[23] *Liber pontificalis*, pp.451–53.

[24] K. Hampe, 'Eine Schilderung des Sommeraufenthaltes der römischen Kurie unter Innocenz III in Subiaco, 1202', *Historische Vierteljahrschrift*, viii (Leipzig, 1905), 509–35.

[25] *Ibid.*, p.531.

[26] S. Kuttner and A. Garcia y Garcia, 'A New Eyewitness Account of the Fourth Lateran Council', *Traditio*, xx (1964), 115–78.

to record his account of what he saw.[27] He describes the papal visit to that city on Sunday 1 May 1216, where Innocent's charismatic preaching encouraged more than 2,000 men and women of every sort to take the Cross. The Orvietan canon even tells us of Innocent's physical appearance within two months of his death. At fifty-seven the pope, of middling height, shone with interior as well as exterior beauty.[28] This description, reminiscent of St. Francis, matches contemporary Mendicant perceptions and accords well with the *Gesta*, whose author speaks similarly of Innocent's medium height and attractive and inspiring appearance.[29]

The *Gesta*'s value as an historical source goes far beyond these chance survivals about the personality of the pope which serve only to enhance its contents, not to diminish them. It is not merely a diary recounting day-to-day events during the first ten years of the pontificate. Instead it is a single author's presentation of carefully organised themes, rigorously selected. The biographer must have lived and worked at the Papal Curia. He certainly had privileged access to the Papal Registers and they were, in fact, his only documentary source.[30] At all times he followed his subject as a skilled and sensitive diplomatist. He begins with a short section on the pope's early career, his education and cardinalate, his election and consecration. He moves rapidly and in an ordered fashion to deal with his chosen themes. He examines in sequence Innocent's policy for the recovery of the Papal States and the reform of the church in Rome. He considers the influence of the church throughout Christendom and includes in this theme relations with Greeks in the East and the Fourth Crusade of 1204. The account concludes with the continuing struggle against the commune for control of the city of Rome. The last six chapters enumerate Innocent's charitable activities and benefactions, not only to churches and religious institutions within the city of Rome but throughout the Patrimony and beyond. These and the list of promotions amongst his household and familiars provide information which is to be found only in this source.

The biographer's first theme is the desperate situation which arose from the German occupation of the Papal States. A harsh and tyrannical repression of the pope's subjects approached the gates of Rome itself.[31] Innocent's purpose was to return the Patrimony to the sphere of influence of the church. It was to be a programme of *recuperatio* or recovery but could not be undertaken without many qualms on the pope's part.[32] Here the author of the *Gesta* comes closest to understanding his subject's innermost

27 Pierpont Morgan Library M. 465, fo. 90v; M. Maccarrone, *Studi su Innocenzo III*, Italia Sacra, xvii (Padua, 1972), pp.3–9.

28 *Ibid.*, p.9, 'Statura modicum, formosum interiori et exteriori pulcritudine vegetavit'.

29 *Gesta*, I, col. xvii, 'statura mediocris et decorus aspectu'.

30 Lefevre, 'Innocent III', 243.

31 *Gesta*, VIII, cols. xxi-xxv; IX, cols. xii-xxv.

32 *Ibid.*, XVII, cols. xxix-xxx.

feelings, expressed through the text from Ecclesiasticus 13:1, 'Whosoever touches pitch shall be defiled'.[33] Innocent's anguish reveals his disquiet, *sollicitudo*, at the impropriety implicit in this armed recovery of his temporal power. The sense of danger and of the limitations on papal power are clearly articulated by the biographer. So well is this point made that the pope may have actually spoken of his anxieties to the author. In the event, papal rule brought positive benefits. Innocent made the roads safer and did not exact those harsh tolls taken by his German predecessors in the area.[34] He was, however, well aware of the heavy burdens he would have to place upon his subjects in the Patrimony and aimed to make these more acceptable by claiming that 'his yoke is easy and his burden light'.[35]

Accepted literary form is given dramatic expression in Innocent's conflict with Markward of Anweiler, the villain and anti-hero of the *Gesta*.[36] The hatred Innocent here displays is unique. Markward, German adventurer, *dapifer regis* and seneschal to the late Emperor Henry VI (1190–97), was duke of Ravenna, margrave of Ancona and count of Molise. Markward not only claimed his right to the regency and the Regno on behalf of the young Frederick II but also initially wrecked Innocent's plan to rebuild the Patrimony. After his siege of the great Benedictine abbey of Cassino in January-February 1199 and his subsequent excommunication,[37] Markward's activities are closely documented by the author of the *Gesta*. On the whole the biographer seems to have selected his information carefully. In July 1199 Markward is shown attempting to make a secret and underhand agreement with Archbishop Conrad of Mainz. If he agreed to represent Markward at the Curia he would receive 20,000 ounces of gold from the customary *census* usually given to the pope in the Patrimony.[38]

Markward made a dramatic attempt in August of the same year at Veroli to prevent the issuing of Innocent's sentence of excommunication. The *Gesta* shows that this very nearly succeeded when Markward threatened force against the cardinals concerned. Only Hugolino's courage managed to save the situation when he is reported as saying 'Behold the mandate of the Lord Pope. We cannot do otherwise'.[39] Innocent's propaganda campaign is continually highlighted. Not only is Markward *perfidius* but

[33] Maccarrone, *Studi*, pp.9–12.

[34] *Gesta*, xv, col. xxix.

[35] O. Hageneder and A. Haidacher eds., *Die Register Innocenz III*, i, *Pontifikatsjahr 1198–99* (Graz-Koln, 1964), pp.127–28; *PL*, cciv, 76; Maccarrone, *Studi*, pp.14–15.

[36] Van Cleve, *Markward*, pp.108–23; E. Kennan, 'Innocent III and the First Political Crusade: a Comment on the Limitations of Papal Power', *Traditio*, xxvii (1971), 231–49.

[37] *Gesta*, XXIII, cols. xxxviii-xlii.

[38] *Ibid.*, col. xlii.

[39] *Ibid.*, col. xliv; 'Ecce mandatum domini Papae. Nos aliud facere non valemus'.

also *ingeniosus et subdolus*.[40] Memories of previous cruelties by the Germans in the peninsula doubtless helped to rally the people against him. The fortuitous discovery by papal forces of Markward's baggage lost in his flight from defeat was used to the full in the *Gesta*.[41] In a cloak, the suppressed will of Henry VI complete with a golden bull was discovered. This will gave all to the church and, forgery or not, it suited Innocent's case. Markward's only claim to legality was the Declaration of Speyer where he was named as the Staufen regent in Sicily.[42] Markward's invasion of Sicily in October 1199 and his alliance with the local colony of Saracens had further fuelled the Pope's fury. This was a threat coming from the 'other Saladin'.[43] When Markward died in September 1202, the *Gesta*'s anti-hero description concludes with the agony he suffered in his final illness, reflecting vividly the view that the sinner was being suitably punished.[44]

Resistance continued in spite of Markward's death. When the pope fell gravely ill at Anagni in 1203, news spread that he had died.[45] An uprising took place in the Regno where Matera, Brindisi and Otranto were lost to him. German influence in the south lasted until 1205 when Innocent's former confessor, the Cistercian and papal diplomat Brother Rainier, received the homage of a number of leading nobles including Diepold of Acerra and another Markward, this time of Laviano.[46] The theme ends with the creation of Innocent's brother Richard as count of Sora, an important lordship at the frontier between the Patrimony and the Regno.[47] Finally Innocent, as the overlord, was able to take oaths of homage and fidelity from all the counts and barons. It was an important and highly symbolic ceremony that was held at S. Germano in June-July 1208 marking the full recovery of the southern part of the Patrimony.[48]

The second theme of the biographer is the power, influence and probity of the Roman church throughout all Christendom. He explains the reforms

[40] *Gesta*, IX, col. xxiii.

[41] *Ibid.*, XXVII, col. lii; Pfaff, '*Die Gesta* Innocenz' III', 79–90.

[42] *Regestum Innocentii III papae super negotio Romani imperii*, ed. F. Kempf, *Miscellanea Historiae Pontificiae*, xii (1947), pp.33–38.

[43] *Die Register Innocenz III*, ii, *Pontifikatsjahr 1199–1200*, eds. O. Hageneder, W. Maleczek and A. Strnad (Rome-Vienna, 1979), pp.411–14; *PL*, ccxiv, col. 780; Potthast, 877. Markward is also 'Dei et Ecclesiae inimicus', *Register*, i, pp.811–13; *PL*, CCXIV col. 516; Potthast, 601. Compare Innocent's letter of June 1212 to James, the papal marshal in *PL* ccvi, cols. 624–25 where the same title is used, even ten years after Markward's death.

[44] *Gesta*, XXV, col. lxvi.

[45] *Ibid.*, XXVII, col. lxvi; CXXVII, col. clxxxviii.

[46] *Ibid.*, XXXVIII, col. lxviii.

[47] *Ibid.*, XXIX, cols. lxxi-lxxiii.

[48] *Ibid.*, XL, cols. lxxiv-lxxx, with the text of his ordinance and a letter to the faithful of the Regno. 'Cum propter necessitatem urgentem in regnum personaliter descendimus . . . ut in ipso videlicet pacem et justitiam reformemus'.

which Innocent had instituted for the spiritual wellbeing of the church. Whilst curial officials were forbidden from taking fees, a sliding scale was established for scribes and *bullators*.[49] Porters were to allow free access to the notarial chambers without taking *douceurs* for themselves, and within the Lateran Palace Innocent, *solertissimus pontifex*, threw out the moneychangers' tables. The Consistory was to meet three times a week where the pope himself would hear the most significant cases, *cum multa maturitate*.[50] The biographer then lists those major cases: Compostella versus Braga; the Canterbury monks in their dispute over Lambeth Palace; the archbishop of Milan against the abbot of Scozula. This last case clearly intrigued the biographer.[51] He gives details, to add to evidence from elsewhere, of Innocent's ever-present concern to establish the validity of documents. He describes the pope's flamboyant act of seal-breaking as part of his campaign to root out forgery wherever it should appear.[52] Another case was the abasement of the excommunicated Conrad of Hildesheim who spread himself on the floor in front of the pope in the shape of a cross.[53] Anticlimax followed with a description of the bishop's open attempt to influence Innocent by presenting silver vases. The quick-witted Innocent immediately responded with a greater gift, of a more precious gold cup, and in so doing showed that he could not be corrupted. Both episodes, seals and vases, are used by the biographer to increase the liveliness of his reporting. After listing other significant cases of papal arbitration the biographer concludes with the case of Ingeborg of Denmark, the divorced wife of the king of France who had appealed to Rome.[54] Her case with its notoriety and pathos and her cries of *mala Francia, mala Francia* and *Roma, Roma*, shows the extent of the problems which Innocent had inherited and is used by the author to expand further on the marital theme, including incestuous marriages in Iberia and in the east.[55]

The second theme concludes with Innocent's desire in the tenth year of his pontificate to visit personally the now peaceful northern part of his Patrimony.[56] In Viterbo in September 1207 he held his great three-day parliament, receiving homage, hearing disputes and on the third

[49] *Ibid.*, XLI, cols. lxxx-lxxxi.
[50] *Ibid.*, XLII, cols. lxxxi-lxxxxii.
[51] *Ibid.*, col. lxxxiv.
[52] R.L. Poole, *Lectures on the Papal Chancery down to the Time of Innocent III* (London, 1915), pp.147–62. See also the case of 19 May 1198 in *Register* i, pp.333–35; *PL.* cciv, cols. 202–3.
[53] *Gesta*, XLIV, cols. lxxxvii-lxxxxviii; Pennington, *Pope and Bishops*, pp.32–33.
[54] *Gesta*, XLIX, cols. xciv-xcv.
[55] *Ibid.*, LVIII, cols. ciii-cviii.
[56] *Ibid.*, CXIII, cols. clxi-clxii.

day enacting several statutes against heresy.[57] The derelict monastery of S. Martino al Cimino nearby was given 'magnificent privileges' and its incorporation into the Cistercian order encouraged in order to help in holding the line against heresy.[58] Innocent's peacemaking and pastoral roles were evident in ending the local conflict amongst the citizens of Todi and providing suitable pontificals for the poverty-stricken archbishop of Ravenna.[59] After visiting his newly fortified palace at Montefiascone, where he spent twelve days,[60] he moved on to Tuscania to the new palace he had built at S. Niccola. There he demanded and received the oaths of his subjects. From Vetralla he went to Sutri, where he remained three days solemnly dedicating the cathedral before returning to Rome.

Further cases of Innocent's wider role as peace-maker are detailed in a small sub-section:[61] Henry, king of Hungary, brought to peace with his brother Andrew; the Milanese with the citizens of Pavia; the Lombard communes and the kings of France and England aided by the special effort of the Cistercian, Gerald, abbot of Casamari.[62] This peace-making often entailed ecclesiastical reform. Long list of provinces visited by papal agents and of bishops removed from their sees are provided.[63] Control by Rome is always evident. Even in its 'profound servitude', the church in England is shown to be ultimately responsible to Innocent. His consecration of Stephen Langton, cardinal-deacon of S. Crisogono is given as evidence of this.[64]

The third and major theme of the *Gesta* is the pope's relationship with Rome, its prefect, its commune and its citizens. From the biographer we have a clear eyewitness account of Innocent taking possession of his city after his consecration when 'all the city was crowned' and rejoicing.[65] Although the prefect, Peter de Vico, a former imperial supporter, is shown performing his act of homage and receiving a red mantle from the pope, the Romans were much less easily won over. They demanded their traditional money gifts given at the election of a new pope and bitterly protested against the

57 For the texts of the three statutes promulgated, see *PL*, ccv, cols. 1226–28; Maccarrone, *Studi*, pp.51–61.

58 *Gesta*, CXXVI, cols. clxii-clxiv; *PL*, CCV, cols. 1309–12; Potthast, 2997. For the gift of a red and gold altar frontal and 100 pounds in money of Siena, *Gesta*, CXLV, cols. ccviii, ccxxvii.

59 *Ibid.*, CXXVII, cols clxv-clxvi.

60 *Ibid.*, XIV, cols. xxviii-xxix; *PL*, cciv, col. 112; Maccarrone, *Studi*, pp.21–22.

61 *Gesta*, CXXVIII, cols. clxviii-ix.

62 *Ibid.*, CXXX, col. clxix. Gerald, abbot of Casamari (1183–1209) was a nephew of Gerald, sixth abbot of Clairvaux.

63 *Ibid.*, CXXX, clxxii-clxxv.

64 *Ibid.*, CXXXI, cols. clxxv-clxxvii.

65 *Ibid.*, VII, cols. xx-xxi; 'Coronata est tota civitas'.

parish by parish oath enforced on them to prevent fraud.[66]

Nor were the nobles any less docile. Using the imagery of the Psalms (63:90), as the virtue of gold is proved in the fiery furnace,[67] a text incidentally used later by Innocent in his call to crusade,[68] the *Gesta* shows the pope, wounded more by his enemies' tongues than by their arrows, successfully resisting the harmful taunts of hiis chief enemies, John Pierleone and John Capocci. They accused him of misusing and despoiling the properties of the city as a sparrowhawk might strip the feathers from a smaller bird.[69] They in their turn tried to extort money from the pope who steadfastly refused to submit to what he regarded as a *pessima consuetudo*.[70] The *Gesta* is at pains to show Innocent as the strong defender of Rome.

In the Romans' two difficult wars against Viterbo his brother Richard gave 1,000 pounds to provision the small, embattled fortress-town of Vitorchiano.[71] The pope himself showed where he stood by insisting upon the return of the bronze doors and fountain grills which the Viterbans had broken and removed from St. Peter's in 1167.[72] The impression given here is that the biographer is struggling hard to show Innocent and the Romans working together. The other side of the picture which he also reports, is a grim catalogue of physical molestation and downright humiliation – of masses disrupted at St. Peter's: of physical attacks on the person of the pope; and of open rebellion during his absence at Velletri in 1202. There is no underestimation of the violence of the Tower Wars between the clans of the Orsini-Boboni-Capocci-Pierleone on the one hand and the papally-supported Conti-Annibaldi-Romani de Scorta (Scotti) on the other.[73] The widespread distaste felt by the Romans for Richard Conti is clearly described including his territorial ambitions which extended from Poli near Tivoli to Sora.[74] In July-August 1208 he was invested as count of Sora at the hands of his brother. From those dark days, the pope, the Bishop of Rome, is shown as emerging triumphant. John Pierleone is publicly excommunicatted and Innocent shows that he is not 'like a dumb dog who does not know how to bark',[75] words identical to those he

66 *Ibid.*, VIII, cols. xxi-xxii.

67 *Ibid.*, CXXXIII, col. clxxvii.

68 In *Quia maior.* J. and L. Riley-Smith, *The Crusades: Idea and Reality, 1095–1274* (London, 1981), p.119.

69 *Gesta*, CXXXIII, col. clxxxiii; 'sicut anceps deplumat avem omnibus pannis'.

70 *Ibid.*, col. clxxix.

71 *Ibid.*, CXXXIV, col. clxxxii.

72 *Ibid.*, CXXX, col. clxxxiii; 'Praecipiens Viterbiensibus ut portas aereos quos de cantharo ante basilicam dicebantur extulisse, vel confregisse, tempore Frederici imperatoris, facerent restauri'.

73 *Ibid.*, cols. clxxxiv-cxcvi.

74 *Ibid.*, XXXIX, cols. lxx-lxxiii.

75 *Ibid.*, CXLII, col. cxcvi.

so frequently used to his own bishops. The steps of the basilica of St. Peter on the feast of its dedication was a most fitting setting for such a declaration where pope and commune finally came to terms.

The language of the *Gesta* is neither highly coloured nor overelaborate. It is surely written, as Lefevre suggested, by a single well-placed curial official whose exposition flows easily along maintaining his readers' interest.[76] The papal registers are the only written source which the biographer appears to have used and he moves stylistically from personal account to the straightforward citation of papal correspondence. Clearly, the *Gesta* is an official work produced by a cleric with privileged access to the chancery and its flow of documents. Up to this point most historians have agreed. On questions of motive and dating there has been far less unanimity. Elkan believed that the text was written between June and August 1208 by a close relative of Innocent himself with the aim of justifying papal policy towards Sicily.[77] Lefevre (1949) dismissed Elkan's examination of the *Gesta* as both incomplete and partial.[78] He agreed that the author was well-placed in the curia but was no relation and had composed his work in two separate stages. A primitive text of *c.* 1203 in biographical form with supporting documents, *pièces justicatives*, was completed in draft. The reason for the speed of this compilation must have been the severe illness and rumoured death of the pope at precisely that time in Anagni. By 1208 a second version had been created without any alteration to the primitive text save the insertion of paragraphs here and there to update his information. In 1207 the biographer had access to the papal registers and incorporated large extracts directly into his work correcting and amplifying the primitive version but without modifying the early form of the text.

Lefevre has argued that this evolution of the *Gesta* indicates the historian working rigorously to select events he wished to highlight and waiting to write about them until he had access to the documents. He would thus diminish the risks of misinterpretation.[79] Lefevre has also suggested that this is the reason the author never deals with the imperial question or the situation in Germany as the outcome is always too uncertain. He considers that the approach to the Fourth Crusade also confirms the policy of waiting to use relevant documents until the registers were written up. The Crusades are written about not in 1203 but in 1208, when the use of the pope's correspondence confirm the author's reliability and trustworthiness in

[76] Lefevre, 'Innocent III', p.245.
[77] *Ibid.*, p.244
[78] *Ibid.*, pp.244–45.
[79] *Ibid.*, p.244.

regard to the capture of Zara.[80] Lefevre has concluded that the author of the *Gesta* wished to present a clear but classified exposition of events. Through his use of papal documents he echoes curial thought and opinion. In a very real sense, therefore, his is a 'view from Rome'.[81]

More recent discussion of the *Gesta* by Pfaff and Imkamp has concentrated on specific issues such as the reported will of Henry VI, whether suppressed or forged, and the accuracy of the details of Innocent's early education and his training in theology. All this is valuable but adds little to our attempt to understand why the *Gesta* stops in 1208 or 1209 and why the biographer selected the themes he did.

One almost contemporary work which may help in this attempt is Boso's *Life of Alexander III* (1176).[82] This history of the Papal Schism of 1159–76 has a classic hero in the pope and an equally classic anti-hero in Frederick Barbarossa. The subject matter is rigorously selected with an eye to dramatic effect, for this is indeed a drama. There is a hero, a villain, a beginning and an end. Far more literary in form than the *Gesta*, it was intended to describe Alexander's formal repossession of Rome. It finished in 1176 before the pope's death not, as was once thought, because Boso himself had died but because the work's purpose had been accomplished.[83] The *Gesta* may have been the same: a work deliberately designed to carry a message about the celebrated achievements of a pope. There is no evident break or sharp change at any point in the narrative which might have been expected had the anonymous biographer died suddenly. The work proceeds to its conclusion calmly and purposefully, ending with a long balance sheet of the benefactions which had been achieved during the period.[84] This is a piece of justicative writing, a prose *geste* directed to a local audience in the Patrimony to show Innocent, a true Roman with roots in the Campania, surmounting tribulation, overcoming the machinations of villains, particularly that 'other Saladin' and at length taking possession of the lands, rights and subjects of the Patrimony of St. Peter. By 1208 it must have seemed both to Innocent and to his biographer that he was at last more or less secure in his homeland. Ten years of struggle had been carefully and honestly described and documented; reverses included as well as triumphs. In the

80 *Gesta*, LXXXIII, cols. cxxxi-cxxxii; A.J. Andrea and I. Motsiff, 'Pope Innocent III and the Diversion of the Fourth Crusade Army to Zara', *Byzantinoslavica*, XXX (1972), 6–25, especially 8–15.

81 Lefevre, 'Innocent III', p.245.

82 *Boso's Life of Alexander III*, intro. P. Munz, trans. G.M. Ellis (Oxford, 1973), especially pp.1–39.

83 *Ibid.*, pp.1–5.

84 *Gesta*, CXLIX, cols. ccxxv-ccxxviii.

carefully structured thematic approach of our author persons and events of Roman and Campanian interest take first place against a background of events of wider significance in contemporary Christendom. The reshaping of the Patrimony demonstrated what its people owed to their bishop, the pope *Innocentius PP III*.

Tor de'Conti
(Photograph: Kate Warren.)

# V

## PHILIP AUGUSTUS AND JOHN: TWO SONS IN INNOCENT III'S VINEYARD?

MY debt to Michael Wilks is great indeed. A valued family friendship for over twenty years has survived interminable power-struggles played out on the Monopoly board, his two sons taking the lead. One other event involving his two sons forms part of Bolton family folklore when, following a barbecue in St Albans, a hedge suddenly went up in flames. Michael Wilks was soon to the fore in quelling the conflagration. Our friendship still survived! I have always been grateful for his wise advice and constant support in academic matters as in other ways. Since April 1985, we have shared a Special Subject on 'The Pontificate of Innocent III', each respecting the other's opinions where they differed. This divergence was always grasped by our students, who have teasingly played us off against each other to the great enjoyment of all. My contribution to his *Festschrift* contains much that he will recognize. Here were two other sons, whose fire needed to be doused if the hedge of the Lord's Vineyard was not to be destroyed.[1] But more time for action was needed in Rome at the turn of the twelfth century than in St Albans in 1975!

The biblical image of the vineyard has always held an honoured place. During Innocent's pontificate it was frequently used, whether in letters addressed to lethargic bishops to halt the spread of heresy,[2] in sermons such as his *Sermo X de tempore*,[3] composed for Septuagesima Sunday, and, in particular, in his vital circular letter, *Vineam domini*, the vineyard of the Lord of Saboath.[4] This was sent out on 19 April 1213 to summon all archbishops, bishops, abbots, priors, and various secular rulers to his proposed great General Council of the whole Church to be held in November 1215.[5]

[1] C. R. Cheney and W. H. Semple, *Selected Letters of Pope Innocent III* (London and Edinburgh, 1953), p. 144 [hereafter *SLI*].

[2] O. Hageneder, W. Maleczek, and A. Strnad, *Die Register Innocenz III, II, 2 Jahrgang (1199/1200)* (Rome and Vienna, 1979), pp. 3–5 [hereafter *Register* II]; *PL* 214, cols 537–9.

[3] *PL* 217, cols 353–8.

[4] *PL* 216, cols 823–7; *SLI*, pp. 144–7.

[5] B. M. Bolton, 'A show with a meaning: Innocent III's approach to the Fourth Lateran Council, 1215', *Medieval History*, 1 (January 1991), pp. 53–67.

Throughout his pontificate, Innocent makes frequent reference to his twin desires for the vineyard: the recovery of the Holy Land, lost to Christians since the Battle of Hattin in 1187, and the reform or renewal of the Church and its message.[6] To achieve success in these tasks, it was vital to re-establish peace and friendship where dissension and rivalry were rife.[7] The maintenance of a stable peace, or at least a long truce, between rulers was thus essential. Unfortunately, during his pontificate of eighteen years, six months, and eight days, there can have been few, if any, occasions when he could have felt totally sure of the support of the Emperor and of the Kings of France and England, the Capetian Philip II and the Angevin John—in traditional papal terms, his two sons. Indeed, he calls Philip his 'special son'[8] and John his 'well-beloved son'.[9] Diplomatic language, then as now, is sometimes useful! Neither were far removed from him in age. Innocent, thirty-seven in 1198, was possibly the youngest pope ever elected:[10] Philip was thirty-two at the time,[11] and John thirty-one on his accession in 1199.[12] Although conscious of this closeness in age, Innocent had no qualms about the nature and authority of his position. In the very first letter of his pontificate, addressed to the archbishops and bishops of the Kingdom of France, he reminded all those who might question his youth that in the bestowal of power God sometimes placed the younger before the elder.[13] He explains how those who had elected him had thought in their wisdom 'to find the silver cup in the sack of the young Benjamin'. Any weakness he might have would be strengthened during his task as was St Peter himself, who, in spite of his three denials, still received the charge from Christ to guide his sheep. As his pontificate unfolded, Innocent was responsible for giving the papacy impetus, creating new justifications for the exercise of authority, and for using those justifications in new ways.[14] His use of verbal images, colourful, vigorous, frequently ironic, enlivened by many allusions to the Bible,

[6] L. and J. Riley-Smith, *The Crusades: Idea and Reality 1095–1274* (London, 1981), pp. 118–29.

[7] J. Gaudemet, 'Le rôle de la papauté dans le règlement des conflits entre états aux xiiie et xive siècles', *La Paix, Recueils de la Société Jean Bodin*, 15 (Brussels, 1961), pp. 79–106.

[8] O. Hageneder and A. Haidacher, eds, *Die Register Innocenz' III, I. Pontifikatsjahr 1198/1199* (Graz and Cologne, 1964), p. 5 [hereafter *Register* I]; *PL* 214, col. 2; Potthast, 2.

[9] *PL* 215, col. 1254; *SLI*, p. 97.

[10] C. Morris, *The Papal Monarchy: the Western Church from 1050 to 1250* (Oxford, 1989), p. 417.

[11] J. W. Baldwin, *The Government of Philip Augustus: Foundations of French Royal Power in the Middle Ages* (Berkeley, 1986), p. 379.

[12] W. L. Warren, *King John* (London, 1961), p. 32.

[13] *Register* I, pp. 3–5; *PL* 214, col. 1; Potthast, 1.

[14] K. Pennington, *Pope and Bishops: the Papal Monarchy in the Twelfth and Thirteenth Centuries* (Pennsylvania, 1984), pp. 13–15.

suited contemporary tastes and ideas. With his vast knowledge of the Bible and his inclination for the apt quotation, parables about sons, particularly the two sons in the vineyard,[15] would have been in Innocent's mind when forced, as he constantly was, to consider the activities of these two regal rivals. The parable is short and clear. In the first half, the father of the vineyard, wishing that it should be cared for, asks his sons to undertake the task. 'I will not go', replied the first, whilst the second immediately said, 'Sir, I go.' Surely, graceless John and noble Philip. Later history has judged them thus. Matthew Paris (*c.*1250) depicted John bemused, his crown awry.[16] A French manuscript (*c.*1270) portrayed the infant Philip, *Dieudonné*, being popped from above by divine hands into longing parental arms.[17] Innocent, however, might not have been so sure that he agreed with the distinction.

The characters and personalities of these two sons were obviously important. Contemporary sources and later historians have had little good to say about John until perhaps quite recently.[18] Some have even gone so far as to agree with the judgement of William of Newburgh that John was 'nature's enemy'.[19] All, however, are agreed that inconsistencies were the basis of his personality, swinging backwards and forwards, from one position to another, in irritatingly rapid succession.[20] Philip, on the other hand, in spite of what has been referred to as his opaque personality,[21] has received uniformly good comment. Whilst John veered wildly in his actions from good[22] to reprehensible, Philip is presented in a more consistent light. He was a traditionally devout and law-abiding Capetian, whose energies were concentrated on Paris. He authorized and supported its university and helped towards the completion of the new cathedral of Notre Dame.[23] He gave much needed payments to the city, founded hospitals, and built an *enceinte* or enclosing wall in his circuit of fortifications. Monasteries and nunneries do not seem to have concerned him over

[15] Matt. 21. 28–31.

[16] London, BL, MS Cotton Claudius, D VI, fol. 9v; S. Lewis, *The Art of Matthew Paris in the Chronica Majora = Californian Studies in the History of Art*, 21 (Berkeley, 1987), pp. 156–7, 184–5.

[17] Paris, Bibliothèque Ste-Geneviève, MS 782, fol. 208r; Baldwin, *Philip Augustus*, frontispiece and p. 368 and 'The case of Philip Augustus, *Persona et Gesta*; the image and deeds of the thirteenth century Capetians', *Viator*, 19 (1988), pp. 195–207.

[18] S. Painter, *The Reign of King John* (Baltimore, 1949); Warren, *King John*.

[19] William of Newburgh, *Chronicles of the Reigns of Stephen, Henry II and Richard I*, ed. R. Howlett, 4 vols, *RS* (1884–90), 3, p. 391.

[20] D. M. Stenton, *English Society in the Early Middle Ages* (London, 1951), pp. 48–9.

[21] Baldwin, 'The case of Philip Augustus', p. 195.

[22] For example, his founding of Beaulieu Abbey, *PL* 214, col. 972: *SLI*, pp. 37–9.

[23] Baldwin, *Philip Augustus*, p. 343.

much, except for one occasion when, perhaps slightly out of character, he wished to establish a convent in memory of his controversial mistress, Agnes de Meran.[24]

Whatever differences there may have been in their characters and personalities, there could be no doubt about their thoroughgoing rivalry on every major issue. Unfortunately for Innocent, this rivalry occurred at precisely the time when, either together or even singly, they could have played a vital role in reclaiming the vineyard. How could a crusade against the infidel be mounted at the edges of the vineyard when there was such rivalry between those inside, even going so far as to bring into disrepute the whole concept of the crusade?

Briefly united for once in 1193–4, when they joined together in rebellion against Richard, they soon became irrevocably divided over the question of the imperial succession[25]—Otto IV was John's nephew—and, more importantly, over Philip's claims to Capetian suzerainty,which threatened to weaken and undermine the whole Angevin territorial structure.[26] True to form, John was inconsistent in action, if not in enmity. When he made peace in 1200 by the Treaty of Le Goulet,[27] recognizing the French King's suzerainty for all the lands John held of him in France, Gervase of Canterbury nicknamed him 'Softsword'.[28] This nickname was unfair. The treaty at least consolidated the judgement of Philip's court that John, rather than his nephew Arthur, had rights to Normandy.[29] In 1202, as a result of John's quarrel with the Lusignan brothers, Philip summoned him to account for his actions.[30] Graceless John refused to appear. Philip's court pronounced him contumacious and confiscated all his fiefs.[31] In the subsequent war, Normandy and all the other territories were lost, only the Channel Islands remaining in John's hands.

[24] Baldwin, *Philip Augustus*, p. 86.

[25] *PL* 216, cols 1062–3; *SLI*, p. 24.

[26] J. le Patourel, 'The Plantagenet Dominions', in M. Jones, ed., *Feudal Empires: Norman and Plantagenet* (London, 1984), pp. 289–308; R. W. Southern, 'England's first entry into Europe', in *Medieval Humanism and Other Studies* (Oxford, 1970), pp. 135–57.

[27] *Recueil des actes de Philippe Auguste*, ed. H. F. Delaborde, C. Petit-Dutaillis, J. Boussard, and M. Nortier, 4 vols (Paris, 1916–79), 2, pp. 178–85.

[28] *Historical Works of Gervase of Canterbury*, ed. W. Stubbs, 2 vols, *RS* (1879–80), 2, p. 92; Warren, *King John*, p. 106.

[29] W. Ullmann, 'Arthur's homage to King John', *EHR*, 94 (1979), pp. 356–64; J. W. Baldwin, 'La Décennie décisive: les années 1190–1203 dans le règne de Philippe Auguste', *RH*, 266 (1981), pp. 311–37.

[30] Baldwin, *Philip Augustus*, pp. 265–6.

[31] *PL* 214, cols 984–5; *SLI*, p. 40.

## Philip Augustus and John

It was against this background of Angevin–Capetian relations that Innocent wished to act.[32] He did so with the clear example of Clement III (1188–91) in mind.[33] Not only had his predecessor achieved a truce between warring cities, in this case, Pisa and Genoa, but he had also, through his legate, Henry, Cardinal Bishop of Albano, intervened in 1188–9 to stop those Anglo-French hostilities which threatened to mar participation in the Third Crusade.[34] By 1198, normal Anglo-French hostilities, the *status quo ante*, had been resumed. Innocent considered that since wars within kingdoms and principalities were always fratricidal, he, by virtue of his office, had the right—indeed, the duty—to intervene.[35] This was even more vital when what was needed was not a fratricidal war but a holy war, a crusade. Innocent considered that it was crucial to avoid an armed conflict where the forces concerned ought rather to be united against the infidel. No one, it appears, raised the charge of hypocrisy in regard to his own actions for the recovery of the papal states, the *Patrimonium beati Petri*, close to Rome.[36] Indeed, Innocent might not even have been perturbed by such a charge. His own approach to problems tended to be pragmatic, acting only after a careful examination of all aspects and justifying any intervention with an elaborate structure of reasons. For him, peace within the vineyard was one of the essential missions of the pope. To the pope belonged the right to make peace between Christian princes: 'ad papam pertinet pacem facere inter principes christianos.'[37] Peace was necessary if the Roman Church, 'caput et magistra et fundamentum', the head, mother, and foundation-stone of Christendom, was to exert its full influence. Papal intervention thus sprang from a threefold obligation: humanitarian, evangelical, and practical.[38]

Innocent brings this message home to his recalcitrant sons in a series of

[32] M. Maccarrone, 'La papauté et Philippe Auguste: La décrétale "Novit ille"', in R. H. Bautier, ed., *La France de Philippe Auguste: Le Temps des Mutations = Colloques internationaux du Centre Nationale de la recherche scientifique*, 602 (Paris, 1982), pp. 385–409 [hereafter Maccarrone, 'Novit ille'] and 'Innocenzo III et la feudalità: *non ratione feudi, sed occasione peccati*', *Collection de l'École Française de Rome*, 44 (Rome, 1980), pp. 457–514.

[33] A. Cartellieri, *Philipp II, August. König von Frankreich* (Leipzig, 1899), pp. 296–7; Maccarrone, 'Novit ille', p. 387.

[34] S. Painter, 'The Third Crusade: Richard the Lionhearted and Philip Augustus', in K. M. Setton, ed., *A History of the Crusades*, 2 (Philadelphia, 1962), pp. 45–85.

[35] C. R. Cheney, *Innocent III and England = Päpste und Papsttum*, 9 (Stuttgart, 1976), p. 276 [hereafter Cheney, *Innocent III*].

[36] M. Maccarrone, *Studi su Innocenzo III* (Padua, 1972), pp. 9–22.

[37] Maccarrone, 'Novit ille', pp. 389–91.

[38] Cf. Innocent's decree *Ad liberandum*, given at the Fourth Lateran Council in *Conciliorum oecumenicorum decreta*, ed. J. Alberigo *et al.* (Bologna, 1973), p. 270.

parallel letters. In August 1198 to Philip and Richard,[39] and in May 1203, to Philip and John,[40] he does not mince matters. First, in a direct challenge to their humanity, he points out that dreadful evils result from wars between princes. Not only for the Church but also for the Christian people: destruction of churches, impoverishment of the rich, oppression of the poor, massacres, perdition of souls, and the dishonouring of monks and nuns all follow. All these evils have been visited on their respective kingdoms—in retribution for their sins—but the damage inflicted on the Holy Land is greater still. In 1203, following the crusaders' attack on Zara in October to November 1202, Innocent's letters contrast the situation of the infidel, who, when Philip and John were at peace and friendly, expected daily to be driven out of Palestine. Now, as a result of their quarrels, the Saracens are audaciously attacking Christians in ever greater strength. In this dire emergency for Christendom, Innocent is unable to keep silent 'lest we should seem responsible, in a manner of speaking, for so many deaths, condemning utterly that which calls for condemnation'.[41]

In this way, Innocent wished to shift the political quarrel between Philip and John, centred as it was on feudal issues, on to a religious plane.[42] Indeed, in a letter of 7 May 1205 to the Archbishop of Rouen, he confessed that he was ignorant both as to law and to custom, of the cause of the affair which had led to the deprivation of John in Philip's court.[43] His peace initiative between the two rulers and his desire to arbitrate stemmed from his religious inspiration, reinforced by theological justifications and a wide variety of scriptural texts. In the preamble to his letters, he reminds them that peace is the supreme commandment of Christ to his Apostles, bequeathing peace *as though to his legal heirs*.[44] Peace must therefore not only be 'sought after and pursued', but established by the Pope as vicar of Christ, whose particular and personal task it is 'to preach the gospel of peace, especially to the sons of peace'. On several occasions, therefore, he resorted to practical action, endeavouring in 1198, 1199, 1203–4, 1206, and 1214 to bring his sons to a definite peace or at least a long truce.[45] Roscher has shown us that a subtle change occurred

39 *Register* I, pp. 515–17; *PL* 214, cols 319–20; Potthast, 363.

40 *PL* 215, cols 64–6; *SLI*, pp. 56–9.

41 Ezek. 3, 18–20; *Register* I, 355, pp. 530–2; *PL* 214, col. 65; *SLI*, p. 59: 'Ne igitur sanguis tot populorum de nostris manibus requirantur, ne re tot mortuum . . . videamur.'

42 Maccarrone, 'Novit ille', pp. 392–4.

43 *PL* 215, col. 564: 'Quia vero, nec de jure, nec de consuetudine nobis constat, utpote qui causam modum et ordinem, aliasque circumstantias ignoramus.'

44 *PL* 215, col. 65, 'quasi haereditario jure'; Maccarrone, 'Novit ille', p. 393.

45 Gaudemet, 'Le role de la papauté', pp. 91–3.

between the end and the means in the relationship between peace or truce and the undertaking to crusade.[46] For Innocent, the crusade was now both occasion and pretext for the implementation of his papal peace plan.

These initiatives for a firm peace or suitable truce were entrusted to Cistercians,[47] who with their international links reveal that shuttle diplomacy was by no means a modern invention. Gerald of Casamari,[48] we are told, ran backwards and forwards for a whole year, 'de Francia ad Angliam et de Anglia ad Franciam discurrendo',[49] between 1203 and 1204, while Stephen of Fossanova, later Papal Chamberlain and Cardinal Bishop of 'SS XII Apostoli' was specially commended to John by Innocent.[50] Casamari and Fossanova were important houses south of Rome, and Innocent enjoyed close relations with both.[51] These emissaries served him well, working in tandem in these delicate negotiations, and, in his turn, Innocent contributed generously to their rebuilding campaigns.[52] The Cistercians' international reputation combined with their known interest in crusades may well, in this Italian context, have made them appear neutral and thus acceptable to both kings. That Philip, at least, seems to have required such assurances is indicated by the appointment of Guy II, Abbot of Trois Fontaines, near Chalons-sur-Marne, and Elias, Abbot of Les Dunes, near Bruges, to assist Gerald in his mission to France.[53]

Arguments in favour of peace and against war were very much the meat of academic debate at this time, in precisely those Parisian circles in which Innocent III had been trained. Robert de Courçon, an Englishman and Innocent's contemporary at the University of Paris, discussed at length both the moral aspects and the practical repercussions of the 'just war' in his *Summa*.[54] One particular section of this, on difficult cases,

[46] H. Roscher, *Päpst Innocenz III und die Kreuzzuge = Forschungen zur Kirchen und Dogmengeschichte*, 21 (Göttingen, 1969).

[47] Maccarrone, 'Novit ille', p. 38, n. 1.

[48] Abbot of Casamari (1182–1209), nephew of Gerald, sixth abbot of Clairvaux.

[49] *Gesta Innocentii PP.III*, *PL* 214, cols cxxix, clxix–clxxi [hereafter *Gesta*].

[50] *PL* 215, cols 182–4, esp. 184; W. Maleczek, *Papst und Kardinalskolleg von 1191 bis 1216: die Kardinale unter Coelestin III und Innocenz III* (Vienna, 1984), pp. 179–83. V. J. Koudelka, 'Notes pour servir à l'histoire de Saint Dominique: Le Cardinal Etienne de Fossanova, ami de saint Dominique', *AFP*, 35 (1965), pp. 5–15.

[51] B. M. Bolton, 'For the See of Simon Peter: the Cistercians at Innocent III's nearest frontier', in J. Loades, ed., *Monastic Studies: the Continuity of Tradition* (Bangor, 1990), pp. 146–57.

[52] To Fossanova he gave 100 pounds to complete the new church and was present at its consecration on 19 June 1208, *Gesta*, cols cxlix, ccxxvii; *PL* 215, cols 1435–7. To Casamari he gave 200 ounces of gold *pro fabrica* and 100 pounds in annual rent, ibid., col. ccviii.

[53] *SLI*, p. 59, n. 28.

[54] J. W. Baldwin, *Masters, Princes and Merchants: The Social Views of Peter the Chanter and his Circle*, 2 vols (Princeton, 1970), 1, pp. 206–15, and 2, pp. 145–53.

contains an apparently hypothetical case, setting out a series of mitigating circumstances in a supposed 'war between the kings'. The example used by Courçon involved a sentence of excommunication issued by the pope, through his intermediary, a legate.[55] In these circumstances, what then were the practical and moral issues at stake for bishops when their obligations to king and pope came into conflict? It is clear that, far from being a hypothetical case, Courçon was dealing with a real-life incident. The 'war between the kings' is that between Philip and John, and the legate in question, the Cistercian, Gerald of Casamari.

When he was dispatched by Innocent III to halt what appeared to be overt aggression by Philip against John,[56] it seems that the Pope had badly misjudged the strength of feudal ties within the French Kingdom. Philip's skill had so bound his vassals to him that their oath of fealty to their liege lord overcame any religious arguments advanced by the Pope. On 22 August 1203, in an assembly of the realm at Mantes and in the presence of the papal legate,[57] Philip declared bluntly that he was not obliged to answer to the Pope in a dispute over feudal rights involving a vassal. This declaration echoed his youthful and defiant attitude of 1189 when, before Clement III's legate, he claimed that the Roman Church had no power to consider any sentence given within the realm of France.

Innocent's reply was sent on 31 October 1203.[58] After an evangelical exhortation on the beauty of the feet of those who spread the Gospel of Peace, he reminded Philip of the way in which, during the 1199 negotiations with Peter of Capua, he had joyfully received, *jocunde*, the legate's instructions to make peace with Richard. In so doing, he expressed the wish never to appear contrary to the apostolic will *in this or in anything else*. Warning of the grave damage facing the Church and the faithful, Innocent went on to claim his right and duty to intervene with fatherly affection and pronounce on the broken peace and violation of oaths which John had brought to his attention. He proposed that an enquiry into the matter should be summarily undertaken by the Archbishop of Bourges, not on the feudal issue, for judgement there belonged to Philip, but on the grounds that a sin had been committed, *ratione peccati*. There could be no doubt that the canonical definition of sin and the recognition of the truth belonged to the Pope, and consequently the power of censure.

[55] Ibid., 2, p. 152, n. 56.
[56] Maccarrone, 'Novit ille', p. 394.
[57] Maccarrone, 'Innocenzo III e la feudalità', pp. 473–4.
[58] *PL* 215, cols 176–80; Cheney, *Innocent III*, p. 289.

Letters sent out on the same day to Gerald of Casamari, the bishops of the dioceses of Sens, Bourges, and Rheims, and John, carried a similar message that the Pope would impose severe penalties if a peace or truce were not agreed.[59]

In April or May 1204, Innocent reinforced his case with a letter, *Novit ille*,[60] addressed to the French bishops. He hoped to win their episcopal support for his intervention in the Anglo-French war. This letter was intended to be widely circulated to the magnates of France and was regarded as another route to Philip himself. His usual evangelical exhortation to peace was missing, and Innocent immediately raised his practical preoccupation with the avoidance of open conflict between the two rulers. He quickly reaffirms that he intends no diminution of royal jurisdiction, for when even the Pope cannot fully discharge his own jurisdiction, 'Why then', he asks, 'should we wish to usurp another's?'

He explains, denouncing French aggression, that John had brought his complaint to the Church, and that the French King seems not to have presented any argument to the contrary.[61] Innocent took care to explain that he could not refuse a request addressed in this manner, based on divine decree and canonically sanctioned. The obligation on bishops, not only to spread the word, but also to correct, rebuke, and coerce as part of their office also fell upon the Pope as bishop of Rome.[62] He repeats that it is not his intention to act as judge in any controversy belonging to the feudal sphere. That must be judged according to feudal law—but he goes on to identify an exception, *nisi forte*, where the application of the common law verges on the area of sin.[63] Innocent would like to submit the matter to an enquiry, to see if the *exceptio* is valid or not. He advances two arguments drawn from Gratian's *Decretum*, designed to appeal particularly to Philip, by indicating great historical figures who had submitted themselves to the judgement of bishops: the Emperors Valentinian and Charlemagne, from whose line, says Innocent, King Philip himself is descended.[64]

In reality, Innocent has to face the issue of whether he can validly intervene against the King of France—no ordinary Christian, but a great public figure to whom God has given *potestas regalis*, the power to rule.

[59] *PL* 215, cols 180–4.
[60] Ibid., cols 325–9; Potthast, 2181; *SLI*, pp. 63–8.
[61] Maccarrone, 'Novit ille', pp. 395–403.
[62] Ibid., pp. 397–8.
[63] *PL* 215, col. 326; *SLI*, p. 64; Maccarrone, 'Novit ille', p. 398.
[64] *SLI*, pp. 64–5; Cheney, *Innocent III*, p. 290.

Should kings be treated any differently from other men? His answer is to reaffirm the pope's pastoral duty to correct all sinners equally, bringing them from error to truth and from vice to virtue?[65] Indeed, the pope is specially empowered to act when the sin endangers peace, even against kings. Philip himself had requested papal intervention against Richard, and it had turned out to be in the French King's favour. Now there is more confusion and *discordia*. Not only has a peace treaty been broken, but a sworn oath has not been kept for its full duration. Both this peace and this oath belong without any doubt to the Church's jurisdiction. The Pope has a duty to intervene 'lest he should seem apathetic and ignorant of the grave damage caused to faithful Christians'. He gives no sanction against Philip, but enjoins the French bishops to share in his responsibility to see their King brought to peace or truce.[66] As it was, events overtook him. The war came to an end, and on 1 June 1204 representatives of the Duchy of Normandy submitted to Philip at Rouen[67]—victorious Philip, defeated John!

But it could not be left there. At the end of June, Gerald of Casamari called together all the French bishops at Meaux.[68] This was the academic Robert de Courçon's hypothetical test case in practice. What would the bishops do in meeting their dual obligations to King and Pope? Even if they wished to bring the King round to the point at which he would allow a full discussion on the issues between the two rulers, Philip's success made him unwilling to place in question his conquest of Normandy. The other path would be for them to appeal to Rome for a ruling. Innocent would have the precedent of Philip's earlier successful appeal when, in the consistory of 1191, the ecclesiastical tribunal to which both kings were subject as crusaders[69] had given judgement against Richard. As a young cardinal, Innocent himself had probably been present. The bishops' appeal to the Pope, when it came, was made from Meaux, with the support of the legate. Gerald of Casamari was able to reveal his considerable ability in putting forward an appeal as a way out of their dilemma of being accused of disloyalty to either their king or their pope. The immediate outcome of the letter, *Novit ille*, was thus to strengthen relations between the Pope and the French bishops.

[65] *SLI*, p. 66; Maccarrone, 'Novit ille', p. 400.

[66] *SLI*, p. 68.

[67] *Layette du Trésor des Chartes*, ed. A. Teulet, H. F. Delaborde, and E. Berger, 5 vols (Paris, 1863–1909), I, p. 250; Baldwin, *Philip Augustus*, pp. 191–6.

[68] *Gesta*, col. clxx; Maccarrone, 'Novit ille', p. 403.

[69] Cartellieri, *Philipp August*, 2, pp. 251–2.

Sometime after August 1204, the archbishops of Sens and Bourges, together with the bishops of Paris, Meaux, Chalons, and Nevers, came to Innocent in Rome to wait for the delay prescribed by canon law to elapse before the case between Philip and John could be heard.[70] Although they waited daily for this, John had designated no one to speak for him. As the *Gesta* states, John let his own case fall 'and out of this negligence, much harm came to him for within a short time he had lost all Normandy and Anjou and most of Aquitaine.'[71] Still John failed to turn up, and when the bishops eventually argued their case in consistory, in the fullness of their office,[72] they indicated that they were in no way attempting to avoid papal jurisdiction. They safeguarded their position with Philip by concluding that in this matter, their King did have a just cause: 'in hac parte suum regem justam causam habere.'[73]

By Christmas 1204, the former Angevin dominions lay in ruins. John was in England, and Innocent might reasonably have hoped that his recalcitrant son might now settle down to govern his remaining territory and reassemble his forces for a future and more successful crusade than the recent and disastrous Fourth.[74] Unfortunately, but not surprisingly, inconsistent John now became involved in the dispute over who should succeed Hubert Walter as Archbishop of Canterbury after his death on 13 July 1205.[75] The monks of Canterbury backed one candidate, John another; and when the matter at length came before the Curia, Innocent proposed a third and compromise candidate, Stephen Langton, Cardinal Priest of S. Crisogono.[76] Innocent, having requested and exhorted, only to be met with threats and expostulations, brushed aside 'certain paltry reasons' which had been advanced by John, implying that the King was influenced by trouble-makers seeking to fish in troubled waters.[77] On 17 June 1207, at Viterbo, Innocent consecrated Langton and gave him the pallium.[78] John's rash reaction in expelling the Canterbury monks was

[70] *Gesta*, cols clxix–clxxii; *PL* 215, col. 425; Cheney, *Innocent III*, pp. 290–1.

[71] *Gesta*, clxxi, 'praenominatus rex Anglie pro se neminem destinavit, negligens prosequi causam suam'.

[72] Ibid., col. clxxi, 'tanquam pontifices sunt professi'.

[73] Maccarrone, 'Novit ille', p. 406.

[74] Cheney, *Innocent III*, p. 8, for the view that Innocent failed to understand the situation in England.

[75] Ibid., pp. 147–54.

[76] *PL* 215, col. 1327; *SLI*, pp. 86–90; D. Knowles, 'The Canterbury Election of 1205–6', *EHR*, 53 (1938), pp. 211–20; Cheney, *Innocent III*, pp. 282–91.

[77] 26 May 1207, *PL* 215, col. 1327; *SLI*, pp. 86–90; Potthast, 3111.

[78] *Willelmi Chronica Andrensis*, *MGH*, *SS*, 24, p. 737, 'cuius etiam consecrationi post dies aliquot interfuimus'; Cheney, *Innocent III*, pp. 298–302.

totally in character. The Interdict followed, to take effect from 24 March 1208.[79]

In trying to bring John to his senses, Innocent presents himself as the doctor using the medicine of the Holy See to heal his patient.[80] Oil is to follow after wine, and John must come to realize that this bitter medicine is being administered with genuine love and affection, since those out to corrupt are 'fattening his head with the oil of the sinner and encouraging his disobedience'.[81] Innocent patiently continues to treat the obstinate John, whom he considers to be almost bewitched and totally unresponsive to words suggested to him for his own salvation. On 13 July 1209, John at last responded to Innocent's cajoling and agreed that he would make satisfaction to the Church,[82] but by October, still nothing had happened. What Adam of Eynsham called his 'wanton inertia' had taken over.[83] Innocent lost patience, and the King's excommunication was published on 8 November 1209.[84] He did not, however, release John's subjects from their oath of fealty nor did he depose him. This was to be the next step.[85]

In Rome in February 1213, Langton and the other exiles were consulted, and letters prepared to put John's deposition into effect.[86] Before they had to be used, John finally yielded, issuing Letters Patent on 13 May, agreeing to peace terms, and a Charter on 15 May, handing over the kingdoms of England and Ireland as fiefs to the Pope and promising an annual tribute of 1,000 marks sterling—700 for England and 300 for Ireland.[87] The letters in Langton's possession are most interesting in themselves.[88] One, addressed to all archbishops and bishops in the kingdoms of France, England, Scotland, and Ireland, as well as to the bishops of Liège and Utrecht, beginning 'Until now we have patiently waited: *Expectantes hactenus expectavimus*', was clearly to be used against John if he had rejected Innocent's final terms.[89] In fact, Langton had taken them away

[79] Cheney, *Innocent III*, pp. 303–7; *SLI*, pp. 107–9; *PL* 215, cols 1422–3; Potthast, 3443.

[80] In a variety of letters, *PL* 215, cols 1422, 1526, 1535; *SLI*, pp. 107, 110–14, 117–20; Potthast, 3443, 3622.

[81] Ps. 140.5 (Vulgate, 141).

[82] Cheney, *Innocent III*, p. 318.

[83] *Magna Vita Sancti Hugonis*, ed. D. L. Douie and D. H. Farmer, 2 vols (Oxford, 1985), p. 149. On the value of Adam as a source, ibid., pp. viii–xxii.

[84] *Chronicon S. Bertini*, ed. E. Martène and U. Durand, *Thesaurus Novus anecdotorum*, 5 vols (Paris, 1717), 3, p. 689: Cheney, *Innocent III*, p. 320.

[85] *SLI*, pp. 128–9; Cheney, *Innocent III*, pp. 322–5.

[86] *PL* 216, col. 772; Potthast, 4392, 4395; *SLI*, pp. 130–6.

[87] *PL* 216, cols. 878–80; Cheney, *Innocent III*, pp. 332–7.

[88] *SLI*, pp. 149–51; Cheney, *Innocent III*, pp. 337–41.

[89] *PL* 216, col. 781; *SLI*, pp. 141–2; Cheney, *Innocent III*, p. 340.

with him before John's letters of submission had arrived. These bulls, which Langton had 'in waiting' or as Professor Cheney says, 'up his sleeve',[90] were kept there until the arrival of the legate, Nicholas de Romanis, Cardinal Bishop of Tusculum,[91] who had been instructed by Innocent to have these letters 'immediately torn to shreds and burned to ashes' so that 'no mischief can be started against him (John) because of them'.[92] Perhaps even Langton was not considered to be above suspicion if he thought that he could turn these 'bulls in waiting' to his own advantage. Obviously Nicholas de Romanis, to whom Innocent refers as an 'angel of salvation',[93] did his job well, for no copy of this unused letter has survived—only the instruction as to what was to be done with it. Nevertheless, it had other important ramifications, some of which must have reached Philip's ears. When the submission of John became known he must have been bitterly disappointed to lose the excuse which John's intransigence towards Innocent and the proposed papal deposition had given him for a crusade against England.[94] An assembly of the French barons at Soissons on 8 April 1213 was called to deal with John, who had been forging threatening alliances with his nephew Otto and various princes in the Low Countries. There Philip commissioned his son, Prince Louis, to lead an expedition against England, in spite of Louis's recent vow to crusade against heretics in Languedoc. John's submission to the Pope, only one month later, which some have judged to have been 'a brilliant diplomatic stroke',[95] placed Philip in a quandary. Poor, noble Philip. Suddenly, what had seemed a perfectly justifiable extra crusade against an excommunicate sinner,[96] now had the overtones of a callous attack on a papal vassal. The magic of submission, brought about by apostolic medicine, was already beginning to work, for John was now labouring in the vineyard, whilst Philip's pretence of labouring looked as if it might be blown away. To return to the parable, the son who said he would not, did,

[90] *PL* 216, col. 926; *SLI*, p. 164.

[91] 5 May 1205–14 September 1219, C. Eubel, *Hierarchia catholica medii aevi*, I (Regensburg, 1913), p. 5.

[92] *SLI*, p. 164.

[93] *PL* 216, cols 881–4; *SLI*, p. 150.

[94] C. R. Cheney, 'The alleged deposition of King John', in *Studies in Medieval History presented to Frederick Maurice Powicke* (Oxford, 1948), pp. 100–16. See also *Œuvres de Rigord et de Guillaume le Breton*, ed. H. F. Delaborde, I, p. 109 [hereafter *Rigord*]; Cheney, *Innocent III*, pp. 338–41.

[95] Baldwin, *Philip Augustus*, p. 209.

[96] For example, the use of the phrase, 'iter Anglicanum', *Matthaei Paris Monachi Albanensis Angli, Historia Major*, ed. W. Wat (London, 1684), p. 236 [hereafter *Historia Major*].

whilst the son who said he would, now appeared not to be doing so. Truly is the repentant sinner rewarded.[97]

It is perhaps interesting here to examine briefly what we know of the nature of John's repentance, which has scarcely, if ever, been regarded in a serious light. While Innocent believed that it was never too late to repent, he applied that belief to his dealings with both Philip and John. In the case of John, he never gave up trying, showing more faith than did Professor Painter, who could find no evidence of any act of piety whatsoever on John's part.[98] But the apparently conflicting attitudes to religion displayed by the Angevins, Henry II and all his sons, aroused as much contemporary comment as they have recent debate. No Angevin was ever attentive at Mass, most refused the Eucharist once they reached the age of discretion, and all swore crudely on various parts of God's body.[99] Their morals were a scandal, and their insane rages legendary. Yet Dr Hallam has conclusively demonstrated that Henry II's and Richard's patronage was far wider in scope than has been hitherto realized.[100] Underlying both Henry and his sons is a clear sense that these kings had more than a sneaking respect for the religious life. To this family pattern, John seems to have been no exception. Adam of Eynsham gives an account of John's apparent gaucheness and impiety in the first year of his reign, 1199–1200, which made even Hugh of Lincoln despair.[101] On 27 March 1202, Innocent wrote a firm letter to the King on the subject of sin, rejoicing that in response to what he has said, the King has confessed those sins committed since manhood.[102] Rejoicing more over this one royal sinner than over the ninety-nine just, Innocent applauds the King's undertaking to send a hundred knights to the Holy Land and to build a Cistercian monastery. 'If you busy yourself with works of piety, your kingdom will prosper and your royal honour will be enlarged.' Although there is no record of this contingent of knights going to the Holy Land—for few from England participated in the Fourth Crusade—John did found Beaulieu between 1200 and 1202, granted a hundred marks towards its construction in 1204, and had two Cistercian abbots, John of Ford and Henry of Bindon, as successive confessors.[103]

[97] Matt. 21. 28–31.

[98] Painter, *King John*, p. 153.

[99] *Magna Vita S. Hugonis*, 2, pp. 143–4; Warren, *King John*, pp. 15–17.

[100] E. M. Hallam, 'Henry II as a founder of monasteries', *JEH*, 28 (1977), pp. 113–32 and 'Henry II, Richard I and the Order of Grandmont', *JMedH*, 1 (1975), pp. 165–86.

[101] *Magna Vita S. Hugonis*, 2, pp. 143–4.

[102] *PL* 214, cols 972–3; Potthast, 1650; *SLI*, pp. 37–9.

[103] Ibid., p. 38, n. 12.

Dr Mason has shown that John had a special reverence for St Wulfstan,[104] asking, and indeed succeeding, in being buried before his shrine at Worcester, together with St Oswald, to protect him from the Devil, while his interest in pilgrimage manifested itself in visits to Canterbury, St Albans, and Bury St Edmunds. Why do we not know more about this? Because John was not a great benefactor to larger monasteries which kept chronicles. Unlike Philip, he was inclined to pretend to despise favourable comment, and he had no chronicler to speak well of him. John's gifts as listed in the Pipe Roll for 1204 have been seen by Lady Stenton as 'uncalculating generosity' to those obscure houses, many of them nunneries, which received small sums of money, vestments, and altar cloths. Nor was John's particular attempt at piety linked entirely with the giving of gifts. During the Interdict he borrowed some books from Reading Abbey,[105] taking away with him six volumes of the Bible—including some of the Old Testament[106]—Hugh of St Victor on the Sacraments, St Augustine's *City of God*, the *Sentences* of Peter Lombard, and the *Commentaries* of Origen, and, in return, lending his own copy of Pliny.[107] This was reading of an advanced and sophisticated nature, and unless John used these books to throw at someone in a 'blind Angevin rage', perhaps he actually read and contemplated on them with the object of achieving repentance. Peter Lombard's *Sentences* may even have been recommended by Innocent himself. After all, these *Sentences*, with their definition of the essence of the Trinity, were approved for their particular orthodoxy in canon 2 of the Fourth Lateran Council.[108] If this is mere supposition or coincidence, a closer link can be provided between John's benefactions and Innocent's building projects in the City of Rome.[109] On 25 March 1204 John assigned to Innocent's own hospital foundation of S. Spirito, the former Anglo-Saxon pilgrim hospice by the Tiber, an expectative for the parish church of Writtle, near Chelmsford, 'out of

[104] E. E. Mason, 'St Wulfstan's Staff: a legend and its uses', *Medium Aevum*, 53 (1984), pp. 157–79.

[105] D. M. Stenton, *The Great Roll of the Pipe for the Sixth Year of the Reign of King John, Michaelmas 1204*, *Pipe Roll Society*, ns 18 (London, 1940), p. xxxvii.

[106] Innocent himself used the Old Testament for textual support in his claim to exercise *casualiter* secular jurisdiction: K. Pennington, 'Pope Innocent III's views on Church and State: a Gloss on *Per Venerabilem*', in K. Pennington and R. Somerville, eds, *Essays in Honor of Stephan Kuttner* (Pennsylvania, 1977), pp. 49–67.

[107] *Rotuli Litterarum Clausarum*, ed. T. Duffus Hardy, I (London, 1833), p. 108; Warren, *King John*, p. 157; Mason, 'St Wulfstan's Staff', p. 159.

[108] S. Kuttner and A. Garcia y Garcia, 'A new eyewitness account of the Fourth Lateran Council', *Traditio*, 20 (1964), pp. 115–78, esp. pp. 154–5.

[109] Cheney, *Innocent III*, pp. 237–8.

respect for the Pope', undertaking to pay 100 marks annually until the church should fall vacant.[110] After the Interdict, Nicholas of Tusculum secured John's promise for the continuation of this sum, and he kept it.[111] Payments continued throughout the thirteenth century, recorded in 1218, 1246, and 1291. John really did deserve the memorial he was given in the necrology of Innocent's hospital.[112] In 1213, the Cardinal Bishop of Tusculum also persuaded John to support Innocent's other great foundation, the rebuilding of the Church of S. Sisto and the establishment there of a convent for all the nuns of Rome.[113] John was to pay 150 marks annually towards this significant building project, with its English connection through the Order of Gilbertine Canons, briefly destined to manage it.[114] Royal interest in this project seems to have continued even beyond John's reign. Both these projects, the hospital and the convent, were schemes closest to Innocent's heart. In supporting them, John fulfilled Innocent's injunction to busy himself with works of piety in a way which could only have greatly pleased the Pope. Pious John indeed.

And what of Philip? As Professor Southern has reminded us, the French kings enjoyed the help of a constantly favourable public opinion, inspiring almost continuous affection.[115] Not only had Alexander III bestowed the title of *christianissimus* on Philip's father, Louis VII, as a mark of honour, linking him with the Carolingians, but by the time that it was inherited by Philip, it had become, in Southern's words 'part of the spiritual armour of the French king'. In striking contrast, therefore, to their counterparts in England, especially the Benedictines of St Albans who did so much to destroy the reputation of John,[116] the biographers of Philip positively glowed when they wrote of his exploits. Rigord of St Denis and William le Breton, Philip's chaplain and official historiographer, have much to answer for.[117] Philip, God-given to his parents after twenty-eight years and too many sisters, was also called *Augustus*, not only because he was born in that month, but because he had augmented

[110] *Rotuli Chartarum*, 1 (1199–1216), ed. T. Duffus Hardy (London, 1837), p. 123.

[111] A. Mercati, 'La prima relazione del Cardinale Nicolo di Romanis sulla sua legazione in Inghilterra (1213)', in *Essays in History presented to Reginald Lane Poole* (Oxford, 1927), pp. 274–89, esp. pp. 287–8.

[112] *Liber Annualium di Santo Spirito in Sassia*, ed. P. Egidi (Rome, 1908), p. 105.

[113] B. M. Bolton, 'Daughters of Rome: All one in Christ Jesus', *SCH*, 27 (1990), pp. 101–15.

[114] Ibid., p. 112.

[115] Southern, 'England's first entry into Europe', p. 149.

[116] Warren, *King John*, pp. 17–31.

[117] *Rigord*, I, pp. 1–167; Baldwin, 'The case of Philip Augustus', pp. 195–207.

the realm.[118] The humiliation of his rapid return from the Third Crusade after just two months is passed over, as is his scandalous attempt to divorce the eighteen-year-old Danish bride, Ingeborg, on 15 August 1193, the day after their marriage.[119] One of the totally absorbing problems of medieval history, we can never know why—although Philip's advisers later said the girl bewitched him—she was imprisoned quite literally in a monastery and isolated from her countrymen. Alone, and unable to speak French, she appealed to Rome in basic Latin, according to the papal biographer, weeping and crying out, 'Mala Francia, Mala Francia' and 'Rome, Roma'.[120] Innocent mentioned the case in his very first letter to Philip in 1198,[121] eventually placing him under interdict from January to September 1200.[122] Philip did not take Ingeborg back until 1213, and even then did not grant restoration (if that word applies) of her conjugal rights.[123] Innocent's intervention in negotiations involving Ingeborg brought him to a further realization about the French King. Philip could not read Latin at all well, and Innocent complained on at least two occasions that his letters on this sensitive and intricate matter were being misinterpreted *minus fideliter exponantur*.[124] Unlike the Angevins, Philip had a deep aversion to swearing, and did not give money to *jongleurs* or troubadours, which probably helps to explain why they, in their turn, did not care over much for him.[125] Persistently reluctant to found new churches or to give alms in his lifetime, in death he managed rather better, giving a few pious bequests, but being rather surprisingly associated instead with miraculous signs.[126] As Baldwin has shown, the campaign to sanctify Philip ran rapidly into trouble, and within twenty years of his death he was depicted as being rescued by St Denis himself from demons bent on dragging him down to hell, before being guided by the saint through purgatory to salvation.[127]

Throughout his pontificate, Innocent was never very sure as to Philip's real motives. Nor was he willing, if he had any doubts, to apply the same

118 *Rigord*, p. 6.
119 R. Davidsohn, *Philipp II, August von Frankreich und Ingeborg* (Stuttgart, 1888); Baldwin, *Philip Augustus*, pp. 82–7 and 'The case of Philip Augustus', pp. 202–3.
120 *Gesta*, cols xciii–ciii, esp. xcv.
121 *Register* I, pp. 5–6, 9–12; *PL* 214, cols 2–3; Potthast, 2, 13.
122 *PL* 214, cols 881–3, 896–8; Baldwin, *Philip Augustus*, pp. 178–9.
123 Ibid., p. 379; Cheney, *Innocent III*, p. 343.
124 *PL* 215, cols 1135–6; 216, cols 36–7; Potthast, 3072, 3715.
125 Baldwin, *Philip Augustus*, p. 359.
126 Ibid., pp. 389–93.
127 Ibid., p. 392.

severe strictures he had applied to John. Above all, Innocent's concern remained the maintenance of peace. The legate to France, the Englishman, Robert de Courçon, had been active since August 1213 in trying to establish peace between the kings, with the objective of preparing for the Fifth Crusade, a proposal he renewed in June 1214.[128] After the momentous defeat of John's allies at Bouvines, on 27 July 1214, John was glad to use Courçon's good offices in the worsening situation in Poitou and Anjou in July and August 1214. On 31 August he agreed to a fortnight's truce with Philip, which allowed for a full truce to be made on 18 September and which was supposed to last until Easter 1220.[129]

On 18 November 1214 Innocent wrote to John to thank him for concluding the truce, while exhorting him to prepare carefully and effectively for the Crusade.[130] His persistence at last had been rewarded, and this truce seemed to offer Innocent the prospect of royal support for his crusade. In this he was yet again to be disappointed. The barons in England, far from supporting John more loyally after his submission to Rome, resisted military service in Poitou, whilst the bishops distrusted the King wholeheartedly. Nor was Langton entirely above suspicion in his dealings with the opposition to John.[131] Arrangements to lift the Interdict were slow and protracted, and the clergy's rights only protected by a series of piecemeal bargains. On 21 November 1214, however, John granted a charter permitting free elections in perpetuity to all the cathedral and monastic churches of England, a charter probably drafted by Nicholas of Tusculum.[132] It was a less striking repudiation of royal rights than a similar agreement made by Peter II of Aragon on 30 October 1207.[133] Yet this charter of free election fulfilled one of Innocent's dearest ambitions, and when the Pope confirmed it, on 30 March 1215, he praised John for making this concession willingly.[134]

Thus, not only had John earned Innocent's eventual approval by his acceptance of the truce with France and by his recognition of ecclesiastical liberty, but also, on Ash Wednesday, 4 March 1215, he made a personal response to Innocent's appeal and took the Cross.[135] The relationship

[128] M. and C. Dickson, 'La vie de Robert de Courçon', *Archives d'histoire doctrinale et littéraire du moyen âge*, 9 (1934), pp. 53–142; Baldwin, *Masters, Princes and Merchants*, 1, pp. 19–25.

[129] Cheney, *Innocent III*, pp. 357–9.

[130] *SLI*, p. 192; Potthast, 4325.

[131] *PL*, 217, col. 213; *SLI*, p. 192.

[132] Cheney, *Innocent III*, p. 363.

[133] *Gesta*, clix–clxi.

[134] *SLI*, pp. 198–201; Potthast, 4963.

[135] *SLI*, pp. 203–4.

between Pope and repentant sinner was thus at its highest point. Indeed, Innocent was reminded of this in one or two out of more than 2,000 Latin hexameter lines, in the *Poetria Nova* of Geoffrey of Vinsauf, dedicated in fulsome terms to the Pope and dated to approximately this time.[136] In his epilogue, Geoffrey reminds Innocent that John has proved himself a soldier, both of 'the Cross and of Christ and the sword of the whole Church'. Such devotion, he goes on to say, deserves love not hate, praise not blame, reward not punishment. 'Therefore you', he addresses Innocent, 'who overcame others, allow yourself to be overcome and desire to turn and be reconciled with the King.' Innocent could, with much satisfaction, say that he had indeed done as the poet wished.[137]

How unfortunate it was, therefore, that Innocent now became seriously entangled in his vassal's domestic difficulties. On 24 August 1215 Innocent announced his open condemnation of Magna Carta and annulled it.[138] Much has been written on Innocent's high theories on the source of his authority for such actions, and, as Cheney has said, 'the intensity of this scrutiny might perhaps have surprised and annoyed the pope.'[139] Innocent certainly acted pragmatically through the apostolic authority vested in him. Already, in *Novit ille*, he had claimed to decide on practical grounds when circumstances required his direct intervention in temporal affairs. As vicar of Christ, he tells the rebels that he is bound to provide both spiritually and temporally for the King and the kingdom.[140] The barons have forced the King to settle through force and fear; the terms are not only demeaning and shameful, but illegal and unjust too. But the matter is strikingly simple to Innocent. What he cannot possibly ignore is not only the threat to legal kingship, but also the serious danger to the whole crusade. On 7 July, in a strongly-worded letter against Langton, Innocent had already accused the bishops of a lack of respect for the crusade.[141] They are worse, he says, than Saracens, for they are trying to depose a king who, it was particularly hoped, would succour the Holy Land.[142] Although this is a feudal crisis, involving a breach of an oath of fealty, Innocent regards as even more serious the fact that John, who is

[136] *Geoffrey de Vinsauf, Poetria Nova*, tr. M. F. Nims (Toronto, 1967); M. C. Woods, *An Early Commentary on the 'Poetria Nova' of Geoffrey of Vinsauf* = *Garland Medieval Texts*, 12 (New York, 1985).

[137] Geoffrey de Vinsauf, *Poetria Nova*, lines 2087–95.

[138] *SLI*, pp. 212–16.

[139] Cheney, *Innocent III*, pp. 382–0.

[140] *SLI*, pp. 215–16.

[141] Ibid., pp. 207–9.

[142] Ibid., p. 208.

now a crusader, has the right to be protected in accordance with the form of privilege granted to crusaders.

From April 1213 until the end of his pontificate Innocent had two major concerns on hand—not only to prepare for the Fifth Crusade, planned for 1217,[143] but also the Fourth Lateran Council, held between 11 and 30 November 1215.[144] He aimed to bring all contending parties together in this great assembly to resolve their remaining differences, thus allowing them to devote all their energies to the Crusade. Alas, Anglo-French rivalry intruded even into this great assembly.[145] In the third plenary session of the Council, on 30 November 1215, when plans for the Crusade and the establishment of peace were on the agenda, the Pope publicly excommunicated all those barons who had rebelled against John, explaining how much aid for the Holy Land might have been expected from his vassal had they not behaved thus.[146] Innocent was probably already aware that negotiations were going on between the English barons and the French court. Rumour had it that Philip believed that he had the Lateran Council on his side, and, indeed, the great outcry *multis contradicentibus*, which went up when the barons' excommunication was announced, strongly suggests French attempts to discredit John in the assembly.[147]

By December 1215 Prince Louis had been invited to bring an army and take the throne of England by force of arms. The Pope was both shocked and alarmed at the prospect of the enlargement of the civil war in England and a renewal of Anglo-French hostilities. His replacement of Pandulf with Guala Bicchieri, Cardinal Bishop of S. Martino, may well have represented an attempt to remedy the situation.[148] Guala had already wide experience of reducing hostile elements in the papal states to obedience and in bringing warring factions to peace.[149]

Although the papal registers for the years 1213 to 1216 are now lost, we know from a fourteenth-century table that Innocent had various letters formulated to use as circumstances demanded.[150] Two letters urged Philip

[143] J. M. Powell, *Anatomy of a Crusade 1213–1221* (Pennsylvania, 1986).

[144] Bolton, 'A show with a meaning', pp. 53–67.

[145] Kuttner and Garcia, 'New eyewitness account', pp. 128, 156–62.

[146] *SLI*, pp. 221–3; Potthast, 5013.

[147] *Rigord*, p. 109, 'in eodem concilio excommunicavit idem papa, multis contradicentibus, barones Anglie et complices eorum.'

[148] C. D. Fonseca, 'Ricerche sulla famiglia Bicchieri e la società vercellese dei secoli xii–xiii', in *Miscellanea in memoria di G. Soranzo* (Milan, 1968), pp. 207–65.

[149] Maccarrone, *Studi*, pp. 61–79; Cheney, *Innocent III*, p. 391.

[150] *Vetera Monumenta Slavorum Meridionalium historiam illustrantia*, ed. A. Theiner (Rome,

to give neither help nor favour to the English barons, whilst forbidding his son to do likewise.[151] Another, similar, letter was directed to Louis. Innocent's anger and anxiety at the ruin of his plans is clear. A war between John and Louis had to be prevented at all costs.[152] Louis sent envoys to Rome to justify his actions. Innocent received them cheerfully, but became distressed when he realized the nature of their mission—as one envoy said, 'He turned a sad face on us.'[153] They may have been in Rome at Easter 1216, which fell in that year on 10 April, for they reported back to the prince that they would wait to see if the Pope would give a sentence against them on Ascension Day, 19 May, 'as is his custom'.[154] But by the time the envoys wrote, Louis had already set sail, and arrived in Dover on 21 May, one day after the legate, Guala. Innocent, meanwhile, had set out on his own preaching and pacification campaign to Pisa and Genoa.[155] On Sunday 1 May we know that he was preaching the Cross to an enthusiastic multitude in Orvieto.[156] News of Louis's invasion of England reached him in Perugia in June or early July, and there, too, he probably heard that Genoese ships, which ought to have been used for the crusade, were now diverted to Louis's invasion.[157] Innocent's short temper is well attested on many occasions, but never so much as here and now. With his plans for peace and crusade in ruins, he was, according to William the Breton, inconsolable. Now he turned all his preaching skills—and they were many—into a public discourse and sermon on retribution and vengeance, addressed to the people and clergy of Perugia.[158] Taking a stirring Old Testament theme (Ezekiel 21.28), 'Sword, sword, unsheathe and polish yourself to kill and to shine', he solemnized the sentence of excommunication against Louis and his men for invading a fief of the Roman Church.[159] Then, calling together his notaries, he began to dictate 'harsh and intolerable sentences' against Philip and the Kingdom of France. Wendover refers to these letters as *litterae deprecatoriae*.[160] But William the

---

1863), pp. 47–70, records the lost chancery registers of the pontifical years 3, 4, 18, and 19.

[151] Ibid., p. 63.

[152] Maccarrone, *Studi*, p. 160.

[153] *Historia Major*, pp. 237–8; Cheney, *Innocent III*, p. 392.

[154] Ibid., p. 392.

[155] Maccarrone, *Studi*, pp. 160–3.

[156] Ibid., pp. 8–9, for the account of his sermon.

[157] Ibid., p. 160.

[158] *Rigord*, p. 109, 'ipse Papa de transitu Ludovici in Angliam certioratus, inconsolabiliter'.

[159] Maccarrone, *Studi*, pp. 160–2.

[160] *Historia Major*, p. 235.

Breton, that official Capetian historian, could not resist reporting with satisfaction that God, who was always well disposed towards Philip, now turned the unsheathed sword back upon the Pope himself. Within a short while Innocent had succumbed to what is likely to have been tertian malaria,[161] and his death on 16 July, according to the Breton, generated greater joy than sadness.[162]

Philip's response to the harsh and deprecatory letters transmitted to him by Guala is highly instructive. When the legate stressed the Pope's duty to protect, defend, and cherish John, vassal of the Holy See, whose kingdom had come to belong to the Roman Church, Philip is reported as replying without hesitation 'Regnum Anglie patrimonium Petri nunquam fuit, nec est, nec erit:[163] the Kingdom of England was never part of the Patrimony of St Peter, nor is it, nor will it ever be. Thus it is free of the Pope's jurisdiction.' Such a statement at precisely the moment of French invasion truly reveals the nature of this 'good' son in Innocent's vineyard.

The year 1216 marked no turning-point in Anglo-French relations which confirmed the established pattern of truces, invasion, and attempts at peace. The protagonists, however, were now different. By the end of that year, not only Innocent but John, too, had died. Philip, however, was to live on for a further seven years. Characteristically, he turned some of his attention to a crusade, not the Fifth, which had been so much Innocent's concern, but that which had been waged since 1209 against 'the little foxes' in Languedoc. The fact that this was ultimately more to the advantage of France than to the Vineyard which Innocent had left, must surely have been purely coincidental!

[161] M. Petrucci, 'L'ultimo destino perugino di Innocenzo III', *Bollettino della deputazione di storia patria per l'Umbria*, 64 (1967), pp. 201–7.
[162] *Rigord*, p. 109.
[163] *Historia Major*, p. 235.

# VI

# *VIA ASCETICA*: A PAPAL QUANDARY

'RESCUE us O Lord Pope from barbaric power and subjugation to laymen' was the cry of despair from the clerics of Grandmont which reached Pope Innocent III about the year 1215.[1] It indicated the growth of the appeal to Rome which took place in the Canon Law of the twelfth century.[2] Many other examples of an increase in papal authority occurred at this time. The extension of papal jurisdiction is one of two important developments of twelfth- and thirteenth-century Christendom with which this paper will be concerned.

This jurisdictional extension of papal authority was both a resolution of and a reaction to the second important development, namely the spiritual crisis or ferment of the time, known as the *vita apostolica*.[3] This imitation of the life of the apostles was claimed, not only by the apologists of the monastic tradition to justify their conventional forms of cenobitic life and by the new religious institute of canons regular but also by a whole host of contempor-

[1] 'Eripe nos, Domini, de potestate barbarica et a servitute laicali', Martène and Durand, *Thesaurus* I (Paris 1717) cols 845–7.

[2] For general comments on appeals to the Curia and papal jurisdiction see G. Le Bras, *Les institutions ecclésiastiques de la chrétienité mediévale, Histoire de l'Église* 12 (Paris 1964) 1; [R.W.] Southern, *Western Society [and the Church in the Middle Ages,]* (Harmondsworth 1970) pp. 104–17 and in particular [C.R.] Cheney, *Innocent III [and England,]* Päpste und Papsttum, 9 (Stuttgart 1976) pp. 97–120 and J. Hourlier, *L'Âge Classique (1140–1378): Les Religieux*, Histoire du Droit et des Institutions de l'Église en Occident, 10 (Paris 1974).

[3] E.W. McDonnell, 'The *Vita Apostolica*: Diversity or Dissent?' *CH* 24 (1955) pp. 15–31; G. Olsen, 'The Idea of the *Ecclesia Primitiva* in the Writings of the Twelfth-Century Canonists', *Traditio* 25 (1969) pp. 61–81; [L.K.] Little, *Religious Poverty [and the Profit Economy in Medieval Europe]* (London 1978); [C.H.] Lawrence, *Medieval Monasticism* (London 1984) pp. 125–45; [B.M.] Bolton, *The Medieval Reformation* (London 1983) pp. 18–32 and above all (M.-D.] Chenu, *Nature, Man and Society [in the Twelfth Century: Essays on New Theological Perspectives in the Latin West,]* trans J. Taylor and L.K. Little (Chicago 1968) pp. 239–46.

ary religious movements then beginning to appear.[4] Few of the religious were to remain unmoved by the example of the first Jerusalem community and from the ferment emerged a whole spectrum of different interpretations, variously emphasising simplicity, voluntary poverty, manual labour, and itinerant preaching, but all related to a christocentric piety. For many the *vita apostolica* would only be achieved through a life of strict discipline and sacrifice – to live like Christ through holy effort, based upon acts of inward or outward virtue or through self-imposed hardship and deprivation to achieve greater personal purity. This gave rise to an austere element,[5] a harsher strand of the *vita apostolica* which may perhaps be seen as a *via ascetica*. It was to be a more regular and monastic road to salvation with the many outward and visible signs of asceticism so desired by its participants.

The papacy, in seeking to exercise its increased jurisdiction in both spiritual and temporal matters, faced mounting problems because of the vast complex of religious orders which had come into being in the twelfth century.[6] The responsibility of the pope as *abbas universalis*, which meant bringing monasteries under canonical protection, became an increasingly important part of his duties.[7] When extended to new monasteries, it became a vital instrument for monastic change and reform and was embodied in the Roman chancery formula *Religiosam vitam*.[8] This extended use of such a collection of standardised formulae made it possible for a variety of

[4] *Ibid* pp. 202–38. For further insights into some of these movements see M.B. Becker, *Medieval Italy: Constraints and Creativity* (Indiana 1981) and [H.] Leyser, *Hermits and the New Monasticism: [A Study of Religious Communities in Western Europe 1000–1150]* (London 1984).

[5] O. Chadwick, *Western Asceticism* (Philadelphia 1958) pp. 13–31; H. Chadwick, *The Early Church*, (Harmondsworth 1967); [D.] Knowles, *From Pachomius to Ignatius: [A Study in the Constitutional History of the Religious Orders]* (Oxford 1966).

[6] [M.] Maccarrone, 'Primato Romano e Monasteri [dal Principio del Secolo XII ad Innocenzo III',] in *Istituzioni Monastiche e Istituzioni Canonicali in Occidente (1123–1215), Mendola* (Milan 1980) pp. 49–132.

[7] *Ibid* pp. 63–4. This principle, first enunciated by Gregory VII, reached its highest development with Innocent III. Apostolic protection was transformed into a papal institution, expressing the exercise of the pope's jurisdiction over the whole Church.

[8] 'Religiosam vitam eligentibus, apostolicum convenit adesse praesidium'. For a discussion of the use of this formula see M. Tangl, *Die päpstlichen Kanzleiordnungen von 1200–1500* (Innsbruck 1894) pp. 229–32.

institutions both to be confirmed and also, at the same time, to be enriched by the granting of much valued privileges. This was an innovatory concept, allowing as it did, a shift of emphasis from simple protection to much needed reform.[9] By the mid-twelfth century, a so-called 'clause of regularity' had been further developed as a condition of confirmation.[10] This not only ensured the permanence of established rules such as those of Benedict or Augustine but also applied to those institutions or observances referred to as *ordo* or *religio* and which in themselves represented a new way of life.[11] As a result of this, a profound transformation of the relationship between the papacy and the religious orders was accomplished within the framework of the protection of St. Peter.[12] Thus papal authority was able to penetrate into the cloister in spite of not always being welcome.

The problem, however, was to be particularly acute in those monasteries which were already exempt from episcopal authority and which were attached *nullo medio* to the Holy See.[13] Here, because the spiritual and temporal condition was often deplorable, the papacy was liable to be brought into disrepute by its inability to supervise them.[14] Such calls as existed for their reform and renewal, were met with resentment and sometimes even with rejection. Divergent responses were rife and indeed epitomised the whole papal dilemma of the way of the *via ascetica*. The many natural, individual human quests for the *vita apostolica* and a consequential *via ascetica*, with either a return to the way of the hermit or the founding of new strict orders could so easily lead away from the control and unity of the Church; but all were in need

[9] Maccarrone, 'Primato Romano e Monasteri' p. 74.

[10] J. Dubois, 'Les ordres religieux au xii$^{e}$ siècle selon la Curie romaine', *RB* 78 (1968) pp. 283–309 especially pp. 285–7.

[11] Maccarrone, 'Primato Romano e Monasteri' pp. 74–5; Chenu, *Nature, Man and Society* pp. 225–7.

[12] For a highly significant discussion of the implications of the development of the idea of *protectio Sancti Petri* see Maccarrone, 'Primato Romano e Monasteri' pp. 50–77.

[13] [G.] Schreiber, *Kurie und Kloster [im 12 Jahrhundert. Studien zur Privilegierung, Verfassung und besonders zum Eigenkirchenwesen der vorfranzicanischen Orden vornehmlich auf Grund der Papsturkunden von Paschalis II bis auf Lucius III 1099–1181,]* Kirchliche Abhandlungen 65–68, 2 vols (Stuttgart 1910) 1, pp. 47–55, 207–9.

[14] *[Die] Register [Innocenz' III*, Bd I: *1. Pontifikatsjahr 1198/9]* edd O. Hageneder and A. Haidacher (Graz-Köln 1964) 2a, p. 6. Letter of 9 January 1198 to all abbots, priors and religious of the kingdom of France.

of papal direction.[15] The popes of the period faced this dilemma in varying states of perplexity. Perhaps the least perplexed was Innocent III who, at the age of thirty-seven, as Lothair de Segni, was elected Pope in January 1198.[16] This may have been because of his ability to grasp both the significance and the number of the wide range and diversity of the views being expressed and also to insert them into an ecclesiastical structure. As the incumbent of Peter's chair at this crucial point, he was a man of exceptional vigour and purpose. He has been described as 'the most brilliantly apparent of all thirteenth century popes'.[17] His actions highlighted the competing problems of the nature and extent of papal jurisdiction and the wish to have complete freedom in the form the *via ascetica* should take.[18] He wished to use this jurisdiction to facilitate the operation of an acceptable form of asceticism within the bounds of the Church. Innocent regarded monks as 'his very special sons since it is through them that God finds the highest and worthiest of the glory due to him'.[19] He tells us that as Pope 'there had come to him the mission to maintain religion in the churches of God and to develop it'[20] and that the prosperity, maintenance of standards and reform of monasteries were particularly close to his heart. At first he attempted to work both through the older traditional Benedictine monasteries and also through the newer orders, particularly the

[15] Schreiber, *Kurie und Kloster* 1 pp. 62–3. For a series of valuable studies on the problems of eremitism see *L'Eremitismo in Occidente nei Secoli XI e XII, Mendola* 4 (Milan 1962) and Leyser, *Hermits and the New Monasticism* pp. 78–86.

[16] From the vast range of literature, the following are particularly useful. A. Luchaire, *Innocent III* 6 vols (Paris 1904–8); H. Tillmann, *Papst Innocenz' III* (Göttingen 1954), now available as *Pope Innocent III*, trans W. Sax, *Europe in the Middle Ages*, Select Studies 12 (North Holland 1980); [M.] Maccarrone, *Studi [su Innocenzo III,] Italia Sacra* 17 (Padua 1972); Cheney, *Innocent III*; [W.] Imkamp, *[Das] Kirchenbild Innocenz' III [1198–1216),]* Päpste und Papsttum, 22 (Stuttgart 1983); [S.] Sibilia, 'L'Iconografia di Innocenzo III', *Bolletino della Sezione di Anagni della Società Romana di Storia Patria* 2 (Rome 1953) pp. 65–120; G.B. Ladner, *Die Papstbildnisse des Altertums und des Mittelalters*, 2 (Vatican City 1970) pp. 53–79.

[17] [R.] Brentano, *Rome before Avignon: [A Social History of Thirteenth-Century Rome]* (London 1974) p. 148.

[18] For a brief yet stimulating account of Innocent's policies see B. Tierney, *The Crisis of Church and State* (New Jersey 1964) pp. 127–38; Cheney, *Innocent III* pp. 1–10 and Bolton, *The Medieval Reformation* pp. 97–111.

[19] 'Nos enim, vos tamquam speciales Ecclesie filios, per quos nomen Domini dignus et excellentius praedicatur', *Register* I, 2a, p. 6. Letter of 9 January 1198.

[20] *Register* I, 176, pp. 262–3.

Cistercians.[21] Indeed, he referred to the Cistercians and the Carthusians as 'the best of monks'.[22] It was not long before he was to suffer serious disillusionment in regard to the spiritual aspects of the *via ascetica* although, in more practical matters, he was able to make provision in the Fourth Lateran Council to regulate the application of the Rule of St Benedict through the institution of a triennial General Chapter for individual, autonomous Benedictine monasteries and to do the same for houses of Augustinian canons.[23]

Innocent himself had always shown a particular sensitivity to those aspects of the *vita apostolica* which stressed the increasing demand for a more ascetic, simpler and more personal spiritual life. He appreciated that for many conventional monasticism was not the only road. He was aware that the hermit ideal of withdrawal into a solitary wilderness was in many ways commendable. It could, however, be seen as too personal and private a quest and there was a danger that many individuals and groups might be tempted towards an even more extreme and exclusive form of asceticism.[24] This might even lead to a desire for mortification, an exercise in endurance with no relief and little hope, through the attempt to achieve the annihilation of the individual self. In such cases, a move towards heresy was always a possibility. But there were others, as Innocent was well aware, for whom the *via ascetica* had no attraction at all, while the approach of still more was half-hearted, to say the least. A glimpse at his life and character will enable us to understand more clearly the efforts that this pope had to make to resolve the quandary of an acceptable *via ascetica* with which he was faced.

Some evidence for his early views on the regular life, on his personal *via ascetica* and on the principles underlying his asceticism

[21] [U.] Berlière, 'Innocent III et [la réorganisation des] monastères bénédictins', *RB* 20–22 (1920) pp. 22–42, 145–59; P. Schmitz, *Histoire de l'Ordre de Saint Benoît* 3 (Maredsous 1948) pp. 42–55; R. Brentano, *Two Churches. England and Italy in the Thirteenth Century* (Princeton 1968) p. 259 and Maccarrone, *Studi* pp. 223–6.

[22] 'Cum inter omnes religiosos nostri temporis viros Cisterciensis et Carthusiensis ordinum fratres magna per Dei gratiam polleant honestate...', *PL* 216 (1855) col 469. Letter of 11 October 1211.

[23] *COD* (3 ed Bologna 1973) Canon 12 pp. 240–1; Maccarrone, *Studi* pp. 246–62.

[24] For a discussion of such dangers see Grundmann, pp. 70–127; B.M. Bolton, 'Poverty as Protest', *The Church in a Changing Society*, Publications of the Swedish Society of Church History, New Series, 30 (Uppsala 1978) pp. 28–32; Leyser, *Hermits and the New Monasticism* pp. 18–24.

can be drawn from a number of sources close to him. The *Gesta Innocentii tertii* presents to us the figure of the Pope and his policies through the eyes of an anonymous contemporary cleric in Rome, probably an employee of the Papal Chancery.[25] The biography, whilst written in an admiring tone, has the advantage of being backed by precise dating, although it stops suddenly at the end of 1208 or early in 1209.[26] It is valuable for the information it provides about Innocent's early career and his chosen life style which perhaps owed much to the fact that he was educated at the Benedictine monastery of S. Andrea on the Celian Hill in Rome where the shadow of its great founder, Pope Gregory I, must have been much in evidence.[27] Studies at Paris and Bologna led to a notable reputation as theologian and philosopher[28] and after he returned to Rome, probably during the pontificate of Lucius III,[29] he was ordained a sub-deacon during the brief pontificate of Gregory VIII.[30] When he was twenty-nine he was named Cardinal Deacon by Clement III[31] and given as his title church SS Sergio e Bacco on the Forum.[32] Whilst Cardinal he wrote three books, *On*

[25] *Gesta* [*Innocentii P.P.III,*] *PL* 214 (1855) xvii–ccxxviii. F. Ehrle, *Die Gesta Innocentii III im Verhältnis zu den Regesten desselben Papstes* (Heidelberg 1876) for a highly critical account of this work. For its revaluation and reappraisal, see Y. Lefevre, 'Innocent III et son temps vus de Rome. Étude sur la biographie anonyme de ce pape', *Mélanges d'Archéologie et d'Histoire de l'École Française de Rome*, 61 (Paris 1949) pp. 242–5.

[26] *Ibid* pp. 242–3; [M.] Maccarrone, ['Innocenzo III,] prima del pontificato', *ASP* 66 (1943) pp. 59–134 especially p. 60.

[27] *Gesta* col xvii, I. His biographer remarks that he was well-grounded in liturgical chant and psalmody. 'Exercitatus in cantilena et psalmodia'. Imkamp, *Kirchenbild Innocenz' III* pp. 20–3; Maccarrone, 'Prima del pontificato' pp. 68–81.

[28] *Gesta* col xvii, II. 'Hic primum in Urbe, deinde Parisius, tandem Bononiae, scholasticis insudavit et super coaetaneos suos tam in philosophica quam theologica disciplina profecit'. Imkamp, *Kirchenbild Innocenz' III* pp. 23–46; K. Pennington, 'The legal education of Pope Innocent III', *Bulletin of Medieval Canon Law* NS 4 (1974) pp. 70–7.

[29] Lucius III (1181–1185). Maccarrone, 'Prima del pontificato' pp. 81–3.

[30] *Gesta* col xviii, III. 'Hunc sanctae memoriae Gregorius octavus papa, in subdiaconum ordinavit'. Gregory VIII (21 November–17 December 1187); P. Kehr, 'Papst Gregor VIII als Ordensgründer', *Miscellanea F. Ehrle*, Studi e Testi 38, vol 2 (Rome 1924) pp. 248–76; Maccarrone, 'Prima del pontificato' p. 83.

[31] Clement III (1187–1191). 'Et Clemens III papa promovit in diaconum cardinalem, vicesimum nonum aetatis annum agentem', *Gesta* col xviii, III; Maccarrone, 'Prima del pontificato' p. 84.

[32] *Gesta* cols xviii–iv, III, IV; Maccarrone, 'Prima del pontificato' pp. 81–91; *Die Register Innocenz' III*, Bd II: *2. Pontifikatsjahr 1199/1200,* edd O. Hageneder, W.

*the Misery of the Human Condition*,[33] *On the Mystery of the Mass*[34] and *On the Four Sorts of Marriage*.[35] During his pontificate he produced a *Commentary on the Seven Psalms*[36] and many Sermons, Letters, Registers and Decretals.[37] Both during his time as Cardinal and as Pope, by precept and example, he insisted upon an honest, strict and sparse code of behaviour.[38] The Lateran Palace became a changed place.[39] In all these actions Innocent seems to have been seeking to organise his own life along more ascetic lines and that of his household on the model of a canonical community.[40] The one exception was his private chapel where nothing was too good for the glory of God.[41] Another contemporary view of Innocent comes

Maleczek and A. Strnad (Rome-Vienna 1979), 94, pp. 198–201. For the repairs to this Church see R. Krautheimer, *Rome: Profile of a City 312–1308* (Princeton 1980) p. 203 and M. Bonfioli, 'La Diaconia dei SS Sergio e Bacco nel Foro Romano. Fonti e Problemi', *Rivista di Archeologia Cristiana* 50 (Rome 1974) pp. 55–85.

33 *PL* 217 (1855) cols 702–46. [*Lotharii Cardinalis (Innocentii III).*] *De Miseria* [*Humane Conditionis*] ed M. Maccarrone (Lucca 1955).

34 *PL* 217 cols 773–916; Imkamp, *Kirchenbild Innocenz' III* pp. 46–53; Maccarrone, 'Innocenzo III, teologo della eucarestia', *Studi* pp. 341–65.

35 *PL* 217 cols 922–68; Imkamp, *Kirchenbild Innocenz' III* pp. 53–63. For a discussion of Innocent's significant literary and administrative activity during his cardinalate, see Maccarrone, 'Prima del pontificato' pp. 86–9.

36 *PL* 217 cols 968–1130: Maccarrone, 'Prima del pontificato' pp. 67–71.

37 *Sermons*: *PL* 217 cols 309–690; *Letters*: C.R. Cheney, 'The Letters of Pope Innocent III' in *Medieval Texts and Studies* (Oxford 1973) pp. 16–38 with a particularly significant bibliography pp. 37–8; *Register* I and II; *Decretals: Corpus Iuris Canonici* ed A. Friedberg 2 vols (Leipzig 1879) 2.

38 *Gesta* XLI: he inveighed against all forms of avarice and cupidity; refused all forms of gift and bribery; reformed the Chancery and decreed that no official had any claim to fees except scribes and *bullators* who were to keep to a fixed scale of charges.

39 On his election as Pope, he had removed all the precious furnishings of the papal chambers, substituting simple wooden or glass vessels for gold and silver, *ibid* CXLVIII and having the money changers' tables taken from the kitchen entrance, *ibid* XLI.

40 His own meals were limited to three courses, those of his chaplains to two and lay servants were replaced by clerics, *ibid* CXLVIII. Under Innocent, there were about fifty *capellani* or chaplains who also belonged to the Pope's *familia* and were fed from the papal kitchens, *ibid* CXLVI. See R. Elze, 'Die päpstliche Kapelle', *Zeitschrift der Savigny Stiftung für Rechtsgeschichte Kanonistische Abteilung* 38 (1950) pp. 145–204; W. Ullmann, *The Growth of Papal Government in the Middle Ages* (2 ed London 1965) p. 331 n 4.

41 The Chapel of St Laurence at the Lateran, known as the *Sancta Sanctorum* for its wealth of relics, was so rich *tam in materia quam in forma* that its like had never before been seen, *Gesta* CXLV; [S.J.P.] Van Dijk and [J. Hazelden] Walker, [*The*] *Origins of the Modern Roman Liturgy* (London 1960) pp. 91–5; G. Marangoni, *Istoria della Sancta Sanctorum* (Rome 1747); P. Lauer, *Le Palais de Latran. Étude historique et archéologique* (Paris 1911).

from an anonymous monk away from Rome at the Cistercian house of Santa Maria di Ferraria near Teano in Campania.[42] In addition to describing how Innocent replaced the rich papal vestments with a religious habit consisting of simple white wool and lambskins,[43] he describes how the Pope instituted a universal convent for a better development of the spiritual life of the nuns of Rome.[44]

Two further fragments of evidence survive. One shows us a glimpse of Innocent at Subiaco where he suffered from heat, mosquitos and cicadas without complaint and without disturbing his prayer and contemplation.[45] The other shows his concern for those who might not have been so stalwart in facing such difficulties. While staying 'at that arid Segni' he ordered his chaplains to shorten the Daily Office.[46]

Above all, we have those works written by Innocent himself, though Cheney has warned us about the authorship of the letters and sermons.[47] Nevertheless, an interior consistency in these letters can be discerned to indicate that the overall view was Innocent's.[48] In his theological works, his taste for parallels between words of similar sound and for the transposition of epithets are further indications of his style of writing.[49]

His ascetical work *On the Misery of the Human Condition*, written sometime after the age of twenty-five, is highly relevant here.[50] While it has been described as 'sound, not deep; genuine, not

[42] [*Chronica Romanorum pontificum et imperatorum ac de rebus in Apulia gestis (781–1228) auctore*] *ignoto monacho Cistercensi* ed A. Gaudenzi in *Società Napoletana di Sancta Patria*, 1, Cronache (Naples 1888) p. 34.

[43] *Ibid* p. 34. 'Assumpsit sibi vestos religiosas, id est de lana alba et pelles agniculas'.

[44] *Ibid*, 'instituit etiam universale cenobium monalium Rome, in quo omnes moniales conveniant, nec eis progredi liceat'.

[45] [K.] Hampe, ['Eine Schilderung des Sommeraufenthaltes der Römischen Kurie unter] Innocenz' III in Subiaco 1202', *Historische Vierteljahrsschrift* 8 (Leipzig 1905) pp. 509–35.

[46] Van Dijk and Walker, *Origins of the Modern Roman Liturgy* pp. 97, 267–8 and Appendix 14b pp. 462–4.

[47] Cheney, 'Letters of Pope Innocent III' pp. 22–9.

[48] *Ibid* p. 29.

[49] *Ibid* pp. 31–4; Brentano, *Rome before Avignon* pp. 150–3.

[50] For the suggestion that this work was completed at the beginning of 1195, Maccarrone, *De Miseria*, Praefatio XXXVII. 'Ergo licet assere opus *De Miseria*, a Lothario completum esse initio anni 1195, nempe inter calendas Ianuarias vel diem Decembris anni 1194 ... atque diem 13 Aprilis 1195'.

original',[51] it was a popular and widely read set-piece on the vanity of earthly pretensions and the span of Man's life 'from the heat of love to the meat of worms'.[52] His analytical powers are brought to bear successively on various human conditions, poor and rich; servant and master; celibate and married; good and wicked; each suffering his own particular misery and prevented from being happy.[53] He expounds the consequences which the desire for riches, especially the temptation of money, brings to justice and the outcome of law-suits, of which he had first-hand knowledge.[54] Successive chapters describe examples of pomp and pride resulting in rich clothing and domestic furnishing.[55] The work closes with the traditional scenario of the Last Judgment, the final act of Man.[56]

The material of much of this short work may not have been new, but it contained motifs which are common to all ascetical and moralistic tracts and has the ring of truth and real life about it.[57] His use of language, described variously as 'fantastic, lyrical, funny and crude',[58] his borrowings from Ovid and Horace, as well as his Scriptural allusions, lead us to believe that Innocent enjoyed this playing with words and with the outrageous mocking at the decline of Man into senility.[59] Although there were many jokes at the expense of his readers, the serious nature of this treatise which at first appears to be a transitory academic exercise, remained in Innocent's meditations and its arguments were often repeated in the many letters and sermons of his pontificate.[60] They played a part too in his practical duties, as the examples of the *via ascetica* which he met, ranging from a reflection of the youthful enthusiasm of the

[51] Van Dijk and Walker, *Origins of the Modern Roman Liturgy* p. 91.
[52] Brentano, *Rome before Avignon* p. 151.
[53] Maccarrone, *De Miseria* pp. 7–36 especially pp. 20–7.
[54] *Ibid* pp. 39–72, especially pp. 39–43, 59–62. For law suits and payment for justice, compare *Gesta* XLI and CXLVII. His biographer witnesses that the pope 'inter omnes pestes, habuit venalitatem exosam', *ibid* XLI.
[55] Maccarrone, *De Miseria* pp. 69–72.
[56] *Ibid* pp. 75–98.
[57] Maccarrone, 'Prima del pontificato' pp. 102–4, for a discussion of possible sources and influences.
[58] Brentano, *Rome before Avignon* p. 151.
[59] *Ibid* pp. 150–4.
[60] Maccarrone, 'Prima del pontificato' pp. 103–10 and especially 107–8. 'Si vede questo dall'influenza, veramente notevole, che il *De Miseria* ebbe sugli altri suoi scritti'.

treatise to that of its more depressive aspects. Although his reactions may often have been too immediate,[61] Innocent was careful enough to look for ways of change which, in the result, brought some acceptance from those he was either over-chastising or over-praising. The affair of Grandmont and the meeting with Francis are two examples.

His own practical experience of what he considered to be extreme asceticism, the *via ascetica* which had lost its way, came from Grandmont in the Limousin.[62] Indeed, the earliest reference we have to Innocent before he was pope comes from an eye-witness account of the Chapter at Grandmont by Bernard Ithier, chronicler of Saint-Martial at Limoges.[63] He notes the presence there, in May or June 1187, of the young Lothair de Segni.[64] This was precisely the moment of the first great crisis in the Order: the revolt of the laybrothers or *conversi*[65] which was regarded by

[61] Brentano, *Rome before Avignon* p. 150.

[62] Among numerous articles on Grandmont, the most useful are [A.]Lecler, 'Histoire de l'Abbaye de Grandmont', *B*[*ulletin de la*] *S*[*ociété*] *A*[*rchéologique et*] *H*[*istorique du*] *L*[*imousin*] 58 (1908) pp. 44–94; and the following, all by J. Becquet, 'Les institutions de l'ordre de Grandmont au moyen âge', *R*[*evue*] *M*[*abillon*] 42 (1952) pp. 31–42; 'Les premiers écrivains de l'ordre de Grandmont', *RM* 43 (1956) pp. 127–37; 'L'"Institution": premier coutumier de l'ordre de Grandmont', *RM* 46 (1956) pp. 15–32; 'La règle de Grandmont', *BSAHL* 87 (1958–60) pp. 9–36; 'La première crise de l'ordre de Grandmont', *Ibid* pp. 283–324; *Scriptores Ordinis Grandmontensis*, ed J. Becquet, *CC*, *Continuatio Medievalis* 8 (Turnholt 1968); 'Etienne de Muret', *Dictionnaire de Spiritualité* 4 (Paris 1961) cols 1504–14; 'Gerard Ithier', *ibid* 6 (1967) cols 275–6; 'Le Bullaire de l'ordre de Grandmont', *RM* 46 (1956) 1–75 pp. 82–93, 156–68; *ibid* 47 (1957) 76–93d pp. 33–43, 245–7; Addenda et Corrigenda, *ibid* 53 (1963) pp. 111–33, 137–160. Abbreviated as *BUL*.

[63] *Chronicon B. Iterii Armarii Monasterii S. Marcialis* ed H. Duplès-Agier, *Société de l'histoire de France* (Paris 1874) pp. 30–129 especially p. 62. Bernard Ithier (1163–1225), novice at Saint-Martial in 1177, ordained deacon in 1185 and priest in 1189, held the offices of treasurer, sacristan and librarian (1204). As he only left the Abbey of Saint-Martial at rare intervals and even then on almost exclusively religious journeys, his presence at Grandmont in 1187 seems of particular significance.

[64] *Ibid* p. 62. 'Ego presens in capitulo cum hoc fieret, et Octavianus, episcopus Ostiensis et Hugo *de Nonans* et Lotharius, qui postea Innocentius papa III[us] meruit nuncupari, et Poncius, Clarmontensis episcopus'.

[65] Becquet, 'La première crise' p. 298. On the general institution of laybrothers or *conversi* see K. Hallinger, 'Woher kommen die Laienbrüder, *ASOC* 12 (1956) pp. 1–104; J.O. Ducourneau, 'De l'institution et des us des convers dans l'ordre de Cîteaux (xiie et xiiie siècles)', in *Saint Bernard et son temps*, 2 vols (Dijon 1928–9) II pp. 139–201; J.S. Donnelly, *The Decline of the Medieval Cistercian Laybrotherhood*, Fordham University Studies, Series 3 (New York 1949). For a contemporary comparative view, see M.D. Knowles, 'The revolt of the lay brothers of

Stephen of Tournai as the severest reproach of all; that within 'this extraordinary Order of Grandmont'[66] clerics were subjugated to laymen. Innocent must have been present at the forced resignation of the sixth prior, William de Treignac.[67] He may have witnessed William's departure with two hundred clerics and thirteen *conversi* for Cîteaux and ultimately for Rome to register a complaint at the Curia.[68] This experience, both dramatic and scandalous in his eyes, together with the fact that, later as Cardinal, he was to be personally involved in their suits at the Curia,[69] made a deep impression on Innocent's mind. In 1202 he reminded the abbots of La Ferté, Pontigny, Morimond and Clairvaux, the four daughter houses in dispute with their mother at Cîteaux, of the great dangers of ascetic over-simplification, instancing the scandal of Grandmont, lest through discord they, like it, might fall into ridicule *in derisum et fabulam* and become the laughing stock and talk of all.[70] Nevertheless, Innocent was characteristically still willing to reconsider the way Grandmont had moved through all its crises and to give a new form of approval to the Order,[71] so much so that much later in 1220, Dominic, who owed much to Innocent, was able to consider looking at the reformed Grandmont as an example that might be followed in his Order's institution of conventual mendicancy.[72]

The clerical congregation of the hermits of Grandmont represented a misguided attempt to institutionalise the solitary life at the

---

Sempringham', *EHR* 1 (1935) pp. 465–87 and R. Foreville, 'La crise de l'ordre de Sempringham au xii^e^ siècle: nouvelle approche du dossier des frères lais', *Anglo-Norman Studies* 6 (Woodbridge 1983) pp. 39–57.

66 J. Warichez, *Étienne de Tournai et son temps* (Tournai-Paris 1937) p. 54 n 50. Stephen, Bishop of Tournai (1192–1203). Becquet, 'La première crise' p. 297.

67 *Ibid* pp. 301–2. Prior William de Treignac (1170–1187). For a discussion of his priorate see *ibid* pp. 291–9.

68 *Chronicon B. Iterii* p. 62. 'Grandimontenses gravi dissentione periclantur, ita quod W. prior cum ducentis clericis et xiii laicis de domo sua prosiliens. Rome obiit peregrinus'.

69 Becquet, 'La première crise' p. 317.

70 *PL* 214 (1855) cols 1107–8; Potthast I, 1772 p. 155; *BUL* 46b, 22 November 1202. For another almost contemporary view of this crisis, see *The Historia Occidentalis of Jacques de Vitry*, ed J.F. Hinnebusch, *SpicFr* 17 (1972) pp. 124–7.

71 Privilege of 27 February 1202. The whole text is edited in Lecler, 'Histoire de l'Abbaye de Grandmont', *BSAHL* 58 (1908) pp. 73–6; abbreviated version, *PL* 214 cols 945–8 and *BUL* 38–53 and 53B–61.

72 Becquet, 'La première crise' p. 324; [M.H.] Vicaire, *Saint Dominic* [*and his Times*] trans K. Pond (London 1964) pp. 310–11.

expense of everything else.[73] The original founder, Stephen de Muret (d. 1124), a noble hermit, had quite deliberately left no rule of life for his disciples to follow, explaining that he belonged to the Order of the Gospel and wished to be called neither monk, nor canon nor hermit.[74] This was intended to be a complete return to the *vita apostolica* but there were many aspects which owed their origin to the ideas of the Benedictines, Augustinians, Carthusians and others.[75] The customs of the Order of Grandmont were only consolidated into a Rule during the tenure of the fourth prior Stephen of Liciac (1139–1163)[76] and by that time there had been a considerable expansion in numbers of these mendicant hermits whose modest cells remained faithful to the model of the desert.[77] These hermits had renounced property, buildings and lands, flocks and herds, either for work or consumption, but bees from the forest were allowed.[78] There was a contradiction, however, in that, while they had given up all regular resources, they accepted ownership of the monastery, its chapel and its garden.[79] To allow the clerics to apply themselves solely to the spiritual work of contemplation and prayer, without ever leaving the monastic enclosure, the founder had made provision that the *conversi* should attend to temporal affairs and indeed should have authority over

[73] For a general discussion of the criticism of eremitism, see G. Morin, 'Rainaud l'ermite et Ives de Chartres. Un episode de la crise de cénobitisme au xi$^{e}$–xii$^{e}$ siècle', *RB* 40 (1928) oo 99–115 and J. Leclercq, 'Le poème de Payen Bolotin contre les faux ermites', *ibid* 73 (1958) pp. 52–84. For accessible accounts of the lifestyle at Grandmont see [B.] Lackner, [*The*] *Eleventh-Century Background* [*of Cîteaux*] Cistercian Studies Series 8 (Washington 1972) pp. 196–203 and Little, *Religious Poverty* pp. 79–83.

[74] *Regula Venerabilis Viri Stephani Muretensis*, *CC* 8 p. 66; Little, *Religious Poverty* p. 80; Chenu, *Nature, Man and Society* p. 239.

[75] Becquet, 'La règle de Grandmont' pp. 11–15; *PL* 204 (1855) cols 1136–75.

[76] Becquet, 'La règle de Grandmont' pp. 15–30 and 'L'"Institution": premier coutumier de l'ordre de Grandmont' pp. 15–32.

[77] *Ibid* pp. 18–21; 'La règle de Grandmont' pp. 35–6; *PL* 204 (1855) col 1151 cap XLVI 'Quod fratres in cella permaneant'.

[78] [Walter] Map, *De Nugis Curialium* ed and trans M.R. James, revised by C.N.L. Brooke and R.A.B. Mynors, (Oxford 1983) pp. 52–5, 112–5. 'Animals they have none, except bees; these Stephen allowed because they do not deprive neighbours of food; and their produce is collected publicly once a year all together'. *PL* 204 cols 1142–3 cap VI 'De bestiis non habendis'.

[79] Becquet, 'La règle de Grandmont' pp. 16–19; *PL* 204 cols 1136–62; Lackner, *Eleventh-Century Background* pp. 200–1.

the clerics in this sphere.[80] In addition, although the clerics should not, except in times of scarcity, seek alms, the *conversi* were eventually allowed to do so.[81] The *conversi* were thus given *de facto* supreme responsibility in the administration of the economy and the clerics were, to all intents and purposes, held enclosed as their pensioners.[82] Although the *conversi* were exhorted to fraternal charity and were specifically warned not to resort to domination, a severe imbalance in the relative proportion of *conversi* to clerics, perhaps in the ratio of as much as seven or eight to one in some cells, caused great tension and placed a heavy strain on this potentially weak link.[83] At times the *conversi* used their authority to persecute the clerics by half-starving them. Such a minor matter as to who rang the bell for collation, became, in such circumstances, a crucial point of difference. If it was not rung—and often it was not—no food was had by anyone.[84]

Although at first papal attitudes to Grandmont were generally benevolent, seeing in it a dynamic order which could absorb and institutionalise the growing appeal of the eremitic life,[85] the crises between clerics and *conversi* led the Holy See to affirm its authority over this form of religious life which could, when diverted from its true *via ascetica*, move dangerously out of control. This insistence upon control did not please many contemporary followers of the life of the hermit. It was, in one case at least, considered to illustrate

[80] *Liber de Doctrina*, *CC* 8 pp. 3–62 caps XV and LIX; *BUL* 13; *PL* 202 (1855) col 1416; *BUL* 21; *PL* 204 col 1375; Becquet, 'La première crise pp. 287, 300.

[81] *PL* 204 cols 1143, 1145; Map, *De Nugis Curialium* pp. 114–5.

[82] Knowles, *From Pachomius to Ignatius* p. 33; Map, *De Nugis Curialium* pp. 113–4.

[83] Becquet, 'La première crise pp. 295–6 and n 45 p. 295. An obituary fragment from Grandmont *c.*1140–1150 bears witness to a ratio of one priest to every seven or eight *conversi*. Some degree of balance seems to have been restored by the early thirteenth century with a proportion then of one priest to two or three lay brothers being considered as an *optimum*, *ibid*, pp. 295, 323. See also C. Dereine, 'L'obituaire primitif de l'ordre de Grandmont', *BSAHL* 87 (1958–60) pp. 325–31 in which he deduces from an examination of Paris BN Lat MS 1138 a precise figure for the proportion of laymen to clerics of one hundred and thirty to twenty three and dates the manuscript to *c.*1120–1160.

[84] *BUL* 12, 19, 21, 22, 24; Becquet, 'La première crise' p. 316; Martène and Durand, *Thesaurus* I, cols 845–7; *PL* 202 col 1415, Bull of Urban III, 14 July 1186, 'Liceat vobis unius campanae pulsatione competentibus horis fratres vestros de laboribus ad ecclesiam convocare'.

[85] Becquet, 'La première crise' p. 283–5; Knowles, *From Pachomius to Ignatius* pp. 16–21.

the over-enthusiasm of a too-youthful pope who ought properly to be more concerned with the form of religious life rather than its spirit.[86] Allowing the *conversi* to be in command had led to the dissipation of the possessions of the Order, the refusal to render accounts and quarrels on innumerable minor matters.[87] Other Churchmen saw the brothers of Grandmont as the loiterers of eremitism, enmeshed in a set of bizarre institutions and with at least twice as many *conversi* as clerics.[88] Innocent saw the inherent weakness of the so-called Gospel Rule which could not be avoided by a simple re-classification of the Order of Grandmont amongst the emerging mendicant orders.[89] He stressed the legitimate character of certain corporate possessions, such as tithes, lands, mills and revenues, and allowed some collection of alms and the receiving of bequests.[90] He reduced the number of *conversi*, improved the economic condition of the cells and ordered that, in each one, a named cleric should be empowered to correct clerics and *conversi* alike.[91] This so improved the nature of the Order that later, a second *conversi* revolt was easily suppressed and an order of clerics, analogous to others, came into being after 1219.[92]

With his first reaction to the situation at Grandmont in mind, and after regulating his own household according to his personal *via ascetica* Innocent turned his attention to what was taking place in the monasteries and in the orders. As Pope he had neither the wish nor the capacity to direct the government of each monastery from Rome, but from the beginning of his pontificate he had announced

86 *Walther von de Vogelweide: Werke* ed J. Schaefer (Darmstadt 1972) p. 226. 'Dâ weinte ein klôsenaere, er klagete gote sîniu leit: Owê der bâbest ist ze junc: hilf, hêrre, dîner kristenheit!' 'Far away in a cell, I heard much lamentation. A hermit was weeping there: he was lamenting his sufferings to God: Alas, the Pope is too young: O Lord, help your Christendom!' The date is probably shortly after 1201. I am grateful to Dr W.J. Jones for this reference and its translation.

87 Becquet, 'La première crise' p. 316.

88 *Ibid* p. 322–4.

89 *Ibid* p. 324.

90 *BUL* 40, 41, 44, 45; Becquet, 'La première crise' p. 319; Lecler, 'Histoire de l'Abbaye de Grandmont', *BSAHL* 58 pp. 73–6.

91 *Ibid* p. 74; *BUL* 40, 41, 42, 45, 46, 53 and especially 54 for the Bull of 24 December 1211 in which Innocent III confided the reform of Grandmont to the Archbishop of Bourges and the Cistercian abbots of La Pré and Varennes.

92 Becquet, 'La première crise' p. 324.

that he would wish to favour and develop existing regular religious institutions.[93] He began with the Benedictines.[94]

These monasteries still followed the Rule of St Benedict and maintained their historic role as instruments of the papacy. They were more effective at some times than at others in this role, and in some monasteries more than others. By the end of the twelfth century greater centralisation ought to have resulted from increasd papal jurisdiction but autonomy, built into the Rule itself, still perpetuated the individual nature of each monastery.[95] It must also be said that not all popes had the necessary vigour to reach those on the periphery.

The Benedictine family was very wide. It included traditional Black monk houses, the monastery of Cluny with all its dependencies and the hundreds of Cistercian foundations which sprang up across Europe. In Italy the congregations of Camaldoli, Vallombrosa and Fonte Avellana made up another great religious reserve with a broader Benedictine tradition.[96] Some monasteries were attached jurisdictionally to a mother house but the greater number were without any links at all, remaining isolated, one from another, and united only in their observance of the same rule.[97] Some were firmly under episcopal jurisdiction, others in receipt of papal privileges and some entirely exempt from their diocesan bishop. The degree of internal discipline varied considerably.

The role of the bishops themselves in monastic reform was considered by Innocent in the first year of his pontificate. He wrote to the bishop of Périgueux that since the Pope, who has general control of all churches, could not be everywhere in person, he wished irregularities to be removed by his brethren the bishops who shared his pastoral care.[98] Mandates to individual bishops thus allowed them to discover the moral and material state of religious houses by canonical visitation with subsequent corrections in head

93 Cheney, *Innocent III* p. 180.

94 P. Schmitz, *Histoire de l'Ordre de Saint Benoît* 3 (Maredsous 1948) pp. 42–55; Berlière, 'Innocent III et les monastères bénédictins', *RB* 20–22 (1920) pp. 22–42, 145–59; Maccarrone, *Studi* pp. 223–46.

95 Berlière, 'Innocent III et les monastères bénédictins' p. 22.

96 *Ibid* pp. 23–6.

97 Knowles, *From Pachomius to Ignatius* p. 6.

98 *Register* I, 445, p. 668. Letter of 5 December 1198 to Raymond, bishop of Périgueux 'Et quoniam ubique presentia corporali adesse non possumus'.

and members. While he did not hesitate to grant to monasteries the special protection of the Holy See or to recognise the *libertas* of certain religious houses, he was always watchful in cases of tithe exemption and visitation.[99] He never failed to show respect for acquired rights and particularly exercised this in the promise of obedience made by abbots to their respective bishops.[100] He counted on his legates to supplement the work of diocesan bishops; granting them wide powers of correction and extending their jurisdiction over any exempt houses of Benedictines or even of canons regular which were inaccessible to their bishops and so subject to no other Rule than Rome.[101]

But if Innocent knew how to defend episcopal rights, he wished also to establish a clear distinction, both in principle and in fact, between the discipline of an abbot in his monastery and the jurisdiction of the diocesan bishop.[102] He recognised the right of the abbot to watch over and to maintain discipline, leaving the bishop in full possession of his right to intervene in contentious matters. Once he had established this distinction, Innocent could more vigorously defend the real rights of the monasteries, seeking a balance between those rights and legitimate aspirations. Innocent was most anxious to conserve the distinctive character of monasticism of which solitude and retreat were two essential elements.[103] He regarded journeys and time spent in the world, especially in litigation, as incompatible with the peace of the cloister[104] and was always ready to combat the tendency of the *gyrovagus* or wandering monk to break with the stability of the monastery.[105] Yet he showed himself sympathetic to the concept of *transitus*, the passage from one order to another more severe.[106] Thus a Benedictine

[99] Berlière, 'Innocent III et les monastères bénédictins' pp. 27–33.

[100] *Ibid* p. 28.

[101] Schreiber, *Kurie und Kloster* I pp. 207–09 for some discussion of the emancipation of monasteries from episcopal authority.

[102] Berlière, 'Innocent III et les monastères bénédictins' pp. 29–31.

[103] *Ibid* pp. 33–5.

[104] *Register* I, 161, pp. 229–30. Letter of 30 April 1198, 'Viris religiosis, et his praecipue qui beati Benedicti regulam sunt professi, non credimus expedire, ut, otio claustrali postposito, contra instituta sui ordinis discurrant per curias seculares aut secularibus negotiis involvantur'.

[105] *Rule of St Benedict* ed J. McCann (London 1952) Cap I, De generibus monachorum, pp. 14–17, *semper vagi et numquam stabiles*.

[106] M.A. Dimier, 'Saint Bernard et le droit en matière de *Transitus*', *RM* 43 (1953) pp. 48–82; G. Picasso, 'San Bernardo e il '*transitus*' dei monachi', in *Studi su S.*

could pass to the Order of Cîteaux but it was not possible for a Cistercian to transfer to a Benedictine house.[107] His statement, made in 1206, in the case of a Durham monk, became the classic justification for such a transfer *ad arctiorem ordinem*, to a stricter way of life.[108]

Innocent was well-informed on the financial and disciplinary state of the Benedictines through canonical visitation, details from legates, complaints from bishops or even from monks themselves.[109] He was also uniquely informed through personal experience, acquired through sometimes prolonged visits.[110] In particular, these visits showed him that the general indebtedness of a house was nearly always accompanied by a lowering of disciplinary standards, reinforcing his view that the *via ascetica* required adequate material provision.[111] Such visits were local, within the Patrimony, and made in his capacity as bishop of Rome. Here and close to home, he was assured of producing and sustaining a salutary moral effect.[112]

We know that, in the summer of 1202, Innocent, with a few cardinals, stayed at Subiaco.[113] On the steep cliff above the lakes of Nero,[114] he found two monasteries where he stayed for a few days

---

*Bernardo di Chiaravalle: Nell'ottavo centenario della Canonizzazione* (Rome 1975) pp. 182–200.

107 Berlière, 'Innocent III et les monastères bénédictins' p. 35; *PL* 215 cols 874–5.

108 *Ibid*, 'Cum ergo dilectus filius R. monachus vester, ad fratres Cisterciensis ordinis transmigraverit, non ut ordini vestro aliquatenus derogaret, sed ut apud eos vitam duceret arctionem'. For an interesting discussion of the problems of transfer from Grandmont to Cîteaux, see Becquet, 'La première crise' pp. 295–6.

109 Berlière, 'Innocent III et les monastères bénédictins' pp. 35–8.

110 *Ibid* p. 39; [L.V.] Delisle, 'Itinéraire d'Innocent III, [dressé d'après les actes de ce pontife',] *BEC* (1857) pp. 500–34 especially p. 509.

111 Berlière, 'Innocent III et les monastères bénédictins' pp. 37, 149–56.

112 *Ibid* p. 39. On monasteries in general in the Patrimony see *Monasticon Italiae*, I, Roma e Lazio ed F. Caraffa (Cesena 1981) and for a social and economic background to the region, see the important study by P. Toubert, *Les Structures du Latium Mediéval: Le Latium Méridional et la Sabine du ix à la fin du xii siècle*, 2 vols (Rome 1973).

113 Hampe, 'Innocenz' III in Subiaco 1202' pp. 509–35; *Monasticon Italiae* I pp. 172–5; [Muratori,] *Chronicon Sublacense [593–1369,]* 24, VI, ed R. Morghen (Bologna 1927) pp. 34–7.

114 Hampe, 'Innocenz' III in Subiaco 1202' pp. 519–21. This was the former *Sublaqueum*, site of the imposing imperial villa and the three artificial lakes created by damming the river Anio and only finally destroyed in 1305.

and preached.[115] The upper one, the Sacro Speco, enclosed the cave where for three years, the young hermit Benedict had been instructed in the practice of asceticism.[116] The sight of the excellent discipline maintained there by its monks gave this pope great pleasure.[117] To demonstrate his deep regard for this community, he made a generous gift of six pounds annually from the Apostolic Camera for the use of the prior and brothers,[118] making a special present of a further twenty pounds for new habits for the monks and a two-coloured chasuble to honour God and St Benedict at the altar.[119]

Things were, however, quite different lower down the mountain. At the sister monastery of Santa Scholastica,[120] more important, more richly endowed and more involved with the secular world of the feudal nobility, grave abuses were revealed by Innocent.[121] While there was neither silence nor abstinence, there was embezzling of revenues and a general laxity which included the abbot.[122] Innocent acted quickly to remedy this deplorable situation, at the root of which lay that possession of personal property,

[115] *Chronicon Sublacense* p. 34. 'In illis diebus venit dominus Innocencius papa tercius ... qui personaliter cum paucis cardinalibus venit ad monasterium, visitavit et pluribus diebus stetit; predicavit ibidem et monasterium reformavit...'.

[116] *Monasticon Italiae* I pp. 172–3; *Grégoire le Grand: Dialogus I*, Sources chrétiennes, 251 (Paris 1978); Lawrence, *Medieval Monasticism* p. 19.

[117] *PL* 214 col 1062, September 1202. 'Accedentes causa devotionis ad locum quem beatus Benedictus suae conversionis primordio consecravit, et invenientes vos ibi secundum institutionem ipsius *laudabiliter* Domino famulari ...'. Berlière, 'Innocent III et les monastères bénédictins' p. 40.

[118] *Chronicon Sublacense* pp. 34–6 for the whole text; Potthast I, 1720, 1 September 1202. 'Priori et fratribus iuxta specum b. Benedicti regularem vitam servantibus sex libras usualis monetae de camera b. Petri singulis annis percipiendas concedit'. Also Potthast I, 1835, 24 February 1203.

[119] *Chronicon Sublacense* p. 36 '...et pro vestibus monachorum emendis xx libras presencialiter elargimur, planetam de cocco bis tincto Deo et beato Benedicto ad altaris officium offerentes'. For details of the fresco by ? *Magister* Conxolus depicting Innocent III with St Benedict and this privilege at the Sacro Speco, see Sibilia, 'L'Iconografia di Innocenzo III' pp. 75–8 and Ladner, *Die Papstbildnisse* pp. 68–72.

[120] *Monasticon Italiae* I pp. 174–5; *PL* 214 cols 1064–6; Berlière, 'Innocent III et les monastères bénédictins' p. 40.

[121] Potthast I, 1734, 'Abbati et conventui Sublacensi scribit de quibusdam vitiis emendandis, quae inter monachos illius coenobii irrepserant'. Dated September 1202.

[122] *Chronicon Sublacense* p. 35 'quia abbas et prior circa correptionem delinquentium erant nimium negligentes'. Also *PL* 214 col 1066.

against which St Benedict had so energetically fought in the Rule.[123] In the Decretal *Cum ad monasterium* of February 1203,[124] emanating from his visit to Subiaco, Innocent made the particular declaration that 'since the abdication of all personal property, as with the practice of chastity, is so essential in the monastic rule, even the Pope himself has not the right to abrogate it'.[125] His decree for Subiaco thus became one part of his code of reformed monasticism.[126]

In June and July 1208, Innocent stayed at San Germano[127] in the plain below St Benedict's own monastery of Cassino, midway between Rome and Naples.[128] Several times he went up the mountain to stay at this, the most ancient of monasteries, where he personally examined the accounts, considered the state of the various monastic offices and brought to light certain malpractices.[129] He addressed a severe reprimand to Abbot Roffredo,[130] reminding him of his obligations under the Rule and threatening him with canonical penalties if he did not hasten to revive that discipline lost through his own fault.[131] He also obliged Roffredo to repay the deficit in revenue and to increase the hospitality of the house without recourse to further exactions.[132]

[123] *RSB* Cap XXXIII, Siquid debeant monachi proprium habere, pp. 84–7; *Chronicon Sublacense* p. 35.

[124] *Corpus Iuris Canonici* ed A. Friedberg 2 vols (Leipzig 1879) II, Decretal of Gregory IX, III, 35, 6, cols 599–600. De statu monachorum et canonicorum regularium. *PL* 214 cols 1064–66; Potthast I, 1734; *Chronicon Sublacense* pp. 34–6, Cum ad monasterium sublacensem personaliter venissemus ...'.

[125] *Ibid* p. 36. 'Nec extimet abbas quod super habenda proprietate possit cum aliquo monacho dispensare, quoniam abdicatio proprietatis sicut et custodia castitatis adeo est annexa regule monachali *ut contra eam ne summus pontifex possit licenciam indulgere*'.

[126] Maccarrone, *Studi* p. 225.

[127] *Ignoto monacho Cistercensi* p. 34. 'Mccviij idem papa mense Iulii apud Sanctum Germanum in terra sancti Benedicti curiam tenuit'; *PL* cols 1593–4; Delisle, 'Itinéraire d'Innocent III' p. 521.

[128] For a recent general background to Monte Cassino, see L. Fabiani, *La terra di S. Benedetto: studio storico-giuridico sull'abbazia di Montecassino dell'viii al xiii secolo* 3 vols, Miscellanea Cassinese, vols 33–34 (Montecassino 1968) and vol 42 (Montecassino 1980). More specific is the important work by H.E.J. Cowdrey, *The Age of Abbot Desiderius: Montecassino, the Papacy and the Normans in the Eleventh and Early Twelfth Centuries* (Oxford 1983) especially pp. 1–45.

[129] Potthast I, 3470; Berlière, 'Innocent III et les monastères bénédictins' pp. 40–1.

[130] Potthast I, 374; *PL* 215 cols 1593–1600.

[131] *Ibid* cols 1593–4.

[132] *Ibid*; Berlière, 'Innocent III et les monastères bénédictins' p. 41.

Innocent demonstrated the importance he attached to the reform of Cassino by the energetic repression of abuses which he had already identified at Subiaco. In September 1215, he drew up a series of statutes to be observed at Cassino,[133] including the abolition of all personal property and peculation, formal interdiction against the alienation of revenues and goods, the restoration of discipline in the community, strict enclosure and the provision of revenues for the sick and poor in the hospital.[134]

The case of Cassino highlighted one particular problem. The choice of an abbot was crucial since upon him depended not only the state of discipline but also the state of the monastic economy, paradoxically so vital to the *via ascetica*.[135] Innocent himself called particular attention to the necessity of making a good choice.[136] The lack of precision in the Rule on the election of the abbot was a perpetual source of trouble.[137] Nor was Innocent any less concerned to ensure the strictest supervision of monastic recruitment. He acted to safeguard the freedom of vocation by criticising all constraint, forbidding the entry of young children and by making a one-year novitiate obligatory for all recruits.[138] Although such reforms were of temporary benefit, none could be really thorough or long-lasting, since they depended, in the last resort, upon individual interpretation in different houses, a particular weakness of the Rule itself.[139]

One major experiment and institutional innovation did, however, mark a new stage in breaking down the isolationism and particularism of some old Benedictine houses.[140] In February 1203,

[133] *PL* 217 cols 249–53; L. Tosti, *Storia della badia di Monte Cassino*, 3 vols (Naples 1842–3) 2 pp. 289–92.

[134] *Ibid* p. 289; Potthast I, 4996, 'Ad monasterii Casinensis reformationem plura capitula statuit', 20 September 1215.

[135] Berlière, 'Innocent III et les monastères bénédictins' pp. 149–51.

[136] *PL* 214 col 168, '... gaudemus plurimum et electionis canonicae apostolicum libenter impertimur assensum'.

[137] Knowles, *From Pachomius to Ignatius* p. 6.

[138] *PL* 214 cols 255–6 speaks of forcible entry into Reading Abbey; *PL* 215 cols 1175–6 tells of a recruit taken to the monks of Clairvaux while ill and *PL* 214 cols 429–30 from Pisa 'unde multa mala noscuntur saepius provenire, cum infirmi ad monasterium iam translati et emissa professione, postquam de infirmitatibus convaluerint, habitum religionis abjiciant et ad propria revertantur'.

[139] Berlière, 'Innocent III et les monastères bénédictins' p. 156.

[140] See the important study by Maccarrone, *Studi* pp. 226–46; also U. Berlière, 'Les chapitres généraux de l'Ordre de S. Benoît' *RB* 18 (1901) pp. 364–98; 'Innocent III et les monastères bénédictins' pp. 156–9; Cheney, *Innocent III* pp. 231–4.

he took an initiative to summon monastic heads to meet together in six provincial chapters for the improvement of discipline in those monasteries immediately subject *nullo medio* to the Holy See.[141] In each of the six regions, a small group of abbots and bishops was appointed to nominate visitors with papal authority *vice nostra*, to go round the monasteries, consider reform and make the necessary corrections.[142] Innocent was well aware of the novelty of these solemn chapters and promised that if the experiment should succeed, he would transform it into a permanent institution to be celebrated each year in a different place.[143] Had this programme been realised, it would have radically transformed life within exempt monasteries. That this experiment of 1203 does not seem to have materialised and could not therefore be transformed into a permanent canonical norm, did not cause Innocent to abandon his idea of direct intervention.[144] The idea came from his experience in the Patrimony and had it worked, would have brought the exempt monasteries into a kind of regional or national congregation, united by an annual chapter and controlled by visitors mandated by the same chapter.[145] In November 1208 another more limited apostolic visitation was organised throughout Tuscany and as far south as Viterbo and Rieti.[146]

If some of these attempts were the fruits of Innocent's own ideas and reforming activity, others give an interesting insight on local initiatives, which he was able to enlarge and develop. In 1206, the archbishop of Lund informed the pope that he wished to unite all the Benedictine monasteries of Denmark by instituting an annual chapter with the abbot of Lund as *rector*.[147] They were weak for

141 *PL* 214 cols 1173–4, 'monasteria per Tusciam, Marchiam et ducatum Spoletanum constituta, *nullo medio* ad Romanum Ecclesiam pertinentia'; Maccarrone, *Studi* pp. 328–30.

142 *Ibid* pp. 228–34; Cheney, *Innocent III* pp. 231–5. These provincial chapters were to be held at Perugia and Piacenza for Northern and Central Italy, at Paris, Limoges and Cluny for the kingdom of France and in London for all English monasteries. Notable omissions were Rome and Upper and Lower Lazio, for which the Pope provided directly, the whole of Southern Italy, Germany, the Iberian peninsula, Ireland, Scotland, Scandinavia including the kingdom of Denmark and Hungary.

143 Maccarrone, *Studi* pp. 234–5.

144 *Ibid* pp. 241–2.

145 Cheney, *Innocent III* p. 233.

146 *PL* 215 col 1490; Potthast I, 3539; Maccarrone, *Studi* p. 242.

147 18 January 1206, *PL* 215 cols 775–6; Potthast I, 2663; Maccarrone, *Studi* pp. 244–6.

lack of common customs and this would produce uniform observance.[148] Innocent showed himself favourable but cautious, asking for a report on the institution at the end of four years.[149] In 1207, the canons regular of the diocese of York proposed annual reunions for the discussion of reform[150] while in 1210 a general chapter of all the abbots of the province of Rouen was established.[151] In 1215, at the Fourth Lateran Council, Innocent transformed provincial practices such as these into the law of the whole Church. Canon 12 of this Council, *In Singulis Regnis*, henceforward obliged those abbots and priors, both exempt and non-exempt, of Benedictine and Augustinian houses, to meet together in triennial General Chapters.[152] A more permanent organ of monastic reform, which would maintain monastic discipline and lead towards Innocent's view of a *via ascetica*, had thus been created by giving one particular General Chapter, that of the Cistercians, the status of an approved model.[153]

The presence in the twelfth century of the new order of Cistercians should have represented for Innocent III the ideal *via ascetica* in operation through the first real order in the Church.[154] The Cistercians had faced the problem of autonomous abbeys implicit in the Rule of St Benedict and had succeeded in reconciling this autonomy with the need to preserve standards and ensure uniformity of observance—the need to keep the original ideal from dilution as new foundations proliferated. Their solution was to create a strong federal framework which ensured strict and uniform observance of the Rule by a system of mutual supervision. In this, the chief agencies were the annual General Chapter[155] and the system of filiation between mother and daughter houses.[156] The

[148] Cheney, *Innocent III* p. 233.

[149] *PL* 215 cols 775–6.

[150] *PL* 215 cols 1128–9, 17 March 1207; Potthast I, 3045. Kirkham, Guisborough, Bridlington and Newburgh are all specified by name.

[151] *PL* 216 col 312, 20 August 1210; Potthast I, 4067 'ut semel in anno capitulum celebrent ... ac de quarto in quartum annum apostolorum limina visitent'.

[152] *COD* (3 ed Bologna 1973) Canon 12 pp. 240–1; Maccarrone, *Studi* pp. 246–62.

[153] *Ibid* p. 248.

[154] For a magisterial introduction to the Cistercian Order, see Lawrence, *Medieval Monasticism* pp. 146–66. I am especially indebted to this work. Also Knowles, *From Pachomius to Ignatius* pp. 23–30; Little, *Religious Poverty* pp. 90–6.

[155] J.B. Mahn, *L'Ordre Cistercien et son gouvernement* (Paris 1951).

[156] F. Van der Meer, *Atlas de l'Ordre Cistercien* (Amsterdam-Brussels 1965) and F. Vongrey and F. Hervay, 'Notes critiques sur l'Atlas de l'Ordre Cistercien', *ASOC* 23 (1967) pp. 115–52.

General Chapter was the most distinctive and influential innovation and hence, the most imitated, not only by the Benedictines and canons but later carried to its logical conclusion by the mendicant orders.[157] It made the Cistercians into an international order, whose monks could be used as papal agents, the frontier guards of faith in all parts of Christendom and even beyond.[158] Furthermore, their observance claimed to be of the most literal kind, a return to the primitive usage and exact letter of the Rule of St Benedict.[159] This combination of simple austerity and dynamic central organisation brought spectacular success—but it did not last. Papal privileges were sought and granted; gifts of lands and churches brought demands of exemption from tithe payments and attendance at diocesan synods.[160] The irony was that the Order, having renounced wealth in favour of apostolic poverty, had by the end of the twelfth century, acquired a well-deserved reputation for avarice and acquisitiveness.[161] Furthermore, while the monks held tenaciously to the belief that their privileges were immutable, popes from Alexander III onwards fought strenuously for the principle that such privileges might, in certain circumstances, be revoked.[162] This problem came to a head during the pontificate of Innocent III.[163]

Innocent was particularly familiar with the Cistercians of the Patrimony and, above all, with the two great houses of Fossanova and Casamari, which he singled out for special favour.[164] His

[157] Canivez, I (Louvain 1933); Lawrence, *Medieval Monasticism* p. 160.

[158] B.M. Bolton, 'The Cistercians in Romana', *SCH* 13 pp. 169–81 especially pp. 170–3.

[159] Lawrence, *Medieval Monasticism* p. 147.

[160] Maccarrone, 'Primato Romano e Monasteri' pp. 75–107 for a wide-ranging study of papal privileges to the Cistercian Order.

[161] Severest critic of all was Walter Map, *De Nugis Curialium* pp. 85–113 who calls them the Jews of Europe.

[162] Maccarrone, 'Primato Romano e Monasteri' pp. 80–2 especially n 101.

[163] *Ibid* pp. 106–7.

[164] *I Cistercensi e il Lazio*, Atti delle giornate di studio dell'Istituto di Storia dell'Arte dell'Università di Roma, 17–21 Maggio 1977 (Rome 1978); *Monasticon Italiae* I pp. 104–5. The new altar at Fossanova was consecrated by Innocent III on 19 June 1208, Potthast I, 3465 and he gave one hundred pounds 'pro consummatione aedificii ejusdem ecclesiae', *Gesta* CXLIV; Casamari was given two hundred ounces of gold *pro fabrica ipsius*, *ibid* but the building was only completed in 1217 and consecrated by Honorius III. See P. Pressutti, *Regesta Honorii Papae III* 2 vols (Rome *1888–95) I p. 134;* F. Farina e B. Fornari, *L'architettura cistercense e l'abbazia di Casamari* (Frosinone 1978); Maccarrone, *Studi* p. 224; *PL* 216 col 21.

reputation amongst the Cistercians of this area remained high and the monk of Santa Maria di Ferraria reported that, after his death, there were verifiable healing miracles at his tomb.[165] Not so amongst Cistercians elsewhere! Later Cistercian historiography bears witness to the very real aversion of the Order to this pope. Caesarius of Heisterbach[166] and Ralph of Coggeshall[167] both report how Innocent was called to order by the Blessed Virgin Mary herself for failing in his indulgence to the Cistercians. An unknown Cistercian abbot, who happened to find himself in Perugia in July 1216, at the very moment of the Pope's death, saw in a vision that Innocent was in danger of eternal punishment.[168] Even more telling was the widely diffused vision of St Lutgard of Tongeren[169] to whom Innocent had appeared after his death. He told her of his narrow escape from Hell, which he had deserved on account of three unspecified sins, through the intercession of the Virgin.[170]

Innocent had earned this dreadful reputation amongst the Cistercians for having challenged the nature and extent of many of their

[165] *Ignoto monacho Cistercensi* p. 36. 'Sepultus est in Urbe Perusii provincie Tuscie: ad cuius tumulum, sicut dicitur, ceci, maniaci et aliis infirmitatibus detenti Deo favente sanati sunt'.

[166] *Caesarii Heisterbacensis Monachi Ordinis Cisterciensis Dialogus Miraculorum*, ed J. Strange 2 vols (Köln 1851) 2 Cap VI pp. 7–8.

[167] *Radulphi de Coggeshall Chronicon Anglicanum*, ed J. Stevenson, *RS* (London 1875) pp. 130–3.

[168] *Chronica Minor Auctore Minorita Erphordiensi*, ed O. Holder-Egger, *MGH, SS*, 24, p. 196, 'quidam abbas... Cysterciensis, veniens cum suis ad curiam Romanam, qui cepit sompnum meridie in prato ante Perusium, viditque visionem hunc habens modum. Vidit, inquam, ille abbas in sompno ad orientalem plagam Dominum sedentem in excelso throno, faciem habentem versus occasum, circumstante exercitu angelorum in prato; viditque ab occidentali parte eiusdem prati hominem toto corpore nudum, sed infula pontificali decoratum, currentem velocissime versus sedentem in throno et alta voce clamantem: 'Miserere mihi misero, misericordissime Deus'! Et vidit, quod insequebatur illum currentem magnus draco subito persequens eum, ut devoraret ipsum; et veniens ante sedentem in throno alta voce draco clamavit: 'Iuste iudica, iustissime iudex'. Et cum hoc abbas vidisset et audisset, protinus evigilavit, et visio disparuit, nec illius disceptacionis exitum ullatenus scire potuit. Cumque abbas ascendisset in civitatem Perusii, que in monte sita est, audivit sonitum quasi campanarum et luctum plangencium et voces lamentancium et dicencium: *'Heu dominus papa Innocencius defunctus est'*.

[169] Thomas de Cantimpré, *Vita Lutgardis Virgine* ed G. Henschenius, *ASB*, 3 June (Antwerp 1701) p. 245–7.

[170] *Ibid*, 'Tres causae sunt, quare sic crucior: per has autem eram dignissimus aeterno supplicio tradi: sed per intercessionem piissimae Virginis Mariae cui monasterium aedificavi, in fine poenitu et aeternam mortem evasi'.

privileges.[171] The longest lasting dispute was over tithe exemption, which was not resolved until the Lateran Council.[172] The earliest dispute over the obligation to participate in the General Chapter, broke out in 1198 when he himself excused the abbot of Sambucina whom he had engaged to preach the Crusade.[173] Innocent's differences with the Order were further highlighted by the whole question of crusade taxation. His idea was that the whole Church should participate by means of a subsidy imposed universally and without exception.[174] The open and tenacious opposition demonstrated by the Cistercians in this matter was judged by Innocent to be a scandal for the Church.[175] At the end of 1202, in a letter to the abbot of Cîteaux and the four daughter abbeys, he even issued a veiled threat that he might abolish the Order altogether.[176] He reported that *rumores sinistri* had reached Rome, that the Order was deviating from its distinctive custom of simplicity, *consuetudo simplicitatis*, through endless litigation and assertions of superiority. Furthermore, he feared that in the bitter quarrel between Cîteaux and its daughters, there might be repeated just that discord which had divided the Order of Grandmont.[177]

It was, however, on the matter of preaching, whether in evangelising pagans in Livonia and Prussia, in the struggle against heresy or in announcing the Crusade that Innocent revealed the deepest divergence with the Cistercians in regard to their own conception of their position in the Church.[178] In 1198, he had authorised the Cistercian Fulk de Neuilly to encourage religious of no matter which order *tam de monachis nigris quam albis* to the task of preaching.[179] In April 1200, he launched an appeal to all Cistercian

[171] Maccarrone, 'Primato Romano e Monasteri' p. 112.

[172] *Ibid* pp. 125–31; *COD*, Canon 55 pp. 260 and Canon 57, p. 261; C.R. Cheney, 'A letter of Pope Innocent III and the Lateran decree on Cistercian Tithe-paying', *Cîteaux Commentarii Cistercienses* (1962) pp. 146–51.

[173] *Register* I, 302, pp. 430–33, 343, p. 513, 358, pp. 538–40; Potthast I, 335, 'Abbatem de Sambucino Siculis verbum Dei praedicantem eosque ad obsequium crucifixi citantem pro excusato habeant'.

[174] *Register* I, 257, pp. 488–90; Potthast I, 913 and 915, 28 and 30 December 1199.

[175] Maccarrone, 'Primato Romano e Monasteri' pp. 112–3.

[176] Canivez, I p. 243 n55; *PL* 214 cols 1107–08, 'Eligeremus enim potius paucos offendi, quam *totum ordinem aboleri*'.

[177] *Ibid.* 'Occasionem scandali et dissensionis materiam praecipue fugientes, ne forte, sicut Grandimontenses, in derisum et fabulum incidatis'.

[178] Maccarrone, 'Primato Romano e Monasteri' p. 122.

[179] *Register* I, 398, p. 597.

abbots and monks that they should co-operate in the work of evangelisation being conducted jointly by Bishop Albert of Riga and the Cistercian Theodore of Treyden in Livonia.[180] In a Bull of 1201, Innocent proposed to reunite all the religious missionaries of this area, whether monks, canons regular or professed religious of other orders, into one regular observance *unum regulare propositum*, wearing one single monastic habit so as to adapt them in the most perfect way to their preaching of the Gospel.[181] But such a papal preaching programme was inimical to the Cistercian General Chapter which in 1200 had punished its own monks for introducing such novelty.[182] Innocent countered this disapproval by claiming in October 1206 to have conceded *potestas praedicandi* to Cistercians active on the Eastern frontiers and specially to Poles working amongst pagan Prussians in the regions of Lokno and Gniezno.[183] These monks were preaching *de nostra licentia* said the Pope.[184] He was well aware that they were suffering by being classed as wandering monks and *gyrovagi*, two categories stigmatised in the Rule of St Benedict because they lived outside their monastery.[185] Further, they had been induced to abandon their evangelisation. To avoid both danger and accusation, Innocent presented to the General Chapter in 1212 a new form of discipline for these Cistercian missionaries, placing them under the vigilance of the archbishop of Gniezno whose job it would be to choose those qualified for this office and present them to the Chapter for approval.[186] The General Chapter of 1213 reluctantly approved this papal request but revealed the Order's rigidity towards the concept of the preaching monk.[187] The obstacle lay perhaps in the nature of

[180] Potthast I, 1026; [M.H.] Vicaire, ['Vie Commune et Apostolat Missionaire. Innocent III et] la Mission de Livonie', in *Mélanges M-D. Chenu*, Bibliothèque Thomiste 37, (Paris 1967) pp. 451–66; Maccarrone, *Studi*, pp. 262–72. Albert of Buxhoven, Bishop of Riga (1199–1229); Theodore of Treyden (d. 1219).

[181] Maccarrone, *Studi* pp. 267–70.

[182] Canivez, I p. 251; Maccarrone, 'Primato Romano e Monasteri' p. 123 and n224.

[183] *PL* 215 cols 1009–11; Potthast I, 2901, 27 October 1206; *PL* 216 cols 315–6; Potthast I, 4074; Henry, Archbishop of Gniezno and the monks Christian and Philip, 4 September 1210.

[184] *PL* 216, cols 668–70, 'olim de nostra licentia inceperunt seminare in partibus Prussiae verbum Dei'; Maccarrone, 'Primato Romano e Monasteri' p. 124.

[185] *Ibid*; *RSB* Cap I.

[186] *PL* 216 col 669.

[187] Canivez, I p. 414 n52. 'Taliter temperet rem gerendam, ut et summo pontifici satisfiat, nec rigor Ordinis enervetur'.

the Order itself, preventing it from responding to the new dynamic perspective revealed by Innocent. The contemplative vocation and retirement of the Cistercians 'in the embrace of Rachel' seemed to be forced into radical change by a ministry 'in the service of Leah'.[188] The Order's structure, based on the purity, discipline and rigour of the Rule, caused its lack of mobility. Innocent's ideal of monastic preaching would have to be realised elsewhere.

The way had been pointed by those Livonian missionaries as early as 1201 or 1202. Unless they were to cause scandal amongst newly converted Christians, the missionaries needed to display the deepest unity in faith and charity.[189] This outward conformity of Cistercians and canons regular in dress and observance, displayed all the aspects of the apostolic life, a way of life which Innocent himself spoke of as *superior*.[190] They had not turned their backs on the ideal of monk or canon in order to become pure evangelical preachers but they stressed the pre-eminent apostolic value of unanimity, that community of life for which the apostles had given the model in the Church of Jerusalem.[191] Nor was this always easy, especially for the Cistercians amongst them. Yet in their life of unanimity, there was a very conscious imitation of the apostles which might indeed have served as a point of departure for an equally apostolic ministry.[192]

Innocent III saw that the Church of the 'new' thirteenth century needed to reorientate its religious towards the missionary zeal of preaching the *vita apostolica*, and, by clear example, of living the *via ascetica*.[193] This was especially so in regard to the Cathars of Languedoc where the Cistercians had not matched those severe exponents of asceticism.[194] Nor were the Cistercians mistaken in seeing papal requirements as dangerous to their own traditions.

[188] Maccarrone, 'Primato Romano e Monasteri' p. 130.

[189] Bull of 19 April, 1201 printed in Maccarrone, *Studi* Appendix 3, pp. 334–7.

[190] Vicaire, 'La Mission de Livonie' p. 459; *Corpus Iuris Canonici*, ed A. Friedberg, II, p. 451.

[191] Maccarrone, *Studi* p. 268; Vicaire, 'La Mission de Livonie' pp. 455–6.

[192] *Ibid* pp. 460–1.

[193] Maccarrone, *Studi* p. 334, 'volens *hec moderna tempora* conformae prioribus et fidem catholicam propagae'.

[194] C. Thouzellier, 'La Pauvreté, arme contre l'Albigéisme en 1206' in *Hérésie et Hérétiques*, Storia e Letteratura 116 (Rome 1969) pp. 189–203; B.M. Bolton, 'Fulk of Toulouse: the Escape that Failed', *SCH* 12 pp. 83–93 and B. Hamilton, *Monastic Reform, Catharism and the Crusades (900–1300)* (London 1979).

The place occupied by the cenobitic life within the Church was to undergo a radical revolution in the face of the two new Mendicant Orders, Franciscans and Dominicans.[195]

From the beginning of his pontificate, Innocent had frequently intervened to judge those cases brought to him by individuals or groups who sought papal approval for their way of life.[196] Some of these he warmly commended for their *vita apostolica*.[197] Others he saw as penitential groups, while still more were directed towards diocesan preaching under the immediate vigilance of the local bishop.[198] He dealt with each case on merit, encouraging the presentation of *proposita* or statements of religious intention with a view to inserting them into existing institutions as appropriate. Two particular individuals needed special attention and so could not be dealt with in the normal way. In dealing with Francis and Dominic, Innocent drew on all the lessons he had learned from his experience of monastic and canonical reform. In their differing ways, both men wished to follow a *via ascetica* which would be difficult to formalise. He was helped in his task by the willingness of these two to obey him utterly—and he used this obedience to assimilate them successfully into the Church.[199]

When Francis came to Rome in 1210 with eleven companions to ask for papal approval of their way of life, Innocent acted in a special way to this direct request for confirmation.[200] They were not clerics but only simple laymen who dressed and acted as a penitential brotherhood.[201] They had not been assigned by their bishop any church in which to house their community and it is

[195] Maccarrone, 'Primato Romano e Monasteri' p. 124.

[196] Maccarrone, *Studi* pp. 278–300.

[197] B.M. Bolton, 'Innocent III's treatment of the *Humiliati*', *SCH* 8 pp. 73–82; Guy of Montpellier, 22 April 1198, *Register* I, 97, pp. 141–44; Potthast I, 96 and 102; Hospital of Santa Maria in Sassia, 18 June 1204, *PL* 215 cols 376–80; Potthast I, 2248; John de Matha and the Order of Trinitarians, *Register* I, 252, pp. 354–5; Potthast I, 483, 21 May 1198.

[198] G.G. Meersseman – E. Adda, 'Una communità di penitenti rurali in S. Agostino dal 1188 al 1236', *RHE* 49 (1954) pp. 343–90; Bernard Prim and his penitential community, *PL* 216 cols 289–93; Potthast I, 4014, 14 June 1210; *PL* 216 cols 648–50; Potthast I, 4567, 23 July 1212, sub magisterio et regimine Domini nostri Jesu Christi ac piisimi vicarii eius papae Innocentii et successorum eius'.

[199] A. Matanić, 'Papa Innocenzo III di fronte a S. Domenico e a S. Francesco' *Antonianum* 35 (1960) pp. 508–27.

[200] Grundmann, pp. 127–56; Maccarrone, *Studi* pp. 300–06.

[201] *Ibid* p. 301.

likely that they had already been advised to take the rule of an existing monastic or eremitic order. Within this, they may have been promised recognition as a penitential group. Francis, however, wanted nothing less than full canonical recognition of his way of life. In other words, to found a religious community similar in status and juridical form to those already existing, yet totally new in its inspiration and form of life—completely without possessions.[202] Innocent was aware of the dangers into which a refusal might lead such a passionate and determined seeker after asceticism. Heresy could easily follow. This was clearly a quite singular case to which Innocent gave unique oral confirmation on the understanding that a Rule, no matter how simple, should be written down.[203] He had this confirmation approved by the Cardinals in Consistory without using the accustomed Chancery formula *Religiosam vitam* and the members of this new community, now raised to the status of a *religio* approved by the Holy See, were tonsured, made clerics and granted the *licentia praedicandi ubique*.[204] Francis promised *obedentia et reverentia* to the Pope in an oath usually made only by the bishops of the region around Rome.[205] This was something quite new and showed the willingness of Innocent III to create a special link between the Holy See and this new Order which had arisen in an area immediately subject to the Papacy.[206] Innocent thus reserved to himself the obligations as diocesan bishop of the new community.[207] Once the issue of obedience was settled, Innocent was quite prepared to wait to see how this small group of mendicant lay preachers would develop.[208] It was worth taking the chance of a successful development being able to take root in such urban surroundings.

In September 1215, on the eve of the Fourth Lateran Council, Dominic appeared before Innocent to ask for approval of his

[202] *Ibid* pp. 302–04; Grundmann, pp. 127–35 especially n115 pp. 130–31.

[203] *Opuscula sancti patris Franciscii*, Bibliotheca Franciscana Ascetica Medii Aevii, I (2 ed Quaracchi 1941) p. 79. From St Francis's *Testament*, 'Et ego paucis verbis et simpliciter *feci scribi*; et dominus papa *confirmavit michi*'.

[204] Maccarrone, *Studi* p. 304, 324–6.

[205] *Ibid* p. 304 n2. 'Hic ergo concessis, beatus Franciscus gratias egit Deo et genibus flexis promisit domino papae obedientiam et reverentiam humiliter et devote'.

[206] Maccarrone, *Studi* pp. 304–5.

[207] *Ibid* p. 305.

[208] Grundmann, pp. 133–5.

community of mendicant preachers in Toulouse.[209] In addition to preaching more successfully than the Cistercians against the Cathars, Dominic was already a canon regular and had founded a house for women at Prouille and obtained sustenance from Bishop Fulk through a portion of diocesan tithes.[210] He now requested papal confirmation of the approval already given by his bishop which had already raised the status of the preachers at Toulouse to an *Ordo Praedicatorum.*[211] Innocent warmly supported this way of religious life. Indeed Canon 10 of the Council recommended the formation in each diocese of similar communities of preachers in the service of bishops.[212] He took into papal protection the convent at Prouille,[213] using it as a model for his Roman convent of San Sisto,[214] but was not willing to confirm immediately the *Ordo Praedicatorum.* He asked instead that Dominic and his companions should choose an already approved rule.[215] This agreed literally with the new norm of Canon 13 of the Council. Innocent seems to have made it clear that once Dominic had considered all the possibilities and still wished to have a preaching order, then this would be granted.[216] After Innocent's death, Honorius III confirmed the Bull to the Order of Preachers in December 1216[217] in the traditional Chancery formula *Religiosam vitam* and in 1220, a year before Dominic's death, the Order declared for the principle of corporate poverty.[218]

209 *Ibid* p. 141; Maccarrone, *Studi* p. 305; Jordan of Saxony, *Libellus de principiis ordinis praedicatorum*, ed H-C. Scheeben, in *Monumenta Historica S. Patris Nostri Dominici*, I (Rome 1935) p. 44.

210 *Monumenta diplomatica S. Dominici*, ed V.J. Koudelka and R.I. Loenertz (Rome 1966) pp. 56–8; Vicaire, *Saint Dominic* pp. 115–36; Grundmann, p. 211.

211 Maccarrone, *Studi* p. 306; Vicaire, *Saint Dominic* pp. 217–39.

212 *COD*, Canon 10, p. 239.

213 Grundmann, p. 211; Little, *Religious Poverty* pp. 152–8.

214 *Gesta* CXLIX, Ad costruenda aedificia Sancti Sixti, ad opus monialium, quingentas uncias auri regis et mille centum libras proviniensium. The work was begun *c.*1208. V.J. Koudelka, 'Le *monasterium tempuli* et la fondation dominicain de San Sisto', *AFP* 31 (1961) pp. 5–81; Maccarrone, *Studi* pp. 272–8.

215 M.H. Vicaire, 'Fondation, approbation, confirmation de l'ordre des Prêcheurs', *RHE* 47 (1952) pp. 123–41; Maccarrone, *Studi* p. 306.

216 *Ibid*; *COD*, Canon 13, p. 242.

217 *Monumenta diplomatica S. Dominici* pp. 86–7.

218 Vicaire, *Saint Dominic* pp. 310–11. Dominic had been deeply impressed by the example of Grandmont and had attempted to introduce the institution of *conversi* to take over temporal matters from the preachers. The first Dominican Chapter

*Via Ascetica*

In all these tasks, Innocent sought to maintain and hand on the true purpose and function of the Church. In so doing, he was able to resolve the papal quandary which all popes of the twelfth and early thirteenth centuries had to face. The administration of the Church seemed to many of them to be of paramount importance and the fact that there are no saints amongst the popes of this period may be seen as an indication of the immensity of this task. With Innocent III, however, the path to holiness, the *vita apostolica*, the *via ascetica* and the road to ultimate salvation could only be followed by constant reference to the Church's sure foundation. With such guidance, not only Innocent, but others were to succeed. Indeed, Dominic would perhaps have been acceptable to more than one pope, but without Innocent III there would have been no St Francis.

---

at Bologna in 1220 rejected his ideal, possibly because of Innocent's earlier strictures, choosing instead corporate poverty. *Processus Canonizationis S. Dominici apud Bononiam*, ed A. Walz, *MOPH* 16 (Rome 1935) 32.

Privilege to the Sacro Speco, Subiaco,
with the earliest fresco representation (damaged) of Innocent III
(Photograph: Brenda Bolton; by permission of the Prior of Subiaco.)

# VII

# NON ORDO SED HORROR : INNOCENT III 'S BURGUNDIAN DILEMMA

The final years of the twelfth century had seen, in Rome, the arrival of a new and determined young pope whilst, in Burgundy, the centennial celebrations of the Cistercian Order were taking place at the mother house of Cîteaux[1]. It was to be expected that some form of interaction would occur between the two events. Innocent III's immediate aim was to strengthen Christ's Church, no matter where it operated[2]. On the face of it, the Cistercian Order could have been expected to have been amongst his most important helpers. Unfortunately, the Order itself was facing problems. The original pattern of a mother house surrounded by respectful daughters was experiencing the difficulties which come with age. The daughter houses had grown increasingly more confident, more self-reliant and were inclined to make thrusting demands for more autonomy. Unless these strains were corrected, Innocent's wish to use them as the example by which other groups of monks and canons could be brought into a systematic form of existence would not be realized[3]. He aimed to influence the Cistercians towards an amicable solution as secretly as possible. Too open a discussion would not have helped Innocent in his search for an organisational model. Nor would it have helped the Order

---

1. J.-B. MAHN, *L'ordre cistercien et son gouvernement des origines au milieu du XIIIe siècle (1098-1265)*, 2 éd. Paris, 1951 ; J.-B. AUBERGER, *L'unanimité cistercienne primitive ; mythe ou réalité ?*, Cîteaux : Studia et Documenta, III, Achel, 1986 ; L. JANAUSCHEK, *Originum Cistercensum* I, Vienna, 1877.

2. *Innocentii III* : *Opera Omnia, Patrologia Latina* 214-7, éd. J.-P. MIGNE, Paris, 1855 ; M. MACCARRONE, «Primato romano e monasteri dal principio del secolo XII ad Innocenzo III», *Istituzione monastiche e istituzione canonicali in occidente 1123-1215*, Atti della Settimana internazionale di studi medioevali, Mendola, 28 agosto — 3 settembre 1977, Milan, 1980, pp. 49-132 ; B.M. BOLTON, «For the See of Simon Peter : the Cistercians at Innocent III 's nearest frontier», in J. LOADES éd., *Monastic Studies I*, Bangor, 1990, pp. 146-57.

3. *Ibid*, pp. 148-9 ; J.-M. CANIVEZ, *Statuta Capitulorum Generalium Ordinis Cisterciensis ab anno 1116 ad annum 1786*, 8 vols, Louvain, 1933-41, I, *Ab anno 1116 ad annum 1220*, Louvain, 1933.

to maintain its unity. It was in the interests of both parties to arrange matters discreetly.

The year 1203 was to be the occasion of Innocent's most serious attempt to resolve the issue[4]. He used as agents, Rainier, an outstanding Cistercian who was the Pope's personal confessor[5] and Gerald, abbot of Casamari, a Cistercian of equal standing who was being used at the time by the Pope to help to bring *pax et concordia* to the troubled relations between France and England[6].

Rainier took advantage of two circumstances to advance the Pope's cause. Innocent had decided to send out *litterae memorie*, sternly reminding Cîteaux and her four daughters of the need to give their full attention to organisation and election, particularly of abbots in the Order[7]. This gave the opportunity to Rainier to send an accompanying letter pointing out the seriousness of the situation. The letter was addressed to Arnald-Amaury, recently promoted as Abbot of Cîteaux[8], and was written as one Cistercian to another. About this time, Gerald of Casamari, papal legate to France, was returning from Rome to Paris to continue his attempts at peaceful negotiation between the kings, Philip Augustus and John of England. On the way, he aimed to attend the Cistercian General Chapter meeting at Cîteaux around the Feast of the Exaltation of the Holy Cross on 14 September. He was an ideal carrier for both the Pope's letters and Rainier's special delivery. To emphasize Gerald's credentials in case Arnald-Amaury should be in any doubt, Rainier highlighted the importance of Gerald's uncle, Gerald I, sixth abbot of Clairvaux (1170-1175/6)[9].

---

4. B. GRIESSER, «Rainer von Fossanova und sein Brief an Abt Arnald von Cîteaux (1203)», *Cistercienser Chronik* 60 (1953), pp. 151-67.

5. (?-d. 1207/1209), H. GRUNDMANN, «Zur Biographie Joachims von Flore und Rainers von Ponza», *Deutsches Archiv* 16 (1960), pp. 437-546 ; A. MANRIQUE, *Cisterciensium seu verius ecclesiasticorum Annalium a condito cistercio*, 4 vols, Lyon, 1649-1657, III, pp. 368-70.

6. Abbot of Casamari (1182-1209) ; *Gesta Innocentii PP. III*, PL, 214, cols XVII-CCXXVIII, CLXIX.

7. «Qui iam in registro iussit litteras memorie commendari», GRIESSER, «Rainer von Fossanova», p. 166.

8. Arnald Amaury (d. 1225), abbot of Poblet, Grandselve and Cîteaux (1202).

9. GRIESSER, «Rainer von Fossanova», p. 166 «deferente sibi eas domno G. abbate Casemarii nepote venerabilis ac beatissimi patris nostri Geraldi Clarevallensis sexti abbatis». Gerald I, *patria Lombardus ex abbate Fossanovae*, cruelly murdered, *Gallia Christiana in provincias ecclesiasticas distributa*, 4, Paris, 1728, p. 801.

Rainier's letter has not received the attention it undoubtedly deserves. It was edited for the first time in 1953[10] but has again lapsed into relative obscurity. It is therefore particularly appropriate that its importance to both the work of Innocent III and the Cistercian Order should be discussed in a volume to honour Professor Pacaut, much of whose professional life has been spent in Burgundy, that region of France so important in the history of monasticism.

Over a period of years, Cîteaux, founded in 1098 had become the head of an extensive family, colonizing the surrounding area with four «daughters» : La Ferté (1113), near Chalon-sur-Saône, Pontigny (1114), north of Auxerre, Clairvaux (1115) near Langres and, in the same year, Morimond between Langres and Troyes. A rich Burgundian vintage indeed but with the potential for turning somewhat sour as these elder daughters planted their own offshoots ! By the end of the twelfth century and in spite of the «safety valve» of the General Chapter, insistent demands were being heard from the elder daughters for shared authority with Cîteaux and a system of wider representation. Not only was this power struggle taking place within the Order but Cîteaux's daughters were also quarrelling bitterly amongst themselves. Innocent did not find this situation at all helpful and his *litterae memorie* pointed this out. Rainier's letter, coming as it did from a Cistercian, was a determined, internal and acerbic attempt to resolve the issue. «Truly», he stated, «unless drastic steps were taken to remedy matters, the Cistercians, instead of an Order, would become a horror, *non ordo sed horror*»[11].

Innocent's own earlier letter, of which the *litterae memorie* were somewhat sharp reminders, had been read to the assembled abbots at the General Chapter of 1198[12]. It was an earnest appeal from a new young pope. He set out the hopes and fears of his office, praying that Christ himself should protect the storm-tossed barque of Peter, turning the cold North wind round to the milder south and calming the wild sea. In a phrase he had already used to the cities of the Patrimony, he reminded the Order that, although Christ 's yoke was easy and his burden light, it was, nevertheless, of vital importance to take it up[13]. Martha was needed as well as Mary. He understood the Order's reluctance to be caught up in

10. Discovered in a fifteenth-century manuscript, Troyes 1511, 48 recto — 50 recto.

11. «Iam non ordo sed horror a plurimis estimetur», GRIESSER, «Rainer von Fossanova», p. 165.

12. CANIVEZ, I, pp. 221-4.

13. 16 April 1198. O. HAGENEDER and A. HAIDACHER, eds, *Die Register Innocenz'III, I, Pontifikatsjahr 1198-99*, Graz-Vienna-Köln, 1964-68, pp. 126-8 ; *PL* 214, cols 75-7 ; M. MACCARRONE, *Studi su Innocenzo III*, p. 15, note 1.

the chores of ministry and that they preferred, like Mary, to contemplate at the feet of the Lord but much was needed from them in the situation then facing the Church of Christ. The pope's burden was heavy and he relied upon the Cistercians in helping him to shoulder it[14]. The letter was well-received and it was agreed by the Chapter of 1198 that Innocent's name should be inscribed in the official records of the Order and even on the great Paschal candlestick in the abbey church of Cîteaux[15].

By 22 November 1202, another letter was needed from the Pope[16]. This was an exhortation specifically addressed to the Burgundian heartland of the Cistercian Order, to Cîteaux herself and the first four daughters. «Those who had earlier walked simply, had walked confidently», was Innocent's message. He regretted that the former spiritual footsteps of the Order which had spread its fame from sea to sea had not remained simple but instead had deteriorated into internal squabbling. There had also been interference with local bishops, interrupting pastoral relations with their flocks. The former good reputation of the Cistercians had become tarnished. This was not what he had expected or hoped for following their friendly reception of 1198. He ordered and warned Cîteaux and her daughters to hold fast to the simplicity and purity of their *propositum* or way of life, keeping their hands to the plough or they would risk being judged by other, harsher standards. Indeed, should they persist in quarrelling, they faced the danger that they might fall into the same scandal and derision as the Order of Grandmont[17] : «woe to those from whom scandal comes»[18]. Such woe, inferred Innocent, might mean the abolition of the whole Cistercian Order, something which he would not deliberately choose to do if it were at all possible to avoid. Such a fearsome disagreement was indeed serious, not only to Innocent's aim for a model which all could follow but to the whole concept of the Cistercians as the «new order» of monasticism. It was time for Rainier to act.

He wrote to the Abbot of Cîteaux who was the head of all Cistercians. In return for the spiritual rest and refreshment which he had received as a member of the Order, he begged to be allowed to write of matters both old and new which the Abbot might either use or discard as

14. CANIVEZ, I, pp. 222-4.

15. «Innocentius papa scribatur in canone et in cereo pascali», ibid, p. 232.

16. *PL* 214, cols 1107-8.

17. «Sicut Grandimontenses, in derisum et fabulam incidatis», *ibid*, col. 1108 ; B.M. BOLTON, «Via ascetica : a papal quandary», *Studies in Church History*, 22 (Blackwell, 1985), pp. 161-91, especially pp. 70-4.

18. Matthew, XVIII, 7.

he wished[19]. In some previous monastic community, unspecified in the letter, both he and Arnald-Amaury had together found solace in their study of the Scriptures, drawing out and exploring the hidden meanings. They found that the Order of Cîteaux, as the stable plant of the Lord, would not be easily divided by boldness or childishness. Their beloved Bernard[20], that latter-day Moses or Paul, had ruled the Cistercians for forty years, had fought against both Gilbert de la Porrée and Abelard, had founded Clairvaux and throughout, maintained the stability and ideals of the Order. Under him, the existence of Cîteaux and her four daughters could be compared with the first five churches of the Apostles and with the five great patriarchates. Cîteaux would thus be equated with Rome, both being necessary centres or seats of the spirit of the soul.

Other allusions abounded in the letter. Rainier described Cîteaux as being surrounded by four wheel-like structures : the daughter houses. The whole Church of Rome was similarly surrounded by the patriarchates. These wheels or circles, in each case, both support and are themselves supported, creating the necessary equilibrium and stability. Each is essential to the other for both Order and Church. To develop the biblical symbolism, he related La Ferté, the first daughter house, to Jerusalem and the primitive Church which, if not very populous, was firm in the faith of the first apostles. Pontigny was likened to Antioch, the home of the first christians ; Clairvaux compared with Alexandria and Morimond with Constantinople. «Our Order, with its close likeness to the Church of Christ, must not be allowed to destroy itself by inward-looking, self-centredness so that the true design which the Pope hoped to follow would not be available to him».

Rainier counselled Arnald-Amaury on the special attention which needed to be given to a harmonious relationship between Cîteaux, the centre of the Order and the centre of the four circles, should aim for spiritual equality by stressing the strength and equality of the daughter houses whose safety Cîteaux would support, neither oppressing them with burdens nor leaving them unprotected. He described his fears as to what might happen when mother and daughters came together in the Annual General Chapter. «Not without reason, O Reverend Father, do they use their words like swords for we have heard with perturbation and are disturbed that at your gathering, no longer are you at one, sharing, as it were, the supper of the Cistercian fathers but each one appearing to go his

19. GRIESSER, «Rainer von Fossanova», p. 163.

20. Bernard of Clairvaux (1090-1153).

own way[21]. No longer do you perform in common the necessary works and duties but each, hatefully and contentiously comes with punitive proclamations of accusation which do not proceed from the office of love. Spurious ordinations have been made which have no roots on high, nor are they then able to be established on a stable foundation. We are too much aware of these and similar abuses which are detrimental to the reputation of the whole Cistercian Order. The Pope himself is also aware of it». Rainier singles out for special rebuke the abbots of La Ferté and Pontigny who seem to have led the demands for more independance.

Examples of earlier divisions in the history of the Church, all associated with the number three are described by Rainier as being awful warnings. The three kings and the ten tribes in the times and land of Judah ; the third period of the Early Church when, after the Apostles and the martyrs, the learned doctors fought against the Arians and then, later, when the Greek Church separated from the Latin. He now warns Arnald-Amaury that the Cistercian Order is in a similar state. It too has reached that third age of spirituality and already the seeds of harmful division have appeared. Thirty three and a third years was about the time that Christ lived in the flesh. «If you multiply such a period into three such spiritual states, you will know that the Order itself has recently passed through this third period. We must watch that the divisions which seem to occur in such third periods do not cause the Order to fall into calamitous ruin»[22]. Rainier's aim is to incite the Abbot of Cîteaux to take remedial action. He should receive the letters from the Pope with all meekness and maturity. He should summon together the first four daughter houses and «others as appropriate», possibly using the definitors[23]. «You will treat the matter with all charity. The occasion of the quarrels may be hidden from those not attending so that matters may be resolved away from harmful outside influences». Rainier explains that Innocent will understand the need for this secrecy. «In the love that each abbot bears for his brother abbots and if Cîteaux and the daughters all agree to this, each will receive letters bearing a special seal[24] in which, by agreed custom, peace and concord would be established. It is to be hoped that the houses would not be, either now or in the future, like the sons of Laban and regard the Pope as having taken away their rights. Nor should what the Curia proposes be considered as frivolous, to be disregarded by

21. «Quia convenientibus vobis in unum iam non est cenam patrum Cisterciensium manducare, sed unusquisque (de sic facientibus loquor) cenam manducat proprie voluntatis, animosus, contenciosus, emulator, voce clamosus, operibus remissus», *ibid*, p. 165.

22. *Ibid*, pp. 165-6.

23. «Et aliis quos iudicaveritis advocandos», *ibid*, p. 166.

24. «Litteras remiseritis singulorum signaculis sigillatas», *ibid*.

future generations. When all the daughters have spoken, bringing out their complaints and allegations against each other, it is to be hoped that they, in turn, will agree to be communally elected to work with and through you to sustain the burden of the Order. Unless this is done, the whole Order will be weakened and swept away. The Pope is not forgetful of his responsibilities and has already, *in registro*, reminded you of the consequences. He has wished to communicate with you in such a way that our Jerusalem will be most carefully examined under a light and thereby preserved and not fatally wounded. But something must be done».

Rainier's letter, with its threat of the stark consequences which the divisions in the Order seemed to be bringing to the relationship between the five senior abbeys and also with the Pope, brought forth little response in 1203. At least, little is recorded. Typically Innocent III still held to his determination to use the ideal of the Cistercian Order as the organisational norm for reform and renewal, not only amongst Benedictines but ultimately for all monastic and regular congregations which were still autonomous[25]. The Cistercians in Burgundy might procrastinate and prevaricate but that would not stop Innocent III from using their model in all its earlier purity for others to follow. In February 1203, he embarked on an elaborate scheme to summon the abbots of monasteries, other than Cistercians, immediately subject *nullo medio* to the Holy See, to meet together in six provincial chapters in northern and central Italy, France and England[26]. A start at least was being made even if the plan faltered and came to little at that time. He was later to revive his plans to present the model to the Lateran Council, ignoring as far as he could the tales of dissention amongst the Cistercians.

The Cistercians themselves seem to have planned to raise their bitter internal quarrel at the Fourth Lateran Council of 1215. Innocent was vigorously opposed to this[27] in order to avoid a scandal at the expense of an Order which he was about to hold up as an example[28]. By the enterprise of Nicholas *de Romanis*, Cardinal Bishop of Tusculum[29], papal legate and another of Innocent's agents, the Cistercians retracted and agreed to

---

25. BOLTON, «Via ascetica ; a papal quandary», pp. 180-2.

26. MACCARRONE, *Studi*, pp. 226-46 ; U. BERLIERE, «Les chapitres généraux de l'Ordre de St Benoît», *Revue Bénédictine*, 18 (1901), pp. 156-9.

27. Letter of 26 July 1216, C. HOROY, *Honorii III romani pontificis opera omnia, Medii aevi bibliotheca patristica*, 6 vols, Paris, 1879-80, 2, VIII, p. 10.

28. Canon XII, *In singulis regnis*, COD, 3 ed., Bologna, 1973, pp. 240-1.

29. 5 May 1204-14 September 1219, EUBEL, *Hierarchia Catholica Medii Aevi*, I, Regensberg, 1913, p. 5 ; W. MALECZEK, *Papst und Kardinalskolleg von 1191 bis 1216 : die Kardinale unter Coelestin III und Innocenz III*, Vienna, 1984, pp. 147-50.

accept the wishes of the Abbot of Cîteaux[30] for the time being. This compromise meant that, should the need arise to depose one of the abbots of the first four daughter houses, the Abbot of Cîteaux would select for the purpose a group of abbots who represented the *sanior pars*[31]. He was to choose and if no agreement was arrived at with the others, the «less wise group», the matter was to be referred to the General Chapter and will be corrected by the diffinitors[32]. After a delay of two weeks, he was to summon the daughter abbots of the senior daughter house thus rendered vacant in order not to make proposals likely to provoke a scandal at the General Chapter.

Whilst not resolving the underlying difficulties[33], the Pope and the Order seem to have maintained a rough *status quo,* allowing Innocent to go forward with his plans for the Fourth Lateran Council where Canon XII *In singulis regnis,* recommended the institution of the General Chapter for Benedictines, Augustinians and other groups of religious lacking such organisation. A compromise for 1215 at least !

---

30. 14 March, 1217, HOROY, *Honorii III Opera,* CCLWVI, cols 328-30.

31. C.H. LAWRENCE, *Medieval Monasticism : Forms of Religious Life in Western Europe in the Middle Ages,* 2 éd., London, 1989, p. 187 ; J.-B. VAN DAMME, «Les pouvoirs de l'Abbé de Cîteaux au XII et XIII siècle», *Analecta Sacri Ordinis Cisterciensis* 24, 1968, pp. 17-85.

32. *Ibid,* col. 329.

33. MAHN, *L'ordre cistercien,* pp. 228-38 for the quarrel of 1263-1265.

# VIII

## FULK OF TOULOUSE: THE ESCAPE THAT FAILED

| | |
|---|---|
| E lo dozes sera Folquetz de | And the twelfth one will be Fulk of |
| Marseilla, us mercadairetz | Marseille, a merchant of importance |
| que a fait un fol sagramen | Who made an oath so mad |
| quan juret que chansos no fetz | And swore his songs no more to write |
| et anz dizon que fo per vetz | This seemed to all to be in true sincerity |
| qe·s perjuret son escien | When he so consciously forswore.[1] |

This short piece of a contemporary troubadour's song makes a suitable introduction to Fulk of Toulouse who was first a jongleur and troubadour, a citizen and merchant and later in life a monk and bishop. Underlying most of this varied career was a desire on Fulk's part to retreat from the world in order to achieve the *vita apostolica.*

The father of Fulk Anfos was a genoese merchant who had settled in Marseille and who had left his fortune to his son. When we first hear of Fulk in 1178 he was established as a rich and highly respected citizen, a married man and father of two sons.[2] In addition to this he enjoyed a reputation as a successful troubadour throughout all the courts of the midi especially so in the court of Marseille.[3] This combination of merchant and troubadour was not unusual and indeed reflected the relatively open society of southern France at this time.

Some understanding of what this society was like can be gained by examining the songs and poetry of Fulk and other contemporary troubadours.[4] It is now generally accepted that these poems did not

[1] The song was written by the monk of Montaudon. [S.] Stronski, [*Le troubadour*] *Folquet de Marseille* (Cracow 1910) p 48*. This critical edition of Fulk's poetry contains a short but valuable biographical study. Pages from this section are asterisked thus * while the page references to his poetry have no asterisk.

[2] *Ibid* p 8*.

[3] This court was presided over by Raymond Geoffrey Barral one of the most powerful lords of the midi. He was favourable to the troubadours and supported not only Fulk but Peire Vidal. Bertran de Born thought sufficiently highly of Barral to address one of his *sirventés* to him. *Ibid* pp 15*–18*.

[4] From the very considerable volume of literature on the troubadours I have drawn upon H. Moller, 'The social causation of the courtly love complex', *Comparative Studies in Society and History* 1 (The Hague 1958–9) pp 137–63; W. Powell Jones, 'The Jongleur

portray any personal love experiences. This concentration upon courtly love was a highly stylised method of expression which allowed them to show both a considerable depth of meaning and an emotional involvement in order to emphasise educational and moral uplift. Such poetry was presented at social gatherings and became an intrinsic part of the value system of a significant number of the secular upper classes. This relatively open society allowed a degree of upward mobility and led to an apparent masculinisation of the upper social layers. The consequent imbalance in the sex ratio was further aggravated by the desire to avoid hypogamy. Marriage was regarded as another means of social ascent. Thus the symbolic contents of this courtly love poetry expressed not only hopes of marrying upwards but also reflected the totally competitive way of life of the knightly class. The troubadours conceived of courtly love poetry as a method of indicating ethical and moral behaviour which they often linked with an idealistic participation in a crusade as a possible equivalent to a lady's service. The symbolism had different layers of meaning but there was a common element which may be seen as an anxiety regarding acceptance, assuaged by self-improvement and devoted service. Such attitudes are not uncommon in any society which allows upward mobility.

Fulk was familiar with all these pressures and his life as a troubadour revealed his attempts to come to terms with them. He composed many songs dealing with love and the crusades. Crusading indeed became the major preoccupation in his later poetry. He himself was already beginning to move away from the competitive world. One song written at the court of Marseille between 1188 and 1192 indicated his new train of thought for it showed that he was aware of the inability of money to provide happiness.

| | |
|---|---|
| Que rix diz hom qu'ieu sui e que be·m vai | They claim that I am rich and in good health |
| mas cel quo diz no sap ges ben lo ver | But those who say this are hardly aware of the truth |
| que benanansa non pot hom aver | For happiness only results from what is pleasing to the heart |

Troubadours of Provence' *PMLA* 46 (1931) pp 307–11; H. Davenson, *Les Troubadours* (Paris 1961) and [C.] Morris, *The Discovery of the Individual* [*1050–1200*] (1972) especially pp 107–20.

| | |
|---|---|
| de nulla re mas d'aisso qu'al cor plai | So that a poor man who is contented has more |
| per que n'a mais us paubres s'es joyos | Than a rich man deprived of joy and constantly |
| q'us rix ses joi qu'es tot l'an cossiros | burdened by sad thoughts.[5] |

The last song he wrote dealt with the crusade in Spain and appeared to be so much a call to arms that Fulk's provençal biographer refers to it as the preaching song (the *prezicansa*).[6] In this Fulk exhorted the poor no less than the rich to take the cross and maintained that their salvation would come through death for the christian faith. It was becoming evident that Fulk was ready to move away from this troubadour life. The activities and moralising of that life were not enough to overcome his growing distaste for a life based on material wealth. Neither was it enough to overcome his disillusionment with the life of the courts. He, like other merchants such as Valdes or Francis, had witnessed at first hand the inequalities between rich and poor. As a troubadour his close contact with the courts had enabled him to assess the real worth of the life in which he had played such an intimate part. He found himself expressing his personal *renovatio* through a commitment to asceticism with a growing emphasis on poverty. He came to hold the augustinian view that poverty meant happiness and realised that the surest way to achieve this was by entry into an order. He chose to enter the austere cistercian order which was the one most compatible with his views. In 1195 or 1196 he retired from the world, entering with his wife and two sons the abbey of Le Thoronet in Provence.[7]

By the time that Fulk had entered the order the cistercians had become the leading crusading agents of the papacy. Their specific function was to mount a missionary campaign 'to evangelise a restive populace and a dechristianised world'.[8] Although the order had been somewhat shaken by its early call to the apostolate, many cistercians played a prominent role in the second and third crusades. In spite

[5] Stronski, *Folquet de Marseille* p 7*, song 7 lines 5–10 p 36.

[6] *Ibid* p 88*, song 19 pp 83–6. This poem, preaching crusade against the infidel, was written after the battle of Alarcos in 1195 and the defeat of the cistercian military order of Calatrava. The provençal biographer writes 'en Folquetz de Marceilla qu'era molt amies del rei de castela si fes una prezicansa per conortar los baros e la bona gen que deguessan secorre al bon rei'. *Ibid* p 8.

[7] *Ibid* p 89*.

[8] [M-D.] Chenu, *Nature, Man and Society* [*in the Twelfth Century*] (Chicago 1968) p 213. On the earlier attempt see R. I. Moore, 'St Bernard's Mission to the Languedoc in 1145', *BIHR* 48 (1974) pp 1–10.

of the bitterness engendered by these failures they were ready to embark on an attack upon heresy wherever it appeared. This attack was two-fold, an academic onslaught and a practical operation on both the geographical and spiritual frontiers of orthodoxy. In Languedoc, their recent mobilisation by the papacy against the cathars had presented them with their most severe challenge yet.[9] To preach and engage in debate with these erudite heretics was one reason why the order needed men of talent who could manipulate words. Another reason was that the laity at all levels were generally illiterate and so were incapable of reading the bible or any other text for themselves. They were listeners and not readers and communication came to them through preachers, poets, jongleurs and learned heretics.[10] The troubadours provided men with such talent in communicating and Fulk's conversion was only one example of successful cistercian proselytising amongst them.[11] Perhaps such proselytising was not too difficult. Morris has discussed some of the similarities of troubadours and cistercians and sees in them a common desire to make personal experience and personal relations the focus of life. 'While the poet looked for love to inspire all the virtues of "courtesy", the monk hoped to find in friendship a common mind in Christ. Finally the expression of longing common to both groups must be linked with the assiduous attempts at self-understanding'.[12]

The cistercian order had acquired a political character and it was not appropriate that Fulk should be allowed to remain long in his monastery. Thus on the eve of the albigensian crusade, he found himself thrust into the politics of crusade-preaching. In 1205 he was elected to the bishopric of Toulouse. He took possession of his see on 5 February 1206[13] and so simultaneously became involved in the

[9] *PL* 215 (1855) cols 355–60; *Potthast* 1 no 2229. The bull *Et si nostri navicula* of 1204 confirmed the legation of Renier da Ponza, Guy, Peter de Castelnau, Raoul de Fontefroide and Arnald Amaury abbot of Cîteaux.

[10] H. Grundmann, 'Hérésies savantes et hérésies populaires au moyen âge', in [J.] Le Goff, *Hérésies et Sociétés* [*dans l'Europe pré-industrielle 11–18 siècles*], École pratique des hautes études. *Civilisations et Sociétés*, 10 (Paris 1968) pp 209–14. Also C. Morris, *Medieval Media* (university of Southampton 1972) in which he discusses the use of the song as a way of expressing values and ideas, in particular the cultural media brought to bear upon Valdes who was himself converted after hearing a *jongleur* recount the story of saint Alexis.

[11] Hélinand of Fontefroide a former *trouvère* became an eminent cistercian preacher while Bernard of Ventadour and Bertran de Born both became monks in the same order.

[12] Morris, *The Discovery of the Individual*, pp 117.

[13] [C.] Devic and [J.] Vaissète, *Histoire générale* [*de Languedoc*], 6 (Toulouse 1879) p 244. Fulk took as his sermon for that day the parable of the sower.

business affairs of the diocese. For Fulk to be entrusted with such an important see as Toulouse with all its political, social and religious problems indicated the high opinion which the cistercian order had of his abilities. Fulk himself was not lacking in confidence. Through preaching he hoped to appeal to the intellect of the heretics and through an insistence on episcopal rights accompanied by an attack on usury he hoped to induce an acceptance of the orthodox view of wealth.

The new diocese presented him with many problems. Contemporary chroniclers such as William de Puylaurens and Peter de Vaux Cernay stressed the major role which a large city such as Toulouse played in the diffusion of heresy.[14] More recent consideration has modified this view and Violante has demonstrated the importance of the *contado* as a vital factor in the growth of italian heresy.[15] It was not by chance that Toulouse at the beginning of the thirteenth century, when heresy there was making enough stir to attract outside intervention, was also attempting to conquer an italian-style *contado*.[16] Nevertheless the mobility and dynamism of urban life, the break with traditional groupings and religious structures which were either oppressive or inadequate, all created stresses and tensions for the urban dweller. In this situation heresy could flourish whether the need was religious or not. Wherever an heretical preacher appeared he became the mouthpiece for all those frustrations and discontents with which neither the priests nor the court of Toulouse could deal.[17]

As a cistercian bishop Fulk was well-placed to collaborate with the legates and missionaries of his order against the heretics. In 1207 an influx of preachers brought to Toulouse by the abbot of Cîteaux led to a transformation of evangelical strategy.[18] Languedoc was divided into districts which were then distributed among the principal preachers and supervised by a *magister*. Whilst the cistercians continued

[14] [William of] Puylaurens, *Cronica* ed Beyssier in 'Guillaume de Puylaurens et sa chronique' in *Troisièmes mélanges d'histoire du moyen âge*, ed A. Luchaire, Bibliothèque de la Faculté des Lettres de Paris, 18 (Paris 1904) pp 119–75. Peter de Vaux Cernay, *Petri Vallium Sarnau monachi Hystoria albigensis*, ed P. Guérin and E. Lyon, 3 vols (Paris 1926–39).

[15] C. Violante, 'Hérésies urbaines et hérésies rurales en Italie du 11e au 13e siècle' in Le Goff, *Hérésies et Sociétés*, pp 171–97.

[16] [J. H.] Mundy, *Liberty and Political Power* [*in Toulouse 1050–1200*] (New York 1954) p 68.

[17] For an interesting discussion of this question see the review article by R. I. Moore, 'The Test of Religious Truth', *Times Higher Educational Supplement* 141 (28 June 1974) p 13.

[18] [C.] Thouzellier, *Catharisme et valdéisme* [*en Languedoc à la fin du xii*e *et au début du xiii*e *siècle*] (2 ed Paris 1969) pp 199, 205.

their preaching and attempts at conversion, pope Innocent III had harnessed what he felt might be an effective new method of evangelism. He diverted Diego of Osma and Dominic to aid the preachers in Languedoc by the example of their austerity and by their skill in words.[19] In 1207 Fulk and Dominic preached together at Pamiers in a great debate between heretics and catholics. Fulk was so confident of the success of the debate that he asked a local knight why people in the area did not expel heretics from their lands. The knight replied that this would be impossible since the heretics lived among them, were numbered among their relations and were seen to be living lives of perfection.[20] The eloquence and example of poverty which Dominic and the cistercians displayed were successful in attracting to orthodoxy a group of vaudois led by Durand de Huesca but no cathars appeared to have been converted.[21] In 1208 Fulk and the legate Navarre, bishop of Couserans, were sent to Rome by the southern bishops to ask for help. After hearing their report and learning of the murder of Peter de Castelnau, Innocent proclaimed the crusade against the heretics. He also renewed the special powers granted to the cistercians in 1204 adding the absolute right to exterminate heresy.[22] Peaceful preaching for conversion alone seemed to have failed.

Fulk who had entered a cistercian monastery to escape from the world thus found himself increasingly involved in preaching the politics of the albigensian crusade.[23] Not only did Fulk preach the crusade in Languedoc with Arnald-Amaury, abbot of Cîteaux, but he also travelled three times through France. He reached Flanders on these preaching campaigns and secured valuable help by attracting men and by raising large sums of money.[24] Fulk's role as a crusade-preacher was obviously very important. He preached continually wherever he was and even accompanied the crusaders in battle. By now convinced

[19] *Ibid* pp 194–5; *PL* 215 (1855) cols 1024–5; C. Thouzellier, 'La pauvreté, arme contre l'Albigéisme, en 1206', *Révue de l'histoire de religions* 151 (Paris 1957) pp 79–92.

[20] Thouzellier, *Catharisme et valdéisme* p 203.

[21] *PL* 215 (1855) cols 1510–14.

[22] Thouzellier, *Catharisme et valdéisme* pp 204–12.

[23] Useful reprints and new works on the albigensian crusade include P. Belperron, *La Croisade contre les Albigeois 1209–1249* (Paris 1967); J. R. Strayer, *The Albigensian Crusades* (New York 1971); [W. L.] Wakefield, *Heresy, crusade and inquisition* [*in Southern France 1100–1250*] (1974).

[24] R. Lejeune, 'L'évêque de Toulouse, Foulquet de Marseille et la principauté de Liège', in *Mélanges Felix Rousseau* (Brussels 1958) pp 433–48. Fulk was in Liège in 1211 or 1212, again between January and September 1213 and finally in 1217.

of the usefulness of the crusade in extirpating heresy he supported Simon de Montfort and thus came to be regarded as his accomplice in those acts committed under the pretext of the crusade. Fulk was perhaps not happy with the way things had developed and in 1217 he asked Honorius III to allow him to resign his see and return to his monastery.[25] Honorius would not allow this.

Although politically Fulk had not been happy, there were other related aspects of his crusade-preaching which were more rewarding. On his visit to Flanders, Fulk had marvelled at the group of beguines centred on the new saint, Mary of Oignies, which he found in Liège.[26] His interest in religious women's communities as a bulwark against heresy had led him earlier to support Dominic's foundation at Prouille in his own diocese.[27] It was now at his request that Jacques de Vitry wrote the *Life of Mary*.[28] Mary's vision of the massacre of northern crusaders at Montgey and her strong desire to take the cross herself were, Fulk felt, useful both as a manifestation of contemporary sanctity and as an *exemplum* to be used when preaching against heretics in his own province.[29] Fulk's role as protector and friend of these groups of religious women was of considerable importance both to the women and to Fulk's self-satisfaction in the value of his preaching. Similarly this was so in regard to his support for Dominic's preachers.

His success in the business affairs of the diocese, concurrent with his attack on usury in Toulouse may also have been another factor in reconciling him to Honorius's refusal to relieve him of his office. When he entered his see in 1206 he was immediately forced to deal with business affairs in an attempt to recover both episcopal rights and associated revenues. The diocese of Toulouse, referred to as the 'dead diocese' by William de Puylaurens, was in a deplorable condition.[30] Even the able bishop Fulcrand (1179–1200) had been forced to live as a humble townsman because he could not enforce the

[25] Devic and Vaissète, *Histoire générale* 6 p 502.

[26] Mary of Oignies, the child of rich and respected parents, was married at the age of fourteen but later separated voluntarily from her husband to live in a cell at the augustinian priory of St Nicholas of Oignies in complete poverty. She became the focus of female piety in the diocese of Liège. See my article '*Mulieres Sanctae*', *SCH* 10 (1973) pp 77–97.

[27] Grundmann, pp 209–11. See also [M-H.] Vicaire, *Saint Dominic* [*and his Times*] (trans by K. Pond London 1964) and *Saint Dominic en Languedoc, Cahiers de Fanjeaux* 1 (Toulouse 1966).

[28] *ASB* 5 (1867) pp 542–72.

[29] *Ibid* p 556.

[30] Puylaurens, *Cronica* ed Beyssier p 125.

payment of tithes due to the see.[31] Fulk's predecessor, Raymond de Rabastens, had encumbered most of the demesne to pay for several lawsuits and to make war on his vassal. The diocese was thus largely in pledge to creditors and Fulk's new treasury contained ninety-six sous. Nor dared he allow the episcopal mules to move outside to drink lest they should be seized for debt.[32]

We have seen that Fulk's emphasis on apostolic poverty had led him to become a cistercian, and he would not have been concerned for himself at the state of the diocesan finances. This is aptly indicated by Robert de Sorbon who reported that Fulk was so highly critical of those who sought to please and praise him at a feast arranged to perform his songs that he interrupted his meal to partake only of bread and water.[33] It is also said of him that he wore a hair shirt as a demonstration of his lack of concern for his own comfort.[34] Nevertheless, it was essential for the power and respect for the office of bishop that this impoverished situation be remedied. Although this was one of the greatest periods of public charity in Toulouse, the church seemed unable to retain the economic means to support its spiritual mission.[35] The value of rents was fast diminishing and few new gifts and donations were coming in. Secular clergy and bishops alike had lost much of their temporal jurisdiction and direct coercive power to the more recent orders as well as to the consuls. Previous bishops had lacked property and the power to reform. Fulk had been sent to Toulouse with the specific task of reforming and this he was determined to do. Because of the financial state of his diocese, Fulk had to decide whether or not to continue to use money obtained for the diocese from usurers.

Usury had always presented a problem to the church.[36] Usury, money lending and commerce raised problems of conscience for those who participated in these activities. The gap between new social

[31] *Ibid* p 125; Mundy, *Liberty and Political Power* p 81.

[32] *Ibid* p 82.

[33] Stronski, *Folquet de Marseille* p 112*.

[34] Vicaire, *Saint Dominic* p 387.

[35] J. H. Mundy, 'Charity and Social Work in Toulouse 1150–1250', *Traditio* 22 (1966) pp 203–87.

[36] [J. W.] Baldwin, *Masters, Princes and Merchants:* [*the social views of Peter the Chanter and his circle*], 2 vols (Princeton 1970); J. T. Noonan, *The Scholastic Analysis of Usury* (Cambridge, Mass., 1957) and B. M. Nelson, *The Idea of Usury: from tribal brotherhood to universal otherhood* (2 ed Chicago 1969). A recent article by B. H. Rosenwein and L. K. Little, 'Social Meaning in the Monastic and Mendicant Spiritualities' *Past and Present* 63 (1974) pp 4–33, especially pp 29–31 gives a useful indication of the ways in which justifications for usury were appearing at this time.

realities and orthodoxy fostered many anxieties and this was nowhere truer than when applied to advancing commercial activity. In Toulouse the problems posed by usury coincided with the growth of heresy but usury was not a feature of heresy alone.[37] The form of social structure here led to a weak social control in regard to individuals. This certainly stimulated heresy and no doubt fostered usury. The social frictions characteristic of the town were due to the rise of business and commercial elements and to an accompanying decline in the wealth and influence of patrician families. Some patricians felt themselves so threatened by this loss of wealth and political leadership that their orthodoxy was reinforced. Other patricians especially those from the countryside became heretics. This division is best shown by the Capitedenario family. Its urban branch was a pillar of the orthodox church while the rural knightly branch was heretical and produced at least one usurer.[38] Similar divisions occurred among the artisans, some being perennial enemies of usury and others heretical *textores*. While catharism permitted usury and did not prescribe poverty for believers, other heretical poverty movements represented a strong expiatory reaction against wealth usuriously acquired. Distinctions here are blurred and I can only stress again that usury was not a feature of heresy alone nor even a feature of all types of heresy. Many of the orthodox also indulged in usurious practices and if, in the view of Weber, usury is regarded as incompatible with brotherly love, it may have been this which decided whether or not usury was practised rather than the holding of orthodox or heretical beliefs.[39]

Fulk attributed the state of his lands in part to lax usury laws and certainly his remedies attempted to tighten them. Nevertheless he may have been more influenced in these remedies by the preaching campaign of Robert de Courçon against usury than by the impoverishment of his episcopal estates, although such an example would have been a telling content in his own preaching.[40] He created a tribunal of two judges to hear complaints and charges of usury. This tribunal, active until 1215, was empowered to force usurers to make restitution. It succeeded for example in condemning the deceased

[37] Mundy, *Liberty and Political Power* pp 74–9.

[38] *Ibid* p 290 n 18.

[39] M. Weber, *The Sociology of Religion* (4 ed 1971) pp 215–16.

[40] Baldwin, *Masters, Princes and Merchants* 1, pp 296–7. This preaching campaign was conducted in northern France but was widely supported in other areas.

and orthodox Pons David and forcing the hospitallers, his heirs, to give restitution to the guarantor of a loan.[41]

We know from the chronicler William de Puylaurens that Fulk established or renewed a confraternity devoted to the destruction of heresy and usury.[42] During a period of intense factional strife, this was the agency which more than anything else stimulated trouble in Toulouse. This white confraternity, partly patrician and partly popular, had power to enforce and render judgements against usurers. Its armed bands of righteous citizens excited by a wave of popular enthusiasm destroyed the houses and goods of well-known usurers but found very few heretics. In considering why this should be so, Mundy advances the view that it was a simple question of fear. Usurers would not dare to be heretics also.[43] It is certainly difficult to demonstrate any inherent link between heresy and usury from this experience in Toulouse. The evidence would seem to point to Fulk pursuing heretics and usurers as two separate concerns of his own. Although a rival black confraternity was set up in opposition by the bourg of Toulouse and was probably dominated by the new urban patriciate of commerce and real estate, any success it may have had is uncertain. Under the existing pressure against usury, interest agreements tended to disappear at least from notarial records and merchants trying to avoid open usury resorted instead to fictitious deals. In practice, therefore, and in spite of Fulk's opposition, usury continued in Toulouse although it was driven underground.[44] However the ecclesiastical attack on usury and the popular enthusiasm which accompanied it were the first signs of the rebirth of episcopal authority in Toulouse. This rebirth, and the fact that Fulk's position despite wartime reverses was much strengthened and his office revivified by the end of the albigensian crusade, were not exactly what he appeared to want for himself. This is clear from his attempt to return to the monastery in 1217. With Honorius's refusal to allow this, he turned his energies to what he hoped would be more peaceful, more permanent and more effective ways of destroying heresy. For example in 1229 he established the university of Toulouse in an attempt to defeat heresy by intellectual means.[45] Perhaps he retained his desire

[41] Mundy, *Liberty and Political Power* p 83.

[42] Puylaurens, *Cronica* ed Beyssier pp 131–2.

[43] Mundy, *Liberty and Political Power* p 79.

[44] J. H. Mundy, *Europe in the High Middle Ages 1150–1309* (1973) p 180.

[45] *Ibid* p 466.

to return to the monastery but this was not to be fulfilled. He died in office in 1231.[46]

Thus Fulk who had entered the cistercian order precisely to escape from the world found himself thrust into politics because of the political character which this order had acquired as the leading crusade agency of the papacy. He was also thrust into business affairs because of the necessity of dealing effectively with the financial needs of the episcopal estates of Toulouse. He had consistently and vigorously opposed heretics and usurers by his own methods, achieving some success especially in reviving the episcopal powers in which the office had been previously lacking. It is ironic that Fulk's retreat from the world should in fact have meant for him a greater involvement with society.

[46] Chronicle of William Pelhisson, printed in Wakefield, *Heresy, crusade and inquisition* p 210.

# IX

## A MISSION TO THE ORTHODOX? THE CISTERCIANS IN ROMANIA

IT has been said that Innocent III shared the popular belief existing at the beginning of the thirteenth century that the world would end in 1284.[1] Perhaps this is the reason why throughout his pontificate he was eager to resolve the divisions facing mankind. These divisions were reflected in the deviations of the heretic, the beliefs of the infidel and the schism of the eastern church. In the first of these Innocent was meeting success, albeit in varying degrees, for example in Languedoc.[2] The second and third needed his further attention. He was of the opinion that a renewed crusading effort in both east and west would be able to achieve mass conversions amongst Jews and Muslims. To this end the fourth crusade of 1204[3], mounted mainly by the Cistercians, came into being.

The unity of the church was also regarded as of paramount importance and therefore had to be included in these last aims. To Innocent, with his grand design for the organisation of a single, united and conforming church,[4] this schismatic situation awaited a 'final solution'. The notorious events associated with 1204 did not deter Innocent from diverting the Cistercians to a mission to the orthodox.

This task was taken up with pride by the Cistercians. One of their chroniclers, Caesarius of Heisterbach, writing in the early years of the thirteenth century stated that 'the vine of Cîteaux had been planted in Greece'. His attribution of this to the Latin emperor Henry of Flanders may have been designed as an historically inaccurate tribute to Henry

[1] R. I. Burns, 'Christian-Islamic Confrontation in the West: the thirteenth-century dream of conversion', *AHR* 76 (1971) pp 1386–1412, 1432–34 especially p 1390; R. W. Southern, *Western views of Islam in the Middle Ages* (Cambridge, Mass., 1962) p 42. For Innocent's crusading appeal of April 1213 see *PL* 216 (1855) cols 817–22.

[2] B. M. Bolton, 'Tradition and temerity: papal attitudes to deviants 1159–1216' *SCH* 9 (1972) pp 79–91. [C.] Thouzellier, *Catharisme et Valdéisme* [*en Languedoc à la fin du xii<sup>e</sup> siècle*] (2 ed Louvain 1969) pp 183–212 provides a detailed account of the mission to Languedoc.

[3] The events leading up to the fourth crusade are analysed by C. M. Brand, *Byzantium confronts the West 1180–1204* (Cambridge, Mass., 1968) and [A.] Frolow, [*Recherches sur*] *la déviation de la iv$^{e}$ croisade* [*vers Constantinople*] (Paris 1955).

[4] A. Luchaire, *Innocent III: La Question d'Orient* (Paris 1907) pp 55–75.

but Caesarius was at least correct in noting the expansion of his order in the newly acquired lands of Romania in 1204.[5] To the Cistercians this was one more accepted example that no matter where the boundaries of the Latin world might be extended, there was no country or island where one could not find their order. The church needed them in Spain: they were there. The church needed them in Languedoc: they were there likewise.

Such pride as this, with the accompanying high hopes for success, may have been justified when Caesarius was writing so soon after the event but a clear examination of what actually happened to the Cistercians both during and after the fourth crusade may perhaps suggest that this further planting may have been harmful to the vine.[6] Southern has suggested that the incipient failure of the Cistercian order may have taken place about the year 1200.[7] It may be that the activities of the Cistercians in Romania after 1204 indicate more clearly this failure.

That Innocent should have chosen the Cistercians was only to be expected. Throughout the twelfth century the development of their order and the characteristics of its organisation meant that they filled the gap between two types of order, the military on the one hand and the monastic on the other. The Cistercians had an organisation which was one of the masterpieces of medieval planning.[8] Their military attitude towards their faith was mirrored not only in the discipline of their internal life but also in their practice of it outside their houses. They represented the frontier guards of faith in both a metaphysical and a physical sense. They determined their objectives with absolute rigour and operated to achieve them on both the geographical and spiritual frontiers of orthodoxy. They were ready to attack no matter where these frontiers appeared. Saint Bernard himself had demonstrated the compatibility of military and monastic aims when he praised the *milites christi* who had taken up both the spiritual and the temporal

[5] [A.] Manrique, [*Cistercienses seu verius ecclesiastici Annales a conditio Cistercio*] 4 vols (Lyons 1642–1659) 3 p 6. Caesarius writes 'ita ut jam non sit regio vel insula intra metas latinitatis ubi ordo cisterciensis non sit'.

[6] [E.A.R.] Brown, ['The cistercians in the latin empire of Constantinople and Greece 1204–1276'] *Traditio* 14 (1958) pp 63–120 especially pp 64–78 for a consideration of Cistercian involvement in events leading up to the fourth crusade.

[7] [R. W.] Southern, *Western Society* [*and the Church in the Middle Ages*] (Harmondsworth 1970) p 269.

[8] *Ibid* p 255.

[9] J. F. O'Callaghan, 'The affiliation of the Order of Calatrava with the Order of Cîteaux', *ASOC* 15 (1959) pp 163–93 especially pp 171–4 and 16 (1960) pp 3–59.

swords to combat the devil and his works. Indeed in another frontier area, Iberia, the phenomenal growth of the military religious orders must be attributed to saint Bernard and his followers.[9] Their example had led in the second half of the twelfth century to the great Spanish military orders of Calatrava and Alcantara and to the Portuguese order of Avis.[10] The appeal of these orders was to the knightly classes, converted as saint Bernard put it from *the militia mundi* to the *militia dei.* These orders adopted the severe Cistercian rule, became affiliated to mother houses and strengthened their links with Cîteaux. Thus on the western frontier, the exact relationship between knights and Cistercians was clarified and juridically stated through Cistercian general chapters. As we shall see, a similar situation did not arise in the east and it is interesting to speculate on the part which the presence or absence of land-based internal communications may have played in this. These were present in Spain but not in Greece.

The Cistercians were regarded as the chief papal agents, and so the fourth crusade was largely a Cistercian operation planned and mounted from Cîteaux.[11] In addition to the objectives of Innocent III the Cistercians, who thought that the further intention of any crusade was certainly to initiate some sort of colonising activity,[12] regarded the operation in the east as being specifically a colonising expedition. Innocent wrote of his wish that the order should propagate itself in any conquered lands there might be.[13] Already before the crusade, Innocent considered the orthodox Greeks to be in need of missionary endeavour. Early in 1204 he had found it necessary to write to his Latin subjects in Constantinople reminding them of the virtue of obedience and asking them to work to reunite the Greek and Latin churches 'for the daughter must return to the mother and all Christ's lambs must have only one shepherd'.[14]

[10] *Ibid* p 176; J. F. O'Callaghan, 'The foundation of the order of Alcantara 1176–1218', *Catholic Historical Review* 47 (London 1961–2) pp 471–86; [R. I.] Burns, *The Crusader kingdom of Valencia: [reconstruction on a thirteenth century frontier]* 2 vols (Cambridge, Mass., 1967) 1 pp 173–96 and for a comprehensive bibliography [*The*] *Historia Occidentalis* [*of Jacques de Vitry*] ed J. F. Hinnebusch, *Spicilegium Friburgense* 17 (Fribourg 1972) pp 260–2. Between 1213 and 1221 the knights of Avis adhered to the order of Calatrava.

[11] Brown pp 64, 72–3.

[12] Southern, *Western Society* p 257.

[13] *PL* 215 (1855) cols 636–8 where Innocent appeals not only to Cistercians but to Cluniacs, Augustinian canons and other orders, and *PL* 216 (1855) col 594 where the Cistercians alone are mentioned, 'nos enim volentes ut ordinis Cisterciensis, religio . . . in Romaniae partibus propagetur'.

[14] *PL* 215 (1855) cols 512–17.

Innocent therefore regarded the task of the Cistercians as being preachers and missionaries on the frontiers of Christianity. They were also to keep the objectives of the crusade firmly before the crusaders. As his main crusade agents and experts in controlling heresy, they had by 1204 already mounted a mission in Languedoc where Innocent regarded them as the most effective instrument for the conversion of the southern French cathars. There their conversion methods involved them in preaching and debating supported by a very powerful papal mandate.[15] He knew that the Cistercians themselves may not have found it so easy to differentiate in practice the partly religious and partly military aspects of their work. Although Innocent was perhaps in advance of his time in wanting as little disruption as possible to accompany the process of conversion, it must be borne in mind that the true interpretation of missionary activity in the medieval sense was for one religion[16] to dominate a subordinate religion. In this the Cistercians had already shown themselves to be eminently suitable at organising large tracts of land of uncertain loyalty. It is likely that Innocent would have thought of them as military police and support troops watching over newly conquered lands, as was their function in Spain. In addition, as a quasi-military monastic order, the Cistercians would have been expected by Innocent to be clear about the objectives of the crusade. It is undoubtedly true that in the case of some crusaders they were successful in this. The dedication of Villehardouin to *simplicitas* might be considered to to be a case in point.[17] Others of course were more concerned with *covoitise* and even abbot Martin of Pairis in his piety did not consider the looting of sacred relics from the church of the Pantocrator to conflict with the idea of *simplicitas*.[18]

It has often been said that the diversion of the fourth crusade to Constantinople meant its complete failure. Arguments on the issue

[15] *Ibid* cols 358–60; Thouzellier, *Catharisme et Valdéisme* p 187.

[16] Burns, *The Crusader kingdom of Valencia*, 1 p 9.

[17] [Geoffrey de] Villehardouin, *La Conquête* [*de Constantinople*] ed E. Faral (Paris 1938). For a most interesting analysis of Villehardouin's views see [J. M. A.] Beer, *Villehardouin. [Epic Historian]*, *Études de Philologie et d'histoire*, 7 (Geneva 1968) pp 26–7; C. Morris, 'Geoffrey de Villehardouin and the conquest of Constantinople', *History*, 53 (1968), pp 24–34. For possible influences on Villehardouin, M. R. Gutsch, 'A twelfth century preacher—Fulk of Neuilly', in *The crusades and other historical essays*, ed L. J. Paetow (New York 1928) pp 183–206.

[18] [S.] Runciman, *Byzantine Style and Civilisation* (Harmondsworth 1975) p 158; *Guntherus Parisiensis Historia Constantinopolitana*, ed [P.] Riant in *Exuviae* [*Sacrae Constantinopolitanae*] 2 vols (Geneva 1875) 1 p 119.

abound.[19] But if the objectives of the crusade included dealing with the 'unorthodoxy' of the orthodox, failure may not have been so complete. This however have may been a casuistic argument presented after the event. No matter which is correct, one of the results of the crusade was the arrival in strength of the Cistercians in Romania.

The question that now has to be asked is whether they were suitable for the tasks which confronted them. The differences between Greeks and Latins could be regarded as a purely jurisdictional matter centering on the recognition of a pope or a patriarch. The Greeks believed that their Roman emperor in Constantinople governed and protected the great society of the Christian faith. The Roman church they thought had strayed far from the paths laid down by the early fathers and councils. Before agreement could be reached, the Latins would have to acknowledge that their kings and emperors were only agents of the one true emperor of the Romans and that their pope was only one of the five patriarchs of the undivided Christian church.[20]

The west for its part regarded the Greeks with revulsion. Their failure to accept the pope's line of succession from Peter and the obstinate way in which they clung to what the Latins considered to be their impure rites only confirmed the view that they were perfidious, hostile to the west and hardened schismatics.[21] Men in western Europe were also concerned about the spiritual wealth of Constantinople. By spiritual wealth they were thinking of the huge store of relics housed in the city. The unworthiness of the Greeks to be the custodians of this sacred treasure was one of the arguments used to justify the crusaders' assault on the city.[22] Both sides, therefore, regarded each other as being worse than the infidel and such mutual incomprehension meant that any mission from the west to the east would at least be difficult if not impossible. The west however regarded the goal of conformity itself as being worth the effort and so undertook missionary activity.

There is no evidence that other orders appeared in Romania until

[19] Among the most recent of the secondary works on the fourth crusade are S. Runciman, *A History of the Crusades* 3 vols (Cambridge 1954) 3 pp 107–31; E. H. McNeal and R. L. Wolff, 'The Fourth Crusade' in *A History of the Crusades* ed K. M. Setton, 2, *The Later Crusades 1189–1311*, ed R. L. Wolff and H. W. Hazard (Philadelphia 1962) pp 153–85; D. M. Nicol, 'The Fourth Crusade and the Greek and Latin Empires 1204–1261' *CMH* 4 pp 275–330 and P. Lemerle, 'Byzance et la Croisade' *Relazioni del X Congresso Internazionale di Scienze Storiche*, 3 (Florence 1955) pp 595–620.

[20] D. M. Nicol, *The Last Centuries of Byzantium 1261–1453* (London 1972) pp 7–8.

[21] Luchaire, *Innocent III: la question d'Orient* p 59.

[22] R. W. Southern, *The Making of the Middle Ages* (London 1967) p 62.

the advent of the mendicants. Even so the Cistercians in addition to the other merits mentioned earlier were the only religious order which could speak with conviction to their orthodox counterparts although there was no Greek name for them as there was later for the Franciscans. As we have seen, the order maintained a severe discipline over its members and also enjoyed a high reputation for the simplicity, austerity and sanctity of its life. It was just these qualities which were the basis for the principal force of monasticism in the east.[23] The life and works of saint Basil were read in the Cistercian foundations of Cîteaux and Clairvaux and so the desire to return to the desert and the recognised value of manual work were elements in Cistercian thought which may have derived from eastern ideas on asceticism. They certainly provide most striking parallels between Cistercian and eastern ideas. If any order was to be heard by the Orthodox, then it was the voice of the Cistercians which many in the west considered to be the one most likely. This was in line with the objective put forward by Innocent III who wanted a vigorous campaign of missionary work among the orthodox which might attract the respect of these schismatic people towards the Latin church. The lay conquerors also supported the Cistercians.[24] These lay benefactors hoped to ensure that they had foundations of great stability and corporate strength, capable of imposing a close supervision on a wide area of country. The leader of the crusade, Boniface of Montferrat who adopted the title of king of Thessalonica was the first to act on behalf on the order. So with the encouragement of pope, emperor and lay lords alike, in the years immediately after the conquest, Cistercian houses were established in Constantinople and Greece to colonise, Christianise and control.

The first Cistercian house to be founded was Chortaitou near Thessalonica, granted in 1205 by Boniface of Montferrat to the

[23] J. LeClercq, 'Les relations entre le monachisme oriental et le monachisme occidental dans le haut moyen âge' in *Le Millénaire du Mont Athos 963–1963* 2 vols (Chevetogne/ Venice 1963–5)2 pp 49–80. Also J. LeClercq, *Aux sources de la spiritualité occidentale* (Paris 1964) pp 53–64. Another highly stimulating article which illuminates many aspects of the problem is P. McNulty and B. Hamilton, 'Orientale lumen et magistra latinitas: Greek influences on Western Monasticism 900–1100' *Millénaire du Mont Athos* 1 pp 181–2.

[24] [G.] Millet, [*Le monastère de Daphni: Histoire, architecture, mosaïques*] (Paris 1899) p 27. They included men such as the emperors Baldwin I (1204–1205) and Henry of Constantinople (1206–1216), Boniface of Montferrat, king of Thessalonica (1204–1207) Otto de la Roche, Megaskyr of Athens (1205–1225) and Geoffrey de Villehardouin, lord of Achaia (1209–1230)

crusader abbot Peter of Locedio.[25] Locedio itself lay in the diocese of Vercelli near Boniface's Lombard lands.[26] By the early 1220s Chortaitou had assumed the responsibilities of a mother house towards the Euboean monastery of St Archangelus in Negroponte.[27] The illustrious Greek monastery of Daphni near Athens was given by Otto de la Roche, a Burgundian knight, and megaskyr of Athens, probably in 1207 to the abbey of Bellevaux near Besançon, with which his family had close connections.[28] The monastery of St Stephen, in or near Constantinople, was occupied after 1208[29] and its Venetian mother house, St Thomas de Torcello, also controlled two monasteries in Crete, Gergeri from 1217 and St Mary Varangorum from 1230.[30] By 1213 or 1214 the house of St Angelus in Pera in Constantinople was affiliated to the abbey of Hautecombe near Geneva.[31] In the following year the community of St Angelus was entrusted with the daughter house of Rufinianai near Chalcedon in Asia Minor, an area won by the Latins only as recently as 1211 or 1212.[32] The location of the monastery of Laurus founded in 1214 remains in doubt[33] and little is known of the community at Zaraca near Corinth occupied by 1225.[34] The convent of St Mary de Percheio in Constantinople contained a community of nuns by 1221,[35] then was taken into papal protection and affiliated to Cîteaux. The convent of St Mary de Verge in Modon appears to have been a later foundation since little is known of it until 1267.[36]

[25] [L.] Janauschek, [*Originum Cisterciensium*] (Vienna 1877) 1 pp 218–19; Brown p 79 n 83; See also the history of Chortaitou by A. E. Vakalopoulos, in *Epeteris Etaireias Byzantinon Spoudon*, 15 (1939) pp 281–8.

[26] A. Ceruti, 'Un codice del monasterio cisterciense di Lucedio', *Archivio storico italiano*, 4 ser, 8 (Florence 1881) pp 373–8.

[27] Brown p 8.

[28] Janauschek p 214; Millet p 28 n 2.

[29] Janauschek p 215; R. Janin, *La géographie écclesiastique de l'empire byzantin, premier partie: Le siège de Constantinople et le patriarcat oecuménique III: Les églises et les monastères* (Paris 1953) pp 488–93 for evidence of the location of St Stephen.

[30] *Ibid* p 213; L. Santifaller, *Beiträge zur Geschichte des lateinischen Patriarchats von Konstantinopel* (Weimar 1938) pp 95–6; Brown pp 82–5.

[31] *Ibid* p 87, Janauschek p 219.

[32] Brown pp 88–90.

[33] *Ibid* p 95; Janauschek pp 219–20. R. Janin, 'Les sanctuaires de Byzance sous la domination latine 1204–1261'. *Études byzantines* 2 (Paris 1944) p 181 suggests that the monastery was in Constantinople.

[34] Janauschek p 227; Brown pp93–4 suggests that Zaraca may have been transferred to the Cistercian order on the initiative of Geoffrey de Villehardouin.

[35] Manrique 4 p 240; Brown pp 91–2 nn 152, 153. There is an interesting short section on Cistercian nuns in the east in *Historia Occidentalis*, ed J. F. Hinnebusch, p 268.

[36] Brown p 194 n 164.

What geographical pattern is it possible to see in these foundations? They are all on or near the coastline and bear some relation to a shipping route following a line of ports from Italy all the way round to Constantinople thus showing an external line of communication.

This coastal pattern makes it difficult to equate the foundations in Romania with the usual Cistercian activity on wasteland and frontier. Perhaps because this was an external line of communication their first idea was not to police the area but to establish a line of trading posts as had the Romans in earlier days. If this was so, then it is interesting to note that no trading posts or garrisons were established on the south side of the Black Sea.

Another point which seems strange is that most if not all of the foundations used Orthodox buildings already in existence.[37] There must have been a very large number of vacant Greek monasteries after the conquest only some of which the Cistercians selected for habitation. In this selection instead of following their normal practice of taking wasteland far from habitation, here in Romania they made foundations in the most civilised, developed and populous places.[38] An example is the monastery of Chortaitou which was a rich house with sufficient assets to support two hundred monks.[39] It is true that the Cistercians destroyed the monks' cells, uprooted their olive grove and sold wood and animals belonging to the monastery. Is this simply the viciousness of the Latins of which Nicol has spoken or could this be said to be the deliberate creation of a wasteland at the second stage?[40] Perhaps the terrain of Greece was such that they had no alternative. Of course it must be remembered that the Cistercians were bound to accept these monasteries, coming as they did in the way of gifts from their lay benefactors. Nor is there any evidence that these benefactors provided them with the large tracts of land which they were accustomed to receive in the west.

It is strange that the Cistercians usually such active builders did not themselves create any new houses. But in Constantinople at least, the Latins' reputation was for dismantling and destroying rather than for

[37] Millet p 27. Many of the Cistercian foundations were installed in Greek monasteries and kept a deformed version of their former name. Chortaitou, Daphni, St Angelus in Pera, Rufinianai and St Mary de Percheio were imperial houses while the names of Zaraca, Laurus and St Mary de Verge indicate Greek origins.

[38] *Ibid* p 30 n 2. Millet thought it quite natural that the Cistercians should establish themselves in the richest of the imperial monasteries.

[39] *PL* 216 (1855) col 951; Potthast 1 no 4879.

[40] D. M. Nicol, 'The Papal Scandal', *SCH* 13 (1976) above pp 141–68.

building.[41] In the conquered provinces, the Frankish princes preferred to introduce the style that they knew at home and at Daphni a Gothic porch was added to the monastery.[42] More generally, the Cistercians had to adapt their churches to conform to the western tradition with an altar exposed to view. We know for example that the iconostasis in the church at Daphni was destroyed.[43]

While the chroniclers speak of libraries being burnt,[44] some of the monasteries taken over by the Cistercians had large stocks of books of which at least a few must have survived. Did the Cistercians—could they—make use of these books, or were they, as in the west, reluctant to get involved in the work of the schools?[45] We know that Innocent III was very concerned about the libraries in the east and spoke metaphorically of the treasures of learning in Constantinople which he wished to entrust to a group of scholars and masters from Paris if they would start a new university there.[46] It is impossible to say how far the Cistercians heeded Innocent's words or indeed read or spoke Greek themselves. The evidence we have tells us little save that Martin of Pairis learned some words of Greek during his short stay in Constantinople.[47] Possibly like a certain canon of Amiens, he had the patience to spell out Greek words on the frescoes of churches in order to read the inscriptions on the reliquaries he had found.[48]

The organisational links with the mother houses on which the Cistercians prided themselves were also difficult to maintain in far away Romania. Attempts were made to impose the same stringent conditions which pertained to attendance at the curia on these monks going to Greece. This required them to obtain the consent of the abbot of Cîteaux and at least two of the abbots of the first four houses of the

[41] Runciman, *Byzantine Style and Civilisation* p 166.

[42] Millet, pp 57–8 and plate VI. The Cistercian additions to the monastery church at Daphni, notably the Gothic exo-narthex, are described by E. G. Stikas in *Deltion tis Christianikis Archaiologikis Etaireias*, ser 4, 3 (Athens 1963) pp 1–43.

[43] *Ibid* p 27. The face of the schismatic Pantocrator was pierced by the crusaders' swords. See also C. N. L. Brooke, 'Religious sentiment and church design in the later middle ages' in *Medieval Church and Society* (London 1971) pp 162–3 for discussion of the differences in church design between east and west.

[44] Runciman, *Byzantine Style and Civilisation* p 158.

[45] Derek Baker, 'Heresy and learning in early cistercianism' *SCH* 9 (Cambridge 1972) p 93.

[46] H. Denifle, *Chartularium Universitatis Parisiensis* 4 vols (Paris 1899) 1 pp 62–3; *PL* 215 (1855) cols 637–38; Southern, *Making of the Middle Ages* p 59.

[47] [P.] Riant, *Des Dépouilles Religieuses* [*enlévées à Constantinople au XIII*e *siècle*] (Paris 1875) p 68.

[48] *Ibid* p 67. Walo de Sarton, canon of Picquigny.

order.[49] The importance of the general chapter was further underlined by the requirement on all abbots to be present every September at Cîteaux.[50] Such annual attendance at Cîteaux had already proved to be a heavy burden for distant houses, and had led to occasional concessions and in 1216 the general chapter agreed that abbots of Cistercian houses in Greece should only be required to attend every fourth year.[51] In 1217 they were allowed to attend only every fifth year.[52] There is however little evidence to tell us how often they went in practice.

It is also interesting to speculate whether the papacy was less concerned with the regulation of Cistercian houses in the east than in the west. The displaced Greek monks appeared to be a litigious group, often appealing to the curia to protect them from the misdeeds of the Cistercians and there are cases in which the curia decided in favour of the Greeks.[53] This was something that the Cistercians in the west were not accustomed to, but it is understandable if papal aims are seen to be the maintenance of the façade at least of a reunited church. This situation also suggests that the Greeks were using a form of non-co-operative passive resistance which the Cistercians were not accustomed to find in their opponents and against which they had little understanding of the correct tactics to use. It may also be true that the papacy's attitude to the regulation of houses of Cistercian nuns showed less concern in the east than in the west, an attitude to be expected on a new frontier.[54] All these points and the fact that the Cistercians do not appear to have been instructed to call church councils to reform the clergy, illustrate the fact that the popes appear to have given no very powerful mandates to the Cistercians in the east as they had done to those of the order who had gone into Languedoc.

In spite of this the papacy appears to have used Cistercian abbots as valuable judges and supporters in its struggle with the Latin patriarchs.[55] The pope appointed the patriarchs either directly or by intervening in

[49] J. M. Canivez, *Statuta Capitulorum Generalium Ordinis Cisterciensis ab anno 1116 ad annum 1786* 8 vols (Louvain 1933–41) 1 p 65.

[50] *Ibid* 1 p 28.

[51] *Ibid* 1 p 459.

[52] *Ibid* 1 p 468.

[53] *PL* 216 (1855) cols 594–5 and 951–2. See also Brown, pp 80–1.

[54] *Ibid* p 114. In 1227 the chaplain of the Cistercian convent of St Antony of Paris visited the nuns of his order in Greece. Compare the suggestion of Manrique (4 p 341) that he was there to institute their chaplains in their houses and to inspire them, with his sermons, with the severe attitude taken by the general chapter towards nuns in the west described by Southern, *Western Society* pp 314–18.

[55] Brown p 96.

disputed elections.[56] Both Innocent III and Honorius III were determined that within Romania papal authority would be supreme. Innocent III in particular had always shown himself to be interested in keeping a very tight control over the higher clergy in the west and continued to try to extend this practice in Romania. The popes believed it to be in their interest to keep the Latin patriarchate weak while the patriarchs fought back to bring their actual position more into accord with their theoretical pretensions. In cases involving the patriarchate in 1217, 1218 and 1223, the abbots of Daphni, Chortaitou and St Angelus in Pera were called upon to act as judges for the pope.[57]

One area of Cistercian activity certainly had no parallel elsewhere. This was the acquisition of relics from Byzantium with which they had become involved from the earliest date.[58] After 1204 the traffic in relics assumed great proportions. The possession of these holy objects may have seemed a certain guarantee of obtaining royal charters of protection or imperial privilege such as that obtained from Philip of Swabia by the abbot of Pairis.[59] Among the sacred objects most sought after by the Latins were fragments of the true cross, any relic of the childhood and passion of Christ, relics of the virgin, the apostles, saint John the Baptist and saint Stephen Protomartyr.[60] The Cistercians had done well out of the division of such religious booty. In 1206 Martin of Pairis returned to his monastery in Alsace loaded with the arms of saints James the Less, Bartholomy and Leo as well as various relics of saints Peter, Thomas, Matthias, Mark, Ignatius Martyr, Blaise, Sebastian, Erasmus, Clement, Suzanne, Amelia and Cyriacus.[61] In 1210, Hugh, abbot of St Ghislain, was charged by the emperor Henry of Flanders with carrying to Clairvaux treasures amongst which were a piece of the true cross and John the Baptist's eyelash.[62] In 1263, the monastery of Daphni played a part in the transmission of relics to

[56] R. L. Wolff, 'The organisation of the Latin Patriarchate of Constantinople 1204–1261: social and administrative consequences of the Latin conquest' *Traditio* 6 (1948) pp 33–60 and 'Politics in the Latin Patriarchate of Constantinople 1204–1261' *DOP* 8 (1954) pp 225–95.

[57] Brown pp 97–108.

[58] Riant, *Des Dépouilles Religieuses* pp 1–30; Frolow, *La déviation de la IVe croisade* pp 7–8, 54–55, 58.

[59] Riant, *Des Dépouilles Religieuses* p 6.

[60] *Ibid* p 27; Frolow, *La déviation de la IVe croisade* pp 59, 65–71 for a discussion of the recrudescence of the Cult of the Passion which stimulated the collection of relics.

[61] Riant, *Des Dépouilles Religiéuses* p 185.

[62] *Ibid* p 184.

Cîteaux.[63] In that year Otto de Cicon, lord of Karystos came into possession of the right arm of John the Baptist from the church at Bucoleon and presented it to Cîteaux. The abbot of Daphni and the abbot of its mother house of Bellevaux who was visiting Greece were to take charge of the transportation of this precious relic.[64] In gratitude the general chapter granted the abbot of Daphni for his lifetime the special privilege usually accorded to abbots in Syria of attending its meetings only every seven years.[65]

We are now ready to pose the question as to how far this mission to the Orthodox, if indeed there was such a mission, was successful. There is no evidence to show that the Cistercians ever preached or that they were in any way able to use the conversion methods which they had used in the western frontiers of Languedoc and Spain. They seem not to have overcome the difficulties of external communications and other difficulties, such as a plentiful supply of monasteries to occupy, Greeks and popes full of duplicity, the need for a new pattern of organisation, and the temptations of abundant religious relics. Indeed these relics may well have been the real cause of failure. Without them the Cistercians might have adapted to the second stage of their mission, finding an inward and outward austerity, which might have led to the hoped-for success. With them, *covoitise*, however disguised, may have as surely corrupted the Cistercians as cupidity for secular treasures corrupted the crusaders.[66]

From 1204 until 1261 when all their houses save Daphni, and possibly the two in Crete, had been lost,[67] Romania presents us with an area in which there is an enormous disparity between the usual Cistercian theory and practice. What is so puzzling is their lack of activity. While in Spain Cistercians had been active in colonial settlement and slow reconquest after military occupation, nothing of this

[63] Riant, *Exuviae* 2 pp 144–49; Brown pp 112, 115.

[64] Riant, *Exuviae* 2 pp 147–49.

[65] *Ibid* p 149.

[66] Beer, *Villehardouin* p 24. He regarded *covoitise* as one of the greatest disasters of the expedition. Villehardouin, *La Conquête* p 253 'li uns aporta bien et li autres mauvaisement; que covoitise qui est racine de toz mals, ne laissa: ainz comencierent d'enqui ennavant li covotous a retenir des choses et Nostre Sire les commença mains a amer'. Robert de Clari, *The Conquest of Constantinople*, ed P. Lauer (Paris 1924) pp 101–12, also complains of the crusaders' cupidity for the *quemun de l'ost* got only the leavings of the *rikes hommes*. Also Frolow, *La déviation de la IVe croisade*, p 53.

[67] Rufinianai was probably abandoned soon after 1225 and Chortaitou by 1223 when its daughter house St Archangelus was put directly under the jurisdiction of Locedio. The house at Zaraca was active until 1260 while the nuns of St Mary of Percheio fled to Italy—Brown pp 116–18.

happened in the east. No military religious order emerged, as in Spain, to deal with the situation although in both areas, the knights and crusaders were present in force. It would have been very much in character for Innocent III to have founded such a military order, but it did not happen. It may be that Innocent III took too long to realise the magnitude of the problem. In 1205, he was writing enthusiastically about 'a great part of the eastern church which has in our time changed from disobedience to obedience and from contempt to devotion'.[68] Perhaps when the time came for him to appreciate the real nature of the challenge, it was already too late. Pressed by the hierarchy to tighten the regulations for new orders, harassed by the patriarchs and perplexed by political problems, he was unable to act even though he may have wished to do so. While Cistercian agents quarrelled with the Greeks, collected relics and caused considerable annoyance to subsequent popes, the Latin empire in Greece slipped away from them.

It was to be left to the Franciscans with their particular aptitudes and urban orientation, more representative of the modernity and forward-looking trends of the thirteenth century, to take up the task which the Cistercians had found too much for them.[69] The ageing vine of Cîteaux had perhaps borne too much fruit too quickly on branches which were too far extended from the main stock. In so doing it had become weakened beyond recovery.

[68] Southern, *Making of the Middle Ages,* p 59.
[69] R.L. Wolff, 'The Latin Empire of Constantinople and the Franciscans', *Tradito* 2 (1944) pp 213-37.

# X

# The Cistercians and Leadership in the Second Crusade: St Bernard's *chose pour rire*

The failure of the Second Crusade made demands upon the resilience of those who had been its spiritual leaders. A close examination of a brief entry in the *Continuatio Premonstratensis* of Sigebert of Gembloux,[1] composed before 1155 in the diocese of Lyon or Reims, will reveal some evidence of the consequences of this concern for Bernard and for the Cistercians. The chronicler refers to councils that were held throughout the Kingdom of France. Three were proposed but only two seem to have taken place. The assembly at Chartres on 7 May 1150 was the largest and most solemn.[2] Present were King Louis VII of France, one of the military leaders just returned from the Holy Land and a great collection of senior churchmen, most notably Suger, Abbot of St Denis and Bernard of Clairvaux. The Cistercian pope, Eugenius III, although not present in person, appears to have dominated the proceedings with his letter, *Immensum pietatis opus* dated 25 April 1150 and circulated to

---

1 *Continuatio Premonstratensis (Sigeberti)*, ed.G.H.PERTZ, *Monumenta Germania Historia, Scriptores* (Hannover, 1844) 6, pp. 447-456 especially p. 455. (Cited as *Continuatio Premonstratensis*).

2 M.BRIAL, 'Mémoire sur la veritable époque d'une assemblée tenu à Chartres, relativement à la croisade de Louis le Jeune', *Mémoires de l'Academie des inscriptions et belles-lettres* (Paris, 1818) 4, part 2, pp. 508-529. (Cited as BRIAL).

the whole assembly.[3] Eugenius, aware of all the difficulties, counselled extreme caution and stressed that nothing should be done without the tacit support of the King of France.

The purpose of the Council seems to have been the consideration of a new or third crusade, arising from correspondence between Bernard, now recovering from his despair at the failure of the Second Crusade,[4] and Suger who seems to have been the driving force behind the discussions. Suger had gone to Laon in early April 1150 after the news broke of the seige of Antioch and of the grave dangers which were to follow.[5] These dangers were not only to the King of Jerusalem and the Templars but also, more importantly, to the Relic of the True Cross. To Suger, the need for the Assembly at Laon with some of the archbishops and bishops - and even the Lord King himself - with the nobles of the realm was of vital importance. The Assembly of Laon judged that after the recent misfortunes, any proposal for a new crusade could only usefully be discussed with the attendance of each and every one of the spiritual leaders of the French Church - bishops and abbots from every province. Such a meeting was called, this time at Chartres.[6] It was equally

---

3 *Regesta pontificum romanorum ab condita Ecclesia ad annum post Christum Natum 1198*, ed.P.JAFFÉ, 2 vols (Leipzig, 1885-88) 2, 9385; *Recueil des Historiens des Gaules et de la France* ed. M.BOUQUET, 23 vols (Paris, 1738-1876), 15 (Paris, 1808) pp.457-58. (Cited as *Recueil*).

4 E.VACANDARD, *Vie de St Bernard*, 2 vols (Paris, 1895) 2, pp. 442-450; A.SEGUIN, 'Bernard et la seconde croisade', *Bernard de Clairvaux*, Commission d'histoire de l'ordre de Cîteaux, Etudes et documents, 3 (Paris, 1953) pp. 379-409; E.WILLEMS, 'Cîteaux et la seconde croisade', *Revue d'histoire ecclésiastique*, 49 (1953), pp. 116-151 (Cited as WILLEMS); E.DELARUELLE, 'L'idée de croisade chez saint Bernard, *Mélanges Saint Bernard*, XXIVe Congrès de l'Association bourguignonne des Sociétés savantes: Dijon, 1953 (Dijon, 1954) pp. 53-67; G.CONSTABLE, 'The Second Crusade as seen by Contemporaries', *Traditio* 9 (1953) pp. 213-279. (Cited as CONSTABLE, 'The Second Crusade'). I have not seen E.POGNON, 'L'échec de la croisade', *Saint Bernard: Homme de l'Eglise*, Témoinages: Cahiers de la Pierre-qui-Vire, (Paris 1953) 38-39, pp. 47-57;

5 *Recueil*, p. 523.

6 *Peter the Venerable: Selected Letters*, ed. J.MARTIN in collaboration with G.CONSTABLE, Pontifical Institute of Medieval Studies, (Toronto, 1974), pp. 87-88. (Cited as *Selected Letters*).

Indeed, many times during previous years whilst Bernard was on his various preaching campaigns, they had importuned him by writing pleading letters saying how desolate they were without him.[7] Bernard was always promising to return. Now that he was back with them at Clairvaux, they were loathe to let him go. But go he did!

In spite of having been subjected to constant requests to preach and advise on the crusade, Bernard's reluctance is stated eloquently before 1146 when, in a blunt letter to Eugenius, he writes, 'If someone has suggested to you the thought of imposing a new burden on me, I warn you that I am already overloaded beyond my strength. You know that I have taken the decision not to leave my monastery. I believe that I have never hidden this from you.'[8] Bernard, however, was always willing to concede that the word of God should take precedence over all else. As the Pope spoke for God when he launched a crusade, should the Pope wish him to participate in the *negotium Dei*, then he would surely do so.[9] Bernard's own experience in 1145 of his preaching campaign in Languedoc may well have helped him to overcome his stated reluctance because the need was so great. Much work still to do, had been his verdict when he returned![10]

The Cistercian Order itself could not give full attention to the matter, distracted as it was by the demands of its own major internal reorganization. The phenomenal growth of the Order in its first fifty years had caused grave concern in many quarters. Whether or not it was this concern which lay behind the abdication of Stephen Harding in 1133 may never be clear but whatever the cause, in the ensuing crisis and deposition of Guido, fourth abbot

---

7 Geoffrey of Auxerre, *Vita Prima Sancti Bernardi*, *Patrologia Latina*, ed., J.P.MIGNE, (Paris, 1855) 185, cols 411-412. (Cited as *PL*); R.I.MOORE, 'St Bernard's Mission to the Languedoc in 1145', *Bulletin of the Institute of Historical Research*, 47 (1974) pp. 1-10.

8 *PL* 182, Letter 245, cols 442-443.

9 Mandastis et obedivi, *PL* 182, Letter 247, col. 447.

10 Geoffrey of Auxerre, *Vita Prima Sancti Bernardi*, *PL* 185, col. 412.

of Cîteaux, the Cistercians demonstrated their ability to close ranks, expunging from their records all traces of this brief but disastrous abbacy.[11]

The year 1150 was to mark a very considerable break with what had gone before. The policy of almost unrestrained expansion had led to a major quarrel with the Premonstratensians thus breaking the Pact of 1142.[12] The length and humility of Bernard's letter to Hugh, abbot of Premontré, reveals this to have been a far deeper and more serious quarrel than was generally allowed by the Cistercians.[13] In the same year, when abbot Raynald died and was succeeded by Gozewin, abbot of Bonnevaux in the affiliation of Cîteaux, the General Chapter seems almost immediately to have taken the opportunity to reverse the former policy towards new foundations.[14] The process of retrenchment was taken most seriously. The very first Chapter celebrated by Gozewin in 1151 requested that the pope himself should reconfirm the origins on which the Order was based.[15]

In 1152, in the Bull *Sacrosancta*, Eugenius gave papal approval to the regular institutions of the Cistercians in the *Carta Caritatis* and may well have been concerned with the propagandist *Exordium Parvum* in draft form.[16] The initiative for the reorganization of the Order seems to have come entirely from within. There was a clear wish that those monasteries recently incorporated

---

11 An excellent recent summary of the controversy is given by J.B.AUBERGER, *L'Unanimité Cistercienne Primitive: Mythe ou Realité?*, Cîteaux: Studia et documenta, vol.3, Editions Sine Parvulos. VBVB, B3590, Achel, 1986. See also L.J.LEKAI, *The White Monks: A History of the Cistercian Order*, Our Lady of Spring Bank, Okauchee, Wisconsin, 1953, p. 42. (Cited as LEKAI).

12 J.M.CANIVEZ, *Statuta Capitulorum Generalium Ordinis Cisterciensis ab anno 1116 ad annum 1786*, 7 vols (Louvain, 1933-1938) I, *Ab anno 1116 ad annum 1220*, (Louvain, 1933) pp. 35-37. (Cited as CANIVEZ).

13 *PL*, 182, Letter 253, cols 453-458.

14 LEKAI, pp. 34-47, especially p. 42.

15 CANIVEZ, I, pp. 41-42.

16 A.MANRIQUE, *Annales Cistercienses*, Lyon 1642, *Anno* 1150, Cap.II, PP. 205-206. (Cited as MANRIQUE).

would show that vigour and stability of which the Cistercians were so proud. It was more important to consolidate the strength of the Order than to allow unrestricted growth. To this end it has been suggested that the Cistercians may well have rewritten their decrees to make them seem simpler, more primitive and therefore more original.[17] While this point may never be fully established, it is important to note that the Cistercians were not averse to tampering with their documents - sometimes for the best of motives.[18] Unfortunately, such an approach means that when we would have wished them to say more, their records remain stubbornly silent.

With so much on their minds, the Cistercians had little interest in the Council of Chartres and the prospect of a new crusade. Not so Bernard! In a letter to Suger, he expresses his delight at the news that he has received from the Master of the Temple.[19] Bernard further explains that he has promised Godfrey, Bishop of Langres, that he would be present at the Council. In addition, he would be happy to accompany the Bishop to the assembly for his presence there would be of great value.[20] This was encouraging information for Suger whose circular letter *Orientalis ecclesiae calamitatem* of April 1150 had been the calling notice for the Council of Chartres.[21] In spite of this notice being sent to all concerned we know of at least three absentees from the Council. The first absentee, Peter the Venerable, Abbot of Cluny, had been particularly invited and beseeched by Suger to attend in the name of God - 'for the matter involved not only prison but death'.[22]

---

17 G.CONSTABLE, 'The Study of Monastic History Today', *Essays on the Reconstruction of Medieval History*, edd. V.MUDROCH and G.S.COUSE, McGill-Queen's University Press, Montreal and London, 1974, pp. 21-51, especially pp. 37-39.

18 Idung of PrÜfening, 'A Dialogue between Two Monks', *Cistercians and Cluniacs: the case for Cîteaux* edd. and trans. J.F.O'Sullivan and J.Leahey, Cistercian Fathers Series, Kalamazoo 1977, pp. 51-53.

19 *PL* 182, Letter 380, cols 585-586.

20 *PL* 182, Letter 380, col.586.

21 *Recueil*, Letter 107, 523.

22 *Recueil*, Letter 107, 523.

Bernard also made a special plea for him to be present.[23] But come he did not![24] This in spite of the fact that the Abbot of St Denis had made quite sure that neither he nor any other potential absentee could allege that they had not been warned in good time. The replies of Peter the Venerable and of the Archbishops of Lyon and Bordeaux make interesting reading. Peter writes, 'I am sorry and grieve more than I can say not to be present at the Council of Chartres where the Lord King will proclaim your wisdom and that of others. Believe me, dear friend, believe what I say. I really am unable to come and because I cannot, I am sad. Who would not grieve to miss such a meeting, where the only person to gain thereby - by a new crusade - is none other than Christ Jesus!'.[25] He regrets that even before the beginning of Lent and before he had received Suger's letter of invitation, he had already summoned a General Chapter of the Cluniacs for precisely the day proposed for the meeting at Chartres.

Humbert, Archbishop of Lyon, had received two letters: one directly addressed to him[26] and the other transmitted through Peter the Venerable on Suger's explicit instructions.[27] Humbert said in his reply that although he wished to attend the Council of Chartres in his primatial capacity and be in the presence of the Lord King and the magnates, he was unable to do so as the Archbishop of Sens persisted in refusing to recognize the primacy of the See of Lyon. 'Furthermore', he added, compounding an already weak excuse, 'Hilo, abbot of Saint-Just, just outside the walls of the city was gravely ill and getting worse each day'.[28] As the *castra* and fortifications of the Church of Lyon were Hilo's responsibility, the Archbishop felt that he simply could not

---

23 *PL* 182, Letter 364, cols. 568-570; *Selected Letters*, Letter 163, 87-88.

24 *Selected Letters*, Letter 164, 89-91; BRIAL, p. 516, note 1.

25 BRIAL, 516, note 1.

26 *Recueil*, Letter 108, 524.

27 *Recueil*, Letters 107 and 108, 523-524.

28 *Recueil*, Letter 108, 523-524.

come in person and leave his church thus exposed. He did, however, delegate Stephen, formerly Archbishop of Vienne, to come in his place, He added that once peace had been brought to the churches of Lyon and Sens, then he, as Archbishop, would definitely declare himself ready to give advice and help in God's cause. Suger had by no means underestimated the ability of this archbishop to evade his duty!

Geoffrey, Archbishop of Bordeaux, also excused himself. He was rather ill, he said.[29] Furthermore, Lord Theodoric Galeranni, on behalf of the Lord King and the bishops of the diocese of Bordeaux, had convened a meeting for Good Shepherd Sunday, the second after Easter, at St Jean d'Angely in order to bring peace to the area. Clearly it must have been pointed out to him that he would have ample time to reach Chartres by 7 May. He did indeed set out but another letter to Suger was soon to appear. 'Geoffrey has fallen ill at Fontevrault and must remain there. Brother 'N' will come in his place'.[30] Hardly a satisfactory substitute!

Those who managed to attend the Council of Chartres would have been in no doubt as to the recriminations which abounded after the failure of the Second Crusade, including the fact that it was all Bernard's fault.[31] Some of the complainants had even gone so far as to suggest that money donated for the *negotium Dei* should be returned to those who had given it. A report of a lost sermon, although not contemporary, is nonetheless revealing of Bernard's actions in response to these protesters.[32] On their return from the Holy Land, he immediately hastened to the King and the French troops to give a message to the disaffected, the disgruntled and the plainly shocked. Taking as his text 'God has cast off and put us to shame and goest not forth with our

---

29 *Recueil*, Letter 109, 524.

30 *Recueil*, Letter 110, 524-525.

31 CONSTABLE, "Second Crusade", 266-276; Willems, 146-149.

32 G.CONSTABLE, 'A Report of a Lost Sermon by St Bernard on the failure of the Second Crusade, *Studies in Medieval Cistercian History*, Cistercian Studies Series, 13, Cistercian Publications, Spencer, Massachusetts, 1971, pp. 49-54. (Cited as CONSTABLE, 'Lost Sermon'.

armies', he reminds the soldiers not to forget the truth given in Deuteronomy:[33] if their faith in one rock and one God is firm, they should prevail, even against overwhelming odds! He says that the Psalmist would have understood that the troops felt cast off by God but, rather than mourning over their defeat, they should not abandon hope. And when they had all heard him, the king and the barons were wonderfully comforted by Bernard's preaching and much strengthened in their faith. Even if this account is not strictly contemporary, it has a ring of truth about it and accords well with what we know from Bernard's own accounts of his preaching and its great effectiveness.[34]

For the Church as a whole, the failure of the Second Crusade was a matter of the utmost seriousness. For Bernard in particular it might have seemed like a personal judgment, but one which he had to overcome. In Book II of *De Consideratione*, Bernard represents the failure as an example of the mysterious ways in which God works. 'The judgments of God are just', he wrote, 'but this is so great a blot that I can only declare blessed whomsoever is not scandalized by it'.[35] Others advanced various reasons for the catastrophe - from Old Testament comparisons where God had punished those who had failed to perform his will, to the New Testament approach more favoured by Cistercians such as John of Casamari who stressed in a letter to Bernard that all those who had made the sacrifice would be saved.[36] Bernard took the view that those who survived would be made stronger by this humbling experience - perhaps an understanding which was a direct result of his own involvement in the disaster. With such all-round demoralization, the question of who was to lead any future crusade would be crucial, particularly if churchmen were to bear in mind St Paul's view that, in a sinful world, man

---

[33] Deuteronomy 32:30; CONSTABLE, 'Lost Sermon', p. 52.

[34] CONSTABLE, 'Lost Sermon', p. 49.

[35] *PL* 182, col.745; Bernard of Clairvaux, *Five Books on Consideration: Advice to a pope* trans. J.D.ANDERSON and E.T.KENNAN, Cistercian Fathers' Series, 37, Cistercian Publications, Kalamazoo, Michigan, 1976, Book 2, pp. 47-52 and especially p. 48.

[36] *PL* 182, Letter 386, cols.590-591.

cannot easily govern events. Thus leadership of any new crusade, whilst on the agenda, was overshadowed by the main talking point of the Council of Chartres; the letter received from Eugenius III which damned the project with faint praise.[37]

The Pope's approval for any new expedition to the Holy Land was vital. Should it be given whole-heartedly, it would exercise great influence over the decision of the assembly at Chartres. Eugenius, however, expressed serious reservations. He had already seen the disastrous failure of one crusade. He had no wish to be associated with another. In his letter of 25 April,[38] fifteen days before Chartres, he equivocated. 'He had', he said, 'many fears about this project inspired by King Louis and dared not take the initiative in advising a crusade, deploring as he did, the recent loss and bloodshed of so many thousands of brave men who had perished'. However, so as not to upset the project, he asked Suger to have prior discussions with the King and his barons. If they found themselves disposed towards restarting this perilous undertaking, then he would offer the usual counsel, advice and remission of sins as he had granted five years previously. The last thing that the Pope wanted was to be seen to upset any such plan once it had been agreed.

In the event, and with no successful military leader being available, an exceptional but understandable decision was reached by the Council. Spiritual and military leadership were to be embodied in one person under the guidance of the Holy Spirit.[39] No-one could fulfil this role better than Bernard whose every action seemed to follow such guidance. Having made this decision by a unanimous vote, the Council members rapidly dispersed to deal with other pressing matters, leaving Bernard to ponder their decision. As Watkin Williams suggests, his first reaction must have been to dismiss the whole suggestion as a laughing matter, *une chose pour rire*.[40]

---

37 BRIAL, p. 517, note 1.

38 BRIAL, p. 517.

39 *PL* 182, Letter 256, cols.463-465.

40 W.WILLIAMS, *Bernard of Clairvaux*, Manchester University Press, 1935, p. 287.

There were various other reactions amongst those affected by this extraordinary and unprecedented proposal. The King was more excited than the barons whose reactions were, at best, lukewarm. The Templars and the ordinary soldiers might have been expected to approve, especially as Bernard had so characteristically thought to console them at the moment of their deepest humiliation. But what of those who had not attended the Council of Chartres; what of Bernard himself - and bearing in mind their earlier strictures, what of the monks of Clairvaux and the whole Order of Cîteaux?

First, those who did not attend. In spite of their protestations, we might assume that, like the Archbishop of Lyon, they perhaps knew what was afoot and wished to save themselves the embarrassment of being present to voice their fundamental objections. So far as the pope was concerned we have to take into account the dilemma Eugenius faced by having already agreed to support decisions made at the Council and by upholding the tradition, so clearly expounded by Urban II, that the participation of monks in crusades should be restricted.[41] The attitude of Bernard himself would be crucial. If Bernard were in favour of the proposal, the Pope could raise doubts. If Bernard was against, Eugenius could support the decision without too much harm arising. Papal damage-limitation at its best!

In the last part of his letter 256 addressed to Eugenius, Bernard refers to the decision of the Council to appoint him as military leader of the new crusade - just like a commander or prince.[42] On a matter such as this, Eugenius had to take soundings before coming to a decision to approve or not. He was helped by Bernard's initial reaction. Although the election by the Council, unanimously, was a compliment, powerful reasons prevented Bernard from accepting immediately. His response is that expected of a Cistercian monk. 'You may rest assured', he tells Eugenius, 'not only that such a proposal was made contrary to my advice and my wishes and that I am still of the same mind with regard to it, but that to give it effect is quite beyond my powers in so far as I am able to judge them. Who am I?', he asks

---

[41] CONSTABLE, 'Second Crusade', pp. 269-270, note 290.

[42] Quasi dux et princeps, *PL* 182, col.464; WILLEMS, p. 143.

rhetorically, 'to lead an army into battle, to march at the head of the troops? What could be further from my profession, even if the strength and necessary skills were not lacking in me?'.[43] Here, Bernard places himself in the hands of Eugenius to know God's will. 'Do not abandon me to the will of men', he begs, 'but since it is your particular mission, try to know the plans of God and have his will done on earth as it is in Heaven!' Eugenius eventually confirmed the decision of the Council but mistakenly did not modify the proposal. There were dangers in allowing Bernard, a sixty-year old monk in such ill health to be in supreme military command. It would indeed have been something at which to laugh or to ridicule. However, the extension of his spiritual preaching to his physical presence at the front of the army might well have led to untold benefits. Bernard had by no means lost the power to attract and hold the attention of a crowd and lead them where they should go!

This problem of leadership was inextricably linked to the question of morale. Who else could overcome the absence of this essential quality in the knighthood of the time but Bernard himself?[44] Had not Raynald, abbot of Morimond, on Bernard's own orders, been inspired to call together the lords of Bassigny to take the Cross on Ascension Day 1146?[45] In a letter to Peter the Venerable, written in May-June 1150 Bernard repeats these orders, stressing again the desperate need for men to do God's work.[46] Although Peter had been absent from Chartres his letter had been by no means unfavourable.[47] Bernard reflects that the hearts of the princes are tepid. 'They bear their swords without a cause and the knights have defected. As you know', he writes, 'at the Council of Chartres, little or nothing was done

---

43 *PL* 182, Letter 256, cols.463-465.

44 CONSTABLE, 'Lost Sermon', p. 52.

45 WILLEMS, p. 138.

46 *Negotium Dei*. J.SATABIN, 'Une lettre inedite de Saint Bernard', *Etudes Réligieuses, Historiques et Littéraires*, Paris 1894, pp. 321-327, especially p. 321.

47 *Selected Letters*, 164, 89-91.

and much had been hoped and expected from your presence.[48] I beseech you to be with us at another Council, arranged to be held at the Royal Palace at Compiègne on 15 July where what is right and proper should be done, as necessity requires - and the necessity is great indeed!'

It seems that Eugenius had not fully listened to Bernard. Suger must also have felt the need to tell him what had occurred at Chartres, but we do not have a copy of the letter he wrote. The Pope, in his reply from Albano dated 19 June 1150,[49] praised and thanked Suger for all his concern to get aid for the Holy Land. 'This affair', he said, 'troubles me greatly. I cannot refuse my consent to the demand that you and the others who have written to me have made although it costs me dearly to do any harm to that person chosen unanimously and whose infirmity I know'[50] - obviously here referring to Bernard. Eugenius, still prevaricating, recommended that Suger should act with prudence and discretion. Perhaps this new Council of the Church at Compiègne would consider the matter and, incidentally, also deal with the reform of the highly irregular canons of St Corneille who seemed to be in occupation there.[51] Subsequent documents reveal much activity over the reform of the canons, replaced by monks from St Denis, but nothing more about Bernard's position nor indeed any further details of the Council of Compiègne, set for July 1150. It seems probable that it never took place at all and that the question of Bernard's leadership was to be quietly dropped.

The final piece of evidence is to be found in that brief extract from the *Continuatio Premonstratensis* already cited. The chronicler says that the Pope had enjoined Bernard to place himself at the head of the crusaders to

---

[48] Nostis quod in Carnotensi conventu de negotio Dei aut parum aut nichil factum est SATABIN, 'Une lettre inedite', p. 323.

[49] *Recueil*, Letter 71, 458-459.

[50] Propter imbecillitatem personae in qua omnium vota, Domino favente, concurrunt BRIAL, p. 521.

[51] G.CONSTABLE, 'Suger's Monastic Administration', *Hermits, Monks and Crusaders i[n] Medieval Europe*, Variorum Reprint, London 1988, pp. 1-51, especially p. 15.

encourage the others. Then in the next line he states laconically that the entire proposal was completely wrecked by the attitude of the Cistercians.[52]

Cistercian sources are silent on this matter. They contain no record of a Council at Chartres, nor is any mention made of Bernard's election - with one voice - as the leader of the new crusade. Surely we cannot blame this important yet solitary entry on Premonstratensian hostility alone. The Cistercians themselves had good reasons for wishing to halt this project. These may have combined a concern for the welfare and health of Bernard, a desire that Clairvaux should have the services of its outstanding abbot for as long as possible and that members of the Order should be discouraged from taking on tasks beyond those for which it was originally formed. In all this, given the outstanding qualities of Bernard, it may have been his health and his age which were the deciding factors. Yet, in spite of both, Bernard had, it seems, at Chartres, once more preached a great crusading sermon, irresistibly provoking men to turn towards Jerusalem. But the Cistercians already recognized that they had a saint on their hands - and no saint could be allowed to risk becoming a laughing stock! Is it possible therefore that Eugenius, former monk and Bernard's pupil at Clairvaux, with the full knowledge and encouragement of the Cistercian Order, prevaricated - as we have seen - and in the end withheld his consent? As it happened, it was all for the best for Suger died early in 1151 and Bernard on 20 August 1153. Nearly sixty years later when Pope Innocent III who was accustomed to using the Cistercians in a wide range of activities made a sharp change in papal policy,[53] a St Bernard of the day, in a position of leadership, would have been received very differently. Innocent and Bernard together would have made an irresistible

52 Anno 1150, habitus per Franciam conventibus, jubente etiam Eugenio papa, ut abbas Clarevallensis Jerosolymam ad alios provocandos mitteretur, grandis iterum sermo de profectione transmarina celebratur, sed per Cistercienses monachos, totum cassatur, *Continuatio Premonstratensis (Sigeberti)*, ed. G.H.PERTZ, *MGH*.SS, (Hannover, 1844) vol.6, pp. 447-456.

53 J.A.BRUNDAGE, 'A Transformed Angel (X 3.31.18): The Problem of the Crusading Monk', *Studies in Medieval Cistercian History*, Cistercian Studies Series, 13, Cistercian Publications, Spencer, Massachusetts, 1971, pp. 55-62, especially p. 57.

combination - as Innocent himself recognized through the very special veneration he gave to the Abbot of Clairvaux![54]

[54] *PL* 214, cols 1032-1033 for Innocent's collect in honor of the abbot of Clairvaux.

# XI

## A SHOW WITH A MEANING
## INNOCENT III'S APPROACH TO THE FOURTH LATERAN COUNCIL, 1215

Rome, on the Feast of St Martin, 11 November 1215, was the setting for a truly great show. There were lights, decorations, music including elephant-sounding trumpets and all types of early thirteenth-century razzmatazz but behind it all was a most solemn purpose. All aspects of the show had a liturgical basis. It marked the beginning of the Fourth Lateran Council which was to result in the most important single body of disciplinary and reform legislation ever applied to the Medieval Church.[1]

One man in particular observed it all - or at least as much as could be seen by any one individual at such an imposing performance. This anonymous German cleric from his place right at the back of the great assembly gives such a vivid eyewitness account that our understanding of the event has been transformed.[2] His account was not actually published until 1964, to accompany the calling of the Second Vatican Council. This thirteenth-century so-called Giessen Manuscript had become available on its rediscovery in the eighteenth century but had up to then attracted little attention.[3] Our cleric, highly educated and with the ability to quote the classics, seems to have been quite overwhelmed at all that he saw. Citing the Latin poet Horace, he wishes to explain to his friends back home, the reasons for the lasting impression which he had received. 'What has fallen on the ears', he writes 'excites the mind less rapidly than what the eyes have faithfully beheld'.[4] His belief in the value of visual communication would not surprise the world of twentieth-century media but, for this unknown cleric from north of the Alps, it was the most remarkable event he would ever see. He was eager to convey something of the exuberance of this Mediterranean *festa* but because his ears had not grasped as much as his eyes he, with Teutonic thoroughness, sought out the appropriate documents to back up his account.[5] He was then not only able to communicate the wonder of the show but also the message it was meant to provide. He was not alone in feeling privileged to participate in such a significant occasion. Thousands of others did likewise. Romans and strangers, clerics and laymen, from the Pope himself and all the cardinals of the Roman Church right down to the humblest persons whose names and positions we do not know. Innocent III (1198-1216) must have been well pleased by the success of the arrangements on which he had spent so much time.[6]

---

1 Kuttner and Garcia (1964), 163; Boyle (1985), 30-43.

2 Kuttner and Garcia (1964), 123-9; Eyewitness (1986), 369-76.

3 Kuttner and Garcia (1964), 115-19.

4 Horace, *Ars Poetica*, 180-1.

5 Kuttner and Garcia (1964), 132.

6 Ladner (1983), 903-29, esp. 905-13 for a general intellectual and artistic background to the pontificate. H. Tillmann (1980), *Pope Innocent III*, trans. W. Sax, *Europe in the Middle Ages: Select Studies*, 12. (North-Holland) is not helpful on the Lateran Council although elsewhere there is interesting information on Innocent himself, esp 189-205, 289-304.

SKETCH PLAN OF THE LATERAN COMPLEX: THE BASILICA OF ST JOHN LATERAN, THE PAPAL PALACE AND AUDIENCE HALLS, THE MONASTERY AND ITS CLOISTER

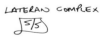

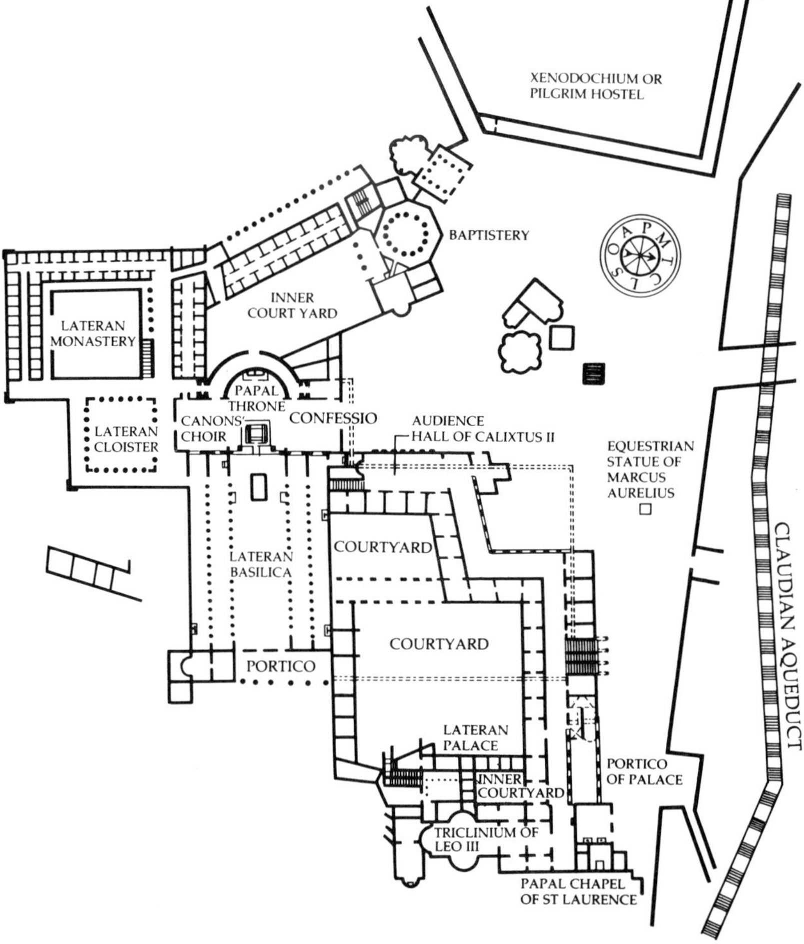


LATERAN COMPLEX
5/5

The cast of this great event could not have been more impressive, including as it did, the greatest ecclesiastical dignitaries of all Latin Christendom. They came from far and near, they spoke in many and varied tongues but it was their faith which united them and it was this on which Innocent relied when he came to prepare his great sermons with which he was to address them. But sermons from the pope in isolation were not sufficient in themselves to reinforce the spiritual message. Preliminary documents had been sent out to all involved so that the participants could prepare contributions of real value to assist in the hard decisions which would have to be made. Possibly too, as news of the great Council spread, pressure groups and individuals with axes to grind may well have tried to influence their local bishops and clergy as they prepared to set out for Rome. They would also have insisted that these clerics should report back after the Council. Indeed, in the middle of the next Lent, the third week of March 1216, our anonymous cleric seems to have made just such a report back to his bishop in Germany, specifically announcing that, as requested, he would describe the solemn masses, the events and the enactments of the Council. The other matters, he says, would await his return.[7]

Innocent, well aware that the councils of the twelfth century had been short on notice - in fact, never summoned more than one year in advance - was determined to avoid the failures inherent in such a brief period of preparation.[8] With a much longer period of notice, the Pope would be able to fix a month and year both 'convenient' to all and which also was to serve his own purpose. These earlier councils had been held during Lent but Innocent decreed that all those attending this new council should present themselves in Rome by the Feast of All Saints', 1 November 1215 with the first full session of the Council being held on St Martin's Day, 11 November.[9] His invitations or calling notices to summon delegates to the Council went out as early as April 1213, two and a half years before the event. He used this tactic lest anyone should claim to be excused from attending on the grounds that they had not known of it or had already made alternative arrangements. Such excuses were by no means unknown in the history of ecclesiastical councils and synods which some preferred not to have to attend, either because they would have to make their contrary positions apparent or carry out any uncomfortable decisions made. Dissension between kings and princes was beginning to abate and the roads, he hoped, should thereby be the safer. Further, summer travel was, by and large, so much easier than that undertaken in winter and thus another potential excuse for absence, namely the difficulty of travelling, was neatly removed.[10] Interestingly, the excuse of poor road conditions seems to have been used by many after the conclusion of the Council to extend the period of their sojourn in Rome. Many did not arrive back home until well into 1216.

The whole environment of the Council was designed to match and enhance its great importance. The three most full and solemn sessions, the plenary sessions, to mark the opening, the halfway point and the ending, were all held in the Church of St John Lateran, otherwise the *Constantiniana* or ancient Basilica of Constantine.

---

**7** Eyewitness (1986), 370.
**8** Robinson (1990), 121-45.
**9** *PL* (1855), 216, 823-7; Cheney and Semple (1953), 144-7.
**10** N. Ohler (1989), *The Medieval Traveller*, trans. C. Hillier, (Boydell Press), 8-9.

This great Church, dedicated to the Saviour, also claimed for itself the prestigious and venerable title of the 'Cathedral of Rome'.[11] Working sessions for smaller groups of Council members took place in the various halls and chambers of the adjacent Lateran palace, all redolent with the history of the popes of the past displayed in a series of frescoes and mosaics.[12] Meanwhile, the whole City of Rome with its own immense layers of history and multitude of churches lay open for all to see, in their capacity either as pilgrims or visitors or both.

St Peter's, in Innocent's opinion at least, somewhat neglected in spite of its possession of the tomb or *confessio* of the Prince of the Apostles, was to be the centrepiece for display and decoration. It was to be the location for a highly significant anniversary commemoration of its dedication. The Pope's own origins as a canon of the Chapter of St Peter's go some way towards explaining his interest in healing the deep divisions between the canons of both great basilicas whose constant bickering was already a grave scandal to Christendom.[13] The decorations that Innocent conceived for St Peter's conveyed religious messages in two distinct forms. Inconspicuous but highly significant were the precious small works for the attention of the archbishops and metropolitans on their private visits to the *confessio*.[14] Conspicuous and also full of meaning were the alterations which had been carried out to the decayed Constantinian apse mosaic.[15] Both these decorations enhanced the solemn mass celebrated on 18 November, the Feast of the Dedication, and helped to raise the status of the Basilica on the Vatican Hill to co-equality with that of the Lateran, a task which Innocent had set himself early on in his pontificate.[16]

The Pope's small works involved the provision of an enamelled screen in Limoges work to protect the focal point of the Basilica, the *confessio* or tomb of St Peter.[17] In this sacred place, the *pallium* or white woollen shawl of each archbishop or metropolitan rested overnight on the tomb of the Saint. Both front and back faces of the lunette above the door by which they entered the so-called 'niche of the *pallia*', as well as the protective screen itself, were covered with small and significant figures of apostles and Old Testament prophets, exquisitely engraved, each giving a special message to the archbishops and metropolitans visiting the Council.[18] The reverse side of the lunette, now in the National Museum of Rome, bears an engraving of simple design but special relevance. Twenty-four enthroned bishops in chasubles and mitres are depicted in animated conversation, as if at a council. Each holds a book in his left hand while with his right, he points in emphasis. In the centre, double the size of the others, sits a bishop wearing his *pallium* and carrying St Peter's keys, with the Dove of the Holy Spirit at his ear. The inscription refers to the Holy

---

11 Krautheimer (1980), 177.

12 C. Walter, 'Papal Political Imagery in the Medieval Lateran Palace', *Cahiers Archéologiques*, 20. (1970), 155-76; *Ibid.* 21, (1971), 109-36; P. Lauer (1911), *Le Palais de Latran*, (Paris).

13 M. Maccarrone (1985), 'La "Cathedra Sancti Petri" nel Medioevo: Da Simbolo a Reliquia', *Rivista di Storia della Chiesa in Italia*, 36 349-447, esp 427-32.

14 Gautier (1968), 237-46.

15 Krautheimer (1980), 203-6.

16 *PL* (1855) 215, 513.

17 Gautier (1968), 237-42.

18 Gautier (1968), 242-46.

Spirit of the Council and the instructions to each bishop read 'Feed your Sheep' and 'This is the Door of the Sheep'; messages entirely in tune with Innocent's aim.[19]

For the very public gaze, in a central position in the lower half of the great apse mosaic, with the Lamb of God on the holy hill, Innocent had placed a chalice to receive the blood of the Lamb, the most symbolic part of the liturgical message which he wished to convey to the universal Church.[20] It is worth noticing that a similar and very small Lamb of God, bleeding into the chalice in the same way, also appears in the cloister of St Paul's outside the Walls, the other great patriarchial basilica, dedicated to the Apostle to the Gentiles.[21] Was Innocent perhaps at work here too? The cloister certainly dates from this period. On the apse of St Peter's, Innocent, the originator of the Council, is represented on the left side of the Lamb with the stylized figure of *Ecclesia Romana*, the Roman Church, on the right - the link is obvious.[22] Decorations and special commemorative service together drew such enormous crowds that Innocent must have been well satisfied.[23] The difficulties he personally experienced in actually trying to enter the Basilica through the crowds could only have enhanced his pleasure.

This Fourth Lateran Council, although the twelfth ecumenical council in the tradition of the Western Church, was the first great assembly of the whole church since Late Antiquity and the Council of Chalcedon 451. Only the Second Council of Nicea 787 could challenge this claim. The first three Lateran Councils held in 1123, 1139 and 1179 respectively were mainly concerned with the development of the earlier Gregorian reforms.[24] It was to be expected that a pope of Innocent's ability and zeal and with considerable experience in the Curia in spite of his youth, would be eager to stage a great new council. The turn of the twelfth century with its explosion of spiritual awareness was just the time for such a council. Contemporary sources describing the Fourth Lateran Council link the significance of the man, the time and the event.

Innocent himself also has much to tell us. In April 1213, he sent a series of letters to all bishops, both in Western Christendom and in the Latin Church in the East. Copies were also sent to other ecclesiastics and secular lords. His aim was clearly stated in the letter beginning *The Vineyard of the Lord of Sabaoth*, dated 19 April.[25] A General Council in accordance with the ancient custom of the Fathers of the Church was needed, not only to consider the recovery of the Holy Land, always urgent since the loss of Jerusalem in 1187, but also the reform of the universal church, a matter which was becoming increasingly important. The Council therefore

---

19 Gautier (1968), 244; J. M. Powell, '*Pastor Bonus*: some evidence of Honorious III's use of the sermons of Pope Innocent III', *Speculum*, 52 (1977), 522-37.

20 G. Grimaldi (1972), *Descrizione della Basilica Vaticana*, ed. R. Niggl, (Vatican City) 169; Krautheimer (1980), 205-6.

21 P. C. Claussen, *Magistri doctissimi romani: Die römischen Marmorkünstler, Corpus Cosmatorum*, I, (Stuttgart) for this and other contemporary cosmatesque works.

22 A. Margiotta (1988), 'L'antica decorazione absidiale della Basilica di San Pietro in alcuni frammenti al Museo di Romana', *Bolletino dei Musei Communali di Roma*, 2, 21-33.

23 Eyewitness (1986), 372.

24 R. Foreville (1965), *Latran I, II, III et Latran IV*, (Paris).

25 *PL* (1855), 216, 823-7; Cheney and Semple (1953), 144-7.

would beseech God to reveal his pleasure and would be concerned with the spiritual health of souls in carrying it out.

Innocent's summons, addressed as it was to all bishops and archbishops, particularly stressed the crucial role they would play at his Council. They were to ensure that all cathedral and other chapters were to send as delegates, deans, provosts or other suitable people to deal with matters of specific concern. In every ecclesiastical province, 'discreet' men were to help in investigating matters which required energetic correction or reform so that each bishop could deliver a 'conscientious' report in writing on his diocese for the scrutiny of the Council as a whole. To press home the grave necessity of the undertaking, Innocent underlines that he will accept no idle excuse for any bishop's neglect of this vital work or reform. This summons to the general council was issued together with *Quia major*, his greatest crusade encyclical, which he had sent out between 19-29 April to every ecclesiastical province of the West save distant Norway.[26]

The spiritual purpose of the Council having been emphasized, Innocent returned to ensuring its perfect organisation. He had first conceived the idea at the beginning of his pontificate in November 1199, expressed in two letters, one to the Patriarch of the Eastern Church[27] and the other to the Emperor at Constantinople. The Emperor had already affirmed that he would participate though his ideas may have been rather different from those which Innocent eventually developed. Even after the violent events of the Fourth Crusade and the attack on Constantinople, the idea of holding a council still held favour in the East. In 1212, the Patriarch of Alexandria was imprisoned by the Sultan of Egypt and several christian strongholds were lost to the infidel. The situation in the Holy Land could wait no longer and if there were to be a council, the time had now surely arrived. Its failure could not be countenanced and the most thorough organization would be required. Carefully constructed schemes of organisation arose from the vast amount of preparatory work which Innocent undertook with the collaboration of his curial colleagues. One innovation in communication and accountability which the pope introduced was that the Council should deal with the reports which the bishops had already been asked to prepare. It was, as Maccarrone has said, the first time in the history of Church Councils that anyone had thought of such a vast preparation of conciliar material and a widespread prior involvement of those called to attend.[28] Never before and perhaps never since has such a thing happened. None of the replies which would have been such a precious source of historical information has survived but Innocent must certainly have worked from them. Personal contact was also important to the pope and he sent his legates to various parts of Christendom, not only to preach the crusade but to collect comments and suggestions on proposals emanating from the papal curia. These would complement discussion and comments provided by the bishops and might even be a check on what they had prepared.

Once the date was set, the organisation prepared and the participants travelling towards Rome, Innocent would have been waiting somewhat anxiously for the first day of November when the roll was to be called. Then the Council would get under

---

**26** Riley-Smith (1981), 118-24.

**27** *PL* (1855), 214, 758-69; Maccarrone (1961), 6-7.

**28** Maccarrone (1961), 9.

way. A great show, a major event with many observers, some of whom were later to provide valuable accounts.

The most important contemporary source - at least until that of the unknown German cleic became widely available in 1964 - was the *Chronicle* of Richard, the imperial notary from San Germano near Monte Cassino who, about the year 1230, wrote the fullest version.[29] He is particularly interesting for the way in which he presents the view from the *Regno*, the southern kingdom of the Emperor, Frederick II. Richard stresses that he was present and saw and recorded the events *seriatim* - in sequence as they occurred.[30] He recounts Innocent's opening sermon verbatim using copies of the text which we know were available to check any lapses of memory he may have had. He also provides details of local interest to his southern audience, for example, the presence and active participation of Berardo, Archbishop of Palermo.[31] His account has been reinforced by that of the unknown German and they complement each other.[32]

In the *Liber Pontificalis* or *Popes' Book*, the entry on Innocent III by Martin of Troppau or Martin the Pole (d.1278), although brief, has been vindicated by the Eyewitness.[33] Previously Martin's mention of the consecration of the Church of Santa Maria in Trastevere, the special event of Sunday 15 November, in the presence of those attending the Council, had been discounted on the grounds that it was nowhere else substantiated.[34]

The vital Registers for the eighteenth and nineteenth years of Innocent's pontificate have not survived and neither is there any official record of the proceedings of the Fourth Lateran Council, such as those made for the First and Second Councils of Lyon in 1245 and 1274. A fragment of only a few lines referring to the numbers of archbishops and bishops who attended was all that was known until 1905 when a more detailed list was discovered in Zurich.[35] From this list we now know that 412 bishops attended together with a further 71 greater ecclesiastics including patriarchs, primates and archbishops. Theiner who, in 1864, attempted a reconstruction of the lost registers for 1213-1216[36] also mentioned Innocent's third and last sermon addressed to the final plenary session of the Council of which unfortunately only a sketchy reconstruction can be attempted. This follows a list he gives of the Council's canons or conciliar decrees, varying between 68 and 71, but usually agreed to be the latter number.[37]

Illustrated evidence of the events of the Council can be found in three manuscripts emanating from England, France and Castile. Matthew Paris of St Albans, in his *Chronica Majora* (c1235-1240) includes a line drawing of one of the

---

29 Richard of San Germano (1888), 88-94.

30 Richard of San Germano (1888), 90, 'seriatim exponam ego qui interfui et vidi Riccardus, huius operis auctor'.

31 Richard of San Germano (1888), 93.

32 Kuttner and Garcia (1964), 147-153.

33 Martin of Troppau (1892), 451-3; Eyewitness (1986) 371-2.

34 Kuttner and Garcia (1964), 143-6; Kinney (1975), 335-47.

35 Zurich Manuscript (1905), 1723-33.

36 *Vetera Monumenta Slavorum meridionalium historiam illustrantia*, ed. A. Theiner, (Rome, 1864), 63.

37 Constitutions (in translation) (1975), *English Historical Documents*, III, 643-76.

sessions.[38] This manuscript, now in Corpus Christi College, Cambridge, depicts two groups of bishops facing each other above a sea of waves. All these bishops are wearing mitres and chasubles and carry pastoral staffs as symbols of their office, yet each one expresses a different mood - some intently involved in the action, others preoccupied in contemplation. An inscription informs us that this is the Lateran Council while beneath, the roll of attendance is given as 61 archbishops, 412 bishops with 800 abbots and priors. Doubtless, Matthew Paris had consulted his own abbot, William of St Albans (1214-1235) who was present at the Council with two fellow monks, Alexander of Appleton and Master Roger Porretanus.[39] We may assume that a chronicler would give the correct number of abbots and priors in attendance even if he was perhaps not quite so accurate about the archbishops.

The manuscript of the anonymous continuator of William of Tudela's *Chanson de la Croisade Albigeoise* written c1275-1280 contains an illustration to accompany the dramatic and poetic account of the protracted debates which took place at the Council throughout the whole period.[40] This shows a crenellated wall and a towerscape designed to evoke an imaginary Lateran Palace and Basilica church. Here the pope sits, his right hand raised in a blessing and holding in his left a book. He faces a crowd of seated persons, including Eleanor of Aragon, wife of Raymond, Count of Toulouse, whose presence is also attested by the German cleric.[41] The great assembly, with its incredible hubbub and confusion of tongues, is described by a short text in verse. The poem, based on first-hand information, provides one topographical detail of much interest. The Count of Toulouse and his young son were made to wait outside the assembly in a marble cloister covered with inscriptions. Surely the Lateran cloister, newly decorated for the Council? The Pope, meanwhile, overcoming his annoyance at the acrimonious discussion taking place inside, walked in the garden of his Palace at the Lateran to recover his composure.[42]

The third illustration of the Council comes from the Kingdom of Castile. In the manuscript known as the *Codex Toledanus* written by two different hands (1235-1255 and 1275), yet very much in the Visigothic tradition, the Archbishop of Toledo, Roderigo Ximenez de Rada (d.1247) is shown centre-stage with the Pope seated at one end of the Audience Hall, flanked by the Patriarchs of Jerusalem and Constantinople and the Archbishops of Compostela, Braga, Tarragona and Narbonne with two more small seated figures opposite Innocent at the other end of the chamber.[43] Professor Foreville has suggested that by the clever device of using only ten figures and no decor, the artist succeeds spectacularly in creating the impression of a vast conciliar assembly whilst concentrating on Archbishop Roderigo. The *Codex Toledanus* is concerned with the verbal record of the session on the third day of the Council, Friday 13 November, at which the Archbishop debated the primacy of Toledo over its rivals, Braga and Compostela. As proof in his vigorous defence, the Archbishop held aloft for all to see privileges from four earlier popes and then read aloud from them including those from Innocent himself. Ximenez

---

38 Foreville (1966), 1122.
39 Matthew Paris (1984), 39-40.
40 *Chanson*, (1957) 40-89.
41 Eyewitness (1986), 371.
42 *Chanson (1957)*, 58-9; Foreville (1966), 1123-24.
43 Foreville (1966), 1125-27.

dismissed his rivals in a highly-charged and emotional speech: the Spanish apostolate of St James at Compostela was nothing but an 'old wives' tale' while Mauricio Burdino, Archbishop of Braga, as the Anti-Pope Gregory VIII (1118-1121), had been merely the 'creature' of the German Emperor, Henry V (1098-1125).[44] Then, in a dramatic gesture, turning to the decorations on the walls of the Audience Chamber of Callixtus II, the Archbishop was able to point to the very fresco, depicting this shameful tale, to the deep embarrassment of Estevâo, incumbent of Braga at this time.

The accounts of these observers, whether written in prose or poetry or even illustrated with drawings, provide glimpses of what may have happened at the Fourth Lateran Council. It is, of course, impossible to be totally accurate but a study of a diary of events will enable us to acquire a good understanding as to how far Innocent's grand design succeeded in its purpose.

One point of interest which emerges clearly is the crucial importance of the date. Innocent had it all worked out! November was a month in which there were several considerable feast days of specific liturgical interest to Rome. His intention was to stimulate the consciousness of the participants and establish in their minds the importance of Rome as a pilgrimage centre, second to none. All were to be present in Rome for the Feast of All Saints, 1 November. Those who had handed in their written reports could then enjoy with clear consciences a variety of local religious spectacles. On 8 November the Feast of the Four Crowned Martyrs was commemorated in the church of the same name while on 9 November, the Feast of the Dedication of the Lateran Basilica provided a great pre-conciliar celebration.[45] The day chosen by Innocent for the opening ceremony of the Council was Wednesday 11 November, the Feast of St Martin, model saint of Western Christendom and a bishop who had worked miracles in his own diocese of Tours. Here was a saint of definite appeal to the episcopate and one on whom Innocent must have wished more bishops would model themselves. On 18 November came the Anniversary of the Dedication of saints Peter and Paul celebrated in the Vatican Basilica.[46] Other feast days followed in quick succession, all particularly appropriate to Rome and with newly restored and splendidly decorated churches just waiting to be visited: the Presentation of the Virgin celebrated at St Mary Major on 21 November, St Cecilia on 22 November, St Clement, third pope and martyr on 23 November and St Crysogono on 24 November whose ancient pilgrimage church with its annular crypt was, by chance, the title church of Stephen Langton, Archbishop of Canterbury and hence of more than passing interest to the English delegates to the Council. The month drew to its close with the Feast of Andrew, Apostle and Martyr coinciding with the last day of the Council.

Other parts of Rome would have been of interest to various groups within that great assembly, meeting at the Lateran. In the best traditions of all well-organised conferences, Innocent was inspired to bring all the participants together on Sunday 15 November for a day out in Trastevere where, on the other side of the Tiber, they might witness his consecration of the 'Church of Our Lady of the Flowing Oil'. For

---

44 P. Linehan, (1971), *The Spanish Church and the Papacy in the Thirteenth Century*, (Cambridge) 8-9.

45 Compare J. M. Powell (1983), 'Honorius III's 'Sermo in dedicatione ecclesiae Lateranense' and the Historical-Liturgical traditions of the Lateran', *Archivium Historiae Pontificum*, 21 195-209.

46 Eyewitness (1986), 372.

the unknown German, this was the highest point of the Council.[47] He had never before seen anything remotely like the spectacle of Roman clergy and nobles, as if on some grandiose religious *passegiata*, moving in procession beneath towers hung with flags and banners. So beguiled was he by the strange musical harmonies and the bright lights that he was able to say almost nothing about the solemn purpose which underlay the ceremony of consecration.

As far as Innocent III was concerned, he had two main tasks to fulfil during the Council. As chairman of the three plenary sessions of the Council held in the Lateran Basilica, his role was to preach a sermon at each one and to maintain strict discipline throughout. The opening and first full session of the Council on St Martin's Day began with a private mass at dawn said by the Pope for his cardinals and the more important bishops. After this, when the remainder of the bishops and the abbots had been settled into their hierarchy of seats, the lesser clergy, together with a huge crowd of observers, were admitted to fill the remaining spaces. Contemporary opinion is unanimous as to the vast numbers and deafening noise. Less reliable are the horror stories that as many as three bishops had been trampled to death in the unseemly rush to enter the Basilica.[48] From where he stood on an elevated platform flanked by his cardinals, Innocent opened the proceedings with a hymn,[49] leading the singing in a strong and melodious voice and following it with a collect.[50] Then he preached the first of the three set-piece sermons he had specially prepared, taking as his text Christ's words to his disciples before the Last Supper.[51] He spoke with characteristic fluency and emotion to move those present to bring about the reform of the universal church and to support the recovery of the Holy Land by all possible means. Once the Pope had prepared the ground, the Patriarch of Jerusalem stepped up to speak about possible aid for the Holy Land, greatly praising Innocent in so doing.[52] The third sermon of the first plenary session was one dealing with heretics by the Bishop of Agde whose see was in the province of Narbonne. To this bishop's heartfelt plea, Innocent responded in a brilliant, off-the-cuff oration.[53] The first day of the Council thus ended with all the major concerns placed squarely in the centre-stage.

Ten days later, on Friday 20 November in the second plenary session, the Pope was introduced by a great fanfare of trumpets for the benefit of those outside as well as those within the Lateran Basilica.[54] Innocent's second set-piece sermon *Si dormiatis* was specifically concerned with reform and the duties of the bishop in his diocese.[55] We have no evidence that he ever got the chance to deliver it for this

---

47 Eyewitness (1986), 371-2; Kinney (1975), 337-9.

48 Kuttner and Garcia (1964), 130-1.

49 'Veni Creator Spiritus'.

50 'Actiones nostras quesumus Domine'.

51 'Desiderio desideravi...'; *PL* (1855) 217, 673-680; Ladner (1983), 903-929, esp 912-13, although I cannot agree that Innocent 'had a premonition of his own death'. This tradition seems to derive from a fourteenth-century chronicler, Kuttner and Garcia (1964), 132. See also Imkamp (1975), 149-79.

52 Kuttner and Garcia (1964), 132.

53 Richard of San Germano (1888), 93.

54 Richard of San Germano (1888), 93.

55 *PL* (1855) 217, 679-688.

session did not go at all according to plan. Instead, it was most rudely interrupted by a riot of bishops - protagonists supporting the rival claimants to the imperial throne, Frederick II and the now deposed Otto IV.[56] Innocent was first forced to intervene with a procedural ruling, dropping into the vernacular with an aside before continuing in Latin.[57] In the end, however, events got completely out of control. While both groups hurled taunts and insults at each other, the Pope first raised his hand for silence and when that failed, he simply got up and walked out.[58]

In contrast, on the final day, Monday 30 November, came the assembly's finest hour. Innocent, that great impressario, had been waiting for this moment since April 1213 when calling notices had first gone out. On this day, the Feast of St Andrew, that alert and conscientious disciple with such great organisational abilities whose life, like his Master's, had also ended on a cross, there was the usual early morning mass for the pope and cardinals. Then Innocent made his final and most impressive entrance, ascending his platform as if he were some great biblical ruler.[59] His third sermon, now lost, was on the Trinitarian Creed.[60] In it he may have singled out for special condemnation the works of Joachim of Fiore (d.1202) and Amaury de Bene. As if to reinforce the message of his sermon and to vindicate the great Paris Master, Peter Lombard, he then had the Creed and each article of faith publicly recited. Asked if they firmly believed, the Council, this time to a man, affirmed with one great shout that they did.[61]

Politics very nearly intruded into this session with the Archbishop of Mainz attempting once more to raise the imperial question. Once again, Innocent raised his hand and this time succeeded in obtaining silence and bringing the archbishop to order.[62] Then the 68 constitutions and the two dogmatic decrees were read out and adopted by the Council. Perhaps it was at this point in the session that the Pope legislated for the organisation of the new crusade in *Ad Liberandum*.[63] Did he now bring the whole assembly to its feet when he promised that he would travel in person to the Kingdom of Sicily by 1 June 1217 to advise and to bless the crusader armies as they embarked from Messina and Brindisi?

Then at the ninth hour of the day,[64] a phrase significant to all christians as being the hour at which Christ had died on the Cross on the first Good Friday and when the veil of the Temple was rent asunder, Innocent presented his master stroke. He held up a relic of the living wood of the True Cross which had been obtained from Constantinople in 1204.[65] He stressed that Christ who had been crucified for

---

**56** Kuttner and Garcia (1964), 147-153.
**57** Kuttner and Garcia (1964), 151.
**58** Kuttner and Garcia (1964), 153, for a discussion of why the Eyewitness does not mention this scene. Did he perhaps slip away early from the session?
**59** Richard of San Germano (1888), 94.
**60** Kuttner and Garcia (1964), 156-63.
**61** Eyewitness (1986), 374.
**62** Kuttner and Garcia (1964), 156-63.
**63** Riley-Smith (1981), 124-9.
**64** Eyewitness (1986), 375.
**65** A. Frolow, *La Relique de la Vraie Croix*, (Paris, 1961), 494-5. The inventory of the Treasure of the Holy See at Perugia in 1311 gives the inscription on the reliquary as + HIC CONTINETUR LIGNUM VIVIFICE CRUCIS DE CONSTANTINOPOLI TRANSLATUM AD URBEM TEMPORE DOMINI INNOCENTII PP. TERTII +

the salvation of all had, at this same hour, suffered and died on this very Cross. The Council members immediately fell on their knees in veneration of this relic, received their absolution from the Pope and returned to their dioceses, determined as never before to maintain the faith wherever it was needed. With this great meaning, so ended the great show of the Fourth Lateran Council.

## BIBLIOGRAPHY

### SOURCES

*Chanson (1957): La Chanson de la Croisade Albigeoise*, ed. E. Martin-Chabot, 2 vols. (Paris, 1957); II, 'Le Poeme de l'auteur anonyme': '*Le Concile du Latran: Débats Contradictoires*', XV (Paris), 7-89.

Cheney and Semple (1953): *Selected Letters of Pope Innocent III Concerning England (1198-1216)*, ed. C. R. Cheney and W. H. Semple, (Edinburgh, 1953).

Constitutions (in Latin): *Conciliorum oecumenicorum decreta*, ed. J. Alberigo et al. (Freiburg-im-Breisgau, 1962) 203-247.

Constitutions (in translation) (1975): *English Historical Documents, Vol. III, 1189-1327*, ed. H. Rothwell, (London), 643-676.

Eyewitness (1986): 'Eyewitness Account of the Fourth Lateran Council (1215)', trans C. Fasolt, *Medieval Europe*, Readings in Western Civilisation, 4, eds. J. Kirshner and K. F. Morrison, (University of Chicago).

Kuttner and Garcia (1964): S. Kuttner and A. Garcia y Garcia, 'A new Eyewitness Account of the Fourth Lateran Council', *Traditio*, 20, 115-178.

Martin of Troppau (1892): *Liber Pontificalis*, ed. L. Duchesne (Paris), 451-53.

Matthew Paris (1984): *Chronicles of Matthew Paris: Monastic Life in the Thirteenth Century*, ed. and trans. R. Vaughan. (New York).

*PL (1855): Innocent III: Opera Omnia, Patrologia Latina*, 214-17, ed. J. P. Migne. (Paris).

*Quia Major* and *Ad Liberandum*, trans in Riley-Smith (1981): L. and J. Riley-Smith, *The Crusades: Idea and Reality 1095-1274*, (London).

Richard of San Germano (1888): *Ryccardi De Sancto Germano Notarii Chronica Priora*, ed A. Gaudenzi, (Naples), 88-94.

Zurich Manuscript (1905): A. Luchaire, 'Un document retrouvé', *Journal des Savants*, 557-68. reprinted as Appendix III, 'Liste des évêchés représentés au Concile de 1215', Hefèle-Leclerq, *Histoire des Conciles*, V (1913) 1723-33.

## BOOKS

Hefèle et Leclercq (1913): C. J. Hefèle et H. Leclercq, *Histoire des Conciles*, Vol. 5, (Paris), 1316-23.

Luchaire (1908): A. Luchaire, *Innocent III: Le Concile du Latran et la Réforme de l'Eglise*, (Paris).

Krautheimer (1980): R. Krautheimer, *Rome: Profile of a City, 312-1308*, (Princeton).

Maccarrone (1972): M. Maccarrone, *Studi su Innocenzo III*, Italia Sacra, 17 (Padua), esp. 246-62.

Robinson (1990): I. S. Robinson, *The Papacy 1073-1198: Continuity and Innovation*, (Cambridge), esp. 121-45.

## ARTICLES

Boyle (1985): L. E. Boyle, 'The Fourth Lateran Council and Manuals of Popular Theology', *The Popular Literature of Medieval England* ed. T. J. Hefferman (University of Tennessee Press, 1985), 30-43.

Foreville (1966): R. Foreville, 'L'iconographie du xiie concile oecuménique: Latran IV (1215)', *Mélanges offerts à René Crozet*, eds. P. Gallais and Y-J. Riou, 2 vols (Poitiers), II, 1121-30.

Foreville (1965): R. Foreville, *Latran I, II, III et Latran IV*, (Paris).

Foreville (1966): R. Foreville, 'Procédure et débats dans les conciles médiévaux du Latran (1123-1215)', *Rivista di Storia della Chiesa in Italia*, 19 (Rome), 21-37.

Garcia (1958): A. Garcia y Garcia, 'El concilio IV de Letran (1215) y sus comentarios', *Traditio*, 14, 484-502.

Gautier (1968): M. M. Gautier, 'La Clôture Emaillée de la Confession de Saint Pierre au Vatican hors du Concile de Latran, 1215', *Bibliotheque des Cahiers Archéologiques*, II, *Synthronon, Art et Archéologie de la fin de l'Antiquité*, (Paris), 237-46.

Imkamp (1975): W. Imkamp, 'Sermo ultimus quem fecit Dominus Innocentius Papa Tercius in Lateranensi Concilio Generali', *Römische Quartalschrift*, 70 (1975), 149-79.

Kinney (1975): D. Kinney, *Santa Maria in Trastevere from its Founding to 1215*, (University Microfilms International, Ann Arbor, Mich.).

Ladner (1983): G. B. Ladner, 'The Life of the Mind in the Christian West around the Year 1200', *Images and Ideas in the MIddle Ages: Selected Studies in History and Art*, Storia e Letteratura, 2 vols. (Rome), 2, 903-29.

Luchaire (1908): 'Innocent III et le Quatrieme Concile du Latran', *Revue Historique*, 98, 225-63.

Maccarrone (1961): M. Maccarrone, 'II IV Concilio Lateranense', *Divinitas* 2, 270-98.

Morin (1928): G. Morin, 'Le discours d'ouverture du concile général du Latran (1179) ... de Maitre Rufin, évêque d'Assise', *Atti della Pontificia Accademia Romana di Archeologia*, Series III, Memorie, 2, (Rome), 113-33.

Marten van Heemskerck, View of the Lateran Basilica and the
Xenodochium or Pilgrim Hostel with the Baptistery in the distance, c. 1535
(Photograph: Frank Salmon; by permission of The British School at Rome.)

# XII

## TRADITION AND TEMERITY: PAPAL ATTITUDES TO DEVIANTS, 1159–1216[1]

THE fourth Lateran council of 1215 represented a watershed in the official attitude towards heresy. It marked the end of a period of considerable flexibility and real experiment in dealing with dissident movements. For nearly sixty years, the Church had been seeking possible solutions to the problems posed by the formation of new religious groups which not only deviated in various ways from orthodox belief but which also failed to conform to accepted social patterns within the christian community. Tradition and temerity were two elements in papal policy at this time. The tentative developments of the pontificate of Alexander III were given positive direction by the energetic actions of Innocent III who examined some of these groups to find a way by which they might be contained within the Church and thus allowed to fulfil their vocation. But at the same time, the Church was becoming institutionalised and its framework more rigid. The freedom of manoeuvre of the pope was limited. The episcopate and the regular orders saw Innocent's actions as inimical to the hierarchical structure of the Church and, therefore, brought the whole weight of traditional opinion and influence to bear against the continuation of such policies.

Before 1215, several groups had presented themselves to the Curia. In 1162, some Flemings came to Alexander III at Tours[2] and Waldes visited him in Rome during the third Lateran council of

[1] The most useful secondary works on heresy and the religious movements of this period have been [H.] Grundmann, *Religiöse Bewegungen* [*im Mittelalter*] (2 ed Hildesheim 1961); [H.] Maisonneuve, [*Études sur les*] *origines de l'Inquisition* (2 ed Paris 1960); [C.] Thouzellier, *Catharisme et Valdéisme* [*en Languedoc à la fin du xii*e *siècle*] (2 ed Louvain 1969) and [J.] Le Goff, *Hérésies et sociétés* [*dans l'Europe pré-industrielle 11–18 siècles*], École pratique des hautes études: Civilisations et Sociétés, x (Paris 1968) which contains an excellent bibliography. W. Wakefield & A. P. Evans, *Heresies of the High Middle Ages* (New York 1969), present a selection of translated sources. Mr John Gillingham, Dr F. D. Logan, Dr Janet Nelson and Dr Colin Tite have read this paper at different stages and my most sincere thanks is due to them for their critical and helpful suggestions.

[2] [M.] Bouquet, *Recueil* [*des historiens des Gaules et de la France*], xv (Paris 1808) pp 790, 792, 799; *PL*, 200 (1855) col 187.

1179.[1] The *Humiliati* of Lombardy came to Innocent III in 1199,[2] seeking recognition of their way of life, and in the same year the evidence of the laymen and women of Metz was heard.[3] In 1208, Durand de Huesca and his followers made a profession of faith.[4] Both Bernard Prim and Francis of Assisi sought Innocent's approval in 1210[5] and details of a penitential community at Elne were investigated in 1212.[6]

A major problem for the Curia was to establish the distinction between heresy and disobedience. The sectarian movement contained two essentially dissimilar elements which demanded different treatment. The Cathars were automatically excluded from the Church, for their beliefs were clearly contrary to christian doctrine.[7] Missionaries were sent to convert them, codes of repressive legislation foreshadowing the Inquisition were enforced and, when these measures showed little or no result, appeal to temporal power was made and crusade preached against them. On the other hand, there were those communities which were formulating new ways of life by attempting to apply the evangelical precept of voluntary poverty.[8] Such groups hovered on the border between heterodoxy and orthodoxy. Could lay preaching organised from an independent centre, be tolerated within the framework of an institutional Church? This was the main point at issue. Separation from the Church was a gradual process. A refusal to submit

1 *Chronicon Universale Anonymi Laudunensis*, [ed A. Cartellieri et W. Stechèle] (Paris 1909) pp 28–30; Walter Map, *De Nugis Curialium*, [ed M. R. James], I, xxxi, *Anecdota Oxoniensia*, Medieval and Modern Series, XIV (Oxford 1914) pp 60–2.

2 *PL*, 214 (1855) col 921; G. Tiraboschi, *V*[*etera*] *H*[*umiliatorum*] *M*[*onumenta*] (Milan 1766–8) II, p 139.

3 *PL*, 214 (1855) cols 695–9; *PL*, 216 (1855) cols 1210–14.

4 *PL*, 215 (1855) cols 1510–14; Potthast I, nos 3571–3, p 308.

5 *PL*, 216 (1855) cols 289–93; Potthast I, nos 4014, 4015, p 346. On Francis's visit to Rome see Grundmann, *Religiöse Bewegungen*, p 127 note 111 and p 132 note 116.

6 *PL*, 216 (1855) col 601; Potthast I, no 4505, p 389.

7 There is a very clear account of cathar beliefs in S. Runciman, *The Medieval Manichee. A Study of the Christian Dualist Heresy* (Cambridge 1947). See also A. Borst, *Die Katharer*, *MGH* SS, XII (Stuttgart 1953).

8 Some of the problems which such groups experienced are dealt with by M. D. Chenu, 'Moines, clercs, laïcs au carrefour de la vie évangelique [au xii^e siècle]', *RHE*, XLIX (1954) pp 59–89. See [M.] Maccarrone, 'Riforma e sviluppo della vita religiosa [con Innocenzo III]', *R*[*ivista di storia della*] *C*[*hiesa in*] *I*[*talia*], XVI (Rome 1962) pp 29–72 for an account of Innocent III's interest in religious movements and C. Violante, 'Hérésies urbaines et rurales en Italie du 11^e au 13^e siècle' in Le Goff, *Hérésies et sociétés*, pp 171–97 who attempts an analysis of the movement towards the *vita apostolica*. Also valuable is the volume 'Movimenti religiosi popolari ed eresie del Medioevo', *Relazioni del X Congresso internazionale di scienze storiche Roma 4–11 sett. 1955*, III; *Storia del Medioevo* (Florence 1955) pp 305–541: see R. Morghen, 'Movimenti religiosi popolari nel periodo della riforma della chiesa', pp 333–56; H. Grundmann, 'Eresie e nuovi ordini religiosi nel secolo xii', pp 357–402. Also Grundmann, *Religiöse Bewegungen*, pp 503–13.

to the decisions of the ecclesiastical authorities brought condemnation of the minority while complete submission usually guaranteed a degree of toleration. As these movements proliferated after 1159, the papacy began to recognise that their essential aims were orthodox in principle and attempted to discriminate between such groups and others which rejected outright the priesthood and sacraments of the Church.

The Church's response to the spread of heresy was not simply one of negative repression but a positive attempt to set its own house in order and to meet the requirements of some dissident lay groups by purifying itself. Deviants of all kinds struck a note of simplicity beside the opulence of the hierarchical and elitist prelates. In Languedoc especially, few bishops could command a fraction of the respect given to the Cathar leaders, either for the purity of their lives or for the force of their preaching and the *vita apostolica* of the evangelical groups provided an equally sharp contrast. In 1179 and 1184 papal injunctions specifically warned the bishops to be much more rigorous in their own behaviour and in their attitude to visitation.[1] They were rich, idle and passive. Innocent, rebuking them for their inability to preach, called them 'dumb dogs who don't know how to bark'.[2] Some were merely incompetent but others subscribed to heretical beliefs themselves. Several bishops were in fact removed from their sees.[3]

The ignorance of the lower clergy posed an active problem at a time when there was an increasing demand from the laity for a really effective preaching programme. It was strongly felt that argument and

[1] Caps III and IV Lateran III in *Conciliorum Oecumenicorum Decreta* [ed J. Alberigo *et al*] (2 ed Freiburg 1962) pp 188–9; Mansi XXII, cols 491–2.

[2] Isa. 56: 10. Innocent might well have been referring to Pons d'Arsac, deposed in 1181 by the cardinal of Albano because he was too feeble to enforce measures against heretics, [C.] Devic and [J.] Vaissète, [*Histoire du Languedoc,*] VI (Toulouse 1879) p 5. During his own pontificate, the bishop of Fréjus was declared incapable in October 1198, *PL*, 214 (1855) col 374 and Otto of Carcassone, who was senile, was removed from his diocese in December 1198, *PL*, 214 (1855) cols 457–8.

[3] In December 1203 the bishop of Toulouse was deposed: *PL*, 217 (1855) col 159; in February 1204 the bishop of Béziers was accused of associating with heretics and was deprived: *PL*, 215 (1855) cols 272–3; in June 1204 Peter, bishop of Vence, was removed for his scandalous behaviour: 'quoniam igitur putridi dentes executiendi sunt de faucibus ecclesiae', *PL*, 215 (1855) cols 366–8; in April 1211 the archbishop of Auch was deposed: *PL*, 216 (1855) col 283; together with the bishop of Rodez: *PL*, 216 (1855) cols 408–9. But the most notorious and most difficult to deal with was Berengar, archbishop of Narbonne, illegitimate son of Raymond Berengar, count of Barcelona. In May 1207 an attempt was made to remove him: *PL*, 215 (1855) cols 1164–5; Potthast I, no 3113, p 265; but he was not finally deposed until 1211 or 1213: Devic and Vaissète, VI, p 137. On Italian heretical bishops see A. Dondaine, 'La hiérarchie cathare en Italie', *A*[*rchivium*] *F*[*ratrum*] *P*[*raedicatorum*], XIX (Rome 1949) pp 280–312.

biblical exposition would bring the stray sheep to see their error and no opportunity was lost to engage heretics in disputation. Groups of learned men were authorised to visit Toulouse to confront the Cathars as early as 1165 but they were booed, denounced as apostates or simply ignored.[1] Roland of Daventry acted as arbiter in a discussion of the position of the hierarchy and the nature of preaching in which both Catholics and heretics participated.[2] Alexander III approved the mission of Henry of Clairvaux to Toulouse in 1178 and empowered him to preach.[3] The Cistercian order was once again mobilised and was invited to transform itself into a preaching order. In 1204, the bull *Etsi nostri navicula* confirmed the legation of Renier de Ponza, Guy, Peter de Castelnau, Raoul de Fontfroide and Arnald-Amaury, abbot of Cîteaux and instructed them to convert by preaching and example *in opere et sermone* and to allow nothing in their actions to provoke 'the reprobation of a heretic'.[4] By 1206, however, the Cistercians were ready to return to the cloister. They hesitated to arrogate exclusively to themselves the function of preaching and they found it difficult to fulfil the provision of absolute poverty.

But by this time, Innocent had harnessed what he felt might be an effective new method of evangelism. Diego of Osma and Dominic had been diverted to aid the Cistercians in Languedoc.[5] The one hope of conversion, it was felt, lay in a demonstration of equal austerity and purity of life. The Mendicants were to live like the heretics but teach like the Church. By the example of their conduct and their skill in words, they were to recall the heretic from error. But in the long run, these missionary activities were only partially successful. The attempts at dialogue with the heretics were of little avail and Dominic's preaching was poorly supported by the local clergy. The conversion of Durand de Huesca and his followers was perhaps Dominic's chief success at

[1] Devic and Vaissète, VI, p 5; Maisonneuve, *Origines de l'Inquisition*, pp 127–9.

[2] *Ibid* pp 136–7. See also A. Dondaine, 'Les actes du concile albigeois de Saint-Félix de Caraman', *Miscellanea Giovanni Mercati* V, *Studi e Testi*, 125 (Vatican City 1946) pp 324–55.

[3] *PL*, 204 (1855) cols 223–5; Maisonneuve, *Origines de l'Inquisition*, p 132 note 224; Thouzellier, *Catharisme et Valdéisme*, pp 19–23. See also Y. M. J. Congar, 'Henry de Marcy, abbé de Clairvaux, cardinal-évêque d'Albano et légat pontifical', *SA* (1958) pp 1–38. Other letters about this mission are printed in *PL*, 204 (1855) cols 235–42 and *PL*, 199 (1855) cols 1120–4.

[4] *PL*, 215 (1855) cols 355–60; *Potthast* I, no 2229, p 192.

[5] *PL*, 215 (1855) cols 1024–5. C. Thouzellier, 'La pauvreté, arme contre l'albigéisme, en 1206', *Révue de l'histoire des religions*, CLI (Paris 1957) pp 79–92.

this time.[1] Thereby the Poor Catholics were disengaged from the laity and yet contained within the Church.

Alexander III introduced Bolognese doctrine into the Church and took from it his ideas on the treatment of heretics. They were to be pursued, not in order to burn them but to bring them back to orthodoxy. Any punishment was to be carried out in a spirit of charity rather than vengeance. Penalties of a medicinal nature, such as exile, the confiscation of goods and even excommunication, were aimed at isolating the heretic and *thus* compelling him to recognise his error and return to the fold.[2] Yet attitudes towards those who were doctrinal deviants were beginning to harden. The Councils of Montpellier 1162 and Tours 1163 enacted severe measures against the Cathars in Languedoc.[3] The secular princes were reminded of their duty, *vis coactiva*, towards the Church on pain of anathema. Clerics were urged to do their duty by enquiring into personal beliefs and by encouraging the denunciation of heretics by the laity. In 1178, an inquisitorial tribunal under Henry of Clairvaux functioned in the county of Toulouse, a mission which Alexander regarded as equal in importance to his projected crusade to the Holy Land.[4] The third Lateran council of 1179 empowered the bishops to levy troops and to issue indulgences as if for a crusade against the infidel.[5] Deviation from the basic tenets of the Church and the refusal to swear an oath were standard marks of heresy but on the questions of preaching and voluntary poverty, papal policy was still to be formulated. In 1162, a group of Flemings, accused of heresy by the archbishop of Rheims, came to seek a papal judgement on their case.[6] They may have felt that this was less well-defined and, therefore, less severe than that which they might expect to receive from Louis VII. Although there is evidence that they had access to a considerable sum of money, their way of life was undoubtedly praiseworthy and they refuted the accusation of heresy when they presented themselves to the pope. Alexander wrote that he received them *with asperity* but

1 *PL*, 215 (1855) cols 1510–14.

2 'Ut solatio saltem humanitatis amisso ab errore viae suae respiscere compellantur', Cap XXIII, Council of Tours. Mansi XXI, col 1178; Maisonneuve, *Origines de l'Inquisition*, p 127 note 198.

3 Mansi XXI, cols 1159–60 and cols 1177–8; Maisonneuve, *Origines de l'Inquisition*, p 126.

4 *Ibid* p 133.

5 Cap XXVII Lateran III in *Conciliorum Oecumenicorum Decreta*, pp 200–1.

6 Bouquet, *Recueil*, XV, 790, 792, 799. I am indebted to Mr Robert Moore for allowing me to see his translations of these texts in proof-copy. Alexander III's position was difficult. The archbishop of Rheims was Louis VII's brother while the pope was merely an exile in France, dependent for help and recognition upon the French king.

his attitude softened when he saw how earnest was their desire to have the matter sorted out, not in Rheims, but in the Curia. He instructed the archbishop to investigate the Flemings' case carefully – with the help of *religiosi viri*—and declared that he would then give judgement. Meanwhile they themselves were not to be molested and their property was to be guaranteed. The outcome of their request is unknown but Alexander's attitude towards them is interesting. He warned the archbishop of Rheims that it was better to absolve the guilty than to condemn the innocent and advised him not to be overscrupulous in his examination of heretics.[1] Alexander was obviously dissatisfied with episcopal judgement alone, and in a letter of 1170 to the archbishops of Rheims, Bourges, Tours and Rouen suggested that 'wise and religious men' should also participate in such decisions.[2]

In 1179, Alexander was visited by Waldes whose popular preaching and translations of the gospels *in vulgari* had reached the attention of the archbishop of Lyons.[3] Waldes and his followers wanted papal recognition and felt that the episcopal ban imposed on them, contradicted the biblical admonition to preach and live an apostolic life. Alexander responded warmly to Waldes's voluntary renunciation of property and approved his way of life. The translations, which were submitted to the Curia for inspection, were tested neither for accuracy nor for orthodoxy but the right to preach was made dependent on theological examination. The Waldenses were declared deficient in their understanding of doctrine and Alexander refused to grant them the right to preach *unless asked to do so by priests*.[4] This was virtually an unconditional ban since preaching was strictly forbidden to all save those specifically ordained or commissioned.[5] Walter Map, who carried out the examination, was presumably one of those *religious men* whom the

1 'Scire autem debet tuae discretionis prudentia quia cautius et minus malum est nocentes et condemnatos absolvere quam vitam innocentiam severitate ecclesiastica condemnare', *PL*, 200 (1855) col 187.

2 'Quia negligentiae praelatorum Ecclesiae posset attribui, si non curarent evellere quae sunt ab universis fidelibus penitus resecanda', *PL*, 200 (1855) cols 684–5; Bouquet, *Recueil*, xv, 888; *Jaffé*, no 11809, p 237. The *religiosi viri* were by no means necessarily churchmen.

3 Guichard, a cistercian monk and archbishop of Lyons 1165–81. Thouzellier, *Catharisme et Valdéisme*, p 17. *Chronicon Universale Anonymi Laudunensis*, p 28.

4 'Nisi rogantibus sacerdotibus', *ibid* p 29. The scriptural justification is to be found in Rom. 10: 15 'Quomodo praedicabunt, nisi mittantur?' and was used by St Bernard in his Toulouse campaign: *PL*, 182 (1854) col 436.

5 For a discussion of this prohibition see Grundmann, *Religiöse Bewegungen*, p 64. See also B. Marthaler, 'Forerunners of the Franciscans: the Waldenses', *Franciscan Studies*, XVIII (New York 1958) pp 133–42; A. Dondaine, 'Aux origines du Valdéisme: Une profession de foi de Valdès', *AFP*, XVI (1946) pp 231–2.

bishops called in to aid them.[1] He was scornful of these *idiotae et illiterati* who believed themselves called to preach and rejected their arrogant mendicity. They had tampered with scriptural dynamite by using written translations which would persist for use by others. This represented a tremendous threat to tradition: in the last resort, the interests of the pope were not separate from those of the secular clergy and Alexander did nothing to contain Waldes within the Church.

In 1184, with the support of the emperor, Lucius III agreed to take radical and severe measures against all forms of heresy. The decretal *ab abolendam* may be seen as the first attempt to define the official attitude to manifest dissent.[2] A whole group of heretics listed as Cathars, Patarines, *Humiliati* or those falsely named Poor of Lyons, Passagians, Josephines and Arnaldists were indiscriminately anathematised. Two distinct groups of deviants are mentioned: the first are those who have arrogated to themselves the right to preach either publicly or privately without papal authorisation; and the second, those who have taught doctrines contrary to the Catholic Church on sacramental questions. As a result of the decretal, Waldes and his followers were not strictly speaking heretics but anathematised schismatics. Judgement was made not on their doctrines but on their tenacious *contumacia*.[3] They would not observe the proscription on preaching and had lapsed into disobedience. Yet they, and other groups, remained impenitent, certain of their apostolic vocation and their right to represent the true Christian Church. Other provisions of the decretal declared that clerics were to be degraded and handed over to the secular power if they themselves were found to subscribe to heretical beliefs or to know of the existence of heretics. Bishops who did not publish these penalties were to be suspended for three years. Three respectable people in each diocese were to denounce, on oath to their bishop, those who held secret conventicles or who differed in their way of life from the faithful. For the first time, regular *inquisitiones* were to be held and the guilty punished by the secular power according to the *animaversio debita*.[4]

Innocent III's attitude to heresy was drawn from both imperial and

[1] Walter Map *c* 1140–*c* 1208. *De Nugis Curialium*, pp 60–2. See also Grundmann, *Religiöse Bewegungen*, pp 64–5 for a critical view of Map's beliefs.

[2] Mansi xxii, cols 476–8; *PL*, 201 (1855) cols 1297–1300. C. Thouzellier, 'La répression de l'hérésie et les débuts de l'Inquisition', in A. Fliche et V. Martin, *Histoire de l'Eglise*, x (Paris 1950) pp 291–340. Maisonneuve, *Origines de l'Inquisition*, pp 151–5.

[3] Thouzellier, *Catharisme et Valdéisme*, p 46.

[4] Maisonneuve, *Origines de l'Inquisition*, p 154.

canonical tradition. In 1199, in the decretal *vergentis in senium*, addressed to the clergy and people of Viterbo, heresy was for the first time equated with treason.[1] Thus the confiscation of lands and goods was radical and final and the heirs of the heretics, even if they themselves were orthodox, were totally and perpetually disinherited. But like Alexander III, Innocent showed that he could be merciful. 'When those isolated desire reconciliation with the Church and when temporal punishment corrects those untouched by spiritual punishment, then to these converted people will be restored civil and political rights and also their goods'.[2] Only after 1208 was the spiritual sword cast aside, 'iron was to conquer those whom persuasion would not convince' and the obdurate heretics of Languedoc were given up to the envious lords of northern France.[3] The radical departure from traditional theory stemmed not only from the revived study of Roman law but also from the unitary, theocratic conception of christian society towards which the papacy tended.

Innocent III possessed a breadth of vision which enabled him to put into perspective the problem of the rapidly increasing number of dissident groups. He attempted to contain several such movements by fairly consistent procedures, some of which develop from those used by his predecessor, Alexander. He asked these groups to present *proposita* or short statements to indicate their willingness to devote themselves to lives of christian piety. He set up commissions, usually of three men drawn from the regular and secular orders, to investigate this evidence. While the inquiries were proceeding, the bishops were warned to cease penalties against these groups and to protect their goods and property. Permission to preach was granted on definite terms and under episcopal licence and, whenever appropriate, these movements were placed in some sort of rule. Innocent seems to have regarded previous episcopal policies as too severe. He urged his bishops to act like doctors. Mere diagnosis of the symptoms was insufficient; effective treatment of each case was urged whether by the amputation of a malignant limb to save the body or by the soothing of wounds, though with oil not wine. Innocent, like Alexander, urged that the

[1] For elucidation on this point see W. Ullman, 'The significance of Innocent III's decretal *Vergentis*', in *Etudes d'histoire du droit canonique dediées à G. Le Bras*, I (Paris 1965) pp 729–41.

[2] Maisonneuve, *Origines de l'Inquisition*, p 157 note 37.

[3] 'Ideoque, cum ferro abscidenda sint vulnera quae fomentorum non sentiunt medicinam et qui correctionem ecclesiasticam vilipendunt brachio sint saecularis potentiae comprimendi, auxilium tuum...invocandum duximus'; *PL*, 215 (1855) cols 1246–8; *Potthast* I, no 3223, p 275; Thouzellier, *Catharisme et Valdéisme*, pp 204–12.

guilty should be acquitted rather than that the innocent should be condemned, and warned his bishops that they would turn piety into heresy by harsh and precipitate action.[1] A way back into the Church was to be opened for those unwillingly or unjustly excluded.

In 1199, Innocent wrote to the bishop of Verona ordering him to cease discrimination against the *Humiliati* and to give them absolution if they were prepared to acknowledge their error and to submit to papal authority.[2] He declared himself unable to grant their request for official recognition without considerable thought and investigation since their way of life was so different from that followed by any existing religious community. A commission composed of two cistercian abbots and one bishop was set up to examine them and reported favourably.[3] The *Humiliati* were given permission to preach as long as they avoided theological questions and dealt only with exhortations to a pious and earnest life. Innocent showed flexibility by retaining the essential form of their movement, yet disciplined and regulated them so that they could be reabsorbed into the Church.[4]

But it was more difficult to find a place for the followers of Waldes. They were wandering preachers, widely dispersed, who basically rejected Church organisation and believed that the right to preach and administer the sacraments was based on *meritum* and not on *ordo* or *officium*.[5] The best that Innocent could do was to deal with the individual groups of Waldenses which came to him and to treat each case on merit.

In 1199, a group of laymen and women in Metz was accused of reading from a French translation of the Scriptures and of disobedience to their bishop.[6] Innocent's attitude to them was similar to that of Alexander towards Waldes. He approved of their desire to understand the Scriptures and acknowledged that they were not entirely uninformed but pointed out the depth of meaning of the texts which not even learned men could understand. He emphasised that the Church possessed doctors specially charged to preach whose function the

[1] 'Quia vero non est nostrae intentionis innoxios cum nocentibus condemnare', *PL*, 214 (1855) col 789.

[2] *Ibid* col 789.

[3] The cistercian abbots of Lodi and Cerreto and the bishop of Vercelli: *PL*, 214 (1855) col 922; *VHM*, II, p 136.

[4] On the *Humiliati* see L. Zanoni, *Gli Umiliati nei loro rapporto con l'eresia, l'industria della lana ed i communi nei secoli xii e xiii*, Biblioteca historica italia, Serie II, 2 (Milan 1911); H. Grundmann, *Religiöse Bewegungen* especially pp 70–97 and pp 487–538 and my article 'Innocent III's treatment of the *Humiliati*' in *SCH*, VIII (1971) pp 73–82.

[5] Grundmann, *Religiöse Bewegungen*, p 95 and note 46.

[6] *PL*, 214 (1855) cols 695–9; *PL*, 216 (1855) cols 1210–14; *Potthast* I, no 781; Grundmann, *Religiöse Bewegungen*, pp 97–100.

laity had no right to usurp.[1] Although he disapproved of their conventicles and ideas on the priesthood, Innocent sensed that to act peremptorily might weaken the faith of these simple people.[2] He refused to judge them before he possessed all the facts of the case as he could not tell whether the matter centred on a slight error in faith or in notorious doctrinal differences.[3] The bishop of Metz was instructed to inquire into the authorship and intention of the biblical translations, the beliefs of those who read them and the teachings of these people. Finally he was to ask whether due respect was shown for the pope and the Church. The bishop reported the continued disobedience of the Metz sectaries but Innocent still felt that he possessed insufficient evidence and again turned to a commission for advice.[4] Three cistercian abbots declared the writings heretical and apparently the books were burned.[5] In this case, Innocent was attempting to establish the *distinctio* between believers and irrevocable heretics. He gave the Metz sectaries a fair chance but, as in the case of Waldes in 1179, written translations and the rejection of the priesthood could not be tolerated by the hierarchy.

In 1208, Durand de Huesca, a former Waldensian, and his companions received official confirmation of their *propositum conversationis*.[6] Innocent praised their work as mendicant preachers but pointed out that the Church could make no concessions on certain points. The fundamental conditions for the existence of the Poor Catholics were that their members should accept the validity of the hierarchical Church and that they should recognise the sacraments which could only be administered by an officially ordained priest, irrespective of his worth.[7] While accepting these conditions, the Poor Catholics gave up few of their former tenets and habits. They could live in voluntary poverty and could preach as a community as long as they conceded that this was linked with their specific papal commission. The Poor Catholics soon met with hostility from the hierarchy. Innocent warned the

1 *PL*, 214 (1855) cols 697; Potthast I, no 780.

2 'Sic *enervari* non debet religiosa simplicitas', *PL*, 214 (1855) col 699.

3 *Ibid* col 699. Innocent recognised that the Metz sectaries were erudite men and appreciated their *scientia*.

4 This commission was composed of the abbots of Cîteaux, La Crête and Morimond; *PL*, 214 (1855) cols 793–6.

5 'Item in urbe Metensi pullulante secta quae dicitur Valdensium, directi sunt quidam abbates ad praedicandum, qui quosdam libros de latino in romanum versos combusserant et praedictam sectam extirpaverunt', Aubry de Trois Fontaines, *Chronicon*, *MGH* SS XXIII (Hanover 1874) p 878.

6 *PL*, 215 (1855) cols 1510–14; Potthast I, nos 3571–3, p 308.

7 Grundmann, *Religiöse Bewegungen*, pp 107–8.

archbishops of Narbonne and Tarragona to act charitably towards them[1] and informed Durand de Huesca of the complaints against him.[2] In spite of Innocent's support, the Poor Catholics did not survive long in the face of this essentially parochial prejudice. In 1210, Innocent accused his bishops of driving people away from the Church by their severity, a warning reminiscent of that made by Alexander III.[3]

In 1210, Bernard Prim undertook to obey papal and episcopal authority and assured Innocent that he and his group of lay penitents would behave respectfully towards the Church.[4] He promised to defend the Church vigorously *usque ad animam et sanguinem* against all heretical sects and to try to prevent simple believers from becoming hardened heretics. His *propositum* was confirmed in 1212.[5] In the same year, a penitential community at Elne was to be approved if the bishop of Elne could guarantee purity of belief among its members.[6]

When Francis came to the Curia in 1210, Innocent had to formulate his attitude to a movement which, like others, was developing in response to the spiritual needs of the time but which, unlike the Waldenses and the *Humiliati*, had not been accused of disobedience.[7] Whereas in the case of the more developed movements, he had asked for evidence and had called upon outside advice, Innocent decided to wait and see what form the new community might take. Francis had already indicated his unwillingness to accept an existing rule but he was allowed to continue on the condition that he and his companions, tonsured like clerks, promised to be 'in all things obedient to the Holy See'. Innocent granted him oral permission to preach and allowed him to transmit this right individually to each brother.[8]

In 1215, the Lateran council stated its attitude towards heresy quite

1 *PL*, 216 (1855) cols 73–4.

2 *Ibid* cols 75–7.

3 'nolentes, sicut etiam nec velle debemus, ut qui trahi gratia divina creduntur, per duritiam vestram ab infinita Dei misericordia repellantur', *ibid* cols 274–5.

4 *PL*, 216 (1855) cols 289–93; Potthast I, nos 4014, 4015, p 346.

5 *PL*, 216 (1855) cols 648–50; Potthast I, no 4567, p 394.

6 'sub disciplina et visitatione catholicorum pauperum permansuri', *PL*, 216 (1855) cols 601–2; *Potthast* I, no 4505, p 389.

7 Grundmann, *Religiöse Bewegungen*, pp 127–35. The question of Francis's acceptance by the Holy See is dealt with by T. Manteuffel, 'Naissance d'une hérésie', in Le Goff, *Hérésies et sociétés*, pp 97–103 especially p 99. He attributes to Innocent III the credit for the farsighted and flexible policy adopted towards Francis and his followers. The crucial issue was that of obedience to the Holy See. Francis not only had episcopal support but had also submitted to the decisions of the ecclesiastical authorities.

8 Grundmann, *Religiöse Bewegungen*, p 133 notes 117 and 118.

unequivocally.[1] Catholic doctrine had become increasingly well-defined as it was defended against the challenge of dissident groups. Henceforth dogma was to be the criterion for distinguishing between orthodox belief and heresy. All heretics were to be condemned '...no matter by what names they are known: they may have different faces but they are all tied together by their tails since they are united by their emptiness'.[2] The creation of new religious orders was banned and founders of new religious houses were to accept the rule of an approved order.[3] This proscription was justified on the grounds that too great a differentiation of orders would cause confusion in the Church. The council, therefore, presented little in the way of choice to those who deviated. They could either return to the fold or suffer persecution. These decisions were totally at variance with the earlier policies of Innocent. Two forces militated against him. On the one hand were the bishops and prelates who saw not only their pastoral rights but their purses threatened and on the other were the Cistercians and representatives of the traditional, regular orders who thought their rules sufficient for anyone truly seeking sanctity.

Since 1159 then, the Church had been continuously assessing the various measures by which it could deal with deviants. It had attempted definite reform rather than purely negative repression and had ordered its clergy to live and preach on the same terms as the heretics. It had contained some groups like the *Humiliati* and the Poor Catholics by setting up commissions to investigate belief and practice and had reversed the anathema of 1184 which had forced them into heresy. Finally it had taken measures against those like Waldes and the Metz sectaries who were not prepared to enter on official terms. In the process, it had emerged, almost incidentally, with its doctrines defined and

[1] There is no evidence of the names of individual bishops at the council or of their attitudes towards heresy but 'A new eye-witness account of the Fourth Lateran Council', Stephan Kuttner and Antonio García y García, *Traditio*, xx (New York 1964) pp 115–78 especially lines 168–78 p 128 shows Innocent III in a very human light, making sarcastic remarks and ordering Siegfried, archbishop of Mainz, to sit down three times in the course of one session.

[2] Caps I and III, Lateran IV in *Conciliorum Oecumenicorum Decreta*, pp 206–7, 209–11. Translated by B. Pullan, *Sources for the History of Medieval Europe* (Oxford 1966) p 91.

[3] Cap XIII, Lateran IV in *Conciliorum Oecumenicorum Decreta*, p 218. See also Maccarrone, 'Riforma e sviluppo della vita religiosa', *RCI*, XVI (1962) pp 60–9. Grundmann, *Religiöse Bewegungen*, pp 135–56 discusses Innocent III's reaction to the Council's decision and attempts to trace the means whereby the Franciscans became an approved order without adopting a recognised rule as required. Innocent seems to have taken steps to ensure their survival and papal protection was willingly granted to them in return for their obedience to the Holy See.

redefined. In 1215, after almost sixty years' experience in the formulation of different approaches to heretics, the Church had to decide on one particular policy and one particular path. Which direction would it take? It took the most traditional way and reversed those policies which seemed to create a dangerous precedent. Innocent III's temerity was not tolerated by the hierarchy which had continually expressed resentment against repentant heretics. The bishops saw their teaching and preaching authority under attack and knew that it was only possible for the Church to survive by keeping to the rules. Tradition triumphed. After 1215, the structure of the Church became too rigid to contain the contemporary phenomena of new religious groups and such spontaneous movements were, like the non-christian heresies, placed almost inevitably outside the communion of the Church.

Domenico Taselli, Atrium and Façade of Old St Peter's
(Photograph: Frank Salmon; by permission of The British School at Rome.)

Marten van Heemskerck, Façade of Old St Peter's and the Vatican Palace
(Photograph: Frank Salmon; by permission of The British School at Rome.)

# XIII

# Poverty as Protest: Some Inspirational Groups at the Turn of the Twelfth Century

n 1184 the decree *ad abolendam* excommunicated several groups who were onsidered by the Church to be dangerously active in their protest against the urity of the Church's precepts.[1] In seeking to bring about discipline and nity, Lucius III thus ensured that the immediate future of these groups would e one of official conflict with orthodoxy. even though it was not the wish of heir members that this should be so. The decree dealt with a whole series of roups quite indiscriminately on the pretext that they preached illegally, both penly and in secret and that their views on the articles of faith and acraments were erroneous. Covered by the decree were not only the dualistic athars who were in serious error but also groups of *humiliati* and waldensians vho only wished to lead lives according to the *vita apostolica*, communicating eir experience of this christian way of life to others.

In 1198 Innocent III became pope and the effects of the decree *ad bolendam* soon came to his attention. Such an arbitrary and all-embracing xcommunication was not in line with his aim of increasing the unity of the hurch. As he saw it, groups who were simply misguided would only crease the true unity of the Church if they were allowed to work inside its amework rather than being officiously excluded.[2] This paper, although ealing with the tensions arising from the situation in which these groups

---

Mansi XXII, cols 476-8; *PL* 201 (1855), cols 1297-1300.

For a discussion of Innocent's policies see H.GRUNDMANN, *Religiöse Bewegungen im Mittelalter* (2 ed., Darmstadt, 1970), pp. 70-2.

found themselves and investigating their inspirational sources, mainly examines Innocent's methods of leading them back into the Church whilst at the same time it suggests some possible reasons for the willingness of these groups to adjust to his gestures of reconciliation.

Who precisely were the members of these groups and where were they to be found? To their contemporaries, particularly those uninitiated in the niceties of theological disputation, they were no different from openly avowed heretics.[3] To themselves they were groups or associations of like-minded individuals, searching within the Church for ways in which Christ's example could be more closely followed. Thus, they had no wish to be in conflict with orthodoxy but it is perhaps true to say that they did not seek to avoid such a conflict at all costs. These groups were often found in towns, especially in those facing a more than average degree of social and political stress. Some were also to be found in rural areas so the consequences to these groups of any interaction of Church and Society in urban environments should not be over-emphasised. Although the groups were located in two main geographical areas, certain parts of France and Italy, the names given them arose either from their founders or from the mode of life which they themselves developed. In France there were the waldensians or Poor Men of Lyon followers of Valdes.[4] In Languedoc, also following Valdes were the Poor Catholics led by Durand de Huesca[5] and a group of *vaudois* led by Bernard Prim.[6] An additional group of laymen and women was to be found in the city and diocese of Metz in Eastern France. They were interesting because as we shall see, they were at the extreme edge of these non-heretical protest

---

3 Walter Map, *De Nugis Curialium*, ed. M.R.JAMES (Oxford, 1914), pp. 60-2.

4 K.-V.SELGE, *Die ersten Waldenser* (Berlin, 1967); C.THOUZELLIER, *Catharisme et Valdéisme en Languedoc à la fin du xiie et au début du xiiie siècle* (2nd ed., Louvain, 1969) and GRUNDMANN, *Religiöse Bewegungen*, pp. 107-8.

5 *PL* 215 (1855), cols 1510-14; *PL* 216 (1855), cols 73-7; Potthast I, nos 3571-3, p. 308; Grundmann, *Religiöse Bewegungen*, pp. 107-8.

6 *PL* 216 (1855), cols 289-93, 648-50; Potthast I, nos 4014, 4015, p. 346 and no. 4567, p. 394.

groups.[7] In the troubled area of Lombardy, the *humiliati* were most important[8] but we should not omit reference to Umbria where Francis and the first friars appeared for these groups grasped many of the points which the Franciscans were later to develop and institutionalise in their order.

The identification common to the membership of these groups was their desire for voluntary poverty and their adoption of a life style immediately and radically different from that which they had led previously. Valdes's first and personal inspiration was to go and sell all that he had acquired usuriously and to live on alms.[9] The *humiliati* would not beg and they aimed to be self-supporting through the work of their hands. Jacques de Vitry tells us that they 'gave up all for Christ' and we may deduce from their name that this required the exercise of a considerable self-restraint and a life far more austere and demanding than that of the ordinary layman.[10] Bernard Prim and his followers also whilst willing to work with their hands, stressed in their determination to be poor, that they would only accept what was necessary for their daily existence.[11]

The *avaritia* and competitiveness current at the time must have appeared to these groups to be in direct contradiction to the form of life they were seeking. They attempted to express their reaction to these weaknesses of contemporary society in an ardent desire for personal expiation through the ideal of renunciation. Thus, in the case of these groups, voluntary poverty

---

7 *PL* 214 (1855), cols. 695-9; *PL* 216 (1855), cols. 1210-14; Potthast I, no. 781; GRUNDMANN, *Religiöse Bewegungen*, pp. 107-8.

8 On the *humiliati* see especially L.ZANONI, *Gli Umiliati nei loro rapporti con l'eresia, l'industria della lana ed i communi nei secoli xii e xiii*, Biblioteca historica italia, Serie II, 2 (Milan, 1911); GRUNDMANN, *Religiöse Bewegungen*, pp. 70-97, 487-538 and my articles 'Innocent III's treatment of the *humiliati*', *SCH* 8 (1971), pp. 73-82; 'Sources for the early history of the *humiliati*', *SCH* 11 (1975), pp. 125-33 and D.FLOOD ed., *Poverty in the Middle Ages*, *Franziskanische Forschungen* 27 (Werl-Westfalia, 1976), pp. 52-9.

9 *Chronicon anonymyi Laudunensis*, ed. G.WAITZ, *MGH SS* 26 (Hannover, 1882), p. 447.

10 *Lettres de Jacques de Vitry*, ed. R.B.C.HUYGENS (Leiden, 1960), P. 73.

11 *PL* 216 (1855) col. 290.

represented a personal and social *renovatio*, a renewal of spiritual triumph through the adoption of a new life style, the *vita apostolica*.[12] If poverty and abasement were both chosen and experienced from a basis of religious inspiration, indeed the only inspiration open to them at that time, doing without possessions and turning away from social responsibility were implicit in the decisions of these groups.

The Church did not object to those who wanted to live in this apostolic style, Alexander III having warmly commended Valdes on his way of life.[13] The question of disobedience arose when the adepts of voluntary poverty referred directly to the Bible and began to tell others of this knowledge and experience. In other words, to preach.[14] The issue was further confused when the Church authorities realised that similar life-styles were common amongst those sects which were unquestionably heretical.

The common inspiration of all these groups was the Bible. Their radical dynamism of spirit could be attributed to the literal observance of biblical texts.[15] The use of Latin was intentionally restricted by the Church to the limited and controllable clerical section of the community.[16] We know that many members of these groups were clerics and therefore *litterati* and that the reading and interpreting of texts in Latin would have been little problem to them. Such a situation, however, could not be acceptable to groups where it was an individual's responsibility to search for salvation. The Scriptures were in absolute terms the rule of these religious groups so they would have had to

---

12 B.M.BOLTON, '*Paupertas Christi*: old wealth and new poverty in the twelfth century', *SCH* 14 (1977), pp. 95-103.

13 *Chronicon anonymi Laudensis*, p. 28; THOUZELLIER, *Catharisme et Valdéisme*, p. 17.

14 *Chronicon anonymi Laudunensis*, p. 29 and Rom.10:15 'Quomodo praedicabunt, nisi mittantur?'.

15 M.-D.CHENU, *Nature, Man and Society in the Twelfth Century: Essays on New Theological Perspectives in the Latin West*, ed. and trans. by J.TAYLOR and L.K.LITTLE (Chicago, 1968), p. 247.

16 M.RICHTER, 'A socio-linguistic approach to the latin Middle Ages', *SCH* 11 (1975), pp. 69-82.

read and practise them *sine glossa* and without dilution of meaning.[17] Their primary wish would be to understand the Scriptures and in so doing they would need to have the texts to hand. Although the New Testament was becoming increasingly available by the end of the twelfth century and although some small pocket volumes on thin parchment were in circulation, yet the availability of such vital texts was not a matter which could be left to chance.[18]Valdes for one commissioned a *scriptor* and a translator to produce a vernacular version of the gospels, together with some other books of the Bible and also books by the Church Fathers.[19] By 1199, the laymen and women of Metz possessed their own French translations of the gospels, the Pauline epistles, Gregory the Great's *Moralia in Job* with its fundamental discussion of man's situation in the world and 'many other books'.[20] In addition there were the *scholae*. These local *scholae* were places where reading aloud from the gospels took place and where groups met to discuss the interpretation of scriptural passages and it was these local *scholae* which could be expected to be in charge of these translations from the vernacular.[21]

Literal observance of these texts in addition to arousing dynamism of the spirit may have led them to act in an anti-social manner by disregarding many of the institutions of existing society. Their revulsion to oath taking was justified by reference to James[22] and they were in radical opposition to the shedding of blood, a right which they denied, even to the temporal powers. Their views on marriage may have indicated a desire to loosen any earthly ties

---

17 CHENU, *Nature, Man and Society*, p. 247.

18 R.LOEWE, 'The medieval history of the Latin Vulgate' in G.W.LAMPE ed., *The Cambridge History of the Bible*, 2, (Cambridge, 1976), p. 146.

19 A.LECOY DE LA MARCHE, *Anecdotes historiques, Légendes et Apologues tirées du Recueil inédit d'Etienne de Bourbon, Dominicain du xiiie siècle*. Société de l'Histoire de France, 185 (Paris, 1887), p. 291.

20 *PL* 214 (1855), col. 695.

21 CHENU, *Nature, Man and Society*, p. 249 and C.MORRIS, *Medieval Media* (University of Southampton, 1972).

22 Jas.5.12.

which could hamper them in the achieving of their religious goal. From this it was not far to a loosening of the automatic assumption that society's existing structure could not and indeed should not be changed. These anti-social attitudes were exemplified by their pessimistic view of the world and its future and for this, they drew much upon the authority of the texts. That they did not go on to include the Church as part of the world as did the cathars and many other later groups seems to indicate both their weakness as a powerful protest movement and their strength as reformative groups acting as yeast within the body of the Church.

In this situation, Innocent III was eminently approachable. He understood both the weakness and the strength and used their inherent wish to remain in conformity with the Church as a basis for his actions. In so doing he was able to get them to agree to urgent and necessary oaths; to the shedding of blood when those in authority could not otherwise avoid it; to the need for strong family groups and to put forward declarations of their orthodox intent in the form of *proposita*.[23]

It is from these *proposita* that we are able to deduce not only the fact that these groups were not strongly anti-clerical in spirit but also an indication of the beliefs and practices held by them prior to their reconciliation with the Church. For example, if in the *proposita* it was agreed to take sacraments from unworthy priests, it can be assumed that this was something which previously their protest had made them unwilling to do. If they agreed to stress their obedience to and respect for bishops and priests, it can be assumed that where previously they had considered certain bishops and priests to be both sinful and ignorant they had them been unwilling to be obedient and respectful. In such attitudes incipient anti-clericalism may have existed. We may also deduce other aspects from their *proposita*. If they had to confirm their orthodoxy by the acceptance of the sacraments, perhaps such sacraments had not previously been much stressed by these groups. There are also other examples where ritualisation of aspects of orthodox belief and practice had to

---

[23] For a discussion of the *proposita* of one such group see BOLTON, 'Innocent III's treatment of the *humiliati*', *Studies in Church History* 8 (1972) pp. 73-82.

be accepted and so we can deduce that previously they had been antagonistic to ritual, the hallmark of any protest movement.

In dealing with these *proposita* Innocent III showed that he was prepared to encounter these protest groups as no other pope had done. He sought to bridge the gap between the groups and the hierarchical Church by allowing them a place within the Church as long as it could be considered that orthodox belief remained untouched and hierarchical authority was basically recognised.[24] His achievement in so doing was to create a host of communities and groups in which the movement towards voluntary poverty was thus legitimised. This was especially so in regard to the mendicant preachers who were the forerunners of the friars. This policy did not represent a change in the general attitude of the religious leadership of the Church but came personally from Innocent's clear insight into the Church's task in the face of the proliferation of protest movements. He not only established the *distinctio* between irrevocable heretics and those who were merely disobedient but also pointed out the supreme folly of excluding the latter as well as the former from the Church.[25] Grundmann has shown how Innocent was able to incorporate those disobedient groups skilfully with foresight and energy into the hierarchical Church. His policy revealed a sensitive approach to those whom he on no account wanted excluded from the Church as heretics. He recognised that because of their austere lifestyle, they were able to speak to heretics on equal terms and so he was willing to allow them to preach as long as they conceded that this right was linked with the special permission which he had given them. By this right, the *humiliati* tertiaries were able to witness to the faith and to preach on their experience of christian life but were not allowed to teach doctrine.[26] The followers of Durand de Huesca and Bernard Prim presented Innocent with a more difficult problem and when their leaders went personally to the Pope they were

---

[24] GRUNDMANN, *Religiöse Bewegungen*, pp. 107-8.

[25] *Ibid.*, p.73.

[26] G.TIRABOSCHI, *Vetera Humiliatorum Monumenta* 3 vols (Milan, 1766-8), II, pp. 133-4.

subjected to a test of belief and made to take an oath.[27] Once they conceded that the right to preach was linked to a papal commission they received approval to preach as a community. Francis was allowed to preach on rather different terms. As clerics, he and his followers could be given the *licentia praedicandi ubique* and the question of leadership became regulated when Francis promised obedience to the Pope and his companions promised to obey Francis.[28]

Another difficulty which Innocent III had to face was the existence of texts in the vernacular which was generally considered to be a real threat to the Church. Early in his pontificate and when dealing with the extremist Metz group, Innocent considered such translations to be the casting of pearls before swine. He stressed the profound nature of the holy scriptures and compared the group to babies capable of digesting only milk and not solid food. he recommended to them that they needed only to know of 'Jesus Christ and him crucified' as the simplest and yet deepest tenet of the christian belief.[29] Thus, although he did not wish to weaken their faith by acting peremptorily he did not stop from being carried out the orders of the Commission which inquired into the group that their books should be burned.[30]

The turn of the twelfth century therefore brought an abatement in the conflict between the Church and these groups. In addition to the actions of Innocent III, it is perhaps possible that there were other less obvious reasons for the social docility of these groups. It may be that these groups, once they had achieved accommodation of their views with Innocent and papal attitudes were no longer important, were able to resolve their internal tensions and

---

27 *PL* 215 (1855), col. 1510; *PL* 216 (1855), col. 289.

28 GRUNDMANN, *Religiöse Bewegungen*, p. 133.

29 *PL* 214 (1855), col. 696 and also C.MORRIS, 'Christ after the Flesh', *Ampleforth Journal* 53 (1975), pp. 44-51.

30 'Item in urbe Metensi pullulante secta quae dicitur Valdensium, directi sunt quidam abbates ad praedicandum, qui quosdam libros de latino in romanum versos combuserant et praedictam sectam extirpaverunt', Aubrey des Trois Fontaines, *Chronicon*, *MGH SS*, XXIII (Hannover, 1874), p. 878.

conflicts on a lower and more personal level. I should like to suggest that these like-minded individuals attempted to solve their own particular protest in an intensely personal way; by attempting to share the actual bodily suffering of Christ as well as adopting voluntary poverty. The mainspring of their lifestyle was the example of voluntary poverty, exemplified in Christ's call to the rich young ruler to give up all that he had and, in following him, achieve salvation.[31] Thus inspired by their knowledge of the gospels, those who deliberately chose poverty saw themselves as successors of the apostles in attempting to live in the way of life of the first christian community as it could best be lived in the twelfth century. By changing his life style a man could find a personal response to the torments of the age through spiritual renewal. Voluntary poverty thus represented a means whereby individuals could make both their protest and obtain personal rebirth or *renovatio*. Their mediation of the scriptures led them to consider both the Church, the body of Christ in which they all shared and the part to be played by their own bodies in the *vita apostolica*. If they were to share the sufferings of the crucified Christ their own natural bodies could do so as surrogates of the Church. In the salvation imagery of his epistles, Paul had developed the idea of the natural body and the spiritual body seen in terms of the old man, Adam, and the new man, Christ.[32] In order to become a new man fit to be part of the body of Christ, the old man has first to be beaten down. Were these groups, by the mortification of their bodies, following Paul's instruction to beat down the old man and bring about the new man? The old self would be denied, the Pauline new self brought about and the body yielded to God for his disposal as implements for doing right.[33] Sin would no longer be the master. A careful reading of Ephesians would have encouraged them to believe that if they could create a new self, they would be worthy members of Christ's body,

---

[1] Matt. 19: 21-22.

[2] 1 Cor. 15:44.

[3] Rom. 6:13.

the Church.[34] In so doing, poverty would have appeared to exemplify the new man whilst the old man was characterised by wealth.

How far does this relate to the protest of these groups against the Church and against society? Were they visiting on themselves the corrections and deprivation which they really wished to apply to society itself? Were they regarding their bodies as surrogates for society? Could it be that by their own mortification they would be able to bring about not only their personal rebirth but also in some mysterious way, they hoped for purification and rebirth of society?[35]

Does this treatment of themselves provide us with explanations why the waldensians and *humiliati* did not really develop unorthodox relationships with the Church? We do not find their criticisms leading to active attempts on their part to change society. Indeed, instead of protesting against the Church, we find them insisting on their desire to conform. It may be that by the time they had taken out their hostility to society on their own bodies, they had largely relieved the symptoms which at first provoked their attitudes. Perhaps the fact that they had vented all their dislike and venom on themselves may help to explain the lack of written evidence from these groups.[36] There was no point in so doing if their poverty and physical suffering could be seen by all.

The Church in fact was rather inclined to admire these groups, especially their voluntary poverty and did not really interfere with them. It regarded them as the latest in a long line of Christian sufferers which included Alexis,

---

[34] Eph.2: 14-17.

[35] A similar idea may be found in the seventh-century Irish treatise *De duodecim abusivis saeculi* which stresses the notion of self-correction by kings and princes before they can correct others. This text was included by Jonas of Orleans in his *De institutione Regia*, *PL* 106 (1864), col. 288. See C.THOUZELLIER, 'Hérésie et pauvreté à la fin du xiie et au début du xiiie siècle' in M.MOLLAT, *Etudes sur l'histoire de la pauvreté*, Publications de la Sorbonne, *Etudes* 8, 2 vols (Paris, 1974), I, pp. 371-88, especially p. 374 for a similar suggestion.

[36] On the lack of written evidence for the *humiliati* see BOLTON, 'Sources for the early history of the *humiliati*', *SCH* 11 (1975), pp. 125-33.

the inspiration of Valdes[37] and so long as they understood that spiritual triumph could only be reached through Christ's body, the Church, their activities were indeed welcomed.

But perhaps it is not in the nature of true protest to prosper if it welcomed by those against whom the protest is made. Mankind's search for a truly inspirational *vita apostolica* may not in the long term have been satisfied by the activities of these groups. It needed Francis with his deeper understanding and stronger challenge for the movement of protest to be taken into the thirteenth century.

---

[37] A.GIEYSZTOR, 'La légende de Saint Alexis en Occident@ in idéal de pauvreté', *Histoire de la Pauvreté*, I, pp. 125-39.

# XIV

## THE POVERTY OF THE HUMILIATI

The renewal of interest in the *vita apostolica,* which had occurred by 1200, was expressed not only through the *vita communis* of monks and regular canons but also through the activities of various groups of laymen and women[1]. They were laymen who wished to lead a religious life after the manner of the apostles and based their ideas on a return to the principles of the early church as might be lived out in the twelfth century. A renunciation of worldly goods and a life of both poverty and manual labour were thus prescribed for individual members of such groups. The greatest problem for these individuals was to achieve this poverty since they had to have limited possession of goods in order to survive. Their poverty was, by definition, personal and more akin to the poverty of the hermit than to that of the monk. In legal terms, a monastic order could be absolutely poor and monks could have use without possession of goods. The problem therefore was far simpler for the monk who could attain absolute poverty through this device of corporate possession. A lay group, on the other hand, could only experience personal poverty in a limited sense. The desire for poverty thus had to be expressed in very different ways by monks and laymen. One group, the Humiliati, attempted to resolve this by offering a choice to its adherents. They could either live in conventual com- munities, renouncing all possessions or, alternatively, they could remain laymen practising limited personal poverty within the framework of the movement and yet at the same time, receiving the approbation of the hierarchical church.

The Humiliati of Lombardy were a lay group from the upper levels of society having an appeal which was both widespread and popular[2]. We find this name used officially for the first time by Lucius III in the decretal *ad abolendam* of 118- which indiscriminately anathematised a whole group of sects classed as heretical

---

[1] An account of the way in which these groups practised the *vita apostolica* is give- in M.-D. Chenu, *Nature, Man and Society in the Twelfth Century* (Chicago, 1968), Cha- VI: "Monks, Canons and Laymen in search of the Apostolic Life", and Chap. VII: "Th- Evangelical Awakening".

[2] G. Tiraboschi, *Vetera Humiliatorum Monumenta* I-III (= VHM) (Milan, 1766-176- contains the main collection of documents on the Humiliati. Important secondary works in- clude L. Zanoni, *Gli Umiliati nei loro rapporti con l'eresia, l'industria della lana ed communi nei secolo xii e xiii,* Milan, 1911; A. de Stefano, "Delle origini e della natur- del primitivo movimento degli Umiliati" in *Archivium Romanicum* 2 (1927) 31-75; G. Volp- *Movimenti religiosi e sette ereticali nella società medievale italiani secoli x-xiv,* Florenc- 1961. I have drawn on the invaluable work of H. Grundmann, *Religiöse Bewegungen i- Mittelalter* (Berlin, 1935 and Hildesheim, 1961), 70-97, 487-538 for my article, "Innoce- III's treatment of the Humiliati" in *Studies in Church History* 7 (1971) 73-82.

[3] Mansi 22, 476-478. The decree *ad abolendam* distinguished between those wh- preached privately or in public without papal or episcopal consent and those who taug- false doctrines.

Yet their only error was apparently failing to observe the prescription of lay preaching rather than the teaching of false doctrines. In this preaching, the Humiliati concentrated on their experience of Christian life. Their poverty was voluntary and religious and very different from the involuntary poverty of the towns in which they lived.

Innocent III was aware of their basic orthodoxy and, in 1199, wrote to the bishop of Verona to warn him that the Humiliati in his diocese were being excommunicated and asked that measures against them should cease[4]. At much the same time, two leading members of this group came to the pope to seek approval and recognition of their way of life[5]. Innocent however declared himself unable to grant their request without deep thought and considerable investigation. He considered the character of their life to be vastly different from that followed by any existing religious community as it contained both lay and clerical elements[6].

The original and strongest branch of the Humiliati comprised a group of laymen, living at home with their families and practising strict evangelical precepts. These were the Tertiaries who had caught the eye and imagination of several chroniclers. The Chronicler of Laon confirmed the importance of family life, prayer, preaching and mutual support in the life of this group[7]. Humbert de Romans praised their austere life-style, their simple mode of dress and quiet domesticity, considering them to be aptly named because they were leading this humble life of manual work[8]. The chosen framework for the Tertiaries was the fraternity which corresponded to the exigencies and uncertainties of urban life and which provided mutual benefits in an atmosphere of piety[9].

The Humiliati later organised themselves into two further groups which were referred to as orders[10]. These were the first and second orders, led by *praepositi* and

[4] *PL* 214, 789.

[5] *PL* 214. 921-922. They are named as James de Rondineto and Lanfranc de Lodi.

[6] There were however some precedents. In a bull of 1091, Urban II confirmed the *vita communis* of certain laymen according to the form of the early church: PL 151, 336. Bernold of Constance lists three categories of convert to this primitive life, both men and women who had vowed obedience, celibacy and poverty in a communal life and married couples who lived according to strict religious precepts: *PL* 148, 1407-1408. A similar group appears to have been founded in 1188 at St. Didier near Vicenza: G. G. Meerssseman et E. Adda, "Pénitents ruraux communitaires" in *RHE* 49 (1954) 343-390, especially 363,

[7] *Chronicon Universale Anonymi Laudunensis*. Ed. A. Cartellieri et W. Stechèle (Paris, 1909), 28-30.

[8] Printed in L. Zanoni, *Gli Umiliati,* 261-263.

[9] The third order is addressed as *societas, fraternitas* and *universitas: VHM* II, 132-133. On fraternities in general see the valuable study by G. Le Bras, *Etudes de sociologie réligieuse* (Paris, 1955-1956), II, „Les confreries chrétiennes", 418-462. Fraternities acted as support groups to a society in which existing ecclesiastical organisation could not easily adapt. The Tertiaries were encouraged to continue their custom of providing essential care or material aid for those who were ill or in need. Elaborate arrangements for funerals were also laid down for them.

[10] VHM II, 135, 139.

*praelati* respectively. They were composed of priests and unmarried laymen and women who lived separate and ascetic lives in religious communities according to a form of rule which at first was unrecognised by authority. The problem thus facing Innocent was considerable. While it was relatively easy to discipline, regulate and draw into the church the conventual orders of Humiliati, it required an entirely different treatment to organise those who wished to lead special lives in family groups. His attitude to them was therefore cautious. He asked the leaders of the movement to present short statements or *proposita,* indicating their willingness to devote themselves to a life of Christian piety. A special commission was established to receive, examine and pronounce authoritatively on these *proposita*[11].

As a result of this enquiry, papal confirmation was given to the *proposita* of the Humiliati in three documents issued in June 1201[12]. The first order was specifically recognised as a religious community and its obligations and privileges were recognised in its *ordo canonicus*[13]. The *institutio regularis* of the second order also received papal approval and the jurisdictional status of *religiosi* was conceded to these unmarried laity[14].

Innocent's letters to both these conventual groups make it quite clear that from their inception they were regarded as purely monastic communities. Thus, while individuals might be without property, the houses of the orders had to maintain themselves by a sufficient income from corporate possessions. Specific instructions were given to the *praepositi* and *praelati* of both orders to retain for the use of their successors all goods and possessions, held legally and canonically, both in the present and in the future[15]. The conventual houses belonging to these orders were well-endowed with lands and possessions given to them by aristocratic patrons. Innocent III certainly assumed that they would attract gifts from kings, princes and nobles as well as from the papacy. Many such lands appear to have continued to bear the names of their noble donors[16]. The granting of tithe exemption was a valuable privilege for the Humiliati. The first order was granted remission on its lands and granges according to the formula *sane novalium* and with diocesan permission was allowed to possess tithes for its own use[17]. The second order was free from payments on its own lands used for animal husbandry but was still obliged to pay tithes on other land[18].

---

11 *Ibid.*

12 The letters to the third and second orders are dated respectively 7 and 12 June *VHM* II, 128-138. The privilege to the first order was sent on 16 June: *ibid.,* 139-148.

13 *Ibid.,* 139.

14 *Ibid.,* 136. For discussion on this point see M. Maccarrone, "Riforma e sviluppo della vita religiosa con Innocenzo III" in *Rivista di storia della Chiesa in Italia* 16 (1962), 29-72.

15 *VHM* II, 136, 141.

16 *Ibid.,* 141.

17 *Ibid.,* 141-142.

18 *Ibid.,* 136-137.

The third order received papal approval of their *norma vivendi* but because of their way of life and not unmarried state were never accepted into the church as *religiosi*[19]. Nevertheless, the papacy showed itself to be responsive and adaptive to the religious needs of this lay group. Innocent III was concerned with containing as many fringe groups as possible for it was only with such groups that the church could meet dissidents on their own ground and could offer an adequate reply to the fervour of heretical sects[20]. Innocent was also aware of the paradox that the relative poverty of limited personal possession was more arduous to achieve than the absolute poverty of corporate possession. Because of this, and as he could not prevent them from having possessions, he gave the Tertiaries considerable encouragement and advice on the subject of self-restraint. Perhaps he realised that in allowing such limited relative poverty, he was recognising the aspirations of laymen and women coming from the upper levels of society.

The Humiliati, in fact, do not appear to have been the impoverished workers which Zanoni seems once to have taken them for[21]. Indeed, the evidence points in quite another direction. The poverty of the Tertiaries appears to have been of a variable nature. Innocent's instructions were based upon the view that they should be more concerned with avoiding excess rather than emphasizing the absence of necessities. For example, they were to have only two meals a day and were to take food sparingly[22]. This was hardly an instruction which could possibly be taken seriously by anybody who had to live at subsistence level. Other instructions followed similar lines. They were to give to the indigent all income from alms and oblations in excess of their own needs[23]. They were to avoid all forms of usury and were to return all unlawful gains to their original sources[24]. Again, these do not suggest to us a group of people unfamiliar with the use and abuse of money. They were specifically warned against finery and ostentatious display[25]. The poverty thus practised by the Humiliati involved considerable personal restraint and was of a kind which was acceptable to the noble and rich urban classes. It represented a way of life more austere and demanding than that of the normal layman and at the same time avoided the severity of monasticism. Indeed, this group of the Humiliati would have been right in stressing that, not only was their poverty the only realistic form possible for them, but it also required none of the legal fiction surrounding corporate possession.

The fact that the Tertiaries became involved in the wool and cloth industries should not necessarily lead us to presuppose that they were either artisans or the

---

19 M. Maccarrone, "Riforma e sviluppo", 47-49.

20 B. M. Bolton, "Tradition and temerity. Papal attitudes towards deviants, 1159-1216" in *Studies in Church History* 9 (1972) 79-91.

21 L. Zanoni, *Gli Umiliati,* 157.

22 *VHM* II, 132. Fasting was prescribed twice a week unless ill or weak or unless it would impede their work. They had to pray before and after they had eaten.

23 *Ibid.,* 131-132.

24 *Ibid.,* 131. See also J. T. Gilchrist, *The Church and Economic Activity in the Middle Ages,* London, 1969 (especially 68).

25 *VHM* II, 133.

lowest group of workers. Spinning and weaving were relatively simple skills which even the rich might acquire. Cloth was in universal demand and involved women as well as men in its production. Such work, operated on a domestic basis, was quite compatible with Innocent's instruction to the Tertiaries to remain with their families[26]. This work was also respectable and would not have been considered too arduous for those who were fairly high up in the social scale. Indeed, it might have represented a deliberate act of humility on the part of those who did not have to work. Grundmann confirms the view that they were not impoverished workers but emanated from a wider and altogether richer cross section of society[27]. That they wished "to be poor and to live with the poor" suggests not only an attempt to bridge the gulf between the classes but presupposes their awareness of the existence of such a gulf.

The Humiliati were thus an important urban movement in early thirteenth century Italy. Jacques de Vitry, an experienced observer of religious groups, recorded his admiration for them in 1216 when they stood out as almost the only orthodox group in heretical Milan[28]. We also know of houses in Como, Lodi, Pavia, Piacenza, Bra, Brescia, Bergamo, Monza, Cremona and Verona[29].

At this time, Lombardy was an area of relatively weak political authority with considerable social mobility[30]. There was thus no strong authority to control the effects on the individual of exposure to such new types of social experience as urban growth. There was a considerable inbuilt opposition to episcopal authority, not only from lords in commune and *contado* alike but also from churches and monasteries with strong particularist tendencies, all seeking to evade the juristiction of the bishop. Because of this, it would be tempting to accept the recent suggestion of Violante that this increased mobility was translated into a state of mind which, in the search for a more austere life, displayed an intolerance towards existing ecclesiastical structures and which in itself constituted a danger to the church[31].

The new urban populations further reflected this problem. Recent immigrants, who lived outside the walls at some distance from the town centre, had no provision made for them by the diocesan church. In addition, as Lombardy was served by first foundation or baptismal churches, a whole town might form one parish with a clergy who led semi-communal lives and performed liturgical as well as pastoral duties[32].

---

26 *Ibid.*, 132.

27 See H. Grundmann, *Religiöse Bewegungen*, 157-169, who discusses the religious reaction amongst the upper classes to social and economic developments. It is interesting to compare this view with that of M. Weber, *The Sociology of Religion* (London, 1971), 95-96, who sees the Humiliati as a lower middle class group.

28 *Lettres de Jacques de Vitry*. Ed. R. Huygens (Leiden, 1960), 72-73.

29 *VHM* II, 128.

30 J. L. Nelson, "Society, theodicy and the origins of heresy. Towards a reassessment of the medieval evidence" in *Studies in Church History* 9 (1972) 72.

31 C. Violante, „Hérésies urbaines et rurales en Italie du XI^e au XIII^e siècle" in J. Le Goff, *Hérésies et sociétés dans l'Europe préindustrielle* (Paris, 1968), 175-179.

32 G. Addleshaw, *The Early Parochial System and the Divine Office*, London, 1957.

Many townsmen therefore were completely untouched by the ministrations of these local clergy.

It was not by chance that the Humiliati were part of a movement towards voluntary apostolic poverty which was most highly developed in the towns and amongst just those circles which might reasonably have expected to benefit most from increasing prosperity. At the outset, at least, large numbers of nobles and members of the urban patriciate appear to have participated[33]. Possibly they experienced a spiritual reaction against the sudden and often usurious accumulation of riches. It has been suggested recently that thirteenth century Italy saw a growth, both in competitive spirit and in *avaritia* which led to "money-mindedness"[34]. The Humiliati, along with others, considered this to be in direct contradiction to the primary demands of the gospels and expressed their reaction through an ardent desire for expiation. Such expiation could be achieved by these new apostles through ideals of renunciation. But who could renounce unless he had possessions? The obligation to *humilitas* and the commitment to voluntary poverty would have been a meaningless gesture if made from the impoverished ranks of society. If poverty and abasement were chosen and experienced for their religious value, doing without possessions and turning from social respectability was implicit in this decision[35]. It seems likely that poverty represented for the Humiliati a personal and social *renovatio*--a spiritual renewal through the adoption of a new life-style- -the *vita apostolica*[36].

A closer examination of the evidence shows that the movement included nobles, powerful citizens and some clerics. Guy de Porta Orientalis, minister of the Tertiaries, is described as *vir nobilis* and *capitaneus*[37]. In Lombardy there was a strong tradition of alienation among the lesser nobility, especially the *vavassours,* who were usually excluded from any positive role in either political or ecclesiastical affairs[38]. Some may have been tempted to join the Humiliati amongst whom they could more easily achieve the eminence denied them by the church. In the towns, the nobility of feudal origin was closely linked through marriage and commerce to the urban patriciate. This urban nobility was highly mobile, reflecting its links with the *contado* and frequently returning to it. Rural lords too were interested in the foundations of the Humiliati and possibly maintained this interest even when later they moved into the towns[39]. Here it might be suggested that the town gave leadership while the country perhaps supplied the leaders[40].

---

33 H. Grundmann, *Religiöse Bewegungen,* 160-163.

34 A. Murray, "Piety and Impiety in thirteenth-century Italy" in *Studies in Church History* 7 (1971) 89.

35 H. Grundmann, *Religiöse Bewegungen,* 168.

36 J. L. Nelson, "Society, thedoicy and the origins of heresy", 75.

37 *PL* 214, 921; *VHM* I, 44.

38 C. Violante, *La Società Milanese nell'età precommunale* (Bari, 1953), 176.

39 C. Violante, „Hérésies urbaines et rurales", 179.

40 N. Gras, "The Economic Activity of Towns" in *The Legacy of the Middle Ages.* Ed. C. G. Crump and E. F. Jacob (Oxford, 1962), 437.

Further evidence confirms this good social standing of the Humiliati. Jacques de Vitry thought that almost all of them were literate[41]. The members of the first order were granted the right to wear a habit *ut laicos litteratos,* presumably similar to that worn by Italian civil lawyers[42]. They could not have known the primary demands of the gospels unless they were able to read for themselves, nor could they have understood the *vita apostolica* simply by being told about it. We know that they organised *schola* to offer training in preaching and teaching and in order to be able to refute error, they must have known scriptural texts[43]. This presupposes the utility to the church of the more civilised, more literate, upper strata of society. Whereas before their value had consisted in donations and pious benefactions, now they were becoming increasingly spiritually minded and thus increasingly useful to the ecclesiastical establishment.

Innocent III's contact with the Humiliati showed him that such movements could be of value if carefully controlled. He used the Tertiaries to supplement the deficiencies of the local clergy by allowing them extraordinarily liberal powers of preaching in direct contravention to the very fierce legislation of the twelfth century[44]. Lay preaching on such a scale was unheard of but, in giving them this permission, Innocent was far from altruistic. Once the crucial question of obedience was settled[45], the Humiliati were allowed an existence within the church because they were already acting as supernumerary clergy in the urban situation.

Innocent III had thus taken the most versatile of one of a number of previously condemned groups in the voluntary poverty movement and brought it into the church. This group, the Humiliati, members of a pious fraternity and adepts of religious poverty, had adapted themselves both to the needs of an urban society and to the requirements of a hierarchical church.

What makes their activities so interesting is their attempt to spiritualise the laity by concentrating on the *vita apostolica.* The Humiliati lived like apostles; acted like apostoles; and in so doing, achieved a quite extraordinary success. This success evidently impressed Jacques de Vitry who in 1216 counted no less than 150 conventual houses in Milan alone while the number of family groups was so many that he could not begin to estimate them[46].

---

41 Jacques de Vitry, *Jacobi de Vitriaco libri due quorum prior orientalis sive Hierosolimitanae, alter occidentalis historiae nomine inscribitur.* Ed. F. Moschus (Douai, 1597), 335.

42 *VHM* II, 142.

43 M.-D. Chenu, *Nature, Man and Society,* 249.

44 *VHM* II, 134. The Tertiaries were allowed to gather every Sunday at a suitable place at which those "wise in faith and expert in religion" could preach as long as they ignored theological questions and dealt only with exhortations to a pious and earnest life. Like the mendicants, the Humiliati appear to have settled outside the town walls built during Barbarossa's wars and to have concentrated their preaching activities at the gates. In Milan they had houses at every gate.

45 B. M. Bolton, "Tradition and temerity", 87.

46 *Lettres de Jacques de Vitry,* 73.

Whether he was correct to be so impressed by numbers is open to question. We should rather judge the Humiliati by the opportunity for challenge which their movement gave to the view that only through a conventual system could the highest order of poverty be achieved. The Tertiaries provided an alternative in giving a lead to the people of the Lombard towns who wanted to live a life of poverty centred on the nuclear and domestic family. They displayed a guilt about possessions derived from a literal view of the New Testament and were not satisfied that the legal fiction of monastic possession was other than a device to achieve the outward sign of poverty without its inward substance. The corporate ownership of property, allowing for its use without possession was not regarded by them as meeting the need for a true life of poverty by individuals. Their limited poverty and retention of some possessions made them akin to the involuntary poor of the towns even though they themselves had come from the upper levels of society.

The Humiliati Tertiaries can be regarded as the forerunners of the mendicants. The ideas put forward by Francis, although of a more inspirational nature, were themselves unable to escape institutionalisation. The attempt of the Humiliati therefore to achieve personal poverty in the prevailing conditions of the early thirteenth century must not be regarded as an insignificant part of the movement towards the *vita apostolica*.

Anonymus Escurialensis, Forum of Nerva and View of the Tor de'Conti
(Photograph: Frank Salmon; by permission of The British School at Rome.)

# XV

## SOURCES FOR THE EARLY HISTORY OF THE HUMILIATI

THE task of understanding the significance of any religious movement in its historical context normally depends upon documents being available for description and analysis. In the case of the *humiliati* this is almost impossible.[1] Such documentary evidence as exists for the period 1179 to 1216 comes not from the *humiliati* themselves but from others whose reasons for mentioning them varied considerably – suggestions as to why this is so will be made as the paper develops. Analysing these sources for information about the *humiliati* will thus be difficult. Nevertheless, as these documents cover certain aspects peculiar to the movement, they can be used to indicate such information as the *humiliati* might themselves have given. Indeed, if carefully pieced together, an even more coherent whole can appear on the principle that onlookers see more of the game than the players. The scope of this paper therefore is to examine the sources available in an attempt to show something of the early history of the *humiliati*; bearing in mind all the time, the limitations involved; the inevitable omissions in such accidental or incidental evidence; and the demonstrable bias which will be found to exist. That these documents are few in number and only rarely rich in detail increases the difficulty.

The documents which exist fall into three categories; general papal decrees and letters recorded in the registers of Innocent III;[2]

[1] General books and articles on the *humiliati* are few in number. But see A. de Stefano, 'Delle origini e della natura del primitivo movimento degli Umiliati', *Archivium Romanicum*, 2 (Geneva 1927) pp 31–75; E. Scott Davison, *Forerunners of St Francis* (London 1928) pp 168–200; M. Maccarrone, 'Riforma e sviluppo della vita religiosa con Innocenzo III', *Rivista di storia della Chiesa in Italia*, 16 (Rome 1962) pp 29–71 especially pp 46–50; [H.] Grundmann, *Religiöse Bewegungen* [*im Mittelalter*] (2 ed Darmstadt 1970) pp 70–97, 487–538 and my article 'Innocent III's treatment of the *Humiliati*' in *SCH*, 8 (1971) pp 73–82.

[2] A detailed introduction to Innocent III's letters is given by [C. R.] Cheney, *Medieval Studies and Texts* (Oxford 1973) pp 16–39; there is also a useful general chapter on sources in J. H. Mundy, *Europe in the High Middle Ages 1150–1309* (London 1973) pp 1–21.

contemporary twelfth- and thirteenth-century accounts made by interested observers and chronicles written in the fifteenth century by two members of the conventual *humiliati*. Many of these documents are available in two important printed collections both published in Milan, the *Vetera Humiliatorum Monumenta* compiled between 1766 and 1768 by Girolamo Tiraboschi[3] and the appendix to Luigi Zanoni's work on the movement published in 1911.[4]

When the papal documents are looked at in more detail it will be seen that they themselves fall into two groups. The first of these indicates prevailing papal attitudes varying from hostility to support and based mainly on the *humiliati*'s supposed heterodoxy or orthodoxy. The earliest official mention occurs in Lucius III's decretal *ad abolendam* of 1184 where they are included amongst a whole group of sects classed as heretical.[5] A papal letter of 1199 shows Innocent III asking the bishop of Verona to cease the excommunication of *humiliati* in his diocese until their views had been reconsidered by the papacy.[6] Yet in 1203 an incidental piece of evidence obtained from a local record shows that, at Cerea in the same diocese, the *humiliati* were still being expelled and their goods confiscated by archidiaconal licence.[7] A papal letter of 1214 shows that Innocent, while considering them still orthodox, was forced to admonish them for appearing to have deviated from their original austere and humble life.[8]

The second group of papal documents deals with the acceptance and formal recognition of the *humiliati*. In a letter of 1200 Innocent refers to an earlier request he had made to the leaders of the movement to indicate their willingness to devote themselves to a life of christian piety by presenting *proposita* or short statements of intent.[9] Although these *proposita* have not survived it is possible to deduce their content from Innocent's separate letters to the three orders of the *humiliati* in

[3] [G. Tiraboschi] *V*[*etera*] *H*[*umiliatorum*] *M*[*onumenta*], 3 vols (Milan 1766–8).

[4] [L.] Zanoni, *Gli Umiliati* [*nei loro rapporti con l'eresia, l'industria della lana ed i communi nei secoli xii e xiii*], Biblioteca historica italia, Serie II, 2 (Milan 1911). The appendix includes the *Chronicle of John de Brera 1421* pp 336–44 and the *Chronicle of Marcus Bossius 1493* pp 345–52.

[5] *VHM* I p 79; Mansi 22 cols 476–8; *PL* 201 (1855) cols 1297–300.

[6] *PL* 214 (1855) col 789. Here the *humiliati* are listed with cathars, arnaldists and poor men of Lyons.

[7] C. Cipolla, 'Statuti rurali veronesi', *Archivio veneto* 37 (Venice 1889) pp 341–5.

[8] *VHM* II pp 156–7; Potthast I no 4945.

[9] *PL* 214 (1855) col 921; *VHM* II p 139.

1201.[10] In giving papal approval to these orders the letters tell us much of what we know about the characteristic features of the movement.[11] These documents, together with comments made by the fifteenth-century chroniclers regarding the fear of some *humiliati* that they would be adjudged as heretics, indicate a preoccupation with the reconciling of the *vita apostolica* and the orthodox views of the Church.[12] Herbert Grundmann, in undertaking a careful exploration of the critical themes underlying the religious movements of the twelfth, thirteenth and fourteenth centuries, concluded that the *humiliati* represented a part of the widespread religious reaction which Chenu has later referred to as the 'Evangelical Awakening'.[13] Grundmann, although pointing out that Innocent's letter to the third order said nothing about the danger of heresy,[14] was the first to suggest that Innocent, when he wrote to the bishop of Verona in 1199, was attempting to achieve a distinction between irrevocable heretics and those who could be drawn back into the church.[15] He referred to Innocent's treatment of the *humiliati* as the first attempt to bridge the gap between the hierarchical church and new religious movements.[16] Perhaps the *proposita* of the *humiliati* convinced Innocent that their views were not heretical which accounts for the omission of a reference to heresy in the letter of 1201.

The documents remaining from this correspondence between Innocent III and the *humiliati* all emanate from the papacy. If, as will be dealt with later, they were indeed literate, then there is every reason to suppose that there was a *humiliati* side to the correspondence. In fact in his letters Innocent asks them to write their responses to his proposals. What then happened to the relevant material? Could there perhaps have been a systematic destruction of *humiliati* writings similar to that which had certainly occurred in Metz in 1199 when the books and vernacular biblical translations of a literate lay group were ordered to

[10] The letters to the third and second orders are dated respectively 7 and 12 June: *VHM* II pp 128–38. The privilege to the first order was sent on 16 June: *ibid* pp 139–48.

[11] The original and strongest branch comprised a group of laymen living at home with their families. These were the tertiaries or third order. The first and second orders were composed of priests and unmarried laymen and women who lived separate and ascetic lives in religious communities.

[12] Zanoni, *Gli Umiliati* pp 341, 350.

[13] [M.-D.] Chenu, ['The Evangelical Awakening'], in his *Nature, Man and Society* [*in the Twelfth Century*: *Essays on New Theological Perspectives in the Latin West*] ed and translated by J. Taylor and L. K. Little (Chicago 1968) pp 239–69.

[14] Grundmann, *Religiöse Bewegungen* p 88 note 33.

[15] *Ibid* pp 72–5.

[16] *Ibid* pp 90–1.

be destroyed?[17] We know that Pandulf, papal legate in England, ordered the destruction of all evidence about Magna Carta in 1215 to facilitate the development of an official papal line.[18] Was it also the intention of the church that there should be such an official line in regard to the *humiliati*? Other alternatives could be that the *humiliati* were either illiterate or simply did not wish to express their views in writing.

We should perhaps at this point consider how literate were these early *humiliati*. Although in the opinion of Burchard of Ursperg, a premonstratensian canon, they were *rudes et illiterati* he appears to be alone in this.[19] Other evidence points to a high rate of literacy. In 1199, as we have seen, Innocent III instructed them to write down their *proposita* for him whilst in 1201 he allowed members of the first order to wear a habit *ut laicos litteratos* presumably similar to the habit worn by Italian civil lawyers.[20] Jacques de Vitry, one of the contemporary observers, was of the opinion that almost all of them were literate.[21] If we conclude from this that they were literate we cannot at the same time deduce much about the uses to which this literacy was put. Even if they did not wish to express their views in writing there is no doubt that they wished for formal sanction of their way of life. To obtain this they would need to put something in writing. As with Francis 'some rule however simple must be drawn up'.[22]

We can link the question of their literacy with the permission to preach given to them by Innocent III. His letter to the third order or tertiaries showed his support for them by allowing them to preach and to give their personal witness to the faith.[23] Although he was not prepared to allow them to teach doctrine this was a considerable concession. It will be remembered that it was their insistence on preaching

[17] *PL* 214 (1855) cols 695–9; *PL* 216 (1855) cols 1210–14; Potthast I no 781; Grundmann, *Religiöse Bewegungen* pp 97–100.

[18] Cheney, *Medieval Studies and Texts* p 253.

[19] *Burchardi et Cuonradi Urspergensium Chronicon* ed O. Abel – L. Weiland, *MGH, SS* 23 (Hanover 1874) p 377. Burchard was in Italy in 1210 and must have encountered the *humiliati* there: Grundmann, *Religiöse Bewegungen* p 90 note 37.

[20] *VHM* II p 142.

[21] Jacques de Vitry, *Historia Occidentalis* ed F. Moschus (Douai 1597) p 335. I have unfortunately not been able to use the new edition ed J. F. Hinnebusch, *Spicilegium Friburgense* 17 (Fribourg 1972).

[22] J. Moorman, *A History of the Franciscan Order from its origins to the year 1517* (Oxford 1968) p 16.

[23] *VHM* II pp 133–4.

which had first resulted in anathematisation by the decree of Lucius III in 1184. This authorisation to preach was in direct contravention to the very fierce legislation of the twelfth century and was in its way unique. Although episcopal licence was necessary for preaching, Innocent expressly commanded the bishops not to refuse. Their only concern was to be the question of place and time.

For reactions to this exceptional privilege we can usefully turn to our eye-witness observers of the *humiliati*. The anonymous premonstratensian canon of Laon, whose chronicle may be dated at some point between the third lateran council of 1179 and Lucius III's decree of 1184, recorded the *humiliati*'s refusal to abandon their preaching and their subsequent excommunication.[24] Burchard of Ursperg of the same order also mentioned this papal prohibition saying that the *humiliati* by their preaching were 'thrusting their sickle into the harvest of others'.[25] This he claimed led to the pope's establishment and confirmation of the dominicans as the order of preachers. Jacques de Vitry who was the most detailed, vivid and enthusiastic of the eye-witnesses recorded his impressions of the *humiliati* first in a letter of 1216 and later in his *Historia Occidentalis*.[26] He was convinced of their opposition to heresy and said that the pope had granted them the right to preach in squares, open spaces and secular churches. There they 'prudently convinced the impious from holy scripture and publicly confounded them'.[27] Such a concentration upon the holy scriptures reflected their wish not only to live by the gospels but to preach by the gospels. They would be more concerned in preaching the word than in diffusing biblical texts and vernacular translations. They would have shown little interest in writing on doctrinal points of theology and so Innocent's prohibition on doctrine would not have troubled them. Such a concentration on preaching the word would mean that they would tend to make use of oral (rather than written) communication. Preaching the word would mean to them that the bible was the only necessary written record.

How far was this correct? Innocent had specifically given the *humiliati* the power to witness to the faith and preach on their experience of christian life but had denied them the right to teach doctrine. But was he really able to distinguish between theological and moral questions

[24] *Chronicon Universale Anonymi Laudunensis*, ed A. Cartellieri and W. Stechèle (Paris 1909) pp 23–30.

[25] W. Wakefield and A. P. Evans, *Heresies of the High Middle Ages* (New York 1969) p 229.

[26] *Lettres de Jacques de Vitry* ed R. B. C. Huygens (Leiden 1960) pp 72–3.

[27] *Historia Occidentalis* p 335.

as far as their teaching was concerned? It seems likely that they must indeed have touched upon doctrinal issues and that Innocent later became suspicious.[28] The evidence here is lacking. We do not even know whether they stressed one gospel more than another although Innocent in his letter to the tertiaries most frequently cites James.[29] Chenu interprets this acceptance of lay preaching as part of the church's long struggle to give juridical and sacramental authenticity to the apostolic drive amongst not only the *humiliati* but also some waldensians, Poor Catholics and later the franciscans.[30]

Should the definition of lay groups mean that normal life is still carried on in the world? The chronicler of Laon tells us that the *humiliati* considered family life to be of prime importance but it is Jacques de Vitry who again is our main source. He reported that many *humiliati* remained physically in the world with their wives and children while yet humbly abstracting themselves from worldly affairs.[31] Their religious motivation compelled them to live by the work of their hands. The working of cloth involved women as well as men in its production and was operated on a domestic basis. It was thus quite compatible with Innocent's instructions to the tertiaries to remain with their families.[32] In spite of this instruction, the family element in the life of this group is stressed only by contemporary observers who seem to have considered this the distinguishing feature of the *humiliati* and not in the papal documents. Innocent's letter of 1201 to the tertiaries gives more emphasis to the fraternity aspect of their life. This fraternity strengthened vertical as well as horizontal social bonds. It did so by binding the tertiaries together in communal prayer as well as in a mutual assurance society which ensured the provision of material welfare for the sick and needy.[33]

[28] Grundmann, *Religiöse Bewegungen* p 81 thinks it unlikely that the *humiliati* had attempted to expound dogma because they were more interested in moral questions but sees a new distinction between clerical and lay sermons.

[29] *VHM* II pp 128–34.

[30] Chenu, *Nature, Man and Society* pp 260–2.

[31] *Historia Occidentalis* p 335.

[32] *VHM* II p 132. For valuable insights into the medieval family see P. Ariès, *Centuries of Childhood* translated by Robert Baldick (London 1973) especially pp 327–99.

[33] *VHM* II pp 132–3. On fraternities see the study by G. Le Bras, *Études de sociologie réligieuse*, 2 vols (Paris 1955–6) II 'Les confréries chrétiennes', pp 418–62; Robert Moore, 'History, economics and religion: a review of the Max Weber thesis' in *Max Weber and Modern Sociology*, ed Arun Sahay (London 1971) pp 82–96. Compare Chenu, *Nature, Man and Society* pp 261–4.

Can we perhaps see here Innocent's wider policies in microcosm? It was greatly in the church's interests to promote these solidarities which cross-cut the family both vertically and horizontally. Such fraternities, although modelled upon the prevalent ideal of the kin-group were not equivalent to the family but rather an alternative. Might it have been a deliberate move on Innocent's part to avoid an over-commitment to kin solidarity which in the context of lombard society with its family feuds, internal tensions and recent patarine past could have proved highly dangerous?[34] In this he may have been successful for after 1216 we hear nothing more of the family groups as a significant feature of the *humiliati* movement. This view is carried further by the chroniclers of the fifteenth century who were instead concerned in writing about the conventual *humiliati* and their place in society.

Various other sources help to throw light on the social composition of the *humiliati*. Zanoni in examining these sources sought to explain their movement as a reaction to social and economic events basing his argument on an incidental account by Humbert de Romans, minister general of the dominicans, who referred to them as *laborantes*.[35] Developing this point Zanoni viewed them as impoverished workers from the lowest stratum of society and so excluded from political influence. There remained for them religious association as their only possible form of organisation.[36] Grundmann however considered that the evidence pointed to a religious reaction in the upper levels of society in a search for the *vita apostolica*.[37] Innocent's letter to the tertiaries about the avoidance of excess[38] and the evidence showing how the *humiliati* organised *schola* seem to bear out Grundmann's view.[39]

A closer examination of the evidence shows that the movement initially at least contained those of good social standing. Jacques de Vitry tells us that it included nobles, powerful citizens, aristocratic matrons and young girls from rich families.[40] Guy de Porta Orientalis, member of one important lombard family and *minister* of the tertiaries is

[34] J. K. Hyde, *Society and Politics in Medieval Italy: the Evolution of the Civil Life 1000–1350* (London 1973) pp 120–1. See also the excellent bibliography.
[35] Printed in Zanoni, *Gli Umiliati* pp 261–3; Grundmann, *Religiöse Bewegungen* pp 158–61.
[36] Zanoni, *Gli Umiliati* p 157.
[37] Grundmann, *Religiöse Bewegungen* pp 158–69.
[38] *VHM* II p 132. They were to have only two sparse meals a day, to give back all wrongfully acquired possessions and to give all income in excess of their own needs to the poor.
[39] Chenu, *Nature, Man and Society* p 249 n 12.
[40] *Historia Occidentalis* p 334.

described as *vir nobilis* and *capitaneus*.[41] In northern Italy and especially in Lombardy there was a strong tradition of alienation among the lesser nobility, particularly the *vavassours* who were usually excluded from any positive role in either political or ecclesiastical affairs. Just as some had supported the patarines of the eleventh century or, in the twelfth, the emperor Barbarossa, so some may have been tempted to join the *humiliati* where they would have had a better chance of achieving the eminence denied them in other spheres. We can neither show any consequent antipathies or tension in local relationships nor show that, if they existed, they were being healed by membership of the fraternities of the *humiliati*. The only possible evidence might be that about the name *humiliati* which was given to them by others. We do not know for certain when they accepted the name *humiliati* nor indeed what it implied to them. Both the chronicler of Laon and the fifteenth century *humiliati* chroniclers tell us that their name derived from their plain clothing while Jacques de Vitry elaborates this by citing the example of humility which they displayed. We know from Innocent's letter of 1199 to the bishop of Verona that they were called *humiliati* by the people.[42] Grundmann maintained that those reconciled with the church were not called *humiliati* officially until 1211 or 1214 and stated that they in fact objected to the name.[43] Certainly there is confusion in two papal letters of 1206 when Innocent appears to be using patarine and *humiliati* as alternatives.[44] Jacques de Vitry confirms that this confusion was still deliberately maintained by ill-willed people as late as 1216.[45]

The evidence in regard to the geographical location may also be of help in examining the question of local antipathies and tensions. All of the *humiliati* were to be found in the towns around Milan in northern Italy and there is considerable general evidence to show that these antipathies and tensions were a common feature of life in these towns. Belonging to the *humiliati* therefore may have meant belonging to a fraternity which safeguarded them from the ill-effects of such a social climate.

Using these documents on the *humiliati* in this way gives a reasonably satisfactory picture. Although this may be so it would be wrong to remain content. What further fields of enquiry are open to us? Field work in the *humiliati* towns might produce local records which would

[41] *PL* 214 (1855) col 921; *VHM* I p 44.
[42] *PL* 214 (1855) col 789.
[43] Grundmann, *Religiöse Bewegungen* p 89 n 34.
[44] *PL* 215 (1855) cols 820, 1043.
[45] *Lettres de Jacques de Vitry* pp 72–3.

improve the documentary situation. The techniques of medieval archaeology might also provide another dimension. It is my opinion, however, that what is really needed is a new approach to the existing evidence by using the insights of the social sciences. These would give us fresh awareness of the part played by the *humiliati* in the religious ferment of their time and greater understanding of the way in which the members of this informal religious congregation were able to live devotional lives at grass roots level. If this is done, it would be true to say that 'while few people are asking interesting questions the raw materials for doing so are becoming better understood'.[46]

[46] See the review article by L. K. Little in *Speculum* 48 (Cambridge Mass., 1973) p 345.

# XVI

## DAUGHTERS OF ROME: ALL ONE IN CHRIST JESUS!

JACQUES DE VITRY (*c.* 1160–1240) was a most perceptive and sympathetic observer of all that the religious life meant to women at the beginning of the thirteenth century. He thus took care to address some of his preaching to particular groups of these women.[1] In his *Sermones vulgares*, probably set down at some time after 1228, he put forward messages appropriate to each of these groups.[2] He was uniquely qualified to do so.

An Augustinian canon from St Nicholas of Oignies, in the diocese of Saumur (1211–16),[3] he became in succession, Bishop of Acre (1216–27),[4] auxiliary Bishop of Liège (1227–29),[5] the centre of Beguine piety, and then Cardinal-Bishop of Tusculum (1229–40).[6] The latter was to be his last and most prestigious position. Interestingly, he was a successor to Nicholas *de Romanis* (1204–18/19),[7] known as the 'angel of salvation and peace',[8] who had also realized the importance of addressing women

[1] For a complete bibliography and an excellent summary of the career and writings of this popular preacher see J. F. Hinnebusch, *The Historia occidentalis of Jacques de Vitry = Spicilegium Friburgense*, 17 (Fribourg, 1972), pp. x–xiii, 3–15. Also B. Z. Kedar, *Crusade and Mission: European Approaches towards the Muslims* (Princeton, 1984), pp. 116–31.

[2] Paris, BN, MS latin 17509, fos 140v–7r. A partial edition is given by J. B. Pitra, *Analecta novissima spicilegii Solesmensis. Altera continuatio*, 2 (Tusculana–Paris, 1888), and for those sermons specifically directed to women, see J. Greven, 'Der Ursprung des Beginenwesens', *HJ*, 35 (1914), pp. 26–58, 291–318.

[3] Hinnebusch, *Historia Occidentalis*, p. 4, n. 6.

[4] R. B. C. Huygens, *Lettres de Jacques de Vitry (1160/70–1240), évêque de Saint-Jean d'Acre* (Leiden, 1960), pp. 72–3. He received episcopal consecration from Honorius III in July 1216 at Perugia. Huygens, 'Les passages des lettres de Jacques de Vitry rélatifs à Saint François d'Assise et à ses premiers disciples', in *Homages à Leon Herrmann = Collection Latomus*, 44 (Brussels, 1960), pp. 446–53. C. Eubel, *Hierarchia Catholica Medii Aevi*, 1 (Regensburg, 1913), p. 6.

[5] Hinnebusch, *Historia occidentalis*, p. 7. Bishop Hugh Pierrepont (3 March 1200–12 April 1229) must have been extremely old; Eubel, *Hierarchia Catholica*, p. 301.

[6] *Ibid*., p. 6 mentioned between 29 June 1229–23 June 1239; Potthast, 1, 8441.

[7] Confusion has been caused by two bishops of the same name, Nicholas *de Romanis*, 5 May 1205–14 September 1219, and his successor, Nicholas de Claromonte, O.Cist., 15 December 1220–9 May 1226; Eubel, *Hierarchia Catholica*, p. 5. W. Maleczek, *Papst und Kardinalskolleg von 1191 bis 1216: die Kardinale unter Coelestin III und Innocenz III* (Vienna, 1984), pp. 147–50; P. Pressutti, *Regesta Honorii Papae III*, 1 (Rome, 1888), p. 358.

[8] *Angelus salutis et pacis, PL* 216, cols 881–4; C. R. Cheney and W. H. Semple, eds., *Selected Letters of Pope Innocent III concerning England* (London and Edinburgh, 1953), pp. 149–54.

directly.[9] Jacques de Vitry, throughout all his normal pastoral and administrative duties, no matter where they were undertaken, was constantly influenced by what he considered to be a task of the greatest importance: encouraging the faith and improving the standing of women in the life of the Church.[10] All were to be 'one in Christ Jesus'.[11]

The responsible position of Cardinal-Bishop of Tusculum, located a few miles south of Rome, also entailed high office in the Curia. His office enabled him to develop his ideas on women, and must have given him great personal satisfaction, as he had been subjected to harsh criticism when he left Liège for Rome in 1229. His disciple, Thomas de Cantimpré, had considered that the Church of Lotharingia still needed his help to continue its pursuit of the *vita apostolica*. This was reinforced when Jacques de Vitry's 'spiritual mother', Mary of Oignies, expressed her regret and dismay when she appeared to Thomas in a vision.[12] Jacques de Vitry's exciting and dangerous mission over the Alps in 1216, when he set out to draw to Innocent III's attention the life being led by such Northern religious women, was still remembered and recounted.[13] Jacques de Vitry was needed at home. The newly appointed Cardinal-Bishop of Tusculum thought differently. He was now to turn his attention to religious women in the south and, in particular, to the daughters of Rome.[14]

Of Jacques de Vitry's many *ad status* sermons which he gave to particular groups or categories of society, two were particularly addressed to virgins about to reach the age when marriage would have to be considered. The first, based on the Song of Songs, well known to the daughters of Jerusalem, used the text: 'I am the rose of Sharon and the lily of the valleys' to put forward the joys of marriage.[15] This sermon was

[9] A. Mercati, 'La prima relazione del Cardinale Niccolo *de Romanis* sulla sua legazione in Inghilterra', in H. W. C. Davis, ed., *Essays on History presented to R. L. Poole* (Oxford, 1927), pp. 274–89; *Monumenta Diplomatica S. Dominici*, ed. V. J. Koudelka, *MOFPH*, 25 (1966), pp. 90–8.

[10] H. Grundmann, *Religiöse Bewegungen im Mittelalter*, 2nd edn (Darmstadt, 1970), pp. 208–19; E. W. McDonnell, *The Beguines and Beghards in Medieval Culture with Special Emphasis on the Belgian Scene* (Rutgers, 1984) and for an important critique of this and other relevant works, J. Ziegler, 'The *curtis* beguinages in the Southern Low Countries and art patronage: interpretations and historiography', *Bulletin de l'Institut Historique Belge de Rome*, 57 (1987), pp. 31–70, esp. n. 5 and pp. 48–54. For Jacques de Vitry's role, B. M. Bolton, '*Mulieres Sanctae*', *SCH*, 10 (1973), pp. 77–96; *ibid*, '*Vitae Matrum*: a further aspect of the *Frauenfrage*', in D. Baker, ed., *Medieval Women, SCH.S*, 1 (1978), pp. 253–73, and 'Some thirteenth-century women in the Low Countries', *Nederlands Archief voor Kerkgeschiedenis*, 61 (1981), pp. 7–29.

[11] Galatians 3.28.

[12] Thomas de Cantimpré, *Vita B. Mariae Oigniacensis, Supplementum, Acta SS*, June 4, pp. 675–6.

[13] Huygens, *Lettres de Jacques de Vitry*, p. 72.

[14] Song of Songs 3.5 for a text applicable to all groups of women.

[15] Song of Songs 2.1.

addressed specifically to those who both accepted the fact of marriage and were eager to enter into it. The second sermon was addressed to those young girls who might not wish to marry, and certainly did not wish to be forced into it.[16] To them, for whatever reasons, the religious life held out attractions. His theme, from the Apocryphal Book of Wisdom, praised chastity and the chaste generation.[17] He urged these discreet and devout girls to avoid any occasion which would allow their detractors, 'those dogs who fouled the Cross' the opportunity to criticize their intentions and divert them from their aim.[18] This was to guard their virginity, avoid marriage, and lead a religious life devoted to Christ. He advised them whenever possible to take refuge in established religious houses, 'which the Lord has now multiplied throughout the world', or else to try to live together in single, private houses under a self-imposed form of discipline.[19]

In this sermon Jacques de Vitry developed themes similar to those which he had already put forward in his *Life of Mary of Oignies* (d. 1213), the 'new saint' of the diocese of Liège.[20] There he spoke of shameless men, hostile to all religion, who were calling these holy women by malicious and disparaging 'new names'.[21] His sermon went on to supply a list of these new names which is most interesting in revealing the geographical spread of the women he was addressing: *beguina* in Flanders and Brabant; *papelarda* in France, *humiliata* in Lombardy, *coquenunne* (cooking nun) in Germany, and *bizoke* in Italy.[22] Clearly he saw all these women as generically similar to the Beguines of Liège, whom he knew so well. The examples in Italy are interesting for their regional variations.[23] *Bizoke* was used in Lazio, mainly the Papal States and central to southern Italy, whilst their sisters further north included not only the *pinzochere* of the Veneto and Tuscany, but also the *humiliatae* of Lombardy, whom Jacques de Vitry had himself seen on his journey south in 1216. His sermon developed into a little *exemplum*. He demonstrated both the absolute stability of their faith and the efficacy of their works, repeating

16 Greven, 'Der Ursprung', pp. 43–9.
17 Book of Wisdom 4.1.
18 Greven, 'Der Ursprung', p. 48.
19 *Ibid.*, pp. 46–7.
20 Jacques de Vitry, *Vita B. Maria Oigniacensis*, pp. 636–66.
21 *Ibid.*, p. 637.4, 'nova nomina contra eos fingebant, sicut Judaei Christum Samaritanum et Christianos Galilaeos appellabant'.
22 Greven, 'Der Ursprung', pp. 44–5.
23 R. Guarnieri, 'Pinzochere', *Dizionario degli Istituti di Perfezione*, ed. G. Pelliccia and G. Rocca, 6 (Rome, 1980), cols 1721–50.

his description of the *humiliatae* in 1216 in a word-for-word application to Beguines or whatever was the appropriate name of the groups described.[24] He used the device of a vision, that of a Cistercian monk who asked the Lord whether these religious women, known to him as *zoccoli* (obviously *bizoke*) had a good name.[25] The reply was strongly affirmative: 'No one slanders or speaks evil against them'. Perhaps detractors were less common amongst the men of Rome!

In the Italian context at least, these *bizoke* or *zoccoli* seem to have been particularly associated with the Dominicans. Constantino da Orvieto, in his *Biography of St Dominic* (*c.* 1243–6),[26] speaks of women called *bizoke fratrum praedicatorum*, whilst the chapter of 1240, in Bologna, had referred to them as *mulieres religiosae*.[27] In the Roman dialect *zoccoli* were those women who went around without shoes, or only the barest minimum of leather thongs on their feet[28]—perhaps a kind of medieval flip-flop!

Real difficulties faced those many young Roman women, the *bizoke* or *zoccoli*, who, whilst remaining in their parents' homes had to resist extreme pressure towards wealthy secular marriage. In such circumstances Jacques de Vitry's advice, although apposite, was difficult to follow. Escape from the dire prospect of marriage seemed impossible. The juridical requirements of the Church for any religious organization to be institutionalized also worked against them. Three pragmatic solutions were developed.[29] Firstly, the women could live together in common houses, mutually exhorting one another. Secondly, they could accept the imposition of the *clausura*, strict enclosure within a convent. Thirdly, the most pragmatic, but the most difficult: they could take a solemn and binding vow of chastity, and yet proceed to attempt to live an otherwise normal life. The danger to the dedication of these consecrated virgins who remained within the family home was of exposure to temptation and lack of discipline. This led to the eventual adoption of yet more common houses. In northern Europe attempts were made to have some form of rule for these women. In southern Europe, where the monastic reforms of

[24] Huygens, *Lettres de Jacques de Vitry*, p. 74.

[25] *Vita B. Maria Oigniacensis*, p. 637.4; Greven, 'Der Ursprung', pp. 47–8. 'Invenientur in fide stabiles et in opere efficaces'.

[26] Constantino da Orvieto, *Legenda S. Dominici*, ed. H. C. Scheeben, *MOFPH*, 16 (1935), p. 350.

[27] *Acta Capitulorum Generalium: ordinis praedicatorum*, 1, *1220–1303*, ed., A. Fruhwirth and B. M. Reichert (Rome, 1898), pp. 13–18; Guarnieri, 'Pinzochere', col. 1723.

[28] *Ibid.*, col. 1723.

[29] Ziegler, 'The *curtis* beguinages', pp. 52–9; J. Pennings, 'Semi-religious women in fifteenth-century Rome', *Mededelingen van het Nederlands Institutut te Rome*, 48, ns 12 (1987), pp. 115–45.

the mid-tenth century had not been so rigorously followed, life was less formal.[30]

By AD 1000 just three convents had been established in Rome for religious women.[31] These were Santa Bibiana,[32] Santa Maria in Campo Marzo,[33] and Santa Maria *in Tempuli*.[34] This scarcity should be no surprise. Ferrari has shown that the Rule of St Benedict was still not fully observed in Rome at that time, and therefore Roman women enjoyed greater freedom than was customary in other parts of Latin Christendom.[35] The convents fulfilled a purely religious function, and only the truly dedicated entered them, albeit still with a somewhat relaxed attitude. This freedom became even more widespread as the number of religious women in Rome itself increased. In the early thirteenth century Dominic, with his reputation and special concern for women, attempted some modification, vividly described by Sister Cecilia in the *Miracula B. Dominici* (*c.* 1260).[36] He sought to enforce and extend enclosure, commonly seen as the essential characteristic of a 'good' monastery or nunnery. All existing nuns were expected to renew and follow their profession to an enclosed life.[37]

30 B. Hamilton, 'The House of Theophylact and the promotion of the religious life among women in tenth-century Rome', in *Monastic Reform, Catharism and the Crusades 900–1300* (London, 1979), pp. 35–68. For important comparative literature on a later period, R. Guarnieri, 'Beghinismo d'Oltralpe e bizochismo Italiana tra il secolo xiv e il secolo xv', in R. Pazelli and M. Senci, eds, *La beata Angelina da Montegiove e il movimento del terz'ordine regolare Francescano femminile, Atti del Convegno di Studi Francescani, Foligno 1983* (Rome, 1984), pp. 1–15; A. Blok, 'Notes on the concept of virginity in Mediterranean societies', in E. Schulte van Kessel, ed., *Women and Men in Spiritual Culture XIV–XVII Centuries: A Meeting of North and South* (The Hague, 1986), pp. 27–33.

31 Hamilton, *Monastic Reform*, p. 43; P. Caraffa, *Monasticon Italiae*, 1: *Roma e Lazio* (Cesena, 1981), p. 90.

32 L. Duchesne, *Le Liber Pontificalis*, ed. C. Vogel, 2nd edn (Paris, 1955–7), 2, p. 24; *Monasticon Italiae*, 1, p. 46; G. Ferrari, *Early Roman Monasteries* (Vatican City, 1957), pp. 379–407.

33 *Liber Pontificalis*, 2, p. 25; *Monasticon Italiae*, 1, p. 64; E. Carusi, *Cartario di S. Maria in Campo Marzio (986–1199), Miscellanea della Società Romana di Storia Patria* (Rome, 1948); Ferrari, *Early Roman Monasteries*, pp. 207–9.

34 *Liber Pontificalis*, 2, p. 25; *Monasticon Italiae*, 1, pp. 68–9; V. J. Koudelka, 'Le "*Monasterium Tempuli*" et la fondation dominicaine de S. Sisto', *AFP*, 31 (1961), pp. 5–81. See also Hamilton, *Monastic Reform*, pp. 195–217; Ferrari, *Early Roman Monasteries*, pp. 225–7.

35 *Ibid.*, pp. 379–407; Hamilton, *Monastic Reform*, esp. pp. 46–9, 195–217.

36 A. Walz, 'Die "Miracula Beati Dominici" der Schwester Cäecilia', *Miscellanea Pio Paschini = Lateranum*, ns, 2 vols, 1 (Rome, 1948), pp. 293–326; S. Tugwell, ed., *Early Dominicans: Selected Writings* (London, 1982), pp. 391–3.

37 Walz, 'Die "Miracula Beati Dominici"', pp. 323–4; Koudelka, 'Le "*Monasterium Tempuli*"', pp. 48–51, 55–6. Cf. S. Tugwell, 'St Dominic's letter to the nuns in Madrid', *AFP*, 56 (1986), pp. 5–13 and 'Dominican profession in the thirteenth century', *AFP*, 53 (1983), pp. 5–52 esp. p. 43 for the formula used at Prouille.

It was widely believed at the time that to reform nuns without enclosing them would be a contradiction in terms. However, many Roman nuns living in these venerable convents, by now seven or possibly eight in number,[38] simply ignored attempts at enclosure. Those of Santa Maria *in Tempuli* were a case in point.[39] Their daily wandering in the streets of the City represented the persistence of ancient customs, a sort of religious *passegiata*.[40] They were often accompanied by those religious women who were living in private houses—the *bizoke* and *zoccoli*. Dominic hoped that when they again became truly professed these women would no longer want to leave the cloister, and others would be eager to enter. The habit of visiting sisters nearby and many others on the way would cease. When those whom they used to visit heard what Dominic had proposed, they came to the convent and began vehemently to protest to the abbess and the sisters. Why did they wish to destroy so noble a convent, *tam nobile monasterium*, and, what was even worse, why did they wish to commit it into the hands of an unknown scoundrel, a *rascal*, as they considered Dominic to be?[41] When this happened some of the sisters regretted the renewed professions they had made, and hearing this, Dominic said, 'Sisters, do you really have regrets? Do you wish to withdraw your feet from the way of the Lord? You who wish to enter have done so of your own free will, *voluntate propria*. Come now and be truly and finally professed by my hand'.[42] This the abbess and all the sisters, save one, did. When they had done so, Dominic took the precaution of confiscating all their keys, so that henceforth he held actual power over the convent, *potestas plenarie*.[43] As a further precaution he established *conversi*, who guarded the convent day and night, providing the sisters with food and necessities. The women were forbidden to talk to them, nor were the *conversi* allowed to speak to any of their friends outside. Our source, Sister Cecilia, then aged seventeen, whose *Miracles of St Dominic* have usually—and perhaps unfairly—been regarded as histrionic rather than historic, seems to have had exciting memories of this period of transition and to

[38] S. Andrea in Biberatica, S. Agnese, S. Ciriaco, S. Maria in Campo Marzo, S. Maria *in Tempuli*, S. Bibiana, and S. Maria in Maxima: Koudelka, 'Le "*Monasterium Tempuli*"', pp. 46–8.

[39] Walz, 'Die "Miracula Beati Dominici"', pp. 323–4; V. J. Koudelka, 'Notes pour servir à l'histoire de S. Dominique', *AFP*, 35 (1965), pp. 5–20.

[40] Cf. Pennings, 'Semi-religious women', p. 117 for the later period: 'The women wandered along the streets and across the squares, stopping at shops'.

[41] Walz, 'Die "Miracula Beati Dominici"', pp. 323–4; 'quod tam nobile monasterium destruere vellent et se in manu ignoti illius ribaldi ultro vellent committere'.

[42] *Ibid.*, p. 324; Koudelka, 'Le "*Monasterium Tempuli*"', pp. 56–8.

[43] Walz, 'Die "Miracula Beati Dominici"', p. 324.

have somewhat relished writing this account in later years.[44] Dominic's intentions, however, were not to be gainsaid. The earlier wishes of Innocent III for the daughters of Rome were at last to be realized.

The first evidence we have of Innocent III's intervention in the affairs of the female convents of Rome is his severe letter of 7 December 1204 to the abbesses of all the convents.[45] He wrote forbidding any alienations from the sale of their goods and properties because, as he said, the houses are 'in our special care'—*cura nobis specialis*.[46] Innocent clearly wanted to halt what was obviously an early example of asset-stripping. No abbess was henceforth to sell, pledge, enfeoff, transfer, or alienate any convent property unless the pope or his 'cardinal-vicar' intervened with a special licence publicly written down. This letter, so firm that its wording verged on the harsh, openly denounced certain abbesses who had been selling their possessions. His grave reproach indicated a state of affairs which Innocent recognized only too clearly.[47] His visit to Subiaco in the summer of 1202,[48] and his initiative in February 1203 in summoning the heads of monasteries to meet together in provincial chapters,[49] had made him particularly well-informed of the consequences to autonomous Benedictine houses of indebtedness. This had nearly always been accompanied by a lowering of disciplinary standards.

These tiny convents in Rome were far from well-off, although they held landed possessions.[50] Family pressures often influenced this desire to realize their assets, which the Pope had now blocked. Yet Innocent realized that adequate material provision was required. His biographer shows that he recognized this poverty by frequently giving generous gifts to nuns, female recluses, and *religiosae*.[51] These female recluses are of considerable interest. They inhabited that stretch of the Aurelianic wall between the Lateran and Santa Croce directly on the pilgrim route where these women, immured for the rest of their lives, could be assured of minimal alms and necessities from passing travellers. We know the names

[44] *Ibid*., pp. 293–305; Koudelka, 'Le "*Monasterium Tempuli*"', pp. 38–40.

[45] *PL* 215, col: 475; M. Maccarrone, *Studi su Innocenzo III* (Padua, 1972), pp. 272–8; Koudelka, 'Le "*Monasterium Tempuli*"', pp. 46–8.

[46] Maccarrone, *Studi*, p. 275.

[47] B. M. Bolton, '*Via ascetica*: a papal quandary', *SCH*, 22 (1985), pp. 161–91.

[48] K. Hampe, 'Eine Schilderung des Sommeraufenthaltes der Römischen Kurie unter Innocenz' III in Subiaco 1202', *Historische Vierteljahrsschrift*, 8 (1905), pp. 509–35; Bolton, '*Via ascetica*', pp. 177–9.

[49] U. Berlière, 'Innocent III et la réorganisation des monastères benedictins', *RB*, 20–2 (1920), pp. 22–42, 145–59; Maccarrone, *Studi*, pp. 226–46.

[50] Maccarrone, *Studi*, pp. 274–5.

[51] *Gesta Innocentii PP III, PL* 214, cols cxcix–cc.

of two of them as examples of holiness and suffering: Sister Bona lived in the Porta Asinaria with her maidservant, Jacobina,[52] whilst Sister Lucia was walled up behind the Church of Sant'Anastasia.[53] Could the Pope ever have visited either of these women? It is possible, but even if Innocent did not, Dominic certainly did, healing them of their horrific disabilities.

Innocent regarded it as his pastoral duty to carry out Christ's instruction to 'feed my sheep'.[54] As Bishop of Rome, this meant all the people of the City. For religious women, the daughters of Rome, convents of nuns would have to be properly organized, while for the *bizoke*, some sort of rule was needed under which they too could live. One of his great projects caught the imagination of the chroniclers.[55] The Anonymous Cistercian Monk of Santa Maria di Ferraria, near Teano, in his chronicle entry for February 1207, says, 'He [Innocent] also instituted a *universale cenobium monialium*, one single convent, into which all the nuns of Rome are to come together, nor are they to be allowed to go out from it'.[56] Benedetto da Montefiascone (*c.* 1318) looking back to this earlier time confirms that 'the women (*mulieres*) of the City and the nuns of the other convents of Rome, instead of wandering about, were to be brought under a strict enclosure—*arcta clausura*—and the diligent custody of the servants of the Lord'.[57]

A most interesting aspect of Innocent's plan was his idea of bringing together and unifying nuns and convents with different disciplinary traditions, from those with a modest degree of enclosure to those with none at all. One great *cenobium* would thus be created. That this initiative was Innocent's alone is apparent from two other attempts he made elsewhere to follow Acts 4.32 and bring multitudes of believers to 'one heart and one mind'. Already, in December 1200, in an attempt to avoid scandal through excessive diversity in religion, he had seriously considered bringing the three separate branches of the Humiliati into one *propositum*.[58]

[52] Walz, 'Die "Miracula Beati Dominici"', p. 322.

[53] *Ibid.*, p. 323.

[54] J. M. Powell, '*Pastor Bonus*: some evidence of Honorius III's use of the sermons of Innocent III', *Speculum*, 52 (1977), pp. 522–37.

[55] Maccarrone, 'Il progetto di un "*universale cenobium*" per le monache di Roma', *Studi*, pp. 272–8; Koudelka, 'Le "*Monasterium Tempuli*"', pp. 38–46; *Chroniques du monastère de San Sisto*, ed. J. J. Berthier (Levanto, 1919–20), 1: *San Sisto 1220–1575*.

[56] *Chronica Romanorum pontificium et Imperatorum ac de Rebus in Apulia Gestis* (*781–1228*) *auctore ignoto monacho Cisterciensi*, ed. A. Gaudenzi, *Società Napoletana di Sancta Patria*, 1: *Cronache* (Naples, 1888), p. 34. Cf. Martin Polonus, *Liber Pontificalis*, 2, pp. 34–5.

[57] Koudelka, 'Le "*Monasterium Tempuli*"', pp. 40–3, and esp. pp. 69–72 for Benedetto da Montefiascone.

[58] *PL* 215, cols 921–2; Potthast, 1, 1192; Maccarrone, *Studi*, pp. 284–90.

Then, on 19 April 1201, in a letter to the Bishop of Riga, he exhorted Cistercians and Augustinians, white monks and black canons, to join together in one *regulare propositum* to overcome their differences and thus avoid confusing the Baltic pagans.[59] Both projects, in Lombardy and Livonia, came to nothing, but the ideas which underlay them must have influenced his attitude to the women of Rome. By virtue of his authority as Bishop of the City, and by exercising his judicial powers *nullo medio*,[60] he was able to impose upon them uniformity of rule, dress, and discipline to counter 'diversity' in religion and serious charges—possibly untrue—of scandal and decadence. That he considered his plan necessary to meet a genuine need for reform is clear from the generous support he gave from his own resources. His apostolic and pastoral ideas were thus to have physical realization.

Underlying this plan was the construction of a great new convent about 1208, just within the walls of Rome and close to the ancient but ruined basilica of San Sisto, the *titulus Crescentianae*. This was very near to the convent of Santa Maria *in Tempuli*, which was to become vital to Innocent's plan. The Pope was so dedicated—*ferventissimo animo*[61]—to the building campaign that his biographer tells us that he set aside a huge sum, 50 ounces of gold of the Regno and 1,100 pounds *provinois*, *ad opus monialium*.[62] As always, he was willing to look beyond Rome for help. In 1213, Nicholas *de Romanis*, Jacques de Vitry's predecessor as Cardinal, 'persuaded' King John in England to set aside 150 marks each year for the work of the convent of San Sisto—*ad opus monasterii S.Sixti*.[63] Outside help was required because the complexities of the scheme must have contributed to the vast cost of the project. The nave of the great basilica church was infilled, the side aisles demolished, and a smaller new church, with an extensive convent to house sixty nuns, erected above. Space surplus to the requirements of the nuns would be exactly what Innocent had in mind for the *bizoke*. The scale of this building campaign was so vast

[59] M.-H. Vicaire, 'Vie Commune et apostolat missionaire: Innocent III et la mission de Livonie', *Mélanges M.-D. Chenu* (Paris, 1967), pp. 451–66; Maccarrone, *Studi*, pp. 262–72, and esp. pp. 334–7 for the text of the letter of 19 April 1201; M. Maccarrone, 'I papi e gli inizi della cristianizzione della Livonia', *Gli inizi del cristianesimo in Livonia-Lettonia* (Vatican City, 1989), pp. 31–80.

[60] Maccarrone, *Studi*, p. 274, n. 3; Bolton, '*Via ascetica*', p. 163.

[61] Koudelka, 'Le "*Monasterium Tempuli*"', p. 69; H. Geetman, 'Richerche sopra la prima fase di S. Sisto Vecchio in Roma', *Pontificia Accademia Romana di Archaeologia, Rendiconti*, 41 (1968–9), pp. 219–28.

[62] *Gesta, PL* 214, col. ccxxvii.

[63] Mercati, 'La prima relazione', pp. 287–8.

that eight years later, on Innocent's death in 1216, the work was still unfinished. Instead, it was carried through to completion by Honorius III (1216–27) and Dominic.[64]

Innocent's aim was to remove the nuns of Rome far from all distractions, and the convent's location, two-and-a-half kilometres from the centre, was ideal for this purpose. An exception was the convent of Sant'Agnese, not only blessed by the absence of distractions, but also on the far side of Rome.[65] Innocent's compromise was to leave the sisters of Sant'Agnese alone, whilst providing adequately for them. Amongst the other houses for women, the convent of Santa Maria *in Tempuli* now came to play a key role in events. A modest establishment, it housed an abbess, first Margarita (1202–5) and then Eugenia (1205–20), and five nuns at this period.[66] In spite of its small size, its past history was both venerable and noble. Originally on the site of a *cella memoria*, the list drawn up in 806 ranked it thirty-ninth amongst the religious houses of Rome.[67] Its properties, two vineyards, three gardens, and the estate of Casa Ferrata on the Via Laurentina, given by Sergius III (904–11) in 905, were probably typical of the possessions of Roman convents, and yet it was still in debt.[68] However, it had in its possession an enviable asset, which set it apart from all the other convents, a miraculous icon of the Virgin, a *brandeum* or associative relic, reputed to have been painted by St Luke himself and brought to Rome from Constantinople.[69] Since the tenth century the nuns of Santa Maria *in Tempuli* had been accustomed to process behind their icon on the great liturgical feast days.[70] Sergius III was believed to have played a key role in one of those earlier processions by actually carrying

[64] Koudelka, 'Le "*Monasterium Tempuli*"', pp. 43–6, particularly that period from December 1219 to Lent 1221.

[65] *Gesta, PL* 214, col. ccxxvii; *Monasticon Italiae*, 1, p. 39; Koudelka, 'Notes pour servir', pp. 16–20.

[66] Koudelka, 'Le "*Monasterium Tempuli*"', pp. 5–38, esp. pp. 32–4. On 3 September 1202, the community comprised Margarita, Eugenia, Cecilia (not Sister Cecilia), Agatha, Scholastica, and Agnes. On 26 November 1219, the names given are Eugenia, Constantia, Domitilla, Maximilla, and Cecilia (presumably our Sister Cecilia).

[67] *Liber Pontificalis*, 2, p. 24; Hamilton, *Monastic Reform*, pp. 197–201.

[68] *Liber Pontificalis*, 2, pp. 100, 104, 106–7; Koudelka, 'Le "*Monasterium Tempuli*"', pp. 12–13.

[69] F. Martinelli, *Imago B. Mariae Virginis quae apud venerandus SS Sixti et Dominici moniales asservata, vindicata* (Rome, 1642), pp. 3–8; L. Boyle, 'Dominican Lectionaries and Leo of Ostia's *Translatio Sancti Clementis*', *AFP*, 28 (1958), pp. 381–94; C. Bertelli, 'L'immagine del *Monasterium Tempuli* dopo il restauro', *AFP*, 31 (1961), pp. 82–111; Hamilton, *Monastic Reform*, pp. 197–9; C. Bertelli, 'Icone di Roma', *Stil und Uberlieferung in der Kunst des Abendlandes* (Berlin, 1967), 1, pp. 100–6.

[70] Koudelka, 'Le "*Monasterium Tempuli*"', pp. 55–7; Walz, 'Die "Miracula beati Dominici"', pp. 323–5; E. Kitzinger, 'A virgin's face: antiquarianism in twelfth-century art', *Art Bulletin*, 62 (1980), pp. 6–19 for other Roman processions with images of the Virgin.

the image on his own shoulders.[71] With the outstanding historical and religious importance of the icon, and the increasing veneration being given to the Virgin Mary at this time, this image must have been seen as the one thing which would make San Sisto a focus for inspiration and a place to which all women would be drawn. If only the nuns of Santa Maria *in Tempuli* with their precious relic could somehow be persuaded to move the few hundred yards to San Sisto, the first stage of Innocent's desired reform would have been completed. Other nuns, *bizoke*, *zoccoli*, and recluses would all be encouraged to come in.

Innocent had wanted to entrust San Sisto to the care of the brothers of the Order of Sempringham. The canonization of St Gilbert in January 1202, after a long process of negotiation, had first brought this English double order to the Pope's attention.[72] Through it he had learned of the 1,500 Gilbertine sisters, constant in the service of God, and of the strict separation of these women from the canons who served them by the actual physical device of a high wall.[73] The brothers of Sempringham, however, were not much interested in this Roman dimension of their activities. Rome was too far, too expensive, and just too hot![74] With Innocent's death, his persuasive powers were ended. Dominic, with the help of Bishop Fulk of Toulouse, had to find alternatives. In January 1218, the incomplete church of San Sisto with its new convent was still awaiting its nuns.[75] Both men had a deep interest in religious women. Indeed, it was at Fulk's request that his friend Jacques de Vitry had written the *Life of Mary of Oignies*.[76] Dominic was already the founder of the house for women at Prouille, in Fulk's own diocese, where daughters of the lesser nobility might, if properly instructed, escape heretical tendencies.[77] The spirit of Innocent's original scheme would now have to be implemented by Dominic, whose Friars Preachers could take the place of the brothers of Sempringham.

71 Koudelka, 'Le "*Monasterium Tempuli*"', pp. 13–19.

72 *The Book of St Gilbert*, ed. R. Foreville and G. Keir, *OMT* (1987), pp. 245–53.

73 *Ibid.*, p. 251.

74 *Ibid.*, p. 171.

75 Koudelka, 'Le "*Monasterium Tempuli*"', pp. 48–50.

76 R. Lejeune, 'L'Évêque de Toulouse, Folquet de Marseille et la principauté de Liège', *Mélanges Felix Rousseau* (Brussels, 1958), pp. 433–48; B. Bolton, 'Fulk of Toulouse: the escape that failed', *SCH* 12 (1975), pp. 83–93.

77 *Monumenta Diplomatica S. Dominici*, pp. 59, 90–3; *Bernardus Guidonis: De Fundatione et prioribus conventuum provinciarum Tolosanae et provinciae ordinis praedicatorum*, ed. P. A. Armagier, *MOFPH*, 24 (1961), pp. 7–9: V. J. Koudelka, 'Notes sur le cartulaire de S. Dominique', *AFP*, 28 (1958), pp. 92–114.

On 3 August 1218 Honorius III gave the Prior of Sempringham one last chance.[78] Unless he could send four brothers to Rome before Christmas 1219 to serve the Basilica of San Sisto, he must relinquish the charge to another order. Representatives arrived at the Curia before 12 November 1219, but on 4 December Honorius III absolved the canons 'R.' and 'V.' from the care of San Sisto as it was too difficult to find any suitable persons to staff it from Sempringham.[79] He also reinforced links with the community of Santa Maria *in Tempuli*. Abbess Eugenia received 35 *sous provinois*, destined to cover the expenses of a *nuntius* to clear the convent's affairs.[80] On 17 December 1219 Honorius ordered the sisters of Prouille to be ready to come to Rome whenever Dominic should require them there.[81] Now began the process of persuading the daughters of Rome to move. The sisters of the community of Santa Maria *in Tempuli* were to be the first. They were very close to San Sisto, and they had their icon. Sister Cecilia remembered it all as if it were yesterday—but her vivid account is also well attested in the cartulary of the convent.[82]

High-status supporters were to be drafted in to lend support to the venture and to provide credibility. And where were such men to be found? Amongst those cardinals who had been close to Innocent III were three well known for their support of women. The first, Hugolino, Cardinal-Bishop of Ostia, was responsible for the enclosure of that wave of religious women imitating St Clare and her community at San Damiano in 1218–19.[83] Later, as Gregory IX, he was to attempt to reform the remaining convents of Rome in 1232, while his bull *Gloriam virginalem* of 1233 enclosed all the consecrated virgins of Germany and the Empire.[84] The second was Nicholas of Tusculum, whose persuasive predecessor of the same name had led John of England to subscribe to both Innocent's favourite projects, the Hospital of Santo Spirito as well as the convent of San Sisto.[85] The third, Stephen of Fossanova, the Papal Chamberlain from

[78] *Monumenta Diplomatica S. Dominici*, pp. 92, 94–5; *CPL*, 1, p. 57; C. R. Cheney, *Innocent III and England*, *Pup*, 9 (1976), p. 238.

[79] *Monumenta Diplomatica S. Dominici*, pp. 112–13; Pressutti, 2283; *CPL*, p. 69.

[80] Koudelka, 'Le "*Monasterium Tempuli*"', p. 52.

[81] *Monumenta Diplomatica S. Dominici*, pp. 117–18; Potthast, 6184; Pressutti, 2303; Koudelka, 'Le "*Monasterium Tempuli*"', pp. 52–3.

[82] Walz, 'Die "Miracula Beati Dominici"', pp. 319–25; Koudelka, 'Le "*Monasterium Tempuli*"', pp. 54–9.

[83] Maleczek, *Papst und Kardinalskolleg*, pp. 126–33; Grundmann, *Religiöse Bewegungen*, pp. 253–71.

[84] Roman nuns were enclosed by a bull of 26 October 1232: Ziegler, 'The *curtis* beguinages', pp. 55–6 and n. 47; Koudelka, 'Le "*Monasterium Tempuli*"', pp. 66–7.

[85] Walz, 'Die "Miracula Beati Dominici"', p. 308; Eubel, *Hierarchia Catholica*, 1, p. 38.

1206, and hence the closest collaborator of Innocent himself, must have followed the Pope's plans step by step.[86] It was through the Chamberlain that the large sums of money for the construction passed, and he may well have been responsible for the works themselves. His particular relations with the new convent made him an obvious choice to work with Dominic, especially as in 1213 he was created Cardinal-Priest of 'SS.XII Apostoli'.[87]

On Ash Wednesday, 24 February 1221, Abbess Eugenia formally abdicated and renounced her rights into Dominic's possession in the presence of the three cardinals, Hugolino, Nicholas, and Stephen.[88] Even the date chosen as the official foundation of the convent was significant, for on Ash Wednesday, according to the *Ordo Romanus*, the cardinals traditionally processed from the Lateran to Sant'Anastasia, where the Cardinal-Bishop of Ostia scattered the Ashes before returning to Santa Sabina on the Aventine for Mass.[89] Their passage to San Sisto would thus have occasioned little attention. However, during the ceremony, Cardinal Stephen's nephew, Napoleon, fell from his horse. Horribly mutilated, he was cured by Dominic in a spectacular healing miracle. What Sister Cecilia reports has a real ring of truth to those familiar with such things. Apparently the boy, once revived, immediately asked the Saint for something to eat.[90] In gratitude, Stephen of Fossanova paid off the chief creditor of Santa Maria *in Tempuli*, one Cencio Gregorio Rampazoli, in the sum of 90 pounds on 15 April 1221.[91]

The whole process, the winding down of the convent's economic ventures, the settlement of its possessions, and the actual transfer of the nuns themselves into the obedience of a provincial superior, was clearly a much longer and more complicated process than either Innocent or Dominic could ever have imagined. Dominic first installed a small group of brothers to serve the community of San Sisto, probably in the former priests' residence of the *titulus* situated beyond the apse of the old

86 Maleczek, *Papst und Kardinalskolleg*, pp. 179–83; Koudelka, 'Notes pour servir', pp. 5–16; *PL* 215, col. 184, and Cheney, *Selected Letters*, p. 62, for his special commendation to King John in 1203.

87 1213–27. Eubel, *Hierarchia Catholica*, p. 39.

88 Walz, 'Die "Miracula Beati Dominici"', pp. 307–9; Koudelka, 'Notes pour servir', pp. 11–12, and 'Le "*Monasterium Tempuli*"', pp. 56–7.

89 *Le 'Liber Censuum' de l'Église Romaine*, ed. P. Fabre and L. Duchesne, 1, (Paris, 1910), p. 294; Koudelka, 'Le "*Monasterium Tempuli*"', p. 57.

90 'Pater, da michi manducare': Walz, 'Die "Miracula Beati Dominici"', p. 309.

91 *Monumenta Diplomatica S. Dominici*, pp. 153–4; Koudelka, 'Le "*Monasterium Tempuli*"', pp. 65–6. For the sale of the farm of one of the convent's vineyards to Cencio on 22 December 1215, *ibid*., p. 21.

basilica.[92] Then he set about recruiting his future community. While Innocent had clearly envisaged new vocations from amongst the *mulieres urbis*, the major recruitment was to come from uncloistered nuns. Dominic's attempt to attract nuns from the other convents of Rome seems to have met with small success. Only at Santa Bibiana did the majority of sisters agree to move—and all but one of those at Santa Maria *in Tempuli*. The occasional reluctance and back-sliding of these sisters seems to have been typical. The implication is that each time Dominic was absent from Rome, his influence over the nuns waned dramatically. Thus, at various times between 1218 and 1220, strong pressures for delay and procrastination were exerted on Abbess Eugenia and her sisters by those former benefactors and friends, who resented the administration of the convent's goods by Dominic's brothers.[93] Possibly this delay explains the three-fold promise of which Sister Cecilia wrote, and the complicated chronology of the whole process of entry, now clarified by Koudelka.[94] The first promise to enter San Sisto seems to have been made at some time between December 1219 and February 1220, and the second, after some back-sliding, a year later. Sister Cecilia tells us that these promises were conditional on their image of the Virgin remaining with them.[95] The third promise implied permanence of location in the new convent and was probably made on 28 February 1221, the first Sunday of Lent.

The actual transfer of the nuns of Santa Maria *in Tempuli* to San Sisto took place after the final removal to Santa Sabina of the brothers' utensils and books.[96] On that Lenten Sunday, the sisters of Santa Maria *in Tempuli*, Sister Cecilia the first in amongst them, took possession of their new convent. By the end of the day, and with the greater part of the nuns from Santa Bibiana, she says that *inter religiosas et seculares* they numbered forty-four in all.[97] Surely some *bizoke* must have been amongst them? On the following night, under cover of darkness and in fear of displeasing the Romans, who did not want it transferred to a place where they could not see it so easily, the image of the Virgin, Santa Maria *in Tempuli*'s treasured icon, was moved in accordance with the earlier promise. Dominic, escorted by two of the three cardinals, Nicholas and Stephen, and with a

[92] *Ibid.*, p. 54.

[93] *Ibid.*, pp. 57–9

[94] *Ibid.*, pp. 53–9.

[95] Walz, 'Die "Miracula Beati Dominici"', p. 324: 'Promittens se cum omnibus intratura si ymago beate virginis cum eis in ecclesia Sancti Syxti permaneret'.

[96] *Ibid.*, pp. 323–5.

[97] *Ibid.*, p. 325; Koudelka, 'Le "*Monasterium Tempuli*"', pp. 59–60.

host of bare-footed followers with candles and torches, carried the image on his own shoulders to San Sisto.[98] And there, says Cecilia, warming enthusiastically to her tale, the sisters were waiting, themselves barefooted and at prayer, as the precious icon was carried into the new church. Nor did it fly out of the window in disgust, as it surely would have done had it been unhappy with its new situation! The relic, too, had accepted its transfer!

A little later, probably in mid-April 1221, and somewhat more firmly founded in reality, Sister Blanche and three nuns, possibly escorted by Fulk of Toulouse, arrived in Rome at Dominic's request.[99] It was now to be the important task of these southern French sisters to assist the daughters of Rome—nuns and *bizoke* alike—to adjust to this strange, new, cloistered environment. Did they perhaps bring with them from Prouille the latest book on their reading-list, the meat and drink of spiritual example—I refer, of course, to Jacques de Vitry's *Life of Mary of Oignies*? It had, after all, been written especially for them at Fulk's request. And when Nicholas of Tusculum was dead and his successor appointed, did he too—as author of the *Life*, supreme authority on Mary herself, and in possession of her finger reliquary, sometimes come to visit the nuns of San Sisto? If he did—and we can surely imagine the frequency of such encounters—we do not hear about them. Our best source, Sister Cecilia, had by 1229 been sent on to the new convent of St Agnes in Bologna as an instructress herself, where the identical process of enclosure of nuns and *pinzochere* of Tuscany began all over again.[100] But as for Mary of Oignies, she had at last and in a manner of speaking—through her finger—well and truly arrived in Rome.

[98] Walz, 'Die "Miracula Beati Dominici"', p. 325: 'Humeris suis ad ecclesiam Sancti Syxti deportavit'.

[99] Koudelka, 'Le "*Monasterium Tempuli*"', pp. 60–1, 70–1, who believes that there were perhaps eight sisters from Prouille.

[100] *Early Dominicans*, pp. 397–8: the *Chronicle of St Agnes*, Bologna, records that Master Jordan wanted four sisters to be fetched from San Sisto. One of these was Sister Cecilia 'who is alive to this day and who was present when St Dominic raised Cardinal Stephen's relative from the dead at San Sisto'. Cf. Grundmann, *Religiöse Bewegungen*, p. 216, 'ut eas docerent ordinam et modum religionis'.

# XVII

## ADVERTISE THE MESSAGE: IMAGES IN ROME AT THE TURN OF THE TWELFTH CENTURY[1]

ON at least three occasions during the pontificate of Innocent III, Gerald of Wales—failed bishop, celebrated story-teller, and inveterate and inventive pilgrim, made the journey to Rome.[2] There, having already carried out his preliminary research, he was always eager to examine two of the most outstanding images in Rome at close quarters. These two images—the Uronica at the Lateran and the Veronica at St Peter's—made such a deep impression upon him that his description and explanation of their importance was to form a central role in his *Speculum Ecclesiae*, which he wrote on his return home.[3] He clearly saw them as a pair, having similar names and being held in equal reverence, although perhaps their authenticity sprang from different roots.[4] His remarks would have greatly pleased Innocent, for this was precisely the approach which the pope aimed to achieve. He considered it essential that the long and damaging rivalry between the two great basilicas of the Lateran and the Vatican, which had existed for much of the twelfth century, should now be resolved.[5] It was a rivalry which had brought scandal to the papacy and grave detriment to the Church.[6] In this

[1] My deep gratitude to Dr Fabrizio Mancinelli of the Vatican Museums for granting me privileged access to the *confessio* of St Peter's and the *Sancta Sanctorum* in April 1989.

[2] Gerald of Wales (*c.*1145–1223), disputed the election to the bishopric of St David's and thereafter pursued his claim relentlessly at the Curia. *Giraldus Cambrensis opera*, ed. J. S. Brewer and J. F. Dimock, 8 vols, *RS* (London, 1861–91). See also *The Jewel of the Church: a Translation of the Gemma Ecclesiastica by Giraldus Cambrensis*, ed. J. J. Hagen (Leiden, 1979), pp. ix–xv [hereafter *Jewel of the Church*] for biographical and bibliographical information.

[3] Gerald of Wales, *Speculum Ecclesiae*, *RS*, 4 (1873), esp. *Distinctio* IV, pp. 268–85 [hereafter *Speculum Ecclesiae*], and *Jewel of the Church*, p. xiii, for the suggestion that this work was possibly his latest, still being added to in 1216.

[4] *Speculum Ecclesiae*, p. 278: 'De duabus igitur iconiis Salvatoris, Uronica scilicet et Veronica, quarum una apud Lateranum, altera vero apud Sanctum Petrum.'

[5] M. Maccarrone, 'La "Cathedra Sancti Petri" nel medioevo: da simbolo a reliquia', *Rivista di Storia della Chiesa in Italia*, 39 (1985), pp. 349–447, esp. pp. 395–432.

[6] Ibid., pp. 430–2; John the Deacon, *Descriptio Lateranensis Ecclesiae*, in R. Valentini and G. Zucchetti, *Codice topografico della città di Roma, Fonti per la storia d'Italia*, 4 vols (Rome, 1940–53), 3, pp. 319–73 [hereafter *Descriptio Lateranensis*]; *Petri Mallii Descriptio Basilicae Vaticanae aucta atque emendata a Romano Presbytero* [hereafter *Descriptio Vaticanae*], ibid., pp. 375–442, and esp. pp. 379–80 for two poems, *Contra Lateranensis*.

controversy the Lateran had some advantages, both historically—as the cathedral of Rome and hence of the world—and in the popular appeal of its fabulous relics.[7] A brief glance at a contemporary inventory shows the outstanding richness of this collection.[8] Innocent's aim was not to diminish the Lateran, but instead to raise the status of St Peter's, so that both became co-equal seats of the pope-bishop of Rome.[9] What Gerald of Wales had written confirmed Innocent's own reading of the *Liber Pontificalis*, which was to form the basis for his important reform of the liturgy at this time.[10] Nor was his approbation merely directed towards Gerald. It went to all observant pilgrims, particularly that small number of highly significant archbishops and metropolitans who came to Rome to collect their pallia on their appointments. That great show, the Fourth Lateran Council of 1215, saw almost all of them in attendance.[11] Here was a wonderful opportunity for Innocent to stress the underlying purpose of his artistic patronage, whereby Lateran and Vatican were to achieve co-equal status whilst, at the same time, the Church's real message was being strengthened.[12]

Innocent III's patronage of the arts, particularly in the field of small-scale works, although performing the task for which it was intended, has been neglected by art historians, with the notable exception of Mme Gautier, whose work well deserves close attention.[13] A full understanding

[7] L. Antonelli, *Memorie storiche delle sacre teste dei Santi Apostoli Piero e Paolo e della loro solenne ricognizione nella Basilica Lateranense*, 2nd edn (Rome, 1852); P. Lauer, *Trésor du Sancta Sanctorum. Extrait des monuments et mémoires publiés par l'Academie des Inscriptions et Belles-Lettres* (Paris, 1906); ibid., *Le Palais de Latran. Étude historique et archéologique* (Paris, 1911); P. Jounel, *Le Culte des Saints dans la basilique du Latran et du Vatican au douzième siècle* (Paris, 1911).

[8] *Descriptio Lateranensis*, pp. 356–8, *De Ecclesia Sancti Laurenti in Palatio*; *Speculum Ecclesiae*, pp. 272–4, for Gerald's own list.

[9] 13 March 1198, O. Hageneder and A. Haidacher, eds, *Die Register Innocenz' III*, I Band, *Pontifikatsjahr 1198/99* (Graz and Koln, 1964), [hereafter *Register* I], pp. 417–18; *Innocentii III: Opera omnia*, 4 vols (Paris, 1855), *PL* 214, cols 254–5; Potthast, 1, no. 46; 18 Jan. 1199, *Register* I, pp. 772–3; *PL* 214, cols 490–1; Potthast, no. 939; 21 Jan. 1204, *PL* 215, cols 513–17, esp. col. 513, 'quia ex tunc fecit Petrum stabilem sedem habere, sive in Laterano, sive in Vaticano'; Maccarrone, '"Cathedra"', pp. 430–1.

[10] S. J. P. van Dijk and J. Hazelden Walker, *The Origins of the Modern Roman Liturgy* (London, 1960), pp. 126–8 [hereafter *Origins of the Liturgy*].

[11] C. J. Héfèle and H. Leclercq, *Histoire des Conciles*, 5 (Paris, 1913), 'Liste des évêchés représentés au Concile de 1215', pp. 1723–33.

[12] B. M. Bolton, 'A show with a meaning: Innocent III's approach to the Fourth Lateran Council, 1215', *Medieval History*, 1 (1991), pp. 53–67.

[13] M. M. Gautier, 'La Clôture Émaillée de la Confession de Saint Pierre au Vatican hors du Concile de Latran, 1215', *Bibliothèque des Cahiers Archéologiques*, II, *Synthronon: art et archéologie de la fin de l'antiquité* (Paris, 1968), pp. 237–46; 'Observations préliminaires sur les restes d'un revêtement d'émail champlevé fait pour la Confession de Saint Pierre à Rome', *Bulletin de la*

of this patronage must surely start with an examination of his attitude to the Uronica and Veronica images and to relics associated with the basilicas. Although Innocent took pains to identify his patronage of several small works, it was by finely incised inscription only.[14] His chief personal identification occurred in his appearance as impresario in the reconstructed apse-mosaic of St Peter's, which was full of meaning for the Christian message.[15] Here, in his own lifetime, he ensured that both the message and his person received due prominence. Some fragments of this mosaic, including his head, have survived the demolition of the basilica which took place in the sixteenth century.[16]

Gerald's account of the Uronica and Veronica sets the scene. Legend attributed the Lateran Uronica to the painter St Luke, whose hand was guided by the Virgin Mary, and the work then completed by an angel.[17] Hence it was also called the *acheropita* or icon not made with human hand.[18] Gerald states that two or three such miraculous icons were made, the one in Rome being in the *Sancta Sanctorum* or papal chapel of S. Lorenzo at the Lateran.[19] This encaustic painting, with its burnt-black, fearsome image, both represented and contained the essential spirit of Christ. The truth of this was confirmed, to Gerald at least, by the blinding of an earlier and unnamed pope who had presumed to peer too closely at the icon.[20] Gerald's description refers to this image being covered with gold and silver, except for the right knee, from which oil constantly flowed.[21] What Gerald is clearly describing is the Uronica after its restoration by Innocent, who added a splendid new cover made of gilded silver,

---

*Société Archéologique et Historique du Limousin*, 91 (1964), pp. 43–70; 'L'art de l'émail champlevé en Italie à l'époque primitive du gothique', *Il Gotico a Pistoia nei suoi rapporti con l'arte gotica italiana = Atti del secondo convegno internazionale di studi, Pistoia, 24–30 aprile, 1966*, pp. 271–93. Cf. F. Vitale, 'Il frontale della confessione Vaticano', *Federico II et l'arte del ducento italiano*, 2 vols (Rome, 1980), 2, pp. 159–72.

[14] Gautier, 'Clôture émaillée', p. 238.

[15] A. Iacobini, 'Il mosaico absidale di San Pietro in Vaticano', *Fragmenta Picta: affreschi e mosaici staccati del medioevo romano* (Rome, 1989), pp. 119–29; A. Margiotta, 'L'antica decorazione absidale della basilica di S. Pietro in alcuni frammenti al Museo di Roma', *Bolletino dei Musei Communali di Roma*, ns 2 (1988), pp. 21–33; R. Krautheimer, *Rome: Profile of a City 312–1308* (Princeton, 1980), pp. 205–6.

[16] Iacobini, 'Il mosaico absidale', pp. 66–8, plates 2, 3, and 4.

[17] Hence Gerald of Wales, *Speculum Ecclesiae*, p. 278; *Descriptio Lateranensis*, p. 357.

[18] H. Grisar, *Il Sancta Sanctorum ed il suo tesoro sacro* (Rome, 1907), p. 49.

[19] Gerald of Wales, *Speculum Ecclesiae*, p. 278, 'Tales fecit duas vel tres, quarum una Romae habetur apud Lateranensem, scilicet in sancta sanctorum.'

[20] Ibid., 'Cum papa quidam . . . inspicere praesumpsisset, statim lumen oculorum amisit.'

[21] Ibid., 'Deinde cooperta fuit auro et argento tota praeter genu dextrum, a quo oleum indesinenter emanat.'

decorated with images portraying the message. Over the centuries this cover became subject to constant elaboration, but there is no record of it ever being removed until Pius X (1903–14) allowed the art historian J. Wilpert to do so.[22] Wilpert's comments bridge the gap between those of Gerald and, indeed, describe what Gerald himself might probably have seen. A full-length figure with traces of polychromy—the purple robe, a brown scroll, and a red cushion: the letters 'E' and 'EL', probably the inscription Emmanuel, in gold, on a *turchino* background: a gold nimbus and cross behind the bearded head.[23] Wilpert also described not only the sun, moon, and stars in the nimbus, but also, on the right side, a great round hole made for unction! Gerald's knee? Eight other holes covered with little silver discs engraved with birds and symbolic animals complete the image (plate 1).[24]

Innocent's cover stopped at neck level, leaving the face free. Flora Lewis is obviously correct when she says that even in full-length images, it is the face of Christ on which the observer focuses his gaze.[25] Today much of Innocent's work on the Uronica's silver cover is overlaid by later additions—a rectangular door for symbolic foot-washing, dating from the fourteenth century, a crown of flames, a baroque angel, and various medallions—but a closer inspection reveals much of the original design.[26] Innocent's cover is divided into four parts with a geometric decoration of stars and rosettes within circles—a complex design reminiscent of the patterns of cosmatesque pavements. Small figures of the highest quality further elaborate the design. At the top, nearest to Christ's face, are the evangelist symbols—Matthew and Mark to the left, Luke and John being identifiable on the right. Beneath them, to the left and right, are St Stephen and St Laurence, with his gridiron, both of whose relics were venerated in the oratory.[27] In the next row and on the left is a medallion with the *Agnus Dei*, matched on the right by a descending angel. The Virgin stands below on the left, and on the right a male figure in the act of

[22] J. Wilpert, 'L'*acheropita* ossia l'immagine del Salvatore della Capelle del *Sancta Sanctorum*', *L'Arte*, 10 (1907), pp. 159–77, 246–62, esp. pp. 162–5.

[23] Cf. W. F. Volbach, 'Il Cristo di Sutri e la venerazione del SS. Salvatore nel Lazio', *Pontificia Accademia Romana di Archeologia, Rendiconti*, 17 (1940–1), pp. 97–126.

[24] Wilpert, 'L'*acheropita*', p. 174 and esp. fig. 9.

[25] F. Lewis, 'The Veronica: image, legend and the viewer', in W. M. Ormrod, ed., *England in the Thirteenth Century, Proceedings of the Harlaxton Conference* (Woodbridge, 1985), pp. 100–6, especially p. 104.

[26] Wilpert, 'L'*archeropita*', pp. 246–62.

[27] *Descriptio Lateranensis*, p. 357.

Plate 1 Innocent III's Silver Cover for the Uronica or *Acheropita* (by courtesy of the British Library).

homage or *proskynesis*.[28] Next comes St Paul, with a pointed beard carrying a book, and opposite him, St Peter, with the pallium over his right hand and keys in the left. Then, nearest to the doorway, for the anointing of the Saviour's feet, are two small female figures, possibly S. Agnese and S. Prassede, whose actual heads were in reliquaries under the oratory's altar.[29] The cover is completed at the bottom with ten small, diamond-shaped champlevé enamel medallions, showing traces of green and yellow colouring.[30] Some of the figures previously encountered are repeated in this marginal frieze, which also includes a mitred bishop and a figure without a nimbus—possibly a donor figure—perhaps even Innocent himself? The inscription shows without any doubt that Innocent, its patron, had the whole cover made.[31]

The second of Gerald's images, this time found at St Peter's, was the cloth with which Christ's brow was wiped on his way to Calvary.[32] A clear and lasting impression of his suffering face had been left upon it.[33] This cloth was called the Veronica, after the Virgin Mary's maid-of-all-work, and meaning the *vera icona*, the true icon or image.[34] Such a play on words would have delighted the eloquent Welshman Gerald. In actual fact, the Veronica image, the so-called *sudarium* of Christ himself may, according to Wilpert, have had a painted image added to it at the end of the twelfth century.[35] Whether this is so or not, it would certainly have been in keeping with Innocent's aim to raise the standing and public veneration of so ancient but obscure an image already in the possession of St Peter's. A bull addressed to the canons of the basilica tells how the

[28] Cf. G. B. Ladner, 'The gestures of prayer in papal iconography of the thirteenth and early fourteenth centuries', *Images and Ideas in the Middle Ages, Selected Studies in History and Art, Storia e Letteratura = Raccolta di Studi e Testi*, 155–6, 2 vols (Rome, 1983), 1, pp. 209–37, esp. pp. 209–11.

[29] *Descriptio Lateranensis*, p. 357, 'et caput Sancta Praxedis et Sanctae Agnese reliquae cum aliis multis'. Wilpert, 'L'*acheropita*', p. 177, suggests that one might be the Magdalene, who herself anointed Christ's feet.

[30] From left to right, Agnes with lamb and crown, St Paul with his sword, John the Baptist, a space, Madonna and Child, Peter with keys and a book, St Laurence, S. Prassede, a bishop, and a donor.

[31] + INNOCENTIVS PP III HOC OPVS FECIT FIERI +.

[32] E. V. Dobschütz, *Christusbilder, Untersuchungen zur christlichen Legende* (Leipzig, 1899), esp. pp. 197–262.

[33] I. Wilson, *Holy Faces: Secret Places* (London, 1991); Lewis, 'The Veronica', pp. 100–3.

[34] E. Delaruelle, 'Le problème de la pauvreté vu par les théologiens et les canonistes dans la deuxième moitié du xii siècle', *Cahiers de Fanjeaux*, 2 (Toulouse, 1967), pp. 48–63, esp. p. 62 for a discussion of Veronica as a poor saint.

[35] J. Wilpert, *Die römischen Malereien und Mosaiken*, 2 vols (Freiburg, 1917), 2, p. 1123; Lewis, 'Veronica', p. 105, n. 15.

Veronica was to be presented to the people, contained within a *capsa* or casket of gold, silver, and precious stones, made specially for this purpose by a silversmith (*fabre facta*).[36]

In both images it was the face which was to convey the message to the people, hence Innocent's concentration on this feature. Yet the Uronica's dark, burnt-black, and fearsome face, with rigid nose, staring eyes, and enormous pupils, seems far less likely than the Veronica to show that Christ had suffered.[37] In the Veronica face the suffering was only too obvious. There were, of course, similarities, and not just in the features. In each, for example, a bruise appeared under the right eye. Perhaps wishing to demonstrate there was humanity in the Uronica image, Gerald speaks also of a scar on the forehead.[38] This he alleged to have been caused by a certain Jew who had thrown a stone at it. The stone thrower died, and many conversions subsequently took place. Gerald cites this story word for word from the *Ordines Romani XII* of Cencio Camerius, of about 1192, and explains that in his day it was still possible to see that the wound had actually bled.[39] We do not know now exactly how the Veronica looked. When Wilpert examined it in 1917 he saw only a square piece of discoloured and stained cloth.[40] Yet it had clearly once existed in a form by which the faithful could be moved to wonder at Christ's message, and its popularity in the later Middle Ages has never been in doubt.[41]

Although these images of the Uronica and the Veronica were the two most impressive in conveying the message, Rome, by the second half of the twelfth century, was one whole great storehouse of images and relics: a unique source of attraction and inspiration to citizen and pilgrim alike.[42] Something of that excitement experienced on being face to face with one or more of these images in the twelfth and thirteenth centuries must have been generated once more when the five surviving Roman icons of the Virgin were brought together at S. Maria Maggiore for two weeks in June

36 3 Jan. 1208, *PL* 215, col. 1270, 'recolitur infra capsam ex auro et argento et lapidibus pretiosis ad hoc specialiter fabrefactam venerabiliter deportetur.' Cf. Lewis, 'Veronica', p. 103, n. 15.

37 Grisar, *Sancta Sanctorum*, p. 51.

38 Gerald of Wales, *Jewel of the Church*, ch. 31, pp. 79–80.

39 *Ordo Romanus XII*, *PL* 78, cols 1063–1106, esp. col. 1097.

40 Lewis,'Veronica', p. 105.

41 For fourteenth-century representations of the pilgrim badge or 'vernicle', see M. Mitchiner, *Medieval Pilgrim and Secular Badges* (London, 1986), p. 273, and plates 1057–8.

42 P. Jounel, *Le Culte des Saints*; *The Blessings of Pilgrimage*, ed. R. Ousterhout = *Illinois Byzantine Studies*, 1 (Urbana, 1990).

and July 1988.[43] The fifth-century icon of S. Maria Nova was the most venerable of them all and owed its miraculous origin to the unseen angelic hand.[44]

Such images were intended to arouse intense spirituality in the worshipping beholder.[45] The effect was heightened as the images were often surrounded by banks of lights—candelabra in the churches and torches in the streets. As Bernard of Clairvaux cynically commented, 'When golden reliquaries catch the eye, the purses open up', and again, 'The brighter the image of a saint appears, the holier the people imagine it to be.'[46] In her study of twelfth-century statues of the Virgin in France, Iylene Forsyth has indicated the importance of the use of precious metals, silver beaten to the thinness of tissue, carefully fastened to a wooden core, and decorated with dozens of precious stones, all producing an awe-inspiring effect.[47] The contours and folds of the metal collected the light and reflected it back, suggesting an intangible, mystical presence. The faithful observer might even have been tempted to endow the effigy with the ability to move, so easily was this shimmering illusion fostered.[48] One Master Gregory, an English tourist visiting Rome at the turn of the twelfth century, could have sworn that the colossal bronze head and hand of Constantine gave the appearance of being about to speak and move![49] A devout worshipper thus built up a close mutual relationship with an image. This was often heightened by the expressive, eloquent, or even terrifying fixed stare in the eyes of the image remarked upon by contemporaries.[50] Indeed, not only Gerald of Wales, but Gervase of Tilbury, who also saw both images, indicated that the *Sancta Sanctorum* image, the

[43] P. Amato, *De Vera Effigie Mariae: antiche icone Romane* (Rome, 1988); C. Bertelli, 'Icone di Roma', *Stil und Überlieferung in der Kunst des Abendlandes*, 2 vols (Berlin, 1967), 1, pp. 100–6.

[44] E. Kitzinger, 'A Virgin's face: antiquarianism in twelfth-century art', *Art Bulletin*, 62 (1980), pp. 6–19; M. Guarducci, *La più antica icone di Maria: un prodigioso vincolo fra oriente e occidente* (Rome, 1989).

[45] E. Dahl, 'Heavenly images. The statue of St Foy of Conques and the signification of the medieval "Cult-image" in the West', *Acta ad Archaeologicam et Artium Historiam Pertinentia = Institutum Romanum Norvegiae*, 8 (Rome, 1978) [hereafter *AAAHP*], pp. 175–92.

[46] *Sancti Bernardi Opera*, 3, ed. J. Leclercq and H. M. Rochais (Rome, 1963), *Apologia ad Guillelmum Abbatem*, p. 105.

[47] L. Forsyth, *The Throne of Wisdom: Wood Sculptures of the Madonna in Romanesque France* (Princeton, 1972), pp. 40–4.

[48] Dahl, 'Heavenly images', pp. 188–91.

[49] Master Gregory, *The Marvels of Rome*, tr. J. Osborne = *Medieval Sources in Translation*, 31 (Toronto, 1987), p. 23.

[50] Dahl, 'Heavenly images', pp. 190–1; S. Sinding-Larsen, 'Some observations on liturgical imagery of the twelfth century', *AAAHP*, pp. 192–212, esp. pp. 208–12.

Uronica, remained covered, possibly by closed doors, because of its fearsome effect on the viewer.[51] Gerald also comments upon the fact that curtains hung before the Veronica.[52] The wide-open eyes, combined with a hypnotic gaze frequently found in reliquary images, indicated to many of the faithful that the Holy Spirit was speaking directly to them.[53] Clearly the danger of idolatry was always present,[54] and steps were taken to protect the images from too frequent a public gaze. The Church legislated consistently against such a threat. Canon 62 of the Fourth Lateran Council decreed that relics were henceforth to be enclosed in reliquaries or behind impenetrable bars.[55] This instruction Innocent had already carried out when he secured the heads of Saints Peter and Paul at the Lateran behind a decorative grille.[56] This had the added advantage of preventing any tampering. Proliferation of relics was to be halted, and the need for solemn authenticity stressed. Sometimes this authentication had to be left to God himself, as Innocent remarked about Christ's foreskin and umbilical cord, both claimed as part of the collection in the *Sancta Sanctorum* of the Lateran.[57] His established practice, indeed, was to concentrate far more attention on images from which the message could be more readily expounded than on relics, the intrinsic characteristics of which were dubious, and which could easily divert attention from the Gospel.

Innocent was eager to bring the two main images out into the streets to meet the people, so following a practice common to all Italian towns in various matters, not merely religious. The Uronica had a venerable history of street theatre, but there is no similar evidence for the Veronica. In bringing the Veronica to the people, possibly for the first time, on 20 January 1208, the second Sunday after Epiphany, Innocent was not only giving them another image of great holiness to venerate, but was also emphasizing the importance of St Peter's, from whence it came.[58] The earliest mention of

[51] Gervase of Tilbury, *Otia Imperialia*, book 3, ed. G. G. Leibnitz, *Scriptores rerum Brunsvicensium* (Hanover, 1707), p. 967; Lewis, 'Veronica', p. 103.

[52] Gerald of Wales, *Speculum Ecclesiae*, p. 279, '. . . a nemine, nisi per velorum quae ante dependent interpositionem inspicitur.'

[53] Dahl, 'Heavenly images', pp. 186–91.

[54] Ibid., pp. 177–8.

[55] *Conciliorum oecumenicorum decreta*, ed. J. Alberigo *et al.*, 3rd edn (Bologna, 1973), pp. 263–4.

[56] Antonelli, *Memorie storiche*, p. 11; Grisar, *Sancta Sanctorum*, p. 24.

[57] *PL* 217, col. 877, 'Melius est Deo totum committere quam aliud temere definire.' Cf. Grisar, *Sancta Sanctorum*, p. 123, who notes that this relic was kept in a gemmed cross inscribed 'PREPUTIUM DNJC'.

[58] *PL* 215, col. 1270, for the privilege to the Hospital.

the ceremony of processing the Lateran Uronica occurs in the *Liber Pontificalis* under Sergius I (687–701).[59] He had laid down that

> from the time of the breaking of the Lord's body, the clergy and people should sing the *Agnus Dei* and on the occasion of the Annunciation, Dormition and Nativity of the Virgin, the procession should go out from the Church of San Adriano gathering people as it went, all meeting up at S. Maria Maggiore.

Stephen II (752–7), barefooted, carried on his shoulders the 'imago Dei et Salvatoris nostri Jesu Christi' across the city to counter the Lombard threat, all the Romans following.[60] By the time of Leo IV (847–55), such processing had become a matter of custom, and the Feast of the Assumption was developing into one of the most grandiose rites of medieval Rome.[61] On the vigil of this feast, 14 August, the procession of the *tabula* or image of Christ—what Gerald had called the Uronica—set out at midnight along lighted streets from the Lateran, past SS Quattro Coronati, the Colosseum, the Arch of Titus, and arrived at the steps of the Temple of Venus and Rome, in front of S. Maria Nova, nowadays S. Francesca Romana.[62] On its arrival, the feet of the image were washed with *basilicum*, whilst the people prostrated themselves and the *Kyrie* and *Christe eleison* were sung a hundred times.[63] At this climax, the image of the Virgin at S. Maria Nova met the image of her Son, which had been carried through the streets to her. By the twelfth century the Uronica was carried on a *portatorium*, borne high, surrounded by lighted candles and torches, to the accompaniment of psalms. It was led by twelve of the best-regarded dignitaries in Rome and twelve officials of the papal chapel.[64] The procession continued to S. Adriano, where the ritual foot-washing was repeated, and S. Maria Maggiore was finally reached as dawn was

[59] *The Book of Pontiffs* (*Liber Pontificalis*), tr. R. Davis (Liverpool, 1989), pp. 87–8; A. Mancini, 'La chiesa medioevale di S. Adriano nel Foro Romano', *Pontificia Accademia Romana di Archeologia, Rendiconti*, 40 (1967–8),pp. 191–245.

[60] *Liber Pontificalis*, ed. L. Duchesne, 3 vols (Paris, 1886–92), 1, p. 443; Grisar, *Sancta Sanctorum*, p. 50; Kitzinger, 'A Virgin's face', p. 12. Cf. D. de Bruyne, 'L'origine des processions de la Chandeleur et des rogations à propos d'un sermon inédit', *RBen*, 34 (1922), pp. 142–26.

[61] *Liber Pontificalis*, 2, pp. 110, 135; Volbach, 'Il Cristo di Sutri', p. 116.

[62] Grisar, *Sancta Sanctorum*, pp. 55–7; Kitzinger, 'A Virgin's face', pp. 12, 17; Mancini, 'S. Adriano nel Foro Romano', p. 223; Sinding-Larsen, 'Liturgical imagery', p. 211; Volbach, 'Il Cristo di Sutri', pp. 116–18.

[63] J. Mabillon, *Museum Italicum seu collectio veterum scriptorum ex bibliothecis Italicis*, 2 vols (Paris, 1724), 2, pp. 131, 134, 174; Kitzinger, 'A Virgin's face', p. 12.

[64] Benedictus Canonicus, *Liber Politicus*, in P. Fabre and L. Duchesne, *Le Liber Censuum de l'église romaine*, 3 vols (Paris, 1905–10), 2, p. 158.

breaking on 15 August. By tradition, the liturgical station for the Feast of the Assumption then followed, and Innocent used this occasion to preach his Sermon XXVIII on the Dawn.[65] The Virgin Mary was the dawn, marking the end of night and the beginning of day, the end of vice and the beginning of virtue in the world. Her Son was the Day-Star on high.[66]

This ceremony of the vigil of the Assumption was seen by Grisar,[67] and more recently by Kitzinger, as representing in a literal sense a visit by Christ to his mother on her great feast day.[68] This cult of the *acheropita* or Uronica seems to have been unique to Lazio, and the *ordo* and rite, as well as the image, were initiated throughout the little towns of the region around Rome.[69] Tivoli appears to have been particularly blessed, for as recently as August 1978, in the so-called *inchinata*, the Saviour and his mother bowed to each other as they met.[70]

Innocent wished to arrange something similar for the Veronica, which was first processed in January 1208. In the procession the special portable reliquary for the image was carried by the canons of St Peter's to Innocent's new hospital foundation of S. Spirito, by the Tiber, and its adjacent church of S. Maria in Sassia.[71] The Veronica was there venerated by 'a flood' of people, who heard a sermon of exhortation from the Pope.[72] In his Sermon VIII, for the First Sunday after Epiphany, Innocent stresses that in this place, too, the mother of Christ is also to be found.[73] At this newly established liturgical station of the Veronica he speaks of the Virgin finding her Son, whose effigy, on being carried around the hospital, encouraged the faithful sick and pilgrims to be amazed at his glory.[74]

Although processions had become so important, Innocent was aware of the necessity of stimulating in small groups of significant people the true importance of Christ's message. The Uronica and the Veronica, sparklingly impressive as they were when seen either by candlelight or sunlight, also possessed a solemn and more contemplative dimension when seen in

[65] *PL* 217, cols 581–6.

[66] Ibid., col. 584: 'Quia vero ad diluculum poenitentiae surgit, respiciat auroram, deprecetur Mariam, ut ipsa per filium cor ejus ad satisfactionem illuminet.'

[67] Grisar, *Sancta Sanctorum*, pp. 56–7.

[68] Kitzinger, 'A Virgin's face', pp. 16–17.

[69] Volbach, 'Il Cristo di Sutri', pp. 104–16.

[70] Kitzinger, 'A Virgin's face', p. 12, n. 46.

[71] *PL* 215, cols 1270–1; A. Albani, *Collectionis bullarum sacrosanctae basilicae Vaticanae*, 3 vols (Rome, 1747–54), 1, pp. 89–90.

[72] *Gesta Innocentii PP III*, *PL* 214, cols xvii–ccxxvi, esp. cols cc–cciii and cci, 'in qua populus illic confluit'.

[73] *PL* 217, cols 345–50.

[74] *Origins of the Liturgy*, pp. 102–3, 460.

their normal locations. The Uronica, by virtue of its position above the altar in the papal chapel of St Laurence at the Lateran, was confined in a very small space. When Mass was celebrated there by the Pope and the seven cardinal-bishops, there was room for no other, and the spiritual awareness of the ceremony in the presence of the image must have provided a religious experience of considerable intensity.[75] The fine decorative work on Innocent's silver cover, perhaps inspired by his reading of Ado of Vienne's *Martyrology*,[76] would have acted as a valuable aid to their meditation. The Easter *ordo* of Cencio Camerarius, in use in Innocent's day, tells how, when the image was opened, the Pope kissed its feet and repeated three times 'Surrexit Dominus de Sepulcro, alleluia', to which the response came back 'Qui pro nobis perpendit in ligno, alleluia.'[77] The cardinal-bishops then kissed Christ's feet, and each received in turn a kiss from the Pope. The ceremony was repeated at all the feasts of the Virgin.

The Veronica was not used in the same way, for at St Peter's Innocent wished to concentrate on the *confessio* or tomb of the Apostle to add a further dimension to the message he wished to convey. At this, the focal point of the basilica, he had a splendid new golden-bronze protective screen made, decorated with small human figures.[78] In antique and rustic capitals mixed with uncials, a one-line inscription identifies Innocent as the patron.[79] His inspiration for the *confessio* may well have come from his readings of the *Liber Pontificalis*.[80] The decoration is there well attested when Sixtus III (432–40) accepted from the Emperor Valentinian a gold image with twelve portals, twelve Apostles, and the Saviour, decorated with the most precious stones, and which was placed over the tomb.[81] Leo III (795–816) inaugurated the disposition later followed by Innocent by inserting a golden grille or *ruga* with a door to give access to the tomb.[82] Leo IV (847–55) renewed the decoration of Sixtus III, destroyed by the Saracens in 846, with a silver *tabula* showing the Saviour enthroned with

[75] *Origins of the Liturgy*, p. 93.

[76] Ado of Vienne, *Vetus Romanum Martyrologium*, *PL* 123, cols 143–82; Van Dijk, *Origins*, pp. 126–8, 226–7, 493–8.

[77] *PL* 78, col. 1077; Grisar, *Sancta Sanctorum*, pp. 50–1.

[78] Gautier, 'La Clôture Émaillée', pp. 237–42.

[79] Ibid., p. 238. + TERCIVS HOC MUNVS DANS INNOCENTIVS +.

[80] On the *confessio* see E. Kirschbaum, *Les fouilles de Saint-Pierre de Rome* (Paris, 1961); *Descriptio Vaticanae*, pp. 375–442.

[81] *Book of Pontiffs*, pp. 35–7, esp. p. 36.

[82] *Liber Pontificalis*, 2, p. 1.

precious gems on his head while, on his right hand, cherubim held the images of the Apostles.[83] Leo IV also seems to have had an altar frontal made in gold and enamel, which Boso claimed was destroyed in 1130 by the antipope Anacletus.[84] Innocent was not only inspired by these decorative precedents when he arranged for the new decoration of the *confessio*, but also took pains to replace the damaged Carolingian enamels with similar work executed by craftsmen from Limoges.[85] His protective screen is simple in the extreme and highly functional. Thirty-eight bars, each a finger's width, are bisected by one horizontal bar, on which is incised the bronze-caster's name, 'OBERT.A.G.'.[86]

Innocent's exquisite and religiously significant small works were designed to impart the message to those important visitors to Rome in November 1215, the 1,200 archbishops, metropolitans, bishops, and abbots attending the Council,[87] but he also took the opportunity to restore the decaying apse-mosaic of St Peter's, which would be visible to all.[88] This mosaic not only claimed equality for St Peter's, now 'the Mother of All Churches', but also revealed the Christian religion in its historical perspective. Innocent's significant alterations showed the importance of the Church and the symbolic purpose of the Eucharist, where the Blood of the Lamb, flowing into the chalice, was for the salvation of all. Such a message, complicated in design, but simple in purpose, was typical of the inspirational approach of Innocent III and deserves further attention elsewhere. His love of street theatre and his feeling for the city of Rome came together spectacularly in the entertainments considered suitable for the delegates to the Lateran Council—the consecration of S. Maria in Trastevere on Sunday 15 November and the Mass in St Peter's on 18 November.[89] Here we have a privileged glimpse of the lights, the music, the trumpets, and the razzmatazz on

[83] Ibid., p. 114.

[84] Ibid., p. 380.

[85] Gautier, 'Observations préliminaires', pp. 43–79.

[86] Gautier, 'La Clôture Émaillée', pp. 238–42.

[87] Ibid., pp. 242–6.

[88] *Gesta*, col. ccv, 'absidam ejusdem basilicae fecit restauri mosibus, quod erat ex magna parte consumptum.' Cf. J. Ruysschaert, 'Le tableau Mariotti de la mosaïque absidale de l'ancien S. Pierre', *Pontificia Accademia Romana di Archeologia, Rendiconti*, 40 (1967–8), pp. 295–317.

[89] S. Kuttner and A. Garcia y Garcia, 'A new eyewitness account of the Fourth Lateran Council', *Traditio*, 20 (1964), pp. 115–78; D. Kinney, *Santa Maria in Trastevere from its Founding to 1215* (Michigan, 1975), pp. 337–9.

which all great impresarios flourish.[90] Innocent III, that much-neglected patron of the small-scale work, merely added the religiosity!

[90] Bolton, 'Show with a meaning', pp. 61–4.

# XVIII

# Hearts not Purses? Pope Innocent III's Attitude to Social Welfare

Innocent III, one of the most powerful and influential popes in medieval history, took seriously both the theory and the practice of his episcopal responsibilities for the poor, already described in the work of Bishop Rabbula. Innocent's ideas, reflecting the medieval theological and canonical tradition, are set forth in his two short treatises, *Book of Alms* and *In Praise of Charity*. Almsgiving is a medicine of salvation that removes the stain of sin and helps to eradicate the desires of the flesh. The natural and social disasters of the early thirteenth century provided manifold opportunities for Innocent to persevere in modeling his theology of charity. Of Innocent's many charitable activities ranging from feeding the poor to ransoming captives, it was his foundation of the Hospital of the Holy Spirit on the banks of the Tiber that epitomized his aspirations for social welfare in Rome, linking past and present, tradition and innovation, care of body and soul. The Hospital's services ranged from the acceptance of unwanted babies, with no questions asked, to an outreach program to the poor in the streets of the city.

In northern Europe, the twentieth century's last decade began with storms, with devastation, but not with total famine. This type of end-of-century phenomena would have been familiar in the decade of the 1190s, and indeed, was perhaps the main preoccupation as the twelfth century gave way to the thirteenth. Contemporary chroniclers described the suffering caused by a succession of natural calamities from 1194 to 1207, which resulted in a series of bad harvests from the Atlantic to the Apennines.[1] The specter of famine, worse north of the Alps before 1198, had moved south to the Mediterranean by the end of the century and plague

[1] *Oeuvres de Rigord et de Guillaume le Breton: Historiens de Philippe Auguste*, ed. H. F. Delaborde, *Recueil des Historiens de la France* 17 (Paris, 1882), 130–41.

followed in its wake.[2] Wolves appeared in inhabited areas where they had not previously been seen and vied with humans for the meager food supplies. In 1202, the Chronicler of the Cistercian Abbey of Fossanova (midway between Rome and Naples) wrote, "In this year, there were great gales, uprooting trees, damaging churches, overturning buildings and wreaking terrible destruction. This year was known to everyone as the year of hunger."[3] This truly disastrous period made a deep impression on contemporaries.

When such disasters occur today, local mayors establish funds to provide and maintain care and welfare for the stricken community. If the disaster is large-scale, national emergencies are declared and international relief agencies rush to the rescue. But what of France in the 1190s or Italy in the early thirteenth century? To whom then might one turn in the hour of need? With whom lay the responsibility of providing succor for the poor and vulnerable, particularly since the disaster was not just one emergency event but a continuous occurrence? Naturally, in the groves of academe and particularly in the University of Paris, there was much intellectual debate, both spiritual and theological, with Peter the Chanter (d. 1197), Robert de Courson (d. 1219), and Stephen Langton (d.1228) well to the fore.[4] A variety of initiatives—which others could take—were put forward.[5] The laity were to be encouraged to perform works of care and welfare.[6] Kings and princes were expected to provide generous gifts, implicit in their double duty to render both justice and charity to their

[2] "1199 ... scilicet fame, gladis et peste," *Auctore ignoti monachi Cisterciensis.* S. M. de Ferraria, ed. A. Gaudenzi (Naples, 1888), 33. The following works have been of great value: J. M. Bienvenu, "Pauvreté, misères et charité en Anjou aux XIe et XIIe siècles," in *Moyen Age* 72 (1966): 389-424; ibid. 73 (1967): 5–34, 189–216; M. Mollat, "Pauvres et pauvreté dans le monde médiéval,"*La povertà del secolo xii e Francesco d'Assisi,* Atti del II Convegno Internazionale, Assisi 17-19 ottobre 1974 (Assisi: Società internazionale di studi francescani, 1975), 81–97; M. Mollat, ed., *Etudes sur l'Histoire de la Pauvreté*, 2 vols. (Paris: Sorbonne, 1974; cited as *Etudes*); M. Mollat, *Les Pauvres au Moyen Age* (Paris: Hachette, 1978); M. Mollat, "Le problème de la pauvreté au XIIe siècle,"*Cahiers de Fanjeaux* 2, (1967): 23–24; M. Mollat, "Hospitalité et assistance au début du XIIIe siècle,"*Poverty in the Middle Ages*, ed. D. Flood (Werl-Westfallen: Dietrich-Coelde, 1975), 37–51.

[3] *Chronicon Fossaenovae Auctore Anonymo ... ad annum MCCXVII* in L.A. Muratori, *Rerum Italicarum Scriptores*, 25 vols. (Milan, 1723-1751), 7 (Milan, 1727): col. 886.

[4] J.W. Baldwin, *Masters, Princes and Merchants: the Social Views of Peter the Chanter and his Circle*, 2 vols. (Princeton: Princeton University Press, 1970); J. Longère, "Pauvreté et richesse chez quelques prédicateurs durant la seconde moitié du XIIe siècle,"in *Etudes*, 1:255–73.

[5] G. Couvreur, *Les Pauvres ont-ils des droits? Recherches sur le vol en cas d'extrême nécessité depuis la "Concordia"de Gratien (1140) jusqu'à Guillaume d'Auxerre (d.1231)* (Rome-Paris: Gregorian University, 1961) and ibid., "Pauvreté et droit des pauvres à la fin du XIIe siècle,"*Recherches et débats du CCIF* 49 (1964): 13-37.

[6] Mollat, "Hospitalité et assistance,"41-42; B. M. Bolton, "The Poverty of the Humiliati," in Flood, *Poverty in the Middle Ages*, 52-59.

subjects.[7] The rich should be induced to give to the poor in time of famine[8] while ecclesiastics, merely stewards of their goods, which belonged to the church, might not only be admonished but actually compelled to distribute alms.[9]

Did any positive results emerge from these high-level discussions? Perhaps not but already, in both rural and urban parishes human need called forth certain practical responses, especially to help those who could so easily fall below subsistence level.[10] Confraternities of like-minded lay people were established for the purpose of supporting those in need, including voluntary acts of manual labor and care for the sick.[11] Indeed, hospital foundations often developed from such spontaneous activities as tending the poor and leprous. Yet in spite of these voluntary initiatives, the chief burden of responsibility in the twelfth century still fell, as in earlier periods, on the church. Monasteries continued to play an important role in hospitality and works of mercy, albeit with an increasingly symbolic rather than strictly practical element.[12] For example, food was distributed in a liturgical ritual to a selected group of the poor. Local priests too could sometimes provide more than just the cure of souls. Julian of Cuenca (d.1207) earned his living by weaving rush baskets, and used all the revenue so gained for charitable works.[13] In such disastrous times, the body needed to be treated and healed before the soul could be attended to. Unfortunately, in the late twelfth century, the bishop in his diocese, who

[7]1195 ... Rex Philippus motus pietate, largiores elemosynas de suo pauperibus erogandas precepit,"*Oeuvres de Rigord, 132; Recueil des Actes de Philippe-Auguste,* ed. E. Berger and A.F. Delaborde, (Paris, 1916), esp. 152, 183.

[8]Most famous of all was Theobald IV, Count of Blois and Champagne (c. 1090–1152). See Sermon XXXIX of Jacques de Vitry, *De comite Campaniae Theobaldo et leproso, Analecta Novissima Spicilegii Solesmensis altera continuatio,* ed. J.B. Pitra, (Tusculum, 1888), II, 449; Couvreur, *Les pauvres,* 165–166, 193–97; Baldwin, *Master, Princes and Merchants,* 1:237, 2:255–56; G. Gracco, "Dalla misericordia della chiesa alla misericordia del principe" in *La carità a Milano nei secoli xii-xv,* ed. M.P. Alberzoni and O. Grassi, (Milan: Jaca Book, 1989), 3–46

[9] B. Tierney, *Medieval Poor Law: A Sketch of Canonical Theory and Its Application in England* (Berkeley: University of California Press, 1959); Couvreur, "Les pauvres," 197–202.

[10]Tierney, *Medieval Poor Law,* 9–16.

[11]G. Ferri, "La Romana Fraternitas," in *Archivo della Società Romana di Storia Patria* 36, (1903) 453-466 (cited as *ASRSP*); G. G. Meersseman, *Ordo, Fraternitatis, Confraternite e pietà dei laici nel Medio Evo,* 3 vols. (Rome: Herder, 1977), 1:24—26; J. M. Bienvenu, "Fondations charitables laiques au XIIe siècle. L'exemple de l'Anjou,"in *Etudes* 1:563–69; G. Barone, "Il movimento francescano e la nascita delle confraternite Romana," *Richerche per la Storia Religiosa di Roma* 5 (1984): 71–80.

[12]M. Mollat, "Les moines et les pauvres XIe-XIIe siècles," in *Il monachesimo e la riforma ecclesiastica (1049–1122)* (Milan: Vita e Pensiero, 1971), 193–215.

[13]Julian, Bishop of Cuenca in the province of Toledo (1179-?1208), *Acta Sanctorum,* January II (Venice, 1734), 893–97.

ought to have been playing a key role, was more often than not so doing.[14]

The task before the church ultimately devolved to the one bishop in Christendom who was both unable and unwilling to shirk this responsibility—the Pope. Innocent III, elected January 8, 1198, was later consecrated as bishop of his city on February 22 in that year.[15] At age thirty-seven (possibly the youngest-ever pope), he approached his formidable task with all the vigor and enthusiasm of his relative youth. He himself had witnessed those famine years between 1194 and 1198 while serving in the Curia and set about providing solutions to what others saw as an intractable problem. As a former student of the University of Paris and friend of all those elegant debaters,[16] he was well aware of their concern and theoretical suggestions. Peter the Chanter in particular had the opportunity to inspire him when this great academic was on a personal visit to the Curia in 1196 or 1197.[17] He was also well aware of the more active work of Fulk of Neuilly, Robert de Courson, and Jacques de Vitry[18] in the fields of popular preaching, pastoral care, and genuine caritative acts.

As Bishop of Rome, Innocent III inherited traditional ideas of welfare and its obligations from his predecessors, particularly Gregory the

[14]One model bishop was William le Donjeon, Bishop of Bourges, known as "the Hermit"(November 23, 1200–January 10, 1209), a Cistercian from Charlieu, diocese of Pontigny, *Acta Sanctorum*, January X: 627-81.

[15]*Gesta Innocentii PP III* in *Patrologia Latina* (hereafter *PL*) 214, ed. J.P. Migne, (Paris, 1855), cols. xvii-ccxxviii (cited as *Gesta*) 5: cols. xix-xx; M. Maccarrone, *Studi su Innocenzo III, Italia Sacra*, 17 (Padua: Antenore, 1972); Idem, "La 'cathedra Sancti Petri' nel Medievo: da Simbolo a reliquia," *Revista di Storia della Chiesa in Italia* 39 (1985): 349–47, esp. 427–29.

[16]M. Maccarrone, "Innocenzo III, Prima del Pontificato,"*ASRSP* 66 (1943): 59–134, esp. 93–108; W. Maleczek, *Papst und Kardinalskolleg von 1191 bis 1216,* (Vienna: Österreichen Akademie der Wissenschaften, 1984), 101–4. Cf. Innocent's work of this period, *De Miseria Conditionis Humanae, PL* 217, cols. 701–46, esp. col. 708. "O miserabilis mendicantis condicio. Et si petit, pudore confunditor et si non petit, egestate consumitur."

[17]Maccarrone, "Prima del Pontificato," 71-79; in Baldwin, *Masters, Princes and Merchants*, 1: 317–43, 336, 343; 2:227 n. 191, 2:233 n. 245.

[18]Fulk of Neuilly (d. 1202), see *The Historia Occidentalis of Jacques de Vitry: A Critical Edition*, ed. J. F. Hinnebusch, Spicilegium Friburgense 17 (Fribourg: Fribourg University Press, 1972): 94–101, 273–274; Mollatt, "Hospitalité et assistance," 467–47; Baldwin, *Masters, Princes and Merchants,* 1:19–25, 36–38, 102, 290; M. and C. Dickson, "Le Cardinal Robert de Courçon: Sa vie," in *Archives d'histoire doctrinale et littéraire du moyen âge* 9 (1934): 53–142, Jacques de Vitry (1160/70–1240), was Augustinian canon of St. Nicholas at Oignies (1211–1216), Bishop of Acre (1216–1227), Auxilary Bishop of Liège (1227–1229) , and Cardinal-Bishop of Tusculum (1229–1240); see *Historia Occidentalis* for a critical bibliography of de Vitry.

Great (590-604).[19] An administrative framework had then existed for the time-honored responsibilities of feeding the poor, *miserabiles personae*, and arranging for the welfare of captives and their ransoming. Linked to the care of the indigent and sick was the upkeep of *zenodochia* or hostels for poor strangers and pilgrims arriving in Rome without lodgings.[20] Innocent aimed to revive and update support for such charitable foundations both within Rome and elsewhere. We know from the Pope's anonymous biographer in his Deeds or *Gesta* of his concern for the poor and disadvantaged, repeating Christ's own exhortation to provide alms and charity for those in need.[21] His ideas are set out in two short treatises, the *Libellus de Eleemosyna* (*Book of Alms*) and the *Encomium Charitatis* (*In Praise of Charity*), which apply the tradition of almsgiving to his time.[22]

It will be rewarding to step aside to examine these two works as the basis for Innocent's reasoning on the care of those in need. His *Book of Alms* consists of two short chapters, full of scriptural texts. Almsgiving removes the stain of sin and washes away vice. Almsgiving benefits, liberates, redeems, protects, seeks out, perfects, blesses, justifies and saves. Innocent demonstrates that one who professes faith in Christ Jesus cannot possibly ignore almsgiving but such giving is worthless if there is no real charity of heart. People have to make themselves ready, eager, and suitable to give in the same way as they would prepare for salvation. Fasting is good but almsgiving is better. While fasting, which starves and weakens the body, is a matter for the individual alone, almsgiving is of positive benefit for it restores the bodies of others. Prayer is good but almsgiving is more universal, affecting one's neighbor before ascending to God. Nor should the poverty of the donor ever be an excuse to avoid almsgiving: the value of the widow's mite is one of Innocent's favorite themes[23]

Innocent is completely in accord with the canonists, conceiving almsgiving as an act of justice or of love but never as a matter of sentimental impulse.[24] He is at pains to stress that effective almsgiving needs prac-

[19] F. Niederer, "Early Medieval Charity,"in *Church History* 21 (1952): 285–95; J. Richards, *Consul of God: the Life and Times of Gregory the Great* (London: Routledge & Kegan Paul, 1980), 95--97. Cf. PL 217, Sermo XIII, *In Festo S. Gregorii Papae*, cols. 513–22, where Innocent III places charity first amongst his great predecessor's qualities. I am grateful to Conrad Leyser who allowed me to read a draft of his Oxford D. Phil. thesis on Gregory's charitable works.

[20] W. Schonfeld, "Die Zenodochien in Italien und Frankreich im frühen Mittelalter," *Savigny-Zeitschrift* 43 (1922): 1–54.

[21] *Gesta* CXLIII, cxcvi-cc. Cf. *De miseria divitis et pauperis*, *PL* 217, cols. 708–9.

[22] Ibid., cols. 745–64. In MS Vat Lat 700, *De Eleemosyna* is incorporated into Innocent's Lenten Sermons between fols. 25r and 28v..

[23] Ibid., cols. 747, 748, 749–50, 752–53; see also A. Albani, *Collectionis Bullarum Sacrosanctae Basilicae Vaticanae*, 1: 79, 82.

[24] Couvreur, "Les pauvres,"121–26.

tical organization—well known by our relief agencies today—and sets down four points to be considered: cause, outcome, means, and order.[25]

1. The cause: an urgent need which must be met by an act of charity.
2. The outcome: should be a blessing for all concerned.
3. The means: almsgiving, which should be carried out joyfully. Here Innocent cites St. Paul (2 Cor. 9:7), "God loves a cheerful giver."
4. The order: almsgiving should be performed regularly.

For a work of charity to be a meritorious act pleasing to God it had to be inspired by right intent, the correct attitude to God and to one's neighbor. While St. Augustine defines two kinds of almsgiving—of the heart and of money, Innocent's definition is fuller. For him it becomes a threefold activity that involves the heart, mouth, and action.[26] Compassion comes from the heart, admonition and encouragement from the mouth, and generosity from actions. Nor is almsgiving ever restricted: alms must be given equally to the good and to the wicked, to the pious and impious, to friend and foe alike. What determines almsgiving is need and opportunity. If at all possible, the circumstances must be weighed and a practical decision made about where and to whom more charitable welfare should be given. In so doing, almsgiving becomes a medicine of salvation against all ills. If one special quality is to be sought in the almsgiver, it is perseverance.[27] Perseverance excludes impatience, eliminates contempt, and fights against obstinacy. Perseverance produces an adult donor of mature habit with no sentimental self-esteem who is the best giver of alms; the spiritual rewards will speak for themselves.

Innocent's *In Praise of Charity* carries further the sentiments of the *Book of Alms* by showing how the spiritual benefits of charitable actions help eradicate the desires of the flesh. The virtue of charity is that it is inseparable from the life of Christ himself, his crucifixion and resurrection, from the love of God the Father, and from the guidance of the Holy Spirit.[28] Yet there are dangers in performing an act of charity when one simply follows one's own wishes and desires in the matter of choice. It is through God's grace that failure will be prevented and the true humility of the virtuous giver ensured. In many ways this brief work by Innocent epitomizes the

[25]*PL* 217, cols. 355–56.
[26]Augustine, *City of God* 1:18; *PL* 41, col. 31; cf. *PL* 217, cols. 355–56.
[27]*Pl* 217, cols. 759–62.
[28] Ibid., cols. 761–64.

*vita apostolica*, the life of the apostles in the Jerusalem community updated to the twelfth century and underpins all his charitable and welfare activities.[29]

Both treatises are deeply serious and thoughtful works, perhaps written in 1202 or 1203 when, as his biographer tells us, Innocent boasted of fulfilling the Lord's work[30] as did the apostles in doing the work of Christ their Savior. The natural disasters of the time were then very much on his mind. In the spring of 1202, after a disastrous winter and little prospect of a harvest to come,[31] the pope, who had been at Anagni, rapidly returned to Rome when he heard of the widespread distress there and began the distribution of alms. This he did in a variety of ways, both organizationally and materially. To those who were too ashamed to beg publicly (perhaps the noble poor who were able to keep such sums safe), he ensured that they received money secretly in sufficient amounts to sustain them for a week at a time. On the other hand, those who begged openly in the streets received sufficient for each day (for they might dissipate anything more than day-to-day handouts). The number of this multitude reduced to such distress exceeded 8,000 of the approximately 30,000 total population.[32] Still more received alms in the form of food in their own homes. Thus the hungry poor were freed from imminent danger, and Innocent could exhort the rich and powerful to follow his example.[33] Here Innocent again shows himself in tune with contemporary canonists who believed that a poor man had a right to the help he received and should not be humiliated in any way.[34] Yet he was not content to leave matters of welfare to his example alone. All bishops and archbishops in the Church were his potential agents.[35]

The letters—and there were many—that Innocent wrote to Berengar II (1190–1212), Archbishop of Narbonne in Languedoc, show clearly the

[29] E. W. McDonnell,"The *vita apostolica*:Diversity or Dissent?" *Church History* 24 (1955): 15–31; G. Olsen, "The Idea of the *Ecclesia Primitiva* in the Writings of the Twelfth-Century Canonists," *Traditio* 25 (1969): 61–81; M. D. Chenu, *Nature, Man and Society in the Twelfth Century: Essays on New Theological Perspectives in the Latin West*, trans. J. Taylor and L. K. Little, (Chicago: University of Chicago Press, 1968), 239–46.

[30] *Gesta* CXLIII, col. cxcvi. Interea dominus Innocentius, suum jactans in Domino cogitatum, operibus pietatis plenius insistebat.

[31] *Chronicon Fossaenovae* 1202, col. 886.

[32] See *Gesta* CXLIII, cols. cxcvi-cxcix.

[33] One such follower was the Roman nobleman Peter of Parenzo, who gave secretly to the poor when he visited them by night. See S. Pietro Parenzo, *La legenda scritta dal Maestro Giovanni, Canonico di Orvieto*, A. Natalini, ed., Lateranum NS 2 (Rome, 1936): 157.

[34] B. Tierney, "The Decretists and the Deserving Poor,"*Comparative Studies in Society and History* I (1958-59): 360–73.

[35]December 5, 1198. *Die Register Innocenz III.*, eds. O. Hageneder and A. Haidacher, (Graz-H. Böhlaus Nachf., 1964), nos. 445, 668; *PL* 214, cols. 421–22; B. M. Bolton, "*Via ascetica*: a papal quandary,"*Studies in Church History* 22 (1985): 161–91, esp. 175–76.

pope's view of the way in which a late-twelfth-century bishop should function.[36] Had not Gratian himself said that a bishop ought to be solicitous and vigilant concerning the defense of the poor and the relief of the oppressed? Charity, generosity, concern for the welfare of his flock, integrity and honesty in the handling of tithes and alms were just some of the necessary qualities of a bishop. Berengar failed spectacularly to match up! In Innocent's eyes he was the worst of offenders—where his heart should have been, there was instead a purse![37] The Pope's letter of 1200 could not have been more scathing in its condemnation. The natural disasters of the age now seemed to be reflected in the religious disasters afflicting the Church of Narbonne. The depths of adversity were marked there both literally and metaphorically by a weeping and shedding of tears.[38] In the darkness of that province, gold had ceased to shine and bright colors lost their hue. Clergy were afflicted with every variety of misery; people saw bishops as no more than a laughing stock, and the church as a whole, the bride of Christ, was held in contempt and utter derision.[39] Fertile ground indeed for the seeds of heresy!

The cause of all this evil was the Archbishop of Narbonne himself. "He it is whose god is money, who lives by avarice and greed and by extorting money from those who sought his services as archbishop."[40] Had he not quite openly charged the Bishop of Maguelonne 50 shillings for his consecration? What Berengar himself had so freely accepted, he was unwilling to pass on to others in the same way. Such a man, says Innocent, has his heart where his treasure is and loves the sight of gold better than the sun. He is far more concerned with the glory of money than the glory of God. In the ten years since Berengar's election, in the shadow of his great predecessors, the Archbishops of Narbonne, he had not once carried out a visitation of his province nor even of his own parish. Pastoral care for the welfare of his flock had been replaced totally by greed. The pope's order to convene a council was met with contempt.

[36] K. Pennington, *Pope and Bishops: The Papal Monarchy in the Twelfth and Thirteenth Centuries* (Philadelphia: University of Pennsylvania Press, 1984), 48–51; C. Morris, *The Papal Monarchy: The Western Church from 1050-1250* (Oxford: Clarendon Press, 1989), 434.

[37] Cujus mens pecuniae avida ... qui habens cor suum ubi est thesaurus suus. See Jacques de Vitry, *Historia Occidentalis*, 78–79. *PL* 214, cols. 902–5. Cf. P. Baumann, "The Deadliest Sin: Warnings against Avarice and Usury on Romanesque Capitals in Auvergne," *Church History* 59 (1990): 7–18.

[38] *PL* 214, col. 903.

[39] Ibid., col. 904.

[40] Ibid., col. 905. Cujus Deus nummus est et gloria in confusione ejus ... a Magalonensis episcopo pro consecratione sua, solidos[*sic*] quingentos exegit.

Berengar feared neither God nor the Holy See and made no attempt to fulfil the papal mandate.[41]

Further letters reveal Innocent's continuing concern that the bishops in the province of Narbonne still followed their archbishop in their lack of care for the welfare of their flocks. In June 1203, Innocent wrote that the church of Narbonne was still in a state of dereliction.[42] The poor were seeking bread but it was not being broken for them. They died and no one cared. Clearly Berengar was still inactive. On 29 January 1204, Innocent wrote once more in even sterner terms. He reminded the Archbishop that the highest place in God's house was reserved for the gospel injunction to charity.[43] He implored Berengar to feed his sheep before he fed himself. Hunger is still in the land and the poor seek bread, both for the body and the spirit. We have no known reaction from Berengar who was perhaps too old and set in his ways either to understand the message or to wish to implement it. The curse of the miser is very strong![44]

By June 1204, Innocent states that the Church of Narbonne had now been without pastoral care for thirteen years.[45] Heresy was spreading because of Berengar's negligence. That hospitality which was expected from a bishop was not forthcoming, nor were alms being given. Now deposition was threatened. Like a barren tree, Berengar deserved to be uprooted and Innocent prepared to send a mission to the region.[46] As was usual in such missions, the Cistercians were chosen as his agents.[47] At last Berengar reacted, protesting that the legates were going far beyond their papal mandate, chiefly in the accusation of heresy.[48] Innocent's response was to concentrate on only two of the worst sins his archbishop had displayed, namely avarice and negligence.[49] At that Berengar came to Rome to see the Pope, full of excuses, promises, and biblical texts of his own. His favorite seems to have been "let him that is without sin cast the first stone."[50] Innocent, possibly glad to have provoked some sort of response

[41] Ibid., cols. 904–5.

[42] June 29, 1203. *PL* 215, cols. 83–84.

[43] *PL* 15., cols. 272–75. Cf. *PL* 217, Sermones XXVIII and XXIX, cols. 439–50 and esp. col. 450, "Tectum est charitas."

[44] Baumann, "Deadliest Sin," 9–11.

[45] May 28, 1204. PL 215, cols. 355–57.

[46] See May 29, 1204. *PL* 215, cols. 360–61 and 358–60.

[47] Led by Arnald Amaury, Abbot of Cîteaux, Peter of Castelnau and Raoul of Fontefroide. C. Thouzellier, *Catharisme et Valdéisme en Languedoc à la fin du XIIe et au début du XIIIe siècle*, Faculté des lettres et sciences humaines de Paris, Recherches 27 (Paris, 1966); *PL* 215, cols. 360–61.

[48] On November 26, 1204, Berengar appealed against the papal legates. C. Devic and J. Vaissète, *Histoire de Languedoc*, 15 vols. (Toulouse, 1872–1892), 8 (1879): 509–11.

[49] December 6, 1204, *PL* 215, cols. 472–74.

[50] May 9, 1206, *PL* 215, cols. 883–85.

at last, excused Berenger. The pope must have taken into account Berengar's own need for charity. (He was, it seems, very elderly and debilitated). Innocent read him a much-needed homily. Profit should not be financial but measured in souls. Instead of illicit exactions and usurious transactions, generous acts of hospitality and kindness should be shown to pilgrims and the indigent alike.[51] Returning to Narbonne, Berengar's memory apparently failed him, and some eight or ten more fierce letters emanated from Rome until 1211.[52] So lax was the archbishop that his removal became vital for Innocent's program of clerical reform. Innocent's denunciations of Berengar have been called vitriolic by some.[53] Indeed, papal language may have been somewhat overstated to achieve a result. All to little effect. At various times, Innocent attempted more indirect approaches. He encouraged the Poor Catholics, the followers of Durand de Huesca, to carry out acts of charity and mercy in the area centered on the diocese of Elne.[54] Berengar was outraged at such activities within his province, but he did not mend his ways. Indeed, the problem was only finally solved on 12 March 1212 when he was replaced by the Cistercian Arnald Amaury, former abbot of Citeaux.[55] By 1213 the purge had been completed. Not only was Berengar's partner in crime, the Archbishop of Auch, deposed, but the bishops of Frejus Carcassonne, Beziers, Toulouse, Vence and Rodez had also been deprived.[56]

With such forcible stricture of his fellow bishops we must consider how far Innocent's own actions matched up to the need to care for the welfare of the flock. Before so doing, however, we need to see what provisions for charity were made by others, including works of charity and mercy, were an integral part of the Rule of St Benedict.[57] Indeed, Benedict had insisted that the poor and strangers should be received in his monastery "as though each one were Christ himself." The problem for each monastery was how it could continue to perform these functions of welfare and

[51] Sed ... peregrinis et indigentibus largus sit et benignus, ibid., col. 884.

[52] May 29, 1207, *PL* 215, 1164–65; July 5, 1209, *PL* 216, 73–4; ibid., cols. 283–84; ibid., cols. 408–9.

[53] See, e.g., Thouzellier, *Catharisme et Valdéisme*, 243.

[54] *PL* 216, cols. 601–02; P. Biller, "*Curate infirmos*: the Medieval Waldensian Practice of Medicine," *Studies in Church History* 19, (1982): 65–77. The hospital at Elne in Rousillon contained fifty beds where the distressed poor, the sick, orphaned and abandoned children and women in childbirth were tended by men and women observing the common life.

[55] Arnald Amaury, Bishop of Narbonne, March 12, 1212–d. September 29, 1225; C. Eubel, *Hierarchia Catholica Medii Aevi*, (Regensberg, 1893), 1:356.

[56] *PL* 214, cols. 374, 456–58; 215, cols. 272–73, 366–68; 216, cols. 283, 408–9; 217 cols. 159–60.

[57] J. McCann, ed., *The Rule of St. Benedict* (London: Burns & Oats, 1952) 26: 91; A. de Vogue, "Honorer tous les hommes. Le sens de l'hospitalité Bénédictine," in *Revue d'Ascétique et de Mystique* 40 (1964): 129–38.

hospitality without diminishing its practice of the contemplative life, as the numbers of the poor increased and their demands became more insistent.[58] By the twelfth century, the shift of emphasis had occurred, doing little to resolve this tension between contemplation and welfare. This new emphasis was increasingly symbolic, involving alms or maintenance of only a token number of selected poor.[59] The Abbey of Cluny, for example, fed eighteen pensioners, the descendants of the *matricularii*, within the monastery; in addition, it distributed food to seventy-two poor men and women at the gate.[60] On certain days, the Abbey provided one night's shelter to pilgrims and gave them bread and wine for their journey. Most symbolic of all was the ritual of the *mandatum*, the traditional washing by monks of the feet of a few chosen poor men, face to face, in a liturgical setting and especially in the ceremony of Holy Thursday. While monasteries may have ceased to function in the fullest sense as charitable institutions, they did nevertheless often provide houses for the poor and infirmaries for the sick and for lepers just outside their gates. These were regarded to all intents and purposes as part of the monastery, subject to the same liturgical provisions and under the control of the almoner acting there for the abbot. The almoner, *eleemosynarius*, was to be chosen for qualities of genuine compassion, ardent charity, mercy, piety, and sincere care for the welfare of orphans and the disinherited.[61]

This system could break down, especially under the strain of two particular conditions. In times of famine, great crowds of the poor and dispossessed could not be prevented from flocking to any monastery for assistance; for example, in 1197 at Val Saint-Pierre, fifteen hundred people crowded to the door of the almonry each day, queuing overnight before distributions of alms were to be made to ensure that they would be first amongst the beneficiaries.[62] Nor were these poor people all from the peasant classes. Nobles, too, were affected[63]—by the loss of vineyards or lands through the calling in of a mortgage or the exactions of a usurer—

[58] M. Mollat, "Les moines et les pauvres."

[59] M. Rouche, "La Matricule des Pauvres: Evolution d'une institution de charité du Bas Empire jusqu'à la fin du Haut Moyen Age,"*Etudes* 1: 83–110.

[60] W. Witters, "Pauvres et Pauvreté dans les coutumiers monastiques du Moyen Age,"*Etudes* 1:177–215, esp. 205–9; M. Plaudecerf, "La Pauvreté à l'Abbaye de Cluny d'après son cartulaire,"*Etudes* 1:217–27.

[61] *Rule of St. Benedict*, 53:119–23; W. Witters, "Pauvres et Pauvreté," in *Etudes* 1: 196–210.

[62] M. Mollat, "Le problème de la pauvreté au XIIe siècle," in *Cahiers de Fanjeaux*, 2 (1967): 23-63, esp. 26.

[63] G. Ricci, "Naissance du pauvres honteux: entre l'histoire des idées et l'histoire sociale," *Annales: Economies, Sociétés, Civilisations* (1983): 158–77; Idem, "Povertà, vergogna et povertà vergognosa," *Società e Storia* 2 , (1979): 305–37; J. C. Peristiany ed., *Honour and Shame: The Values of Mediterranean Society* (Chicago: University of Chicago Press, 1966).

and the increased presence of nobles or those from the upper levels of society now fallen on hard times seems to have been a particular feature of the 1190s which had to be treated with the utmost sensitivity.

The second condition that frequently placed an additional strain on the whole system of welfare was deeply rooted in the Benedictine Rule that allowed each monastery to have a considerable degree of autonomy.[64] This autonomy was a perpetual source of trouble, as Innocent knew to his cost.[65] In June 1208, in his capacity as Bishop of Rome and hence as local diocesan bishop, he visited the great Benedictine Abbey of Monte Cassino, which guarded the southern approaches to the Papal States.[66] Here he found a most unsatisfactory situation, partially caused by the local autonomy on the election of the abbot. Roffredo, Abbot of Cassino (1190–1209), had to be most seriously reprimanded for not fulfilling his duty of hospitality and almsgiving.[67] He was further accused of misappropriating revenues that should have been used for the benefit of the infirmary. On Roffredo's death his successor, Atenolfo, proved to be precisely in the mold of Archbishop Berengar and was deposed in 1215.[68] Innocent's letter to Cassino in September of that year reveals the chaotic state of monastic discipline and the collapse of all charitable functions.[69] Hospitality that had been withdrawn was to be restored so that the sick and the poor fleeing to this refuge for comfort should receive it there fully. Indeed, anyone who has struggled up this particular mountain (alt. 1,707 ft.) will sympathize with those who had been harshly sent away!

The truth of the matter was that while the numbers of the poor were increasing spectacularly, monasteries were becoming far less useful in providing charity than their more flexible rivals who did not feel the same need for withdrawal from the world. These rivals were Canons Regular

[64] M. Maccarrone, "Primato Romano e Monasteri dal Principio del Secolo XI ad Innocenzo III," in *Istituzioni Monastiche e Istituzioni Canonicali in Occidente (1123-1215)* (La-Mendola–Milan: Vita e Pensiero, 1980), 49–132.

[65] U. Berlière, "Innocent III et les monastères bénédictins,"*Revue Bénédictine* 20-22 (1920): 22-59, 145-159; Bolton, *"Via Ascetica,"*161-191.

[66] *PL* 215, cols. 1593-1600; L. V. Delisle, "Itinéraire d'Innocent III dressé après les actes de ce pontife," in *Bibliothèque de l'Ecole des Chartres* (Paris, 1857), 500–34, esp. 509.

[67] *Rule of St. Benedict:*, chap. 64, pp. 145–49; D. Knowles, *From Pachomius to Ignatius: A Study in the Constitutional History of the Religious Orders* (Oxford; Clarendon, 1966), 6; *PL* 213, col. 168 "... gaudemus plurimum et electionis canonicae apostolicum libente impertimur assensum"; 215, cols. 1593–94; Berlière, "Innocent III et les monastères bénédictins," 149–51.

[68] *PL* 217, cols. 249–53; L. Tosti, *Storia della Badia di Monte Cassino*, 3 vols., (Naples, 1842–1843),2: 289–92.

[69] Tosti, *Badia di Monte Cassino*, 2:289.

living according to the Rule of St. Augustine.[70] One such was Jacques de Vitry, a canon from Liège. Trained in the school of Peter the Chanter in Paris, Jacques de Vitry was particularly well qualified to bring together academic theory and practical charitable activity.[71] This popular preacher and sensitive observer of contemporary religious phenomena chronicles in his *Historia Occidentalis* the quite remarkable expansion of works of charity and assistance on behalf of the sick, the poor, the homeless, travelers, pilgrims, and lepers around 1200.[72] In chapter 29, he describes those hospitals for the poor and leper houses founded in his own day by men and women alike, who had renounced the world and dedicated themselves to the care of the infirm. Indeed, his own spiritual mother, Mary of Oignies, the "new saint" of the diocese of Liège, had worked together with her husband in similar fashion in a leper colony at Willambroux on the River Sambre in Brabant.[73] Jacques de Vitry speaks generally of "hospital religious," who observed the Rule of St. Augustine, wore the religious habit, lived separately and chastely, and observed the canonical hours as often as their ministrations allowed. Clearly, those who organized such hospitals were well on the way to becoming full-fledged religious since they were also required to attend a chapter on faults to regulate discipline. Chaplains were to minister to the poor and sick while those too ill to leave their beds could hear the Divine Office, and be exhorted both to grace and to patience. Confessions were heard on death beds, and extreme unction was dispensed. After death, the poor were buried decently by the religious.[74]

Jacques de Vitry extols these hospital brothers and sisters for acting as the ministers of Christ. It requires, he says, a martyr's courage to overcome natural disgust in the face of the unbearable stench of the sick. These good people are sober and upright, dealing with all bodily needs and bearing filth and squalor in this world for spiritual reward in the next. Yet, realizing the weakness and fragility of human beings, Jacques de Vitry adds as a warning a chapter on the known abuses of certain of these hos-

[70] J. C. Dickinson, *The Origins of the Austin Canons and their Introduction into England* (London: SPCK, 1950); *La Vita Communi del clero nei secoli xi e xii, Miscellanea del Centro di Studi Medioevalii* III, 2 vols. (Milan: Pubblicazioni dell Università Cattolica del Sacro Cuore, 1962); C. W. Bynum, *Docere Verbo et Exemplo: An Aspect of Twelfth Century Spirituality,* Harvard Theological Studies 31 (Missoula, Mont.: Scholars Press, 1979), and idem, *Jesus as Mother: Studies in the Spirituality of the High Middle Ages* (Berkeley: University of California Press, 1982).

[71] Baldwin, *Masters, Princes and Merchants,* 1:137–49. All his sermons are listed in J.B. Pitra, *Analecta Novissima Spicilegii Solesmensis Altera Continuatio* (Tusculum, 1888), 2:344–442.

[72] Hinnebusch, *Historia Occidentalis,* 29: 146–51.

[73] *Vita B. Mariae Oigniacensis,* ed. D. Papebroeck, *Acta Sanctorum,* June IV (Antwerp, 1707), 636–66; B.M. Bolton, *"Vitae Matrum*: A Further Aspect of the *Frauenfrage,"* in *Medieval Women, Studies in Church History,* Subsidia I, ed. D. Baker (London: Blackwell, 1978), 253–273.

[74] Hinnebusch, *Historia Occidentalis,* 147.

pital congregations.[75] Under the cloak of hospitality and piety lurk extortion, deception, and lies. Sometimes those who should care do not do so. They collect alms from the faithful on the pretext of giving to the poor, but instead they profit greatly—rather like crafty merchants or cunning innkeepers. Often, those who themselves give little to the poor, receive much under the pretext of alms. So rich are they reputed to be that they grow richer than hunters. But even worse than that is what Jacques de Vitry identifies as external hypocrisy among those he calls *fratres barbati*, bearded brothers, as well as among hirelings and lying priests. All their charity is performed without faith, mercy or affection. They turn houses of hospitality and piety into robbers' dens, prostitutes' brothels, or synagogues of Jews!

In spite of his fierce criticism of those institutions that had gone astray, Jacques de Vitry could only praise certain other hospital foundations for the ardor of their charity, the unction of their piety, the rigor of their discipline, and their upright and honest dignity. And then he provides the names of the very best of his day: the Hospital of Santo Spirito in Rome, the Hospitals of St. Sampson in Constantinople and SS Anthony and Mary, both at Roncevalles in Navarre, the latter being particularly renowned for its special care of sick pilgrims. Paris and Noyon in the Kingdom of France, Provins in Champagne, Tournai in Flanders, and his own Liege in Lotharingia all deserve a mention.[76] Of these hospitals, that at the very top of this list was Innocent III's own foundation, Santo Spirito in Rome.

Innocent's own caritative works within Rome and the Patrimony are very much in the mainstream of what Jacques de Vitry considers important. While initiating new projects, Innocent never fails to make them relevant to past tradition and to his own obligations and duties as Bishop of Rome. From late antiquity the revenues of the Roman Church were divided into four parts, an arrangement known as the *quadripartitum*.[77] The pope retained one part for himself and distributed the second among his clergy, who in Innocent's case, were those canons who served the Basilica. A third part was assigned for the upkeep of the church and the fourth part for the relief of the poor. Just how much Innocent spent on almsgiving, says his biographer, only God himself knew.[78] Immedi-

[75] See ibid., 148–50 and 282–84, for an extensive bibliography. See also M. Revel, "Le rayonnement à Rome et en Italie de l'Ordre du Saint-Esprit de Montpellier,"*Cahiers de Fanjeaux* 13 (1978): 343– 55; E. D. Howe, *The Hospital of Santo Spirito and Pope Sixtus IV* (New York: Garland, 1978).

[76]See Hinnebusch, *Historia Occidentalis*, 150, 279–284; *PL* 216, col. 217.

[77] A. H. M. Jones, "Church Finance in the Fifth and Sixth Centuries," *Journal of Theological Studies* 11 (1960), 84-94.

[78]*Gesta*, CXLV, cciv-ccv. Quantam vero pecuniam in hoc opus expenderit, novit ille qui nihil ignorat.

ately after his election he set aside as alms for the poor not only their traditional portion but also his own income from offerings made in St. Peter's. Besides this he had one-tenth of his total income set aside for charitable work while from what remained he frequently gave alms generously and secretly. All those alms coming to him as pope were received by the papal almoner for distribution according to "ancient custom." Hence, we are told that he fed the hungry, clothed the naked, found dowries for poor virgins, and cherished abandoned children. He frequently gave money to help monks and poor nuns, recluses and hermits, visiting them personally, and in the case of the nuns, freeing them from debt incurred through no fault of their own. His almoner was instructed to go around and diligently to search out the poor and weak (*pauperes et debiles*). In particular, he was to find the noble poor and give to them a special seal or sign so that those who carried and produced it should each week receive money for food. Again, this provision was in tune with the common attitude of the canonists that the church should mitigate the sense of shame felt by a nobleman who had fallen on hard times. Innocent often spent as much as fifteen pounds each week on the distribution of such alms, not counting those who received a daily dole in food, money, or clothing. Poor children were encouraged to come to the papal table when meals were over and were allowed to eat what remained. In commemoration of Christ himself and in imitation of monastic welfare, the Pope performed the *mandatum pauperum* each Sunday by washing, drying, and kissing the feet of twelve poor men. He then ensured that all were fed and cared for, paying 12 pence to each one.[79]

Innocent's great new hospital on the banks of the Tiber epitomized all the pope's aspirations for social welfare in Rome, linking past and present, tradition and innovation, care of body and of soul. All this was underpinned by the literal imitation of Christ's acts on earth, placing a new emphasis on love of one's neighbor and on the corporal acts of mercy.[80] Innocent's foundation of Santo Spirito brought together all these strands in his thinking on social welfare. Even the site was significant, for the hospital replaced or incorporated the Schola Saxonum or pilgrim hostel for the English nation and utilized the nearby Church of Santa Maria in Sassia (Saxia) where several kings of Wessex lay buried.[81] The hostel, or *zenodochium*, was the responsibility of the bishop of Rome, but by the twelfth

[79] See ibid., CXLIII, cciv–cc; B. M. Bolton, "Daughters of Rome: All One in Christ Jesus!" *Studies in Church History* 27 (1990): 101–15; cf. Witters, "Pauvres et pauvreté," in *Etudes* 1:177–215, esp. 198–205.

[80] R. Brentano, *Rome before Avignon: A Social History of Thirteenth-Century Rome* (London: Longman Group, 1974), 19–21.

century the number of English pilgrims was clearly in decline. In 1163, the deacon of the Saxon School wrote to complain that the income from offerings was falling while scarcely anyone from England, either cleric or layman, could be found to serve in it.[82] By 1200, the *zenodochium* was standing empty and derelict—but ripe for development!

The institutional model for Innocent's hospital came from France. In May 1198, he approved the hospitals of Saint-Esprit in Montpellier, Marseille, and Millau together with two small houses in Rome, one at Santa Maria in Trastevere and the other at S. Agatha to serve pilgrims and travelers entering the city.[83] The rector of the Hospital of Montpellier and the brethren were recognized as *religiosi* who observed the Rule of St. Augustine and were taken into papal protection as an *ordo*. Building may have begun as early as 1201 on the site of the abandoned English school, and it was certainly well under way by 1204.[84] From this association Innocent III found a pretext for inviting King John to contribute to his new hospital.[85] An annual payment of 100 marks was made from the English exchequer and the king was remembered in the necrology of the hospital. Yet alms and donations were collected not only from England but from Montpellier, Italy, Sicily, and Hungary, too.[86] To these donations, Innocent added 1,000 silver marks from his own private fortune. As he writes "the superfluity of wealth which is often gathered together for death can be better used to provide necessities for the poor in life—for it is not beneficial to lay up earthly treasure nor to allow mammon to make enemies out of friends." The Church of Santa Maria in Sassia, he adds, is a particularly suitable place for hospitality and almsgiving "for there, in future time, God willing, the poor and infirm will be received and restored to health and other works of piety made manifest." He and his successor popes witness in Christ Jesus "who is about to come to judge the living and the dead, that this hospital, founded with the goods of the Roman Church and amply endowed, ought to be given special care."[87]

[81] W. Levison, *England and the Continent in the Eighth Century* (Oxford: Clarendon Press, 1946), 39–44.

[82] *Materials for the History of Thomas Becket, Archbishop of Canterbury*, ed. J. C. Robertson, 7 vols., *Rolls Series* 67 (London, 1875-1885), 5 (1881), 64-65.

[83] April 22 and 23, 1198. *Register* 1:95, 97, 139–44; *PL* 214, cols. 83–86.

[84] June 19, 1204. *PL* 215, cols. 376–80.

[85] C.R. Cheney, *Pope Innocent III and England* (Stuttgart: Hiersemann, 1976), 237–38; *Rotuli Chartarum...* 1:1(1199-1216), ed. T. D. Hardy, Record Commission (London, 1837), 123.

[86] Tantum Italia, et Sicilia, et Anglia, et Ungaria. PL 215, col. 378. The bishop of Chartres was also prevailed upon to assign the third part of the income of a prebend to the hospital. Ibid., col. 1334.

[87] *Gesta*, CXLIV, cols. cc-cciii, CXLIX, col. ccxxvii, cols. 377, 380.

A fifteenth-century legend held that Innocent had been the victim of a terrible, punishing dream.[88] Fishermen in the River Tiber were catching in their nets, not fish but instead the bodies of babies unwanted by their sinful mothers. These they placed at Innocent's feet. There was perhaps a grain of truth in this legend for the hospital set out to care for unwanted babies and for orphaned children. A box placed next to the door of the hospital allowed for the depositing of infants at any hour of the day or night. It was clearly understood that no awkward questions would be asked and no names traced afterwards. The hospital also catered to female pilgrims in labor, even providing a series of cradles so that each pilgrim baby might sleep alone.[89] Destitute children were raised by the Sisters of the hospital. Boys were apprenticed to a suitable trade while the girls were provided with marriage dowries unless they proved to have a vocation. Female sinners, many of whom were prostitutes, were admitted during Holy and Easter weeks if they were truly penitent.[90] But this hospital was by no means designed solely for mothers and their babies or for women alone. Once a week, the Brothers of the hospital were instructed to go into the streets and were actively to seek out both male and female infirm paupers so that they might be brought back for nursing and care.

Nothing of Innocent's original hospital building stands today. Destroyed by fire in 1471, it was reconstructed and enlarged between 1473 and 1478 by Sixtus IV.[91] All that remains now is the series of frescoes in the Corsia Sistina of the hospital (nowadays a male geriatric ward) depicting its legendary history and its building, first by Innocent and then by Sixtus IV.

In the city of which he was bishop Innocent was able to care for his flock by direct intervention,[92] but he was well aware that care for bodies went hand-in-hand with care for souls, that there was no real difference between material and spiritual welfare. Nowhere is this more clearly demonstrated than in his Sermo VIII De tempore, composed for the first Sunday after Epiphany, when the text for the day is the marriage feast at Cana (John 2:1–11).[93] On this day, probably 3 January 1208, the image of

[88] P. De Angelis, *L'Architetto e gli affreschi di Santo Spirito in Saxia* (Rome, 1961), 130–134; Lowe, *Hospital of Santo Spirito*, 15–92.

[89] PL 217, 1129–58, esp. chap. LIX, *De cunabulis puerorum*, col. 1148.

[90] Ibid., chap. XLVI, *De peccatricibus suscipiendis*, col. 1146.

[91] Lowe, *Hospital of Santa Spirito*, 15–92.

[92] R. Ambrosi de Magistris, "Il viaggio d'Innocenzo III nel Lazio e il primo Ospedale in Anagni," *Storia e Diritto* 19 (1898): 365–78 provides evidence of a further hospital foundation on August 26, 1208, at Anagni, south of Rome.

[93] *PL* 217, cols. 345–50.

the Veronica[94] was carried processionally in its special reliquary from its home in the Basilica of St. Peter's by the canons there to the hospital on the Tiber.[95] Not only did this dramatic representation of Christ signify his willingness to suffer for all people, but it also acknowledged the role of Veronica, who was herself poor, the servant and maid of the Virgin Mary.[96] While the hospital of Santo Spirito represented Innocent's practical concern for the sick and poor, for those who suffered and for pilgrims, so its association with this venerable and precious image was formalized by the creation of a new liturgical station in which the Pope himself was to play the central part, delivering this exhortatory sermon on works of piety and welfare.[97]

Innocent exhorts his audience to consider the threefold marriage of faith, youth, and sacrament, all of which were to be found in the care provided by his new hospital. As the marriage at Cana represented the joining of flesh and spirit, so zeal of charity is united with love of salvation, converting men from error to charity and from vice to virtue.The wine at the feast represents charity, flowing freely at first as does charity in the first flush of its enthusiasm. When the wine begins to run out, then charity grows cold and requires reawakening with a sermon of instruction and exhortation. The miracle of the best wine coming last shows that "charity never fails" (1 Cor. 13:8). The six jars at the feast represent the six corporal works of mercy commended by Christ: feeding the hungry, giving drink to those who thirst, caring for the guest or traveler or the sick or those in prison, and clothing the naked. The jars are made of stone to represent firmness and each jar may contain double or triple measure. Food and drink can be given in three ways: the material, as natural food; the sacramental, through the eucharist; and the doctrinal, through the writings of scripture. The sick may be tended to in two ways, in heart and in body; likewise, the prisoner and the guest. When charitable works are perfectly carried out, the jar is filled to the brim and water transformed into wine. At the marriage feast, continues Innocent, the bridegroom is the Holy Spirit; the bride is grace; Jesus, the Divine Sermon; his disciples, honest habits; the Mother of Jesus, the catholic faith; the master who presides at the feast is reason, which rules amongst the natural virtues of the spirit.

[94]Or Veronica's veil, a relic said to be a cloth that a woman used to wipe the face of Jesus on his way to Calvary, which retained the print of his face.

[95]S.J.P. Van Dijk and J. Hazelden Walker, *The Origins of the Modern Roman Liturgy* (London, 1960), 102–3, 460–61. See also my "Advertize the Message: Images in Rome at the Turn of the Twelfth Century,"*Studies in Church History* 28 (1991).

[96]E. Delaruelle, "Le problème de la pauvreté vu par les théologiens et les canonistes dans la deuxième moitié du xii siècle,"*Cahiers de Fanjeaux* 2 (Toulouse, 1967): 48–63, esp. 62.

[97]*Gesta* CXLIV, cols. cci-ccii.

Cana of Galilee is the conversion of sinners, and the third day is the time of grace. Water is mercy, wine is charity. The six jars are the corporal works of mercy and the ministers who administer these are liberality and happiness. Water becomes wine when the effect of mercy gives shape to the gift of charity. The heretic, too, begins with good wine that is sound doctrine or an honest way of life—but when he has made men drunk, then they are led astray by the disease of error or the ferment of evil in the poor wine.[98] This was the first miracle of Jesus in Cana of Galilee when he justified the impious, converted evil, and won back the sinner—and on account of this his disciples believed in him.

Innocent concludes his sermon by referring to the liturgical station which he has instituted at Santo Spirito, making his hospital just such a place as Cana, where vices are transformed into virtues, where the corporal works of mercy are performed in all their fullness, where the mother of Jesus is to be found, in whose honor the church is dedicated. At the Station of the Veronica the Virgin finds her son whose effigy is carried with reverence to the hospital so that the faithful may wonder at his glory, having come together to celebrate the marriage of piety and mercy. Lest any should leave hungry from the feast, all are to celebrate liberally, joyfully, and healthily, and shall receive one full year in remission of their sins.[99] As a spectacular gesture, one thousand poor pilgrims together with three hundred poor from the surrounding area were each to receive three pence taken from the papal treasury—one for bread, one for meat and the third for wine.

Innocent's vision of the *vita apostolica* included love of one's neighbor in every sense. He combined this with a traditional function of the bishop of Rome, that of arranging for the ransoming of captives from their enemies and their subsequent welfare. He was to give many reminders throughout his pontificate of those thousands of Christians held by the Saracens, in prison or in slavery on the galleys of the Mediterranean.[100] He made frequent exhortations that every possible effort should be made to liberate them. In Rome on December 17, 1198, Innocent had approved the Order of Trinitarians.[101] Its founder, John de Matha, had come from Marseille, where a similar organization already existed for the redemption

[98] *PL* 217, cols. 346–50.

[99] *Gesta*, CXLIV, cols. cc-cciii; Brentano, *Rome before Avignon*, 19–21.

[100] P. Deslandres, *L'Ordre des Trinitaires pour le rachat des Captifs*, 2 vols. (Toulouse-Paris, 1903); "Islam et chrétiens du Midi (XIIe-XIVe siècle)," *Cahiers de Fanjeaux* 18 (1983).

[101] *Register* I, 481, 703-708; *PL* 214, cols. 444–49.

of Christian slaves in Moslem captivity.[102] One-third of all the order's revenues was used to pay for suitable ransoms or exchanges of captured Christians. Another third was used in the order's hospitals for the rehabilitation and care of these former prisoners, while the last third was used to maintain the brothers of the order, who lived according to the Rule of St. Augustine. In 1199, Innocent wrote to Miramolino, the Almohad caliph of Morocco, to commend those Trinitarian brothers sent to ransom prisoners.[103] By 1209 he speaks of the Order's influence as extending "from sea to sea."[104] In that year, the founder of the Trinitarians, John de Matha, retired to become a hermit in the Claudian Aqueduct by the Arch of Dolabella on the Celian Hill, where he remained until his death in 1213.[105] Legend held that he had a vision—of Christ himself holding by his two hands a couple of slaves, one black and one white, both manacled and in fetters. A mosaic of this vision dated 1210 above the gateway of the monastery of San Tommaso in Formis and enclosing the hermit's cell must have arrested the attention of Romans and pilgrims alike. Here was another highly practical and valuable example of charity and welfare, the idea of ransom already well known to Gregory the Great, but updated by Innocent to the realities of the early thirteenth century. Now he turned the minds of all Christians towards the plight of captives and of fellow Christians suffering in the East, exhorting them to perform their charitable responsibilities. He did not seek a totally new system to relieve poverty and suffering; instead, he showed that he was prepared to go to great lengths to support orders like the Trinitarians who were so eager to share in the sufferings of others.

Yet, in spite of all this good work, Innocent himself was not immune from criticism. Indeed, he was frequently parodied in savage terms, quite similar to those he had used against Berengar of Narbonne. The avidity of many churchmen for power, honor, and riches was a constant theme of contemporary satirists. The Roman Church in particular was the object of bitter hatred and scandal on account of its alleged venality and voracious appetite for money. The *Gospel according to the Silver Mark*, a Goliard poem and a frightful—even blasphemous—parody of a sacred text, was an explicit denunciation of all popes up to this time.[106] A particular feature

[102] G. Cipollone, *Studi intorno a Cerefroid, prima casa dell'ordine trinitario (1198-1429), Ordinis Trinitatis Institutum Historicum*, Series prior, I (Rome: Gregorian University, 1978); idem, *La Casa della Santa Trinità di Marsiglia (1202-1547)*, Series prior 2 (Vatican City: Typis polyglottis Vaticanis, 1981).

[103] March 8, 1199. *Der Register Innocenz III, 2 Jahrgang (1190-1200)*, O. Hagender, W. Maleczek and A. Strand, eds. (Rome-Vienna: Abteilung für Historische Studien des Österreichischen Kulturinstituts in Rom, 1979) 9, 16–17; *PL* 214, col. 544.

[104] June 21, 1209,Cipollone, *La Casa della Santa Trinità*, 206–7.

[105] Brentano, *Rome before Avignon*, 14-15.

[106] A. Hilka and O. Schumann, *Carmina Burana, Die Moralisch-Satirischen Dichtungen* (Heidelberg: Winter, 1930): 86.

of much of this satirical writing was its constant reference to biblical texts: the avarice of Gehazi, servant to the Prophet Elisha (2 Kings 4:17–37, 5:20–27) and of Simon Magus (Acts 8:9–24) were especially prominent.

One such anonymous satire, dating from the first quarter of the thirteenth century, Lombard in origin, accused Innocent of precisely those charges of avarice and negligence which he had levied against Berengar. Now, though, it is Innocent's turn to be portrayed as the hireling of the Gospels, who runs from the sheep only to allow the ravaging of the flock (in this case by the growth of heresy). This "new Solomon" reigns in evil times, when all is subordinated to venality. He is no better than the others; indeed, he is far worse precisely because of the position he holds. He rarely observes the Sabbath, caring more for the profit and glory of justice than for the welfare of his people. Such impiety is even more serious when it masquerades as piety. One who calls upon others to bark but does not do so himself is revealed as the shepherd caught out in crime while his sheep are massacred by ravaging wolves. Through his acts, Rome *caput mundi* is irreparably stained and blemished.[107] While established laws and principles have perished in the fire or are fused into the gold of avarice, the church has ceased to care for the faithful. Now it is openly said that Rome "bites the hand that feeds it." The Bishop of Rome is powerless, tossed around like an anchorless ship in a huge storm. When the sinner has sinned, money steps in to wipe away the crime and thus fills Innocent's own purse—although the satirist does not tell us in what part of the papal anatomy we might find this purse. (Innocent was far more specific about Berengar!) Peter, once the peaceful fisherman of souls, is now the predatory hunter, avid for their money.

Such satire is particularly biting as it cleverly echoes the words and phrases that Innocent himself often used. The pope's anonymous biographer was quick to retort to such criticism by showing how Innocent earnestly considered the best means by which avarice could be extirpated. We know from another source, the Collection of Vatican Bulls addressed to the Canons of St. Peter's, that in April 1212 Innocent seems to have been forced to make a quite unprecedented, deliberate, and very public denial of the appalling accusation that he, the pope, was appropriating for his own use those alms given at the high altar and at the tomb of St. Peter.[108] Clearly the criticism, however untrue, hit its mark. Characteristically, after explaining carefully where the money did go, Innocent's final reply

[107] M. T. d'Alverny, "Novus regnat Salomon in diebus malis: Un satire contre Innocent III" in *Festschrift Bernhard Bischoff*, ed. J. Autenrieth and F. Brunholz (Stuttgart:A. Hiersemann, 1971), 372–90; Bibliothèque Nationale, Paris, Ms. Lat. 3236A, fol. 84.

[108] April 24, 1212. *Bullarum Sacrosanctae Basilicae Vaticanae*, 1: 96–97.

to his critics was that God himself would "recognize the lies of these guilty men at the Day of Judgment."

In conclusion, it must be said that the pragmatic nature of Innocent's approach to problems—involving as it did the need for "realism" in achieving what was best for the Church—could often be misunderstood. More than a tinge of hypocrisy can always be found in an office which has to be both political and spiritual.[109] If we examine Innocent's approach to welfare, a series of apparent contradictions, consistent in their inconsistencies, might well appear to a casual or biased observer. This could have been a fatal flaw in his caritative program. But to those who have some understanding of the way of Christ in a fallen world where evil has to be faced, Innocent's approach to welfare may be appreciated as a most successful spiritual activity in a political office.

In considering some of these apparent contradictions, I mention first Innocent's support for the ideal of monastic poverty as the way to achieve salvation. This is matched by his insistence on the need for all such religious institutions to achieve solvency through financial competence.[110] Here, money and no money at all are used in the same breath. He does so because he knows from observation and personal experience that insolvency leads to spiritual decadence, with all that that entails. His decretal *Cum ad Monasterium* of February 1203, with its very firm statement, applauds the sound basis of communal property found in many monasteries but deplores an individual monk's possession of private property, utterly condemned by St. Benedict himself in his Rule and which, as Innocent says "not even the pope himself has the right to abrogate."[111] Innocent thus supported financial rectitude at all times and most especially in the monasteries.

Innocent presents a similar attitude about alms to the poor. We have already seen that in his first treatise Innocent considers the blessedness of almsgiving, yet he is quick to warn against what has been called "the false cloak of destitution," which could mean that those in receipt of alms were content to live a life of perpetual comfort.

He is at pains to point out that the cry of the poor must always be heard but he is also insistent that any answer to such a cry must require that the gospel is preached to them so that they may be fed in spirit as well as in body. Further, he was equally aware that the message of salvation

[109]For a pertinent insight into this problem in a slightly earlier period see J. Anderson and E. T. Kennan, *Five Books on Consideration: Advice to a Pope* (Bernard of Clairvaux), Cistercian Fathers' Series 13 (Kalamazoo: Cistercian Publications, 1976), 16–17.

[110]Bolton, "Via Ascetica," 177–179.

[111]*Corpus Juris Canonici*, ed. A. Friedburg, 2 vols. (Leipzig, 1879), 2: Decretal of Gregory IX,3: *De statu monachorum et canonicorum regularum*, 35, 6, cols. 599–600; *PL* 214, cols. 1064–66; *Chronicon Sublacense 593-1369*, Muratori, 24, VI, ed. R. Morghen (Bologna, 1927), 34–37.

was a mission to individuals, which could become overenthusiastic and unrealistic in its demands. Innocent's solution was usually to form an order or to approve an existing institution of *religiosi* to protect such individuals from the wiles of the Devil. It was in just this spirit that he could enable the new mendicant orders to play their vital role in spite of the strong current of belief among the hierarchy that no such new orders were necessary. It is interesting to conjecture whether St. Francis, with his life of poverty and charity, and St. Dominic, with his immeasurable strengthening of the faith through teaching, would ever have achieved such prominence in the history of the Church without that significant oiling of the wheels on their behalf by Innocent. His pragmatic approach to the welfare of the flock within Christ's church was crucial for future development but it brought him considerable criticism. Like Berengar of Narbonne but with much less reason, he was charged with letting his purse distract him from his duty. Yet, in Innocent's far-reaching approach to social welfare, epitomized by that evocative Baby Box by the Tiber, there can be absolutely no doubt that his heart was in the correct part of his anatomy!

The Baby Box at the Hospital of Santo Spirito
(Photographs: Brenda Bolton.)

# XIX

## 'RECEIVED IN HIS NAME': ROME'S BUSY BABY BOX

INNOCENT III, a proud and learned Roman pope, was well acquainted with the history and literature of the Rome of earlier days.[1] He would have been aware of the prophecy given by Virgil in the *Aeneid* that when the foaming Tiber appeared to run as a river of blood disaster was foretold.[2] In his own day the River Tiber gave him a clear message of a real disaster actually taking place. Far too frequently the fishermen of Rome drew in their nets only to find not a harvest of fish, but the tiny corpses of babies. These had been thrown naked to meet their deaths in the waters of the Tiber. Rome, of course, was by no means a stranger to the problem of abandoned babies. The great legend of the City's origins with the suckling of the babes who were to become its eventual founders was given a daily reminder since, under the portico of the Lateran Palace, was the famous bronze statue of the *Lupa* or *She-Wolf*.[3] In spite of the serious damage caused by a thunderbolt in Antiquity, which had left the Wolf's feet broken and destroyed the group of the twins,[4] the 'Mother of the Romans', as she was known, had come to represent papal jurisdiction over Rome, as well as the nourishing of its children.[5] The River Tiber had always been available for

[1] *Sermo XXII in solemnitate D. Apostolorum Petri et Pauli*, *PL* 217, cols 555–8. M. Maccarrone, 'Innocenzo III, prima del pontificato', *Archivio della Società Romana di Storia Patria*, 20 (1942), pp. 3–78, at p. 16, n. 6, 'Troviamo citazioni di Orazio, Ovidio, Giovenale, Severino Boezio'.

[2] Virgil, *Aeneid*, book vi, lines 86–8; compare Enoch Powell's speech at Birmingham, 21 April 1968, 'I am filled with foreboding. Like the Roman, I seem to see the River Tiber foaming with much blood.'

[3] C. Dulière, *Lupa Romana: Recherches d'iconographie et essai d'interpretation* (Brussels, 1979), pp. 21–43; Master Gregory, *The Marvels of Rome*, ed. and tr. John Osborne (Toronto, 1987), pp. 36, 96–7; P. Borchardt, 'The sculpture in front of the Lateran as described by Benjamin of Tudela and Master Gregorius', *Journal of Roman Studies*, 26 (1936), pp. 68–70.

[4] R. Krautheimer, *Rome: Profile of a City, 312–1308* (Princeton, 1980), pp. 192–7; A. Venturi, 'Romolo e Remo di Antonio Pollaiolo nella lupa capitolina', *L'Arte*, 22 (1919), pp. 133–5; R. Schofield, 'Giovanni da Tolentino goes to Rome: a description of the antiquities of Rome in 1490', *Journal of the Warburg and Courtauld Institutes*, 43 (1980), pp. 246–56.

[5] *PL* 217, col. 557, 'ubi duo fratres . . . Remus et Romulus, qui urbem istam corporaliter condiderunt . . . ibi duo fratres . . . Petrus et Paulus . . . civitatem istam suis patrociniis tucantur'.

the disposal of the many unwanted infants. Why, then, should the macabre catch of the fishermen of his time have been received by Innocent III as a matter in need of his most urgent attention? It might have been that there were more babies than usual. Population pressure was affecting Rome, and, as elsewhere, social problems were increasing with consequent effects on newborn children.[6] What evidence then can be found to link Innocent with Rome's Baby Box as a way of remedying such a dreadful situation?

The Hospital of Santo Spirito is the starting-point. In his papal role and even earlier, through curial responsibilities, Innocent was aware of the need for new large hospitals, which were required by the populations of the growing towns. The Hospital of the Order of St John in Jerusalem provided the outstanding model.[7] Before 1187, some 2,000 sick male and female pilgrims were being taken in annually and cared for within its compound.[8] As Lotario, Cardinal-Deacon of SS Sergio e Bacco, Innocent had personally witnessed the granting of privileges to a European-based hospital of the Order of St John at Sigena on 3 June 1193, which followed the hospital model provided by Jerusalem.[9] The *maisons-Dieu* in France were also similarly influenced.[10] One such was at Montpellier. There Innocent's attention was particularly caught by the Hospital of Saint-Esprit, founded in about 1174, by Guy of Montpellier at Pyla-Saint-Gely, close by the city walls.[11]

[6] John Boswell, '*Expositio* and *Oblatio*: the abandonment of children and the ancient and medieval family', *AHR*, 89 (1984), pp. 10–33, and *The Kindness of Strangers: the Abandonment of Children in Western Europe from Late Antiquity to the Renaissance* (New York, 1988), esp. pp. 322–63. Compare Richard B. Lyman Jnr, 'Barbarism and Religion: Late Roman and early Medieval Childhood', in Lloyd de Mause, ed., *The History of Childhood* (London, 1976), pp. 75–100, and S. Shahar, *Childhood in the Middle Ages* (London, 1990).

[7] J. Delaville le Roulx, ed., *Cartulaire général de l'Ordre des Hospitaliers de St Jean de Jérusalem (1100–1310)*, 4 vols (Paris, 1894–1906) [hereafter *Cartulaire*]; J. Riley-Smith, *The Knights of St John in Jerusalem and Cyprus c. 1050–1310* (London, 1967); Jean Richard, 'Hospitals and Hospital Congregations in the Latin Kingdom during the first period of the Frankish Conquest', in *Outremer: Studies in the History of the Crusading Kingdom of Jerusalem*, ed. B. Z. Kedar, H. E. Meyer and R. C. Smail (Jerusalem, 1982), pp. 89–100.

[8] John of Würzburg, *Descriptiones Terrae Sanctae ex saeculo VIII, IX, XII et XV*, ed. T. Tobler (Leipzig, 1874), p. 159; Timothy S. Miller, 'The Knights of Saint John and the Hospitals of the Latin West', *Speculum*, 53 (1978), pp. 709–33.

[9] *Cartulaire*, 1, 947, pp. 598–9.

[10] Louis Le Grand, 'Les Maisons-Dieux, leurs statuts au xiii siècle', *Revue des questions historiques*, 40 (1896), pp. 95–134.

[11] P. Brune, *Histoire de l'Ordre Hospitalier du Saint-Esprit* (Lons-le-Saunier-Paris, 1892); A. Fliche, 'La

In a letter of 22 April 1198, Innocent praised Guy's foundation, which 'shone out' like a star amongst the new hospitals.[12] It was an outstanding example of piety and the exercise of hospitality through the distribution of alms. The Pope had heard 'from the lips of many' that there 'the hungry were fed, the poor clothed, the sick cared for'. There, too, the Gospel was preached. The abundance of consolation given so much more than matched the misery suffered that the Master and brothers of the hospital were 'not just the protectors of these unfortunates but also their servants'. In recognition of their devotion the Pope specially empowered the brothers of Saint-Esprit to erect oratories and cemeteries. He also ordered local bishops not to hinder in any way the 'pious liberalities' of the faithful on behalf of the hospital. On the following day, 23 April, the bull *Religiosam vitam* took the hospital into papal protection and confirmed Guy's profession to the religious life.[13] The status of an *ordo* was given both to Guy and to his brothers, so that henceforth they were able to live according to a form of rule, *secundum rationabiles institutiones*. Other houses belonging to this new *ordo* were listed as Millau, Clapier, Mèze, Brioude, Barjac, Largentière, Marseille, and Troyes to the north. Beyond the Alps, in Rome itself, were two more—the hospice across the Tiber, next to S. Maria in Trastevere, and S. Agatha *in introitu urbis Rome*. All these were to be subject to the authority of the head of the Order at Montpellier.

Bearing these examples in mind, the site chosen by Innocent for his Roman hospital foundation was to be that of the abandoned Saxon School, with its associations as the former pilgrim hostel for the English nation.[14] He also utilized the nearby church of S. Maria in Saxia, where several kings of Wessex were

vie réligieuse à Montpellier sous le pontificat d'Innocent III (1198–1216)', *Mélanges Louis Halphen* (Paris, 1951), pp. 217–24; M. Revel, 'Le rayonnement à Rome et en Italie de l'ordre du Saint-Esprit de Montpellier', in *Cahiers de Fanjeaux*, 13, *Assistance et charité*, ed. M.-H. Vicaire (Toulouse, 1978), pp. 343–55; B. Rano, 'Ospitalieri di Santo Spirito', *Dizionario degli Istituti di Perfezione*, 6 (Rome, 1980), cols 994–1014.

[12] O. Hageneder and A. Haidacher eds, *Die Register Innocenz' III*, Band I, *Pontifikatsjahr 1198/99* (Graz and Cologne, 1964), 95, pp. 139–40 [hereafter *Register*]; *PL* 214, cols 83–4; *Regesta pontificium Roman – orum inde ab. a post Christum natum 1198 ad 1304*, ed. A. Potthast, 2 vols (Berlin, 1874–5, repr. Graz, 1957) [hereafter Potthast], I, p. 96.

[13] *Register* I, 97, pp. 141–4; *PL* 214, cols 85–6; Potthast I, 102.

[14] W. Levison, *England and the Continent in the Eighth Century* (Oxford, 1946), pp. 39–44.

buried. This *zenodochium* had been Innocent's responsibility as Bishop of Rome, and so prime a site could not be allowed to remain under-utilized for long.[15] Since before the beginning of Innocent's pontificate, the *Schola Saxonum* had stood derelict and ripe for development.[16] With characteristic enterprise, Innocent proceeded to gather resources for the foundation of his hospital. In November 1201, Renaud de Bar, Bishop of Chartres (1182–1217), was persuaded to donate the third part of a prebend from his church to the hospital.[17] In addition, Innocent's letter *Cupientes proplurimis*, of 10 December 1201,[18] led to the acquisition by the new hospital of property which had formerly belonged to S. Maria in Saxia, consisting of various lands and churches.

On 19 June 1204,[19] a detailed and eloquent preface set out what Innocent believed to be the aim and purpose of his hospital. These were those corporeal works of mercy which would be particularly rewarded on the Day of Judgement: feeding the hungry; giving drink to those who thirst; welcoming homeless strangers; clothing the naked; visiting captives in prison, and helping those who have suffered during their lifetime. The brothers of the hospital were not to be content merely to visit the sick, but they were also to provide material care for all those unfortunates, including abandoned children. Like Abraham and Lot, the brothers felt that, in so doing, they would have the honour of giving hospitality to the angels.[20] The benefits of hospitality are listed, together with the need for the renunciation of riches, which might otherwise lead to perdition: all an admirable exchange—the perishable goods of this world in return for the eternal goods of the next. On behalf, therefore, of his predecessors, of his successors, and of the cardinals, Innocent announced the building of the Hospital of Santo Spirito. It was to be a most favoured place for the exercise of hospitality, so that

[15] P. de Angelis, *L'Ospedale di Santo Spirito in Saxia*, 2 vols, 1. *Dalle origini al 1300*; 2. *Dal 1301 al 1500* (Rome, 1960–2).

[16] J. C. Robertson, ed., *Materials for the History of Thomas Becket, Archbishop of Canterbury*, 7 vols, *RS* (London, 1875–85), 5 (1881), pp. 64–5.

[17] De Angelis, *Santo Spirito*, 1, pp. 379–80; *PL* 215, col. 1334, 11 November 1207. Compare *Cum vacetis operibus*, 14 June 1217, cited by De Angelis, *Santo Spirito*, 1, p. 211.

[18] Ibid., 1, pp. 211–14, 380–1.

[19] *PL* 215, col. 380.

[20] Ibid., col. 377.

the poor might be received, the sick tended, and other works of charity performed.[21]

To ensure that the spiritual administration of the hospital was adequately carried out, at least four clerics professed by the Order were always to be in attendance. Santo Spirito was given primacy in the Order and was joined to Saint-Esprit in Montpellier. Guy, named as its Master, was to rule the two foundations on either side of the Alps and was to visit both annually.[22] Provision was made that any future election would depend upon whether Guy died in Rome or in Montpellier.[23] The task of the Master was to manage the finances of the foundations, and he was entrusted with the entire spiritual administration, being responsible only to the pope.[24]

Innocent's Rule for Santo Spirito must have undergone several revisions.[25] The primitive text, part of which is dated to 1213, is associated with two cardinals, Stephen, Cardinal-Deacon of S. Adriano (1216–28) and later Cardinal-Priest of S. Maria in Trastevere (1228–54)[26] and Rainier of Viterbo, Cardinal-Deacon of S. Maria in Cosmedin (1216–50).[27] Stephen was none other than Innocent's own nephew, the son of his brother Richard.[28] He was close to his uncle and had accompanied him on the preaching campaign for the Fifth Crusade in the summer of 1216.[29] Innocent's design for the hospital and its future implementation could not therefore have been left in safer hands. Stephen and Rainier were entrusted with subsequent compilations of the hospital's Rule, possibly between 1228 and 1250. The wisdom they showed in organization and reform at Santo Spirito led to them being used on another occasion by Gervase, Abbot of Premontré, in the matter of S. Maria *de Parvo Ponte* at Brindisi.[30]

21 Compare Luke 7. 22.

22 *Bullarium diplomatum et privilegiorum Sanctorum Romanorum Pontificium*, 3, ed. F. Gaude (Turin, 1858), pp. 320–3, for Honorius III's Bull of 13 May 1217 dissolving this union.

23 *PL* 215, cols 378–80.

24 Ibid., cols 1270–1 and 1424.

25 *PL* 217, cols 1129–58.

26 W. Maleczek, *Papst und Kardinalskolleg von 1191 bis 1216* (Vienna, 1984), pp. 195–201.

27 Ibid., pp. 184–9.

28 M. Dykmans, 'D'Innocent III à Boniface VIII. Histoire des Conti et des Annibaldi', *Bulletin de l'Institut historique belge de Rome*, 45 (1975), pp. 19–211, especially 44–6.

29 M. Maccarrone, *Studi su Innocenzo III Italia Sacra* 17 (Padua, 1972), pp. 8–9, 135–8.

30 C. L. Hugo, *Sacrae antiquitatis monumenta* (Etival, 1725), Letter XXII, pp. 26–7, 'per litteras vestras

Out of the 105 articles of the Rule followed by the brothers at both hospitals, more than one-third have since been identified as literal borrowings from the Rule of the Hospital of St John at Jerusalem.[31] It seems possible, therefore, that the primitive Rule of Saint-Esprit and Santo Spirito was an adaptation of that of St John well before the early thirteenth century. The two or three chapters of the original Rule referring specifically to children are most relevant. Chapter 41, *De orphanis nutriendis et feminis praegnantibus*,[32] simply states that abandoned children, *proiecti*, will be looked after by the hospital, whilst pregnant female paupers will be freely received into its care. Chapter 59, *De cunabulis puerorum*,[33] applies to a slightly different group of children, this time those born in the hospital to female pilgrims. These children were to be placed in individual cradles so that they could sleep alone, lest any accident by overlaying or crushing occurred. Renaud, Bishop of Chartres, is the link here. He seems to have been aware of the little cradles provided at the hospital in Jerusalem by the Statutes of Roger des Molins in 1182[34] and could well have been the driving force behind their introduction at Santo Spirito.[35]

Evidence on the founding and work of the Hospital of Santo Spirito can be deduced by the study of a series of frescos still existing in the hospital itself.[36] These draw attention to Innocent III's connection with the babes drowned in the Tiber. They are to be found in the Corsia Sistina, a vast hall of more than 350 feet in length, which is the largest ward of the hospital. The walls of the Corsia Sistina, named after Sixtus IV (1471–84), who rebuilt it about 1471–5, are decorated with a double row of frescos by Antonio da Viterbo (*c.* 1476). These show the relationship between the foundation of the hospital and papal patronage. It is a narrative cycle, depicting both the historic growth and day-by-

quas in hac parte multum esse efficaciam habituras'; A. De Leo, *Codice Diplomatico Brindisino*, I (492–1299), pp. 62–3, 70–2.

[31] Le Grand, 'Les Maisons-Dieux', pp. 105–6.

[32] *PL* 217, col. 1146.

[33] Ibid. col. 1148.

[34] 14 March 1182, 'Cet si establi que petiz bers fucent fait por les enfans des femes pelerines qui naissent en la maison, si que il gisent à une part soul, et que li enfant alaitant n'en aient aucun ennui por le mesaise de lor mere', *Cartulaire*, p. 426.

[35] Ibid., p. 719, for the meeting of 1185 between Renaud de Bar and Roger des Molins at Chartres.

[36] Eunice D. Howe, *The Hospital of Santo Spirito and Pope Sixtus IV* (Baltimore, 1978).

day work of the institution. The fresco cycle records three aspects which are relevant to the babes in the river. As was to be expected, the contemporary patron, Sixtus IV, is well to the fore, but also, and naturally of considerable interest, are the three representations of the hospital's first founder, Innocent III.[37] On the east wall is the particular depiction which suggests his link with the babes. It had been placed by Antonio da Viterbo in a position accessible to the widest conceivable range of visitors at the time. This central position indicates that, of all the fresco stories, this was the one with a message in constant need of reiteration, namely, that succour was to be given to the innocent victims of sin. This important fresco, set by the Tiber, shows a group of mothers engaged in infanticide by throwing into the river their unclothed and unwanted offspring. Obviously the time which elapsed between the delivery of the babies and their deposition in the Tiber needed to be minimal and so was often done in the full light of day. A second scene depicts two fishermen drawing in their net with its catch of three drowned babies. The fishermen are shown using their creels to carry the corpses to the Pope. Innocent throws up his hands in horror at being so confronted. His distraught countenance and upraised hands display his abhorrence at what is before him. It surely must have been so horrible as to disturb his sleep, and he may have recalled an earlier vision in one of his dreams.[38] This is also depicted by Antonio da Viterbo. Innocent is told by an angel to erect a hospital on the banks of the Tiber. The Pope responds, and in a subsequent scene is shown riding up on his white horse to inspect the progress of the building works.

The next stage of the search for evidence is best undertaken with the help of Professor Bergami, the current Hospital Administrator.[39] When prevailed upon he will show with pride the evidence of the founding Pope's charitable concern for children in general and his practical solution to the problem of the *expositi*, the abandoned infants. Set into the wall, just to the left of the main entrance to the hospital, is the Rota Box, a rotating turntable with an iron grille through which a small, newly-born

[37] Ibid., pp. 336–41.
[38] Ibid., p. 201.
[39] My gratitude to Professor Bergami for privileged visits on 24 September 1988 and 29 September 1990.

baby might be inserted.[40] The baby, instead of being drowned or abandoned, thus ended up on a little mattress in the box behind the grille, placed there for its safe reception to face its life in the world. The sound of the Rota turning or the child crying—or most likely both—often alerted an attendant, who would collect the child, without being aware of the identity of the person or persons who had deposited it through the grille. The Baby Box is certainly there today. It was certainly there in the time of Sixtus IV, when the hospital was rebuilt, but any attempt to link the first box to Innocent III can be met only with the most tenuous evidence. However attractive the possibility might be, the connection between the Box and the Pope was largely a legend which the fifteenth century certainly played to the full, with little regard to the evidence.[41]

The legend seems to have been already widely disseminated before the fifteenth century.[42] A specific manuscript decoration from at least the late thirteenth or early fourteenth century associated Innocent III with the hospital. The *Book of the Rule* or *Liber Regulae*,[43] from about 1290 to 1320, is a superb codex of 248 folios, containing more than fifty miniatures.[44] Amongst these are several representing the legendary facts which induced Innocent to found the hospital—the macabre catch in the Tiber, the Pope's dream, and the angel's revelation. These were currently the beliefs of 1386, when Jacob Twinger of Königshofen attributed the foundation of the hospital to Innocent's desire to prevent the killing of unwanted infants.[45] In the mid-fifteenth century, Philip III the Good, Duke of Burgundy (1419–67), commissioned a series of twenty-two miniatures to commemorate the foundation of the Hospital of Saint-Esprit at Dijon, about 1204, by his predecessor, Duke Odo III (1193–1218).[46]

[40] Brune, *Saint-Esprit*, p. 288.

[41] Ibid., p. 38, 'il paraît avoir frappé bien vivement l'imagination populaire car sa fondation finit par revêtir le charactère d'une légende aux traits merveilleux.'

[42] Howe, *Santo Spirito*, p. 203.

[43] Rome, Archivio di Stato, MS 3193; A. Canezza, *Liber Regulae Hospitalis S. Spiritus in Saxia de Urbe*, IV Congresso Internationale degli Ospedali, 19–26 Maggio 1935, XIII (Rome, 1936); A. F. La Cava, *Liber Regulae S. Spirito, Studi di storia della medicina*, 6 (Milan, 1946).

[44] Canezza, *Liber Regulae*, pp. 7–8.

[45] Jacob Twinger, *Strassburger Chronik* (Strasbourg, 1871), p. 569.

[46] Dijon, Archives of Saint-Esprit, A4; G. Peignot, 'Histoire de la fondation des Hôpitaux du Saint-Esprit de Rome et de Dijon', *Memoires de la Commission des Antiquités du Department de la Côte-d'Or*, 1 (1838), pp. 17–70.

The first ten miniatures from Dijon depict the same sequence of events as for the founding of the Hospital of Santo Spirito—from sinful mothers tossing their babies into the Tiber to Innocent III's institution of the Hospital Order. It is unlikely that the Dijon illuminations served as a direct model for the Corsia Sistina frescos.[47] The settings are French Gothic and have more in common with the local Burgundian style than with anything Roman. They can be dated quite precisely between the granting of a Jubilee privilege to the Order by Nicholas V in 1450 and the death of Duke Philip in 1467.[48] The two series, the *Liber Regulae* and the Dijon miniatures, would seem to have been dependent on some common text, as yet undocumented. Both could have been modelled on fresco scenes from the old Hospital of Santo Spirito, *vetustate pene collapsum* by the time of Sixtus IV.[49] His predecessor, Eugenius IV (1431–47), was the first fifteenth-century pope to revive papal patronage of the hospital,[50] and his renovations may well have included just such a fresco cycle. Exact details of the projects commissioned by Eugenius IV or Nicholas V (1447–55) may never be known, as the literary sources for the hospital narrative pre-date Sixtus's own biography. It is perfectly possible that the Dijon miniatures at least were dependent on an older cycle.[51]

The fifteenth-century Life of Sixtus IV states quite clearly that 'Cruel mothers were killing their illegitimate offspring by throwing them off the bridge into the Tiber where they were caught up in the nets of the fishermen.'[52] As late as 1570, Albert Bassanus, a Pole, in his history of the Order, further embellished this legend. Guided by a heavenly voice, Innocent III had been led to the banks of the Tiber to inspect the bodies of more than 400 dead babies. In 1653, Ascanio Tamburini, Abbot of Vallombrosa, reproduced the account without comment, but added the more reasonable assertion that the hospital's task was to care for 'the

[47] Howe, *Santo Spirito*, pp. 204–7.

[48] Ibid. p. 234, n. 41.

[49] Vatican, MS Cod. Urb. 1023, fols 11b–12a.

[50] Vatican, MS Lat. 9026, fol. 64a.

[51] Howe, *Santo Spirito*, pp. 206–7.

[52] Vatican, MS Cod. Urb. 1023, fol. 11a, 'Qualiter ex damnatu coitu progenitos in lucem veniant, crudeles matres diversimode erucidant. Qualiter infantes de Ponte in Tiberim proiecti a Piscatoribus rete pro piscibus capiuntur.'

sick and pilgrims and for abandoned children and babies'.[53] Sixtus IV, himself a Franciscan, felt a great reverence for Innocent, who had granted approval to Francis of Assisi. Howe has pointed out that there were no precedents for biographical scenes commissioned by a living patron, but Sixtus wished to create a legend in his own day.[54] 'Never before had a pope seen fit to depict his own life from birth to death as a succession of laudatory acts.'[55] The presence of three depictions of the great pope, Innocent III, would have enhanced this—prestige by association! The frescos of Sixtus's early life display a continuous hagiographical sequence—from his mother's vision of her unborn child in a Franciscan habit; his birth near Savona in 1414; his baptism; severe illness; his vesting with the Franciscan habit in order to cure him, and to his infantile blessing of the people in the piazza at Savona.[56] In all these the stress emphatically is upon images of a rewarding childhood.

No contemporary frescos of a like nature exist for Innocent III. Other means will have to be used to try to discover those spiritual and philosophical beliefs which underlay his actions in regard to the poor, the sick, and the helpless, the babies and children in general, and the role to be played by the hospital.[57] He appears to pass through three developmental stages—as cardinal presenting a learned text, as pastoral pope concerned with the saving of souls, and as Bishop of Rome imbued with the *vita apostolica*. These need to be tackled chronologically, even though all were to have formative influences on his ultimate position.

First, as a cardinal who may have felt that publication was an essential qualification for advancement. Between about 1190 and 1198[58] he wrote three interesting works, *De miseria humanae*

[53] *PL* 217, cols 1129–30, where an extract from Tamburini's history is reproduced. Also A. Tamburini, *De Iure Abbatum et aliorum praelatorum*, 2 vols (Lyon, 1640), 2, Disputatio xxiv, Quaest. IV, p. 367: 'Ad Tiberim se contulit et laxatis retibus, prima vice octaginta septem, secunda vero trecentos et quadraginta extraxit infantes abortivos.'

[54] Howe, *Santo Spirito*, pp. 207–20.

[55] Ibid., p. 207.

[56] Ibid., pp. 342–50.

[57] Brenda Bolton, ' "Hearts not Purses": Innocent III's Approach to Social Welfare', *Through the Eye of a Needle: Judeo-Christian Roots of Social Welfare*, ed. Emily Albu Hanawalt and Carter Lindberg (Missouri, 1994), pp. 123–45.

[58] He was created Cardinal-Deacon of SS Sergio e Bacco between 3 June 1189 and 8 January 1190.

*conditionis*,[59] *De sacro mysterio altaris*,[60] and *De quadripartita specie nuptiarum*.[61] Of relevance here is his *De miseria*, with its concern for the human condition. In the first few pages of this ascetic treatise he deals with the evil world into which the young were unfortunately born to suffer the sins of their fathers.[62]

This work, written between 25 December 1194 and 13 April 1195, became one of the most popular and influential works of the Middle Ages.[63] Now seen by some as a 'mirror' revealing the Curia and its corruption,[64] this was only the first of a projected two volumes. The misery of the human condition was intended to be complemented by another, *On the Dignity of the Human Condition*, but this was never completed. No evidence has been found as to its proposed contents.

In *De miseria*, Lotario discourses upon the weak, sad, and sinful condition of the child. From the moment of its conception in sin and lust, the Cardinal sees the child condemned to bear the transgressions of its parents. 'Happy is the child', he says, 'who dies before it is born, experiencing death before knowing life.'[65] In this passage he particularly mentions children with deformities, singled out as they were for ridicule. He then reflects that all children are born weak, unable to speak or understand, or even to crawl on all fours.[66] Indeed, children are less well equipped than animals, who at least can walk soon after they are born. The weakness of the child is further demonstrated when it is born crying, which expresses the misery of its own nature and the world into which it has entered. Lotario cannot resist at this stage indulging in a little sophisticated punning, obviously meant to appeal to his clerical readers. Boys are born saying 'Ah', while girls cry 'E' or '*Eu*'.[67] '*Eu*' and 'Ah' are a play on the name of Eve

[59] *PL* 217, cols 701–46; *De miseria humane conditionis*, ed. M. Maccarrone (Padua, 1955); *On the Misery of the Human Condition*, ed. Donald R. Howard and tr. Margaret M. Dietz; *De miseria condicionis humane*, ed. Robert E. Lewis (Athens, GA, 1978).

[60] *PL* 217, cols 774–914.

[61] Ibid., cols 922–68.

[62] Lewis, *De miseria*, pp. 93–105.

[63] R. Bultot, 'Mépris du monde, misère et dignité de l'homme dans la pensée d'Innocent III', *Cahiers de civilisation médiévale*, 4 (1961), pp. 441–56, esp. p. 442.

[64] J. C. Moore, 'Innocent III's *De Miseria Humanae Conditionis*: a *Speculum Curiae*?', *Catholic Historical Review*, 67 (1981), pp. 553–64.

[65] Lewis, *De miseria*, p. 103, lines 2–4.

[66] Ibid., p. 103, lines 15–18.

[67] Ibid., p. 104, lines 1–19.

or Eva, both interjections expressing the magnitude of sorrow or great pain caused by childbirth. He cites Rachel's death who, whilst dying of this agony, named her son 'Benoni, that is, son of pain', which, incidentally, Jacob quickly changed to Benjamin. There was, too, the sorrow of the child Ichabod, representing 'the glory hath departed', so named by his mother, the wife of Phineas (one of the two disreputable sons of Eli), who was killed at the time when the Philistines captured the Ark of the Covenant. No greater disaster could have been faced by the Israelites. In this early work, Lotario seems to have had little regard for any action that might be needed to ease the pain and suffering of the child born from sin.

In his second stage of development, as pope and pastor, one of Innocent's first tasks was to clarify important and complex matters concerning the spiritual well-being of his flock. The baptism of infants as soon as possible after their birth[68] raised important issues. In a letter of 1201 to Humbert, Bishop of Arles,[69] which entered into the *Decretals* of Gregory IX, Innocent argued strongly against those who asserted that baptism was conferred uselessly on infants who were dying in such numbers every day. He considered baptism an essential pastoral duty to ensure the child's passage into Heaven, having received Christ's salvation.[70] But for the grace of God these little ones would have perished eternally. The saving of souls was even more important than the saving of bodies. The Baby Box was an ideal solution, for it allowed for both. Yet Innocent was bound to approach the 'Babes in the Tiber' problem as would all priests: had these children already been baptized or not? The anonymity which the Box was designed to encourage raised at least the practical problem of finding this out. If, by chance, the custodian of the Baby Box heard footsteps outside, he was immediately to rush to put the question: 'Has this child been baptized?'[71] Failing an

[68] J. D. C. Fisher, *Christian Initiation: Baptism in the Medieval West* (London, 1965), pp. 109–12.

[69] Humbert de Aquaria (1190–1202), *Gallia Christiana*, 1 (Paris, 1715), pp. 564–5. For the letter see H. Denzinger, *Enchiridion symbolorum, definitionum et declarationum de rebus fidei et morum*, 10th edn. (Freiburg, 1908), pp. 180–2.

[70] For similar views, see Innocent's Advent Sermon VII, *PL* 217, cols 341–6, especially cols 343–4. Compare O. Pontal, *Les Statuts Synodaux Français du xiiie siècle* I. *Les statuts de Paris et le synodal de l'Ouest (xiii siècle)* (Paris, 1971), p. 140; Boswell, *Kindness of Strangers*, pp. 322–5.

[71] Brune, *Saint-Esprit*, p. 288.

answer, exposed children were to be baptized, just in case, and their souls would be saved.[72]

It would be a mistake, in considering Innocent III's actions, to neglect any acknowledgement of his social awareness. He was, above all, a pastoral pope, and the building of the hospital was evidence of this, as was the care he gave to pilgrims coming to Rome. Many of these pilgrims were pregnant women, whose babies added to the demands for child-care in Rome. Each pilgrim baby was provided with its own separate cradle, thus protecting it from being overlaid by its worn out pilgrim mother.[73] There was, after all, room at the inn!

Many harrowing tales exist about the mishaps and injury to infants, including those where babies were frequently suffocated or squashed. Innocent had to adjudicate as pope in one such heart-rending case. On 2 May 1207 he wrote to the Bishop of Lubeck and his suffragans about the case.[74] 'H', a priest, had come personally to see him with a tearful confession. Entering the house of his niece, with whom he had to arrange the payment of a debt, the priest apparently sat down, at her invitation, on a heap of clothing placed near the communal seat. Under this seat a certain sick little child, entrusted to the care of his father (no less), had been placed there to sleep. No sooner had he sat down than his niece hastened to warn him of the child beneath the clothing, whereupon the priest in horror leapt up from the place where he had been sitting. Alas, it was too late. Whether because of the weight of the clothing, or the gravity of the illness, or whether because the priest had crushed the child by sitting on him, the babe was found to be dead. The priest 'H' had come to the Pope, not presuming to perform any of the functions of his office until he received forgiveness. Innocent's judgement in this case was that the man had not gravely sinned, but that penance should be performed in a manner compatible with the event.

This third and fundamental aspect brought about by Innocent's social awareness in regard to children would have developed from his support for the *vita apostolica*, the movement which had arisen out of the spiritual ferment of the twelfth

[72] Boswell, *Kindness of Strangers*, pp. 322–5.

[73] *PL* 217, col. 1118.

[74] *PL* 215, cols 871–72.

century. With such spiritual inspiration, Innocent would constantly have had in mind the Gospels and the sayings of Jesus. There, in Matthew[75] and Mark,[76] he would have found the advice to 'suffer little children . . . because of such are the Kingdom of Heaven.' This demanded an approach to children by others than those in the parental relationship, which was perhaps not at all common at the time. What Christ had said was certainly as unexpected in apostolic times and in the early years of the Church as it would have been in Ancient Greece and Rome. It is not clear when Christ's injunction—not to offend against his little ones—became a guiding principle for the Church, but by the turn of the twelfth century some attempts were obviously being made. These seem to have been irregular, often ineffective, perhaps not truly 'Gospel based', and more concerned with the consequences to the parents of their sin than to the foundlings themselves. Innocent III can hardly have been the first, although his anonymous biographer would like us to believe so. This biographer does not mention the Baby Box specifically, but devotes much space to Innocent's support for such causes as Santo Spirito. Indeed, Innocent's overall expenditure on poor orphans, on widows, and the younger sons of impoverished nobles was estimated at the staggering sum of 5,000 pounds in the first ten years of the pontificate.[77] This most pious pope not only allowed, but positively encouraged the very poor children of Rome to come to his own table after meals so that they could eat up the remaining food.[78]

Innocent certainly took the words of Christ as the basis for his actions, as he became increasingly aware of the needs of poor children in general and abandoned babies in particular. What better could the Church to than to receive these little children in his name, so receiving Christ himself and he who sent him? Perhaps the legends of the fifteenth century had more basis in fact than we imagine. The Hospital of Santo Spirito is well documented, but the episode of the Baby Box less so. A deeper examination of the spiritual beliefs underlying Innocent's ac-

[75] Matt. 18.2–6; 19.13–15.

[76] Mark 9.36–7, 42; 10.13–16.

[77] *Gesta* CL, col. ccxxviii.

[78] *Gesta Innocentii P.P.III, PL* 214, ch. CXL, col. cc.

tions may be a logical first step towards finding the evidence we seek.

Lunette of Mentorella, Doorway to the *Confessio* of St Peter,
commissioned by Innocent III, c. 1215 (detail of front)
(By permission of the Soprintendenza per i Beni Artistici e Storici di Roma.)

Inscription reads: + EGO SUM OSTIUM [T] OVILE OVIUM ('I am the door of the sheep', John 10[7]). In the centre, the Lamb of God, looking right and carrying a cross, is surrounded by the symbols of the evangelists; left: St Luke above and St Mark below; right: St John above and St Matthew below; and beneath the centrepiece, Old Testament prophets announce the coming of the Lord.

Lunette of Mentorella, Doorway to the *Confessio* of St Peter,
commissioned by Innocent III, c. 1215 (detail of rear)
(By permission of the Soprintendenza per i Beni Artistici e Storici di Roma.)

ription reads: + SP̄C ALMUS EGO TEGAS UT TEGENDA TE TEGO VIR DICO PASCE :GES QUIA NULLIS EPULIS EGES ('It is I, Holy Spirit of the Council, who invests you what is suitable [?the mitre]. I say to you, man, feed your sheep, because you lack no ', translation adapted from M.M. Gautier, 'La clôture émaillée de la confession de Saint :e du Vatican, lors du concile de Latran IV, 1215', *Synthronon* [Paris 1968], pp. 237–46, :cially p. 244). The central figure, wearing the pallium, holds the keys of St Peter and ns to the Dove of the Holy Spirit, like Gregory the Great, but has no halo; the second ription reads: QUI SITIT VENIAT ('whomsoever thirsts, he should come').

Lunette of Mentorella, Doorway to the *Confessio* of St Peter, commissioned by Innocent III, c. 1215 (front view)
(By permission of the Soprintendenza per i Beni Artistici e Storici di Roma.)

# Select Recent Bibliography


·ances Andrews, *The early Humiliati: the development of an Order c.1176-1270.* Unpublished PhD thesis, University of London (1994).

eonard Boyle, 'Innocent III and vernacular versions of scripture', *The Bible in the Medieval World: essays im memory of Beryl Smalley, Studies in Church History*, Subsidia 4, ed. Katherine Walsh & Diana Wood (Blackwell, 1985) pp. 97-107.

ıilippe Buc, '*Vox clamantis in deserto*?: Pierre le Chantre et la prédication laïque', *Revue Mabillon*, Nouvelle Série 4, 65 (1993) pp. 5-47.

ary Dickson, 'The burning of the Amalricians', *Journal of Ecclesiastical History* 40 (1989) pp. 348-369.

ary Dickson, 'Stephen of Cloyes, Philip Augustus and the Children's Crusade of 1212', *Journeys toward God: Pilgrimage and Crusade* ed. Barbara N. Sargent-Baur (Kalamazoo, Michigan, 1992) pp.83-105.

ary Dickson, 'Clare's dream', *Mediaevistik* 5 (1992) pp. 39-55.

.R. Evans, 'The attack on the Fourth Lateran Council', *Annuarium Historiae Conciliorum* 21 (1989) pp. 241-66.

.R. Evans, 'Exegesis and authority in the thirteenth century', *Ad Litteram* ed. Mark D. Jordan and Kent Emery (Notre Dame, 1992) pp. 93-111.

.L. Jansen, 'Mary Magdalen and the mendicants: the preaching of penance in the late Middle Ages', *Journal of Medieval History* (forthcoming).

ary Macy, 'The dogma of transubstantiation in the Middle Ages', *Journal of Ecclesiastical History* 45 (1994) pp. 11-41.

ernard McGinn, *Apocalypticism in the Western Tradition*, (Variorum, 1994)

C. Moore, 'Lotario dei Conti di Segni (Pope Innocent III) in the 1180's', *Archivum Historiae Pontificiae* 29 (1991) pp. 255-58.

C. Moore, 'Sardinia and the Papal State', *Speculum* 62 (1987) pp. 81-101.

J.C. Moore, 'The sermons of Pope Innocent III', *Römische Historisch Mitteilungen* 36 (1994) pp. 81-142.

A. Murray, 'Confession before 1215', *Transactions of the Royal Historic Society*, Sixth Series, 3 (1993) pp. 51-81.

Kenneth Pennington, *Popes, Canonists and Texts 1150-1550* (Variorun 1993).

*Innocent III: Vicar of Christ or Lord of the World*, 2nd expanded edition b J.M. Powell (Washington, 1994).

I. Ragusa, '*Mandylion-Sudarium*: the 'translation' of a Byzantine relic t Rome', *Arte Medievale* II serie, Anno V (1991) pp. 97-106.

Fiona Robb, 'Who hath chosen the better part? (Luke 10, 42) Pope Innoce III and Joachim of Fiore on the diverse forms of religious life', *Monast Studies: the Continuity of Tradition*, ed. J. Loades (Bangor, 1991) pp. 15 70.

Fiona Robb, 'Did Innocent III personally condemn Joachim of Fiore? *Florensia: Bolletino del Centro Internazionale di Studi Gioachimiti*, (1993) pp. 77-91.

Constance M. Rousseau, 'Pope Innocent III and familial relationships clergy and religious', *Studies in Medieval and Renaissance History*, 1 (1993) pp. 107-48.

Jane Sayers, *Innocent III: Leader of Europe 1198-1216*, (London, 1994).

Maria L. Taylor, 'The election of Innocent III', *The Church and Sovereign c.590-1918: Essays in Honour of Michael Wilks*, ed. D. Wood, *Studies Church History*, Subsidia 9 (Blackwell 1991) pp. 97-112.

Diana M. Webb, 'The Pope and the cities: anticlericalism and heresy Innocent III's Italy', *The Church and Sovereignty c.590-1918: Essays Honour of Michael Wilks*, ed. D. Wood, *Studies in Church Histor* Subsidia 9 (Blackwell 1991) pp. 135-52.

# INDEX